THE LEGACY OF ROME

TEMPLE OF MATUTA (?), ROME

FORUM ROMANUM. From the engraving by Piranesi

The Legacy of ROME

Essays by C. FOLIGNO, ERNEST BARKER, H. STUART JONES, G. H. STEVENSON, F. DE ZULUETA, H. LAST, CYRIL BAILEY, CHARLES SINGER, J. W. MACKAIL, the late HENRY BRADLEY, G. McN. RUSHFORTH, G. GIOVANNONI, W. E. HEITLAND

Edited by

CYRIL BAILEY

With an Introduction by

The Right Hon. H. H. ASQUITH

OXFORD

At the Clarendon Press

OXFORD UNIVERSITY PRESS
AMEN HOUSE, E.C. 4
London Edinburgh Glasgow New York
Toronto Melbourne Capetown Bombay
Calcutta Madras
HUMPHREY MILFORD
PUBLISHER TO THE UNIVERSITY

FIRST PUBLISHED 1923
REPRINTED 1924, 1928
1936, 1940

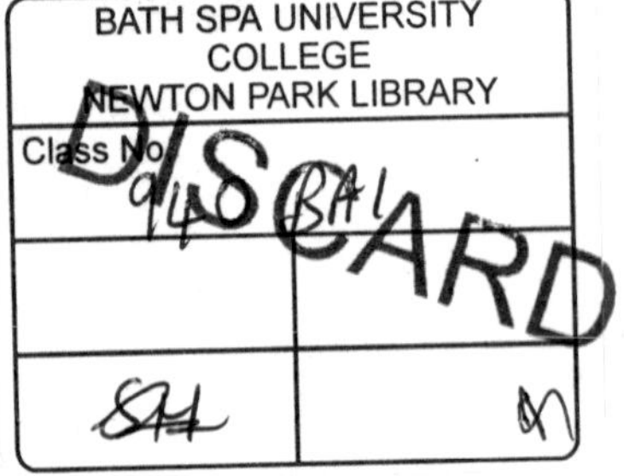

PRINTED IN GREAT BRITAIN AT THE UNIVERSITY PRESS, OXFORD
BY JOHN JOHNSON, PRINTER TO THE UNIVERSITY

EDITOR'S NOTE

THIS book is an endeavour to trace in many fields the extent of the inheritance which the modern world owes to Ancient Rome. The chapters have been written independently, and it will be seen that they are not all on the same plan. Some writers have described the contribution of Rome to civilization, and have left it to the reader to infer the extent of the legacy: others have traced the steps by which the legacy has come to us, and to this subject Professor Foligno has devoted a valuable chapter.

The editor's thanks are due to all the contributors, especially to Mr. Asquith, who found time to write an Introduction to the volume. Also to Mr. Angus Davidson for his assistance in translating Professor Giovannoni's chapter, and to Professor R. S. Conway for the two photographs illustrating the probable site of Virgil's farm.

C. B.

2570

CONTENTS

LIST OF ILLUSTRATIONS

BUILDING AND ENGINEERING

AGRICULTURE

INTRODUCTION

A RUSTY scholar, long ago *rude donandum*, nothing but the relentless and flattering persistence of my friend, Mr. Cyril Bailey, could have constrained me to be responsible for the Prologue to this volume. For though during a busy life I have striven never to lose touch with the studies and interests of my youth, Scholarship in these days, with the new implements which have been forged for it by archaeology, and the many developments of the comparative method, completely outstrips the ardent but belated amateur, who (relatively speaking) has not got much beyond the equipment of the Neolithic Age.

This book is intended to give a comprehensive estimate of the Legacy which Rome has left to the modern world. On what may be called the political side of her activities—the art of government and conquest, the statecraft of consolidation and expansion, the reconciliation of local diversities with imperial unity, the approximation to a world-wide Peace—there is no need to dwell. I endeavoured, some years ago, to give reasons for the opinion that, in the thousand years which followed the birth of Christ, there was no era in which the external conditions of life were so favourable to the happiness of mankind as the reign of the Emperor Hadrian. The great fabric succumbed in time, as all human institutions do, to the law of decay. But it is unique in history, and its memories and examples will not and cannot die.

It is much more difficult to describe the character and appraise the value of the intellectual and spiritual debt which we owe to Rome. The impressions left upon my mind, after reading the learned and penetrating contributions which follow, may be summed up in this way: alike in literature, in art, in philosophy, and in religion, Rome built the bridge over which many of the best thoughts and the finest models of antiquity found their way into the Mediaeval and thence into the Modern World. Her genius was not creative but assimilative; its function was not to originate but to adapt; and not unfrequently, in the process of adaptation, to transmute. Her intellectual activities are, I think, happily described by one of the writers as those of a great 'intermediary'.

Like all generalizations of the kind, this requires many qualifications before it can be made to fit the facts. It may be worth while to see how the case stands in the departments of Literature, Religion, and Philosophy. Roman Law is in a category by itself.

In the domain of Literature our first and greatest obligation to Rome is naturally the Latin language itself. We owe to it (as Mr. Mackail says)—to take only one illustration—'practically the whole vocabulary of our theology and moral philosophy'. Indeed, it is difficult to refuse assent to the larger claim which is advanced by the same eminent authority: that 'European prose, as an instrument of thought, is Cicero's creation'.

It is easy to emphasize and to illustrate the still greater debt which Roman literature owed to Greek. In originality, and real independence, Lucretius and Catullus stand almost alone among the Latin poets. 'Neither,' says Dr. Verrall, 'so far as we know, had any near affinity to predecessors or successors.' But the fact that Virgil and Horace were 'copyists', as they avowedly were, has not in any way impaired the unique influence which, by unique gifts, they have exercised both in the mediaeval and the modern world. There are, indeed, some departments of the art of writing in which, without any antecedent model, the Roman Genius attained to something very near perfection. Satire is one example; it is claimed by Quintilian as a purely Latin product. J. J. Scaliger once said that he would give in exchange for the text of Ennius in its integrity, Lucan, Statius, Silius Italicus, '*et tous ces garçons-là*'.[1]

[1] Scaligerana, 136.

It would perhaps be a more interesting exchange if we could obtain at the same price the outpourings of Lucilius, the founder of Roman Satire. Its greatest master, Juvenal, has never been surpassed, and there are few ancient writers, Greek or Roman, who have been more industriously and on the whole more ineffectually imitated in modern times.

Roman Oratory, again, stands on its own legs. It was, of course, founded upon, and largely fashioned by, Attic and 'Asiatic' examples. The Latin language is in some respects less adapted to oratory than the Greek. As Cardinal Newman has said: 'Latin is comparatively weak, scanty, and unmusical, and requires considerable skill and management to render it expressive and graceful.' [1] It was doubtless for this reason that the great Roman orators, Hortensius and Cicero himself, abandoned the 'plainness' and the sometimes statuesque simplicity of Lysias and Demosthenes, for the amplitude and ornateness of their own carefully built up and sonorous periods. It may be a moot point to decide whether one would rather have heard a speech from Demosthenes or from Cicero. But there can, I think, be little doubt, notwithstanding all the study which Brougham and other great practitioners allege that they have given to the *De Corona*, that Cicero has had a more abiding and pervasive influence upon the methods of modern oratory.

There remains another branch of Literature, less pretentious, but more fascinating, in which Rome can truly be said to have led the way: that of Letter-writing. Cicero was here the pioneer, and in his eight or nine hundred letters he has shown himself a master of all the resources of epistolary Art. They make up the most vivid picture that we possess of social and political affairs, of current topics and conspicuous personages, in the troubled years of the moribund Republic. The younger Pliny, who lived in the tranquil days of the Emperor Trajan, was in every way an inferior artist to Cicero, but his letters

[1] Quoted by Sandys, *Orator*, Introd., p. lxii.

which (after the fashion of the age) he published to the world in his lifetime, in a steady succession of no less than nine books, reveal an amiable character, a faculty of close observation, a retentive memory, much descriptive power, and (in the opinion of competent judges) the possession of a finished Latin style. The literature both of France and England is singularly rich in this form of production, and it goes back to a Latin origin.

The Religion of Rome had little to do with what we call religion, and still less with morality.[1]

For a real understanding of the primitive religion of the Roman people we are indebted largely to the researches and the insight of Warde Fowler. It was Paganism in the most literal sense of the word. Every village settlement was haunted by its own local spirits: spirits of the wood, of the spring, of the hill, of the household. They are grouped together under the generic name of *Numen*, and while in the City of Rome the remodelled and hellenized Pantheon kept open its hospitable doors with a welcome ready for each new-comer from the conquered world, the local deities were never superseded, and never lost their vogue. Some of them, which had more than a merely local prestige, such as Hercules and Silvanus, even grew in popularity in the first two centuries of the Empire.

It is a striking fact that (as is stated by one of the writers in this volume) 'the last fight of Christianity was with the *pagani*, the people of the country villages, clinging to their ancestral cults'. They were worsted; but their saints'-days, their fasts and feasts, even some of their actual rites and ceremonies, were taken over and adopted by the Catholic Church.[2] It is instructive to compare the old Roman Calendar, which has been compiled by scholars from surviving inscriptions, with

[1] It did not 'demand any profession of faith in any theory of the unseen; all it required was ceremonial purity and exactness' (Dill, *Roman Society from Nero to Marcus Aurelius*, p. 544).

[2] See Gibbon, ch. xxviii, and Bury's note at the end of the chapter.

that which is now prefixed by Papal authority to the *Breviarium Romanum.*

One of the signs of the consolidation of these scattered communities, and of the growing authority of a central capital, is the 'generalization' of the local deities and cults, with the ultimate emergence of the Roman or rather Italian Trinity—Jupiter, Juno, and Minerva—and the organization of the hierarchy of Pontifices, Augures, and the rest: what is sometimes called 'institutional' religion.[1] This was the first step in the characteristic Roman process of assimilation. A much longer one was taken when 'captive Greece' succeeded in importing her own Pantheon, and the stiff, archaic figures of the Roman gods were labelled with the names and attributes, and clad in the gorgeous mythological raiment, of the whole company of Olympus. It was to a large extent a literary and spectacular affair: which made little appeal to the man in the street—the *faex Romuli.* But it led, as Rome pushed her conquests farther east, to the domestication of a long series of Oriental cults, from that of the Phrygian Magna Mater,[2] as far back as at the end of the Second Punic War, to that of the Persian Mithra, which was in the third century of our era perhaps the most formidable competitor of the Early Christian Church.

On this side—the official side—Roman religion was latitudinarian and comprehensive.

This rapid survey is sufficient to make it easier to understand what is meant by the 'Religion' which was so passionately denounced by the greatest of Roman poets. It was the superstition, which still haunted the lives and minds even of the educated, that Divinities of one kind or another, whether Capitoline or country-side, had a power of capricious inter-

[1] Every emperor from Augustus onwards was Pontifex Maximus, and this practice continued after Christianity had become the State religion.

[2] She had been enthroned on the Palatine for more than 600 years when St. Augustine denounced hers as one of the most pestilent of the pagan superstitions (Dill, p. 548).

ference, for good or for evil, with the fortunes of men. Lucretius was too good an Epicurean to be an Atheist. He was not for abolishing the gods, but for exiling them. Let them keep to themselves in

> The lucid interspace of world and world,
> Where never creeps a cloud, or moves a wind,
> . . . .
> Nor sound of human sorrow mounts to mar
> Their sacred, everlasting calm.[1]

From the point of view of Theology—I will deal in a moment with the philosophic aspect of the case—there is not much to choose between the banished gods of Lucretius, and the sublimated and kaleidoscopic conceptions of the Deity held by Stoics such as Seneca, who apparently regards it as immaterial whether God is thought of as 'the creator of the Universe, or the incorporeal Reason, or the divine breath diffused through all things, or Fate and the immutable change of inter-linked causation'.[2]

Of all the formative races which have helped to build up the fabric of civilization, there is hardly one which has made less original contribution than the Romans to speculative Philosophy. In 161 B.C. the Senate by decree forbade 'philosophers and rhetoricians' to reside in Rome. It was, of course, a futile proscription; but Greek metaphysics and psychology were never really acclimatized among the Seven Hills. Cicero, who dabbled in an eclectic fashion with the shifting doctrines of the Academy, and gradually drew nearer to the Stoics, makes no pretence to originality. He says, himself, frankly enough, of his copious contributions to philosophic literature: 'ἀπόγραφα sunt . . . Verba tantum adfero, quibus abundo.'[3]

J. J. Scaliger, whose admiration for Cicero as a writer was unbounded—he calls him 'le plus bel auteur Latin que nous

[1] Tennyson, *Lucretius*.

[2] Dill, p. 306. All these hypotheses are grouped by Seneca in a single sentence: *Ad Helv.* viii, § 3.

[3] *Ad Att.* xii. 52.

avons '—is yet constrained to say of his excursions into philosophy 'libros omnes philosophicos Ciceronis nihili facio '.[1]

In the domain of Ethics Greek thought found at Rome a more promising field for exploitation and propaganda. Of Cicero's *De Officiis* Henry Sidgwick says: 'there is probably no ancient treatise which has done more to communicate a knowledge of ancient morality to mediaeval and modern Europe.'[2] But here again the Latin function is that of intermediation and transmission.

The Ethics of the great philosophical teachers of Greece were based upon the identification of the good man and the good citizen. In other words, they were framed for the comparatively small aristocratic minority, which, even in the ἔσχατος δῆμος of Athens, was in exclusive possession both of freedom and of power. 'Even Plato,' writes Sir Samuel Dill,[3] 'requires the elders of his Utopia as a duty, after they have seen the vision of God, to descend again to the ordinary tasks of Government.' But the State-City, federation having proved a failure and representation being still unknown, was submerged by the Macedonian conquests, and annihilated by the dominion of Rome. 'Morals were finally separated from politics' (in the real sense of that term): the individual man, citizen, freedman, or slave, had to make his own soul; and henceforward that became the Ethical problem. The field was thus left clear for the two surviving Schools, both of purely Greek origin and development, which fought for a time for the spiritual supremacy of the Roman world.

The Stoics and the Epicureans, though they differed in phraseology and method, had a common ideal—the complete emancipation of the soul from the yoke of passion and superstition.[4] This was the real significance of the αὐτάρκεια of

[1] Scaligerana, 93.

[2] Sidgwick, *History of Ethics*, p. 95.

[3] Dill, p. 291.

[4] See Sidgwick, pp. 92 seq., Dill: 'the problem of philosophy was to find the beatitude of man in the autonomous Will,' p. 291.

the one sect and the ἀταραξία of the other. In the words which Tennyson puts into the mouth of the dying Lucretius—they were both in search of the

Passionless bride, divine Tranquillity.

The teaching and practice of the Stoics was bound in the long run to gain the ascendency in Rome. It suited best the traditional and inbred *gravitas* of the highest type of Roman manhood. The greatest of the Greek philosophers had supplied no practical corrective to the moral instability which was the fatal flaw in the Athenian character; the public and private careers of some of his most intimate and favourite disciples gave plausibility to the view that, as an ethical teacher, Socrates was an unsettling and demoralizing influence. But, as has been often pointed out, the heroes of the early history of Rome might be fitted almost without modification or manipulation into the Stoic mould: the picture of Regulus in Horace's famous Ode is an anticipation of the ideal Stoic, as he was to be, or ought to have been, in action.

Stoicism reached its finest and ultimate expression, not in the rhetoric of Seneca (whose practice ill consorted with his doctrine), but in the almost Evangelical teaching of Epictetus and Marcus Aurelius. It had as a system no real philosophic basis: God and Immortality were to it, not fixed points either of affirmation or negation, but nebulous and wavering hypotheses: its martyrs and confessors were wont to seal their faith by suicide; it was at its highest and best, an esoteric rule of life, not for the many, but for the few.

If this were all, one might be disposed to conclude that Rome had left little of her own to the modern world of philosophic or even of ethical value. There is, however, one great and conspicuous exception—the legacy of Roman Law. This was the domain in which Rome showed constructive genius. She founded, developed, and systematized the jurisprudence of the world.

H. H. ASQUITH.

THE TRANSMISSION OF THE LEGACY

There are two sources of error which must be guarded against in considering the connexion of ancient with modern civilization: unreasoned worship of the past and unjustified pride in the present. It is as pernicious to overrate the value of ancient civilization and to exaggerate the amount of the heritage which the modern world has actually received, as it is foolish to ignore the great achievements of the ancients and to deny that a portion of their assets has leavened progress in later days. The greater scientific knowledge and mechanical advantages of contemporary civilization need not be sources of pride. It is thus as unjust to measure ancient values by modern standards as to evaluate the legacy of the ancient world by the greatness of the effort which the Greeks and Romans accomplished. The truth is that, apart from modern mechanical progress, the value of which may be questioned, a chasm separates the modern from the ancient world: between these two epochs there were centuries of rapid decadence, of inactivity and progress, and often enough this gap is not studied or explained, but bridged by a superficial statement such as: 'The Middle Ages began with the fall of the Western Empire, and were succeeded by the Modern Era'; sometimes instead of the non-committal words 'Middle Ages' one finds the more emphatic and misleading expression 'Dark Ages'.

One wonders what these mediaeval centuries are thought to have been. Perhaps a period of continuous gloom through which timid individuals groped senselessly and were attacked at each turning by ferocious giants ready for every violence, murder, destruction, and rape; as if one imagined that the moderns owe it to the very darkness of the Middle Ages that anything of the Roman heritage has reached them, because it passed unnoticed by the invaders, and thus escaped being ravished or burned.

Even though such a fanciful view of the actual events were as correct as it is assuredly wrong, it would still be opportune to explain more definitely how and by what means so much of the Roman legacy escaped the destroying fury of the barbarians who were the unconscious instruments of a profound innovation.

In order to give a fairly satisfactory reply to such a question, a distinction must be made. One part of the legacy reached the modern world by a natural process, handed down from people to people and from one generation to another, through traditions which could not be rooted out, through legends, customs, intellectual outlooks, rough elaborations of artistic conceptions; and it is this part of the legacy which, independently of its intrinsic value, bore the best fruits in the modern era. The other part, which was perhaps richer in itself, was gradually recovered by the ceaseless efforts, the toil and study, excavations and investigations of scholars during the last centuries of the Middle Ages and the Modern epoch. Thus the process of transmission was twofold, natural and artificial; and this circumstance modified so profoundly the very essence of the legacy, that it may be assumed that the legacies were two: one which is difficult to make out, but has been active at all times, and has benefited all classes of men, and another, more conspicuous, which is the result of a long collective effort of antiquarian research and seldom benefits those who do not belong to cultured or in some way privileged classes.

The natural legacy escaped destruction because it was constantly in use; and though usage has entailed wear and tear, it has also ensured a considerable influence upon men, which was continuous if varying in degree: such a heritage has been treated by its temporary possessors as a lawful property; it was absorbed, modified, and re-elaborated by them like a thing of their own; and the inherent preciousness of the thing was often obscured by the habit of possession. The remainder of the legacy was first buried under the débris of an enormous upheaval, or sunk in deep waters by the shipwreck of the ancient world, and was only recovered later, after long searching which enhanced its value in the opinion of men of culture, for whose benefit it was placed in museums and imitated.

A profound difference between the direct transmission and the later recovery during the Renaissance is to be found in the altered outlook of the recipients upon the Latin legacy. Mediaeval men accepted all that came to them from the ancients with absolute trust. They were the willing pupils of masters whom they considered infallible. On the other hand, the scholars of the Renaissance, and also some among the later Schoolmen, owing to their wider information about the ancient world, almost unwittingly took up a critical attitude; the classical age was still for them a period immeasurably superior to their own in all ways, but they had to make their choice when they traced a conflict of evidence or theories, and thus to take up the position of critics; they took over what they desired from the ancients, rather than received any gift from them, for taking implies selection and a conscious intellectual activity, and receiving merely denotes acceptance. Once the critical attitude was taken up, it was bound to bring about a reconsideration of traditional values, which caused first a form of rivalry with the ancients and later, during the seventeenth century, the famous polemic concerning the relative merits *des anciens et des modernes*.

Much then has perished, much has been but lately recovered as the result of purely intellectual labours; but much has also survived by the regular process of transmission in a form which is difficult to recognize. Such a distinction could be illustrated in many ways, but a linguistic example may serve the purpose. The Greek κέρασος was transformed into the Latin derivative *cerăsus*, vulgar Latin *cerĕsia*, whence the French *cerise* and the English *cherry*; a full and legitimate heritage; on the other hand *ecclesiastic* is a purely learned word. No doubt all words, whether they come from a popular source or whether they have been imported into the language through literature in more or less ancient days, are legal tender; but the former have been completely anglicized, and the latter are still recognizable by an alien or bookish flavour which renders them less easily acceptable.

One might say that the Roman influence which was, at least in part, instinctive and unconscious, has become, in the course of the centuries, conscious and intellectual. And this is true not of one only but of all modern civilized peoples, though in varying degrees. Easy material and intellectual communications between peoples in peace time, no less than frequent wars, which generally end in the victors borrowing the moral and intellectual outlook of the vanquished, have so welded the different nations with one another, that one cannot nowadays speak of substantial diversities of culture between people and people. It is just a matter of shades and degrees, and there is a profound reason for it. The foundations of modern civilization are common to all people: they are mainly Roman, Greek under certain aspects, and scientific. Common foundations do not imply identity, but a kinship which cannot be denied: just as a form of religion, when it is practised by peoples of different races, cannot avoid being influenced or slightly modified in its expression by the habits of thought peculiar to each race, but remains identical in its substance.

Thus Christianity, which spread originally in Western Europe through Rome, has remained unaltered in its main lines, but has necessarily fallen under the influence of the religious traditions of the several races; and it would not be difficult to discover traces of cults which have disappeared long ago in the minute forms of religious cult and ritual as they are practised in the several countries. In Italy, where Roman traditions were naturally strongest, Christianity has seldom been rent by doctrinal dissensions, thus following the tradition of Roman religiousnesss, which was characteristically tolerant of alien beliefs, and is prone to the reviving of ancient myths by the traditional worship of saints and by more or less superstitious practices. Elsewhere Christians have been more readily swayed by the discussions of subtle questions of doctrine, as in the East, or have become pugnacious and learned as among Germanic races. Thus each race and each generation create their religious beliefs afresh, although men think that they are faithfully following an unalterable creed.

What Christianity acquired through contact with the Roman world is mainly to be traced in the hierarchical organization of the Catholic Church ; it is institutional rather than religious. And it was principally due to Roman influence that the idea of a universal Church arose so soon in the history of Christianity, and that from that idea there so unexpectedly sprung the theory of a universal Empire which had lasting political consequences.

From the time when Constantine the Great accepted Christianity as the religion of the Empire, the election of the Pope was completed by the confirmation, at first of the Western and later of the Eastern Emperors. The recognition by the Popes of the authority of the Byzantine Emperors was only natural, for the creation of two Emperors with separate territorial jurisdiction was never understood to imply the separation of the Empire or the creation of two distinct States ; it was merely intended to establish two capitals from each of which an Emperor, in full accord with his colleague, was to rule a clearly defined portion of a single State. Thus the Popes were merely consistent in their loyalty to the State in never failing to seek confirmation after election from the Eastern Emperors up to the seventh century, and it was only due to the decreased authority of the Byzantine Emperors in Italy and to their unwise interference in purely theological questions, that the Popes freed themselves by degrees from the allegiance to the Eastern Empire. The power of the Popes had so far increased that it was felt at last to have no further need of the protection and corroboration of the lay authorities. But soon a new danger threatened the Church at the hands of the Roman aristocracy and the Lombard kings. As they were no longer restrained by imperial authority, owing to the split between the Church and Byzantium, the more powerful among the Roman nobles endeavoured to subject the papacy to their will and to enmesh it in the ceaseless riots and quarrels which were brought about by their feuds. On the other hand, some of the Lombard kings, endeavouring to establish their authority over the whole of the territory which formed the Lombard State, and anxious to extend it farther, were ready to use military force against the papacy. In such straits the Popes had recourse to the one power which, during the eighth century, possessed military and political strength and showed pious submission to the Church, namely the monarchy of the Franks. Thus they appealed, at first to Pepin and later to Charlemagne, and secured from them the legal recognition of a temporal dominion in the Duchy of Rome and the complete liberation from the Lombard menace. When Charlemagne had swept away the Lombard monarchy and added its territory to the vast lands over which he was already ruling, Pope Leo III, almost without a warning, bestowed the imperial crown upon the King of the Franks who had gone to Rome to celebrate his victories. It was once again the glamour of ancient glory together with the undying recollection of the world power of the Romans which was at work. The Pope did not wish any longer to acknowledge the pre-eminence of the Byzantine Emperors, who were far away, untrustworthy, and continually becoming more eastern in character ; but the Church was universal in theory and aimed at the spiritual direction of the whole world ; it had converted the Arian barbarians, and, with the help of Frankish valour, it was rapidly gaining ground among the German and Slav tribes, while the credit of checking the progress of the Mohammedans into Western Europe had been ascribed to Charles Martel's victory at Poitiers, rather than to the internal feuds of the Moors of Spain. A universal Church needed to be balanced and strengthened by a universal Empire embracing at least the whole of the Western world. And the Frankish king whose State was already rivalling the Roman Empire in extent, after some hesitation, saw the benefits of the papal gift; he took pride in the new crown that had been placed on his head, and allowed himself to be made the first exponent of a theory which had scant foundations in actual politics. The Carlovingian Empire had only two things Roman: its size, and that for a short time, and its name. It was its name more than anything else which lent glamour to the mediaeval Empire, saved it in moments of crisis, and made it most coveted by ambitious princes. Also its immediate origin was Roman in so far as the Roman Church had brought it into existence; but the defender of the Church was soon to become the rival of the papacy and the opponent of its temporal ambitions.

But how had the glamour of Roman power survived in the recollection of men despite the persistent disasters which prepared and caused the downfall of the Western Empire and followed upon it? Between the third and the fifth centuries the boundaries of the Roman State were overrun by hostile tribes, bent inwards by persistent pressure and withdrawn so far as to include in the end little more than the Italian peninsula; and in such territories as had been only recently romanized or had become the home of barbarian tribes which had escaped so far the contact of civilization, it is to be assumed that the recollection of past glories was rapidly dimmed.

But the barbarians were mostly accustomed to live in huts or wooden houses; and the farther they advanced towards the heart of the Empire, the more often were they confronted by cities built of stone, bricks, and marble, boasting decorous public edifices, temples, statues, mosaics, and paintings, linked to one another by paved roads, mostly watered by still efficient aqueducts. It was a sight so overwhelming in its unexpected grandeur, that it may have goaded to fury the destructive impulse of the more savage invaders, but it must have aroused an almost mysterious awe in them, and particularly in those who were less impervious to civilization. The vanquished Romans may have struck them as weak and unwarlike, but the complexity of Roman civilization must by degrees have impressed them. After their occupation the cities must have looked forsaken as if they were vast conglomerations of sparsely inhabited edifices, edifices too which were often crumbling into ruins; every object of gold, silver, or bronze was stolen, the statues were knocked down, but the feeling that they were face to face with a grand product of human effort, more impressive even than their own victories, little by little mastered the uncouth visitors. They could not suddenly change their methods of living, but they did proceed to inhabit those houses whose halls they had emptied of dwellers, and they found the change so pleasant, that they were soon busy erecting stone buildings of their own, or rather having them erected.

For it should not be overlooked that the invaders were not so numerous as one might imagine, and did neither destroy nor drive away the native inhabitants. In this respect there was for the most part a striking difference in the behaviour of the Romans and the invaders. The invaders came from far-off lands and had been on their way for years, fighting, marching, and camping. They were still encamped rather than settled. If other invaders came in their wake and conquered them, they were wont to start on their track once again, making for other lands; but what was left of the Roman or Romanized population did not stir. In the course of time during the decline of the Empire the resources of its subjects had been exhausted by taxation, many had been debased from the status of free citizens to that of men chained to a particular class or a place, small landowners had become serfs or civil servants; but they had not stirred from their abodes when the invasions began, and they had not all died. The upheaval struck them with stupor; they felt helpless; life which had been so harassing became more harassing still; the administration of justice which had been corrupt became a travesty and a mockery, for the scornful ferocity of the new masters ignored the restrictions of such laws as they had issued themselves; the people suffered hunger, violence, and insult but they did not all die. If the crumbling of the massive organization of civil life turned them into beings more enslaved, ignorant and miserable, they certainly would not forget, when still abiding in the cities where they had dwelt for generations, that their forefathers had been more powerful, cultured, and richer than they. If the invaders despised them as cowards, they in their turn scorned the invaders as savages; the recollection of their own past glories became a refuge and a comfort, and thus a source of immense strength and vitality. The more they suffered in the darkness of the present, the more light was reflected upon the past; recollections under such circumstances could not be turned into history, but materialized into legends, and were the more enduring for it.

The period of recurrent invasions occupied more than three centuries, but the waves were intermittent and did not everywhere last so long; in many countries they ceased sooner, and stability was more readily reached. Celts, Britons, Angles, Jutes, Saxons, Normans settled in Britain one after another, and legends of different races became stratified or intermingled, but no amount of fighting and no ferocity of domination succeeded in completely obliterating the recollection of each of the successive stages.

Visigoths and Suebi ceased their wanderings once they had arrived in far-away Spain; stability was reached in Gaul about the sixth century, and in Italy the inrush of migrating tribes may be held to have ceased after the Lombard conquest, though the wars were by no means at an end.

Where the Roman population was still in sufficient numbers at the time of the invasion to retain some organization, the first invaders neither mixed with the Romans nor outnumbered them. Just because the barbarians were relatively few as compared to the inhabitants of the Roman Empire, they ruled the country at first by keeping apart from the indigenous population; thus the ancient customs and organizations of civil life and trade were not swept away of a sudden. The Roman *municipia* disappeared, the village organization was enforced, the corporations of the free workmen and tradespeople lost all legal *raison d'être*; and yet in Rome and in Central and Southern Italy the traditional system of administration was so far from being forgotten, that the names of ancient magistrates occur unexpectedly in documents of the sixth, seventh, eighth, and ninth centuries. Long before the year 1000 there were cities which enjoyed a rudimentary communal administration. During the last centuries of the Empire military authority had been taken away from the civil magistrates of the *municipia*, and the *dux*, or military commander, had acquired an ever-increasing influence. When the power passed into the invaders' hands, in Northern Italian towns there were officials, whether Goth, Lombard, or Frank, under the names of dukes (*duces*), counts (*comites*) or marquises who retained both military and every other authority. The change was thus gradual, and continuity was not totally broken.

The system of administration of the new masters, such as it was, was opposed to free labour, and thus it was antagonistic to the close corporations of the Romans which were linked together by economic legal and religious ties. But if the corporate organization offered little resistance in the minor centres, it was very hard to suppress in the cities, particularly when the corporation exercised a trade of primary necessity. In point of fact *scholae* are mentioned in documents of cities subjected to the rule of Byzantium, and guilds make their appearance everywhere at a fairly early date. The guilds were not identical with the *scholae*, and they were probably not a direct continuation of the Roman corporations, but their appearance seems to prove that old customs and methods had survived despite the unfavourable economic environment.

The land was mostly cultivated for the new masters by the old owners who became *aldii* or serfs; and owing to the great decrease in population which was brought about by the wars of the third, fourth, and fifth centuries, agriculture was mainly extensive rather than intensive; there were woods and pastures and only so much tilled soil as was necessary; but the great monasteries and the great abbeys were founded often in barren, impervious, and unwholesome regions, and the land surrounding them was quickly cleared, broken, drained, and subjected to an exploitation which was far more intensive.

Another stage requires attention. The invaders, who had endeavoured at first to rule the newly occupied lands by holding aloof from the old population, were soon compelled to come into touch with a civilization which, however corrupt and decayed, was immeasurably superior to their own. And, once the first step was taken, the new masters, though retaining the absolute pre-eminence in the government, were rapidly attracted into the cycle of ancient civilization and became assimilated by the native population. One illustration will be sufficient. The Lombards were among the least advanced of the invaders, for they seem to have lacked even epic traditions, and were as ferocious as they were valorous; nevertheless they could not withstand the lure of civilization. They had been Arians and became Catholics; they had no sooner settled in Italy than they wrote their inscriptions in Latin; their kings Rothari and Liutprand, in compiling codes of Germanic law, must have availed themselves of the expert assistance of Latin lawyers, for in the details of their statutes the echoes of Roman Law are unmistakable; little over fifty years after their arrival in Italy they began to intermarry with the inhabitants and, as they numbered from the outset not more than two or three hundred thousand, they were so quickly assimilated by the Latin population, that during the ninth century the Lombard language was not to be heard anywhere in Italy.

That the invaders soon grew accustomed to city life and undertook the building of churches and palaces is proved by the evidence of documents and still extant edifices, most of which bear marks of Roman influence whether they be found in the lands occupied by the Franks or in those where the Lombards ruled. It has been maintained both that their efforts brought about the rise of a new school of architecture and decorative art, and that the work must have been entrusted to specialized corporations of masons who hailed from Northern Italy. The two theories contradict one another so completely that it seems hopeless to suggest a satisfactory compromise. There is scarcely any evidence, however, that Italian workmen were enlisted by Charlemagne, and possibly the Roman elements in Frankish architecture are to be traced to the influence and the study of Vitruvius; on the other hand, it is most likely that the Lombards had recourse to local masons retaining some tradition of the proficiency to which their craft had risen in the past. Such signs of originality as used to be pointed out in Lombard art are now held to be due to local Byzantine influence. And it seems the more likely that the secrets of craftsmanship were traditionally retained and kept alive by some loosely constituted associations which survived despite the hostility of German legislation, or by families, for there is ample evidence that the sovereigns, from the Lombard Ataulf to Otto II, bestowed privileges and extended protection to certain classes of the vanquished races which were of use to them, such as merchants and tradesmen; and it may be assumed that some exemption from the application of existing laws was also made in favour of capable builders and decorators. At any rate, there seems to have been no absolute break of continuity in the development of necessary crafts.

It is at times difficult to trace such fragments of ancient lore as are still with us, so difficult in point of fact that they are only too often ignored. But in most branches of life and culture, however humble or exalted, if one probes deep enough and goes back far enough one can almost always trace the influence of Rome. Thus in a recent book by a glass-maker on glass-making in England it is shown that though no glass was made by the Romans in England, the Anglo-Saxon glasses of the sixth and seventh centuries are directly evolved from Roman forms.

The conversion to Christianity and to Catholicism is a phenomenon which took place wherever the invaders came into contact with civilized races. In the territories where a Roman language was spoken the invaders also adopted the language of their vanquished subjects for the purposes of daily use, while Latin became for them too the official and literary language. This latter change was probably hastened by the influence of the Roman Church, but the Church achieved a much more relevant result. From the fifth to the ninth century it gradually undertook the functions of education and learning, and one may assert that the principal means by which Roman culture passed through the Middle Ages and gave rise to their culture, is to be traced in the powerful organization of the Church.

It was uphill work to save what was left of ancient thought, for the decline of Roman power had been accompanied, as is well known, by a surprising dearth and decadence of literary and scientific output. Already Claudian lamented

> Ei mihi, quo Latiae vires Urbisque potestas
> Decidit ! in qualem paulatim fluximus umbram !

It seems that after a period during which creative work was undertaken rather by provincial than by purely Roman or Latin authors, an epoch followed during which the tendencies and defects which were peculiar to certain provinces gained favour and left a deep mark upon literature. Thus at the end of the fifth and during the early part of the following century there was in Northern Africa a period of recovery from decadence; two Vandal rulers, just like Theodoric in Italy, endeavoured to revive culture as well as peaceful activities; the schools were reorganized and men of letters received encouragement at Court; mediocre poets wrote in praise of their Vandal Kings, and Fulgentius showed the way to an allegorical interpretation of the *Aeneid*; he claimed that he was pointing out 'Virgilianae continentiae secreta physica', and avoided setting down 'illa quae plus periculi possent praerogare quam laudis'. This strange attempt will be less surprising if one recollects that African writers had developed since the second century a tendency to an obscure and almost cryptic style, mistaking difficulty for elegance, so that Virgilius Maro, the grammarian, who was probably a contemporary of Fulgentius, declared in his *Epitomae* that there is not only one sort of Latin, but twelve, in order that one may be enabled (in the manner of nineteenth-century diplomatists) to conceal sublime thoughts from the crowd. The allegorical interpretation of classical works was the necessary counterpart of an ideal of obscurity in writing, for the masterpieces of literature must needs have been held to be merely apparently lucid. Thus the fashion of allegorical interpretation was started in the same province of the Western Empire which had been the first to show signs of decadence.

When the German race began to crowd at the boundaries of the Western Empire and later to move across them and to unhinge the gates of the Empire, Roman literature had admittedly begun to fail, and the turmoil of wars and invasions was not likely to bring about its revival; but it is a grievous mistake to believe that literature was suddenly silenced. Just as men continue to live under oppression, they cannot cease thinking or writing.

Boëthius lived at the court of Theodoric the Ostrogoth, and there wrote his works, which summed up ancient knowledge for the Middle Ages. When he was actually in a dungeon at

Pavia awaiting his death sentence, he composed the most celebrated of his treatises, *De Consolatione Philosophiae*, in which Stoic doctrines find a place alongside of a tendency to allegory, and an uncertain sense of a new epoch is traceable side by side with a deep attachment to the old world. The works of Boëthius, and particularly his last book, were destined to rank among the best known to mediaeval scholars. And Cassiodorus provided them at the same time with a summary of the arts of the *Trivium* and *Quadrivium*. Apart from their importance as sources of the mediaeval knowledge of antiquity, these two men acquire an almost symbolical significance. They lived when the crumbling of the old civilization was apparent to all, but they did not despair. When the sovereign whom he had loyally served threw Boëthius into jail and sentenced him to death, that philosopher, who had translated Aristotle into Latin, found consolation in philosophy, as if he wished to teach the men of his and later ages, that barbarians may oppress and threaten a civilized and innocent people with destruction, but this people will find solace and strength in the pursuit of knowledge; political power may fail, but intellectual force will prove unconquerable.

Worse days were still to come, but the cultural heritage of the ancient world was never completely wiped out. Whatever was left of intellectual life during the gradual decline which occurred in the earlier mediaeval centuries was entirely Latin. One may say that whatever the Middle Ages thought and wrote, was thought and written in Latin, was based on Latin foundations, and was expressed in Latin. And if it is true that the nations of modern Europe were formed during the years between A.D. 500 and 1200, it is necessarily true that they were formed under the guardianship of the great memories of ancient Rome.

An exception may be found in Britain, where the authors of *Beowulf*, *Widsith*, and the *Ruin*, Caedmon and Cynewulf wrote in the vernacular, but did not Alfred endeavour to bring his people into direct contact with the Latin tradition by translating Orosius and Boëthius? And did not Bede or a contemporary write: 'Quam diu stabit Colyseus, stabit et Roma; quando cadet Colyseus, cadet et Roma; quando cadet Roma, cadet et mundus'?

Outside Britain, and soon in Britain also, the language of the schools was the language of Rome. If a man was able to sign his name without the help of some sort of stencil plate, if he was able to read a letter or to write it, he must have had some knowledge of Latin. And he wrote in a hand that was derived from Rome. Mediaeval palaeography could provide by itself a sufficient illustration of the unbroken persistence of the Roman legacy. A superficial observer might think that mediaeval scripts had national origins and should be classified as Lombard, Merovingian, Saxon, &c. But, as Traube pointed out, Maffei has corrected this error long ago. Mediaeval handwriting had one origin only, and that was Roman. Its varieties were due to local developments, and arose in an epoch in which the unity of the Roman tradition was weakened, and the interdependence of its several centres had been loosened by the invaders. The greater the ignorance, the greater was the almost superstitious obsequiousness to the Latin tradition and glories. What matter if the *Aeneid* was inadequately understood, badly transcribed, and allegorically interpreted, if the whole outlook upon the ancient world was influenced by the Roman and imperial conception of it which Virgil had raised above contingency and launched for posterity? What matter if the Virgilian hexameter was at times wrongly scanned or if the fourth *Eclogue* was held to imply that, in some miraculous way, Virgil was a follower of Christ, when one observes that the personality of the poet acquired so great an attraction for the mediaeval mind as to be surrounded with the superstitious halo of necromancy? John of Salisbury laughed at the French clerk of the days of William the Bad who wished to visit Naples in order to dig out Virgil's magic booklet from beneath the poet's skeleton ; but the anecdote shows how great Virgil's personality loomed in the darkness of mediaeval ignorance.

It was not the Homeric tradition which prevailed and found credit in the Middle Ages, but the tradition which Rome and Virgil had started, as is sufficiently proved by the boastful claims to Trojan foundations which were set forward by countless cities of Britain, France, Germany, Spain, and Italy. Virgil found useful allies in Dictys of Crete and Dares of Phrygia, and Trojan lineage was asserted in more works of poetry and prose than can here be enumerated.

With a few exceptions mediaeval literature, at any rate the literature of culture, was Latin and could only be Latin ; and such opposition as it met during the earlier periods was due to ecclesiastics, despite the fact that the principal, and by far the most numerous, agents who spread Latin culture during the Middle Ages belonged to the Church. Vernacular literature was scarcely a rival to be considered.

The opposition was raised for the first time by Jerome and St. Augustine ; Gregory the Great and after him most of those who attempted to reform the customs of the clergy took up the same position during the Middle Ages. Even Boccaccio was assailed with such doubts and had to be comforted by Petrarch. A crusade was started against profane science and literature. From Jerome and Gregory, down to Odo of Cluny, all professed to scorn ancient learning, purity of style, and even syntactical rules ; but their very protests were written in Latin, and their authors showed that they possessed an adequate knowledge of the language and were widely read in its literature. And while they scorned profane learning, they endeavoured to improve the standard of education among the clergy ; and they founded schools with such an object in view. In these schools, however, Latin was taught, and the rules and examples of this language were necessarily taught according to classical models. Thus the road to the acquisition of profane learning was kept open by the work of its principal opponents ; for what could prevent a student more inquisitive than the average from feeling dissatisfied with the fare that religious books provided? The works of St. Augustine were apt to arouse curiosity by the quotation of classical authors and doctrines, and the student could well feel prompted by them to read such ancient books as he happened to find in the library of his monastery. Then as now the training of students was based on anthologies and text-books; these also were apt to suggest to the learner the attractions of classical studies, even if such books were Donatus, the *Disticha Catonis*, or lives and anecdotes of famous men of the ancient world.

It is surely of some significance that a large section of the works which were written in mediaeval French dealt with Latin traditions, from the *Roman de Troie* to the *Roman de Rome* and the *Livre de César*.

If this aspect of the question be considered from a more strictly chronological standpoint the results are the same and equally cogent. The Western Empire fell in the fifth century, and about a hundred years later Gregory the Great, in his indictment of profane learning, pointed out the mistakes which he had committed in spelling, in accidence, and in the application of all grammatical rules; as if he had taken pride in them and echoed the words of the sage: 'Daemonum cibus est carmina poetarum, saecularis sapientia, rhetoricorum pompa verborum.' On the other hand, his words may suggest that he smarted under the limitations of his proficiency, which he was sufficiently learned to measure by the standard of the ancients rather than that of his contemporaries. A gifted contemporary of his, Gregory of Tours, lamented the decadence of learning in Gaul, enumerating his own grammatical mistakes in almost identical words. Need one then accept as irresistible the conclusion that humane studies had become a thing of the past and that creative literature was silent? One may reasonably doubt it, for the ancient biographers of Gregory the Great are loud in the praise of his wisdom, learning, and care for good studies; and about the same time Maximianus, an archbishop of Ravenna, had compiled a famous universal history which unfortunately has not come down to us; Venantius Fortunatus rose to great fame owing to his much too facile muse; Secundus, bishop of Trent, wrote a history of the Lombards, and many authors flourished whose value it is difficult to judge on account of the loss of their works.

The conditions of learning became worse in Rome and in Italy during the following century, when every vestige of Roman civilization in Northern Africa was wiped out by the Arabs; but in Spain a centre of study was formed. At the court of the Visigoth princes there were many scholars, perhaps more notable for their zeal than their accomplishments, and all overshadowed by Isidore, bishop of Seville, who gave proof in his *Etymologiarum libri* of a learning which would be remarkable at all times and was prodigious in his own.

And if the Saracens, by crossing the straits, silenced Latin culture in Spain for a long time to come, learning had already found another refuge in Ireland. Following upon conversion to Christianity, there had been in that island since the fifth century a revival which was connected with Greek learning. The monks, trained during that and the following century, at Clonard, Bangor, and other celebrated monastic centres, were as ardent in their ascetic piety as they were tireless in their pursuit of learning. Some of them went over to Scotland, England, and the Continent in order to bring comfort to the harassed inhabitants and to teach them again to admire 'quae doctiloqui cecinerunt carmina vates', as St. Columban wrote in one of his poems. It was Columban who, leaving Bangor, founded a monastery at Luxeuil, and on being driven out of France, crossed the Alps and founded the abbey of Bobbio which was to become so important a factor in the revival of learning in Italy.

The efforts of the pious and learned monks of Celtic race proved more successful in reviving religious zeal than Latin culture, partly because in all lands where Romance languages were spoken the vernaculars were breaking through the Latin shell, and were straining all grammatical rules. Thus during the sixth and seventh centuries the seeds of Latin civilization survived, but could do little more. It is, however, of some relevance to note that during the sixth, seventh, and eighth centuries Rome was the centre whence the evangelization of a great part of continental Europe was conducted; from Rome Augustine and Theodore of Tarsus were sent to Britain; Wilfrid, Willibrord, and Boniface kept in touch with Rome. They went forth and conquered; and the weapons which assisted them in their missions were the relics of saints and books: the relics providing miracles, the books being used for religious and educational purposes. There is ample evidence that these missionaries were unceasing in their demands, so much so that even the resources of Rome, which was held to have unlimited stores of relics in the churches and of books in the papal library, became strained. By the end of the seventh century the Popes were unable to accede to all the requests for books which the missionaries and converts made. These zealous Christians went in pilgrimage to Rome and returned to their countries, bringing with them, as Saint Gertrude did, 'volumina de Romana urbe'. Rome had by necessity become a centre of book trade and an emporium for all things which are used in churches. There is evidence in the works of Anglo-Saxon and Celtic writers that the unceasing demand called into being industrial undertakings. Books were actively transcribed, vestments and sacred pictures were produced in large quantities. Three Saxons, about whom Ædelwald wrote in his work *De Transmarini itineris peregrinatione*, brought back from Rome 'volumina numerosa', 'vestium velamina' which were finely woven and embroidered, and paintings of Christ and of Mary. The Venerable Bede, in his account of Benedict Biscop's life, wrote that this first abbot of Wearmouth went seven times in pious pilgrimage to Rome and returned with loads of books which he had purchased or received as gifts, with pictures representing Christ, the Holy Mary, the Apostles and the Last Judgement, and beautiful altar frontals made of silk. He assures us that the books were 'omnis generis', and comprised a manuscript of Greek cosmography which was much admired by the King. Theodore of Tarsus had taught Greek as well as Latin to his pupils in Britain, who were refreshingly unable to draw a distinction between sacred and profane learning; thus a pilgrimage to Rome was not only a pious duty for them, but also an opportunity for intellectual enlightenment. And they returned from their pilgrimage with some added knowledge of the classics and overwhelmed with admiration for that wonderful city of St. Peter which still gloried in so many monuments of her ancient magnificence. On reaching their homes these tireless missionaries of faith and learning were not more fervent in their laudation of the teaching of the Church than in their praises of the greatness and learning of Rome. The impression which pilgrims received from a visit to Rome may be measured by such works as the *Mirabilia Romanae Urbis* and the *Graphia aureae urbis Romae*. Rome was still the capital of the world, 'Roma potens, mundi decus, inclyta mater' as Alcuin wrote, 'caput mundi' as the old Prosper of Aquitaine seems to have realized sooner than others:

> Sedes Roma Petri quae pastoralis honoris
> Facta, caput mundi, quidquid non possidet armis
> Religione tenet.

In Gaul there was a period of decline during the reign of the last Merovingians despite the activities of Gregory of Tours, Venantius Fortunatus who became bishop of Poitiers, and others; but before Charlemagne ascended the throne, his father and grandfather had striven to raise the standard of ecclesiastical education; and, with this object in view, they had founded new schools and reformed those which existed already by appointing as directors scholars of merit and trust. Thus during and before the reign of Charlemagne there occurred in Gaul an amazingly rapid revival which was wholeheartedly supported by the Popes. Besides liturgical books Paul I sent Greek treatises on grammar and science to Pepin, and he dispatched to the Frank court the prior of the *schola cantorum* of St. Peter, as he had sent the *praecantor* of the same 'schola' to England. The Roman *schola cantorum* had a history and an importance of its own: its object was the education not of choir boys but of priests; and being placed under the immediate supervision of the Popes it was the object of the greatest care. Thus it is known that the study of Greek was pursued in the *schola* when all knowledge of that language was probably forgotten in all parts of Italy except where Basilian settlements existed; and it is maintained that the pupils of the *schola* who were destined to serve in the papal chancery received instruction in the elements of Civil and Canonical law. Such a school of law is supposed to have had moments of splendour during which it rivalled the school of law which the Byzantines kept up at Ravenna, and the school which was founded at Pavia by the Lombard kings in order to educate a class of 'notaries' capable of drafting and interpreting the royal decrees. Later a famous school of law was established at Bologna and became the kernel of the University; the way for the school of Bologna was prepared, however, by the activities in legal learning of such centres as Ravenna, Pavia, and probably Rome itself.

But the papal support which was freely given to Pepin and Charlemagne would be grievously misunderstood if it were held to imply that the Carlovingian revival of learning took place under Italian influence. At the Frankish court, where men were assembled from all parts of the West, Italians were few, they remained for short periods, and were entrusted with comparatively unimportant duties; only Paulus Diaconus, Peter of Pisa, and Paulinus of Aquileia represented Italian thought in the circle of Charlemagne; and they were summoned to it long after the beginning of his educational reform. It was in Italy that Charlemagne had met his principal adviser, but he was not an Italian. In the year 781 at Parma the king came across Alcuin, and was so favourably impressed with him, that the scholar was thereafter attached to the court and was never allowed to leave it for long. Notker, the monk of St. Gall, did not think of Alcuin, and may have rather exaggerated his description when he wrote that two Scots on landing in Gaul shouted to the crowd: 'If there is any one among you who wishes to acquire wisdom, let him come to us and he will get it, for we have it for sale'; it is certain, however, that Charlemagne's educational activities were influenced by Irish and Anglo-Saxon tendencies and learning, and among the men who were entrusted with the more delicate duties were Alcuin and his friends, Wizzo, Fridugis, Dicuil, Eginhard, Clemens Scotus, Josephus Scotus, and Smaragdus. And just as their treatises were Celtic in type, the best Latin poets at court were the Frank Angilbert and Alcuin himself.

But whatever their immediate origin, their learning was profoundly Latin. Alcuin's treatises are based on Donatus, Cicero's *De Inventione*, Porphyrius' *Introduction* and Aristotle's categories, and his poems are not free from open and frequent imitations of Virgil, Lucan, Statius, and Fortunatus; they retain, however, sufficient individuality not to be comparable to the usual *centones* of the Middle Ages. Creative power was not stunted in them by servile imitation, and the *Versus de cuculo* and *Conflictus veris et hiemis* are charming little poems. Eginhard's *Vita Karoli* was cast in the mould of Suetonius' life of Augustus. The palaces of Worms, Ingelheim, Nimwegen, and Aix-la-Chapelle were decorated with statues and precious marbles which had been removed from Ravenna and Rome, and were probably built after the designs of Eginhard, a man who seems to have possessed all gifts and was a close student of Vitruvius. Further, the writing and illuminating of manuscripts reached in the days of Charlemagne a very high standard of clearness and neatness, but both handwriting and illuminations reveal Anglo-Saxon influence. During the eighth century Latinity went back to Gaul through Britain.

Charlemagne's schemes of educational reform were not allowed to lapse by his sons and successors. It was during their rule that Italy was struck by the tide which had first started from Rome, spreading through the Western Empire, and later had flowed back from Ireland to Northumberland, from Northumberland and Ireland to the Carlovingian kingdom. The delay must be accounted for by political conditions, and by the fact that Italian activities seemed to centre on trade and later on building when the means were provided for it by the pence of a growing number of pilgrims. Schools were established or reformed; Irish monks formed centres of teaching at Bobbio, Pavia, in Venetia, in Piedmont, in Aemilia, at Nonantola, in Tuscany, at Farfa, and more particularly at Monte Cassino. An unknown Irishman copied works of Horace, Ovid, St. Augustine, and Bede at Milan and his manuscript is still extant; the Marquess Eberhard of Friuli had in his library works of religion and writings by Vegetius, Orosius, Fulgentius, Sedulius, Alcuin, and Smaragdus; there is evidence that almost everywhere libraries were put together at this time. Donatus Scotus, who became bishop of Florence, is supposed to have explained to his pupils not only Virgil, but also portions of Hesiod and Democritus; at Naples Lothar II is said to have met thirty-two philosophers, the value of whose theories it is probably merciful that we are unable to judge.

Progress was stunted once more during the tenth century, and a period of decadence followed. The onslaught of Arabs, Normans, and Slavs brought confusion and destruction everywhere; the breaking up of the Carlovingian empire and the struggles in Britain and Italy caused learning to fall into abeyance. But towards the end of the century in France a more settled political condition followed upon the victory of Hugh Capet; and Odo of Cluny undertook to restore discipline and learning among the clergy, drawing inspiration perhaps for some aspects of his reform from Irish traditions; and the movement rapidly spread in all directions. Odo repeated the well-worn charges against profane learning, but his Latin verses show that he did not act upon his own theories. Nevertheless the lack of princely courts where men of learning could find refuge, protection, and the necessary encouragement, might well have rendered fruitless all previous efforts, if a progressive sovereign had not arisen in Saxony, where such an event seemed least likely to occur. Otto I, the Great, added to his circle and attracted to himself the best brains of France, Germany, and Italy: Stephen of Novara, Gunzo, Ekkehart II, and Bernward of Hildesheim who, after the death of Otto II, helped his Byzantine Empress, Theophano, to bring up the youthful Otto III. Schools sprang up in Saxony, in Bavaria, where, at Tegernsee, the learned Froumunt copied in his own hand works of Horace, Cicero, Statius, Juvenal, and Persius, also in Lorraine and in Flanders. It has been observed that few laymen had any part in this Saxon revival, but the clergy had in that epoch so great a share in the management of civil and political affairs that the movement did not exhaust itself in the seclusion of cells or affect only religious learning. No doubt pious texts and theological books claimed the largest attention, but the classics were not ignored, since Roswitha found occasion to decry the coarseness of Terence, and Rahing of Flavigny to copy the *Aeneid*. Latin learning did not penetrate the Saxon world so deeply as it had done the people of Britain; German legends, however, were rendered into Latin and topical poems were composed in Latin for a musical setting. Music had indeed a considerable share in this progressive movement, a fact which is but partly due to the German fondness for song, for Latin influence entered into musical studies. Gerbert has been hailed as the innovator of musical art particularly because he succeeded in explaining the theories of Macrobius and Boëthius for the benefit of the mediaeval world. And it was primarily due to his interpretation and dissemination of the information which he drew from Boëthius and to his direct or indirect connexion with Arab and Jewish scholars of Spain that Gerbert became also the leader of a revival of scientific studies.

Thus there appears to have been scarcely any intellectual movement during the earlier Middle Ages which was not closely dependent on the Roman heritage. Just as a great fire resists the attempts at extinction and after the principal outburst is checked, flares up here and there in secondary blazes, the Latin civilization could not be stamped out. When Italy ceased to be its centre, there were indications of its persistence in Africa, in Spain and Ireland : from Ireland the movement spread to Britain, from Ireland and Britain to France, to Germany and back to Italy ; then from Germany to France and to Italy again.

At last, towards the end of the tenth century, we find a more enduring revival throughout Europe : the improvement was no longer local and temporary, but general and continuous, and announced the dawn of Scholasticism ; there were still ecclesiastics of excessively mundane disposition, and there were countries in which the laymen did not share in the progress of learning ; but even the most corrupt ecclesiastics were widely read in the classics ; so much so that the factious bishop Ratherius of Verona felt bound to justify himself for having cited and imitated too often the works of Virgil, Cicero, and Seneca ; elsewhere laymen vied with ecclesiastics in the pursuit of learning. In Germany, France, and Britain wider knowledge was immediately followed by increased creative activity ; in Italy such a result was considerably delayed, but in the end it took place there also, and before the year 1000, Eugenius Vulgarius of Naples, who was acquainted with Lucan, Horace, Virgil, Servius, and many other authors and books including Boëthius' *Institutio Arithmeticae*, showed himself to be a master of metre, and ventured to employ metrical schemes which had ceased to be used since ancient days. A tendency peculiar to mediaeval culture became at this time increasingly apparent : the culture which was Latin and closely linked to the Church, was catholic by definition and thus unaffected by national or racial distinctions. This is not to be interpreted too strictly, for men did not cease to be men, nor racial and political prejudice to exercise their influence, but it would be difficult to point out such national characteristics in the culture of the centuries from 1000 to 1300. Just as men of all races flocked to the court of Charlemagne to place themselves under the guidance of Alcuin, and just as learned men who were born in France, England, and Italy joined the Germans whom the Ottos protected, so when the centres of study were formed which developed by degrees into the great mediaeval universities, students and teachers flocked to them from every part of Europe. The world of study was never more united and single-minded than in the period of the Schoolmen ; it stood above national associations, a real 'universitas magistrorum' which comprised the men of learning and science of every civilized country.

It is not our purpose to outline a sketch of Latin traditions and culture during the Middle Ages ; it suffices to have shown that there was no definite break of continuity in the tradition of culture from the fifth to the eleventh century ; that learning never became fully extinct, even if in the most perilous and gory periods of strife it had to seek shelter in successive migrations to different countries.

The year 1000 provides a useful landmark. It was once an accepted tradition that men had been terrorized by fearful predictions which forecast the end of the world at that date ; so that the daily expectation of a cataclysm had inflicted a daily repetition of the agonies of death. It is known now that men were never preyed upon by such a terror ; that they never trembled at the thought of the year 1000, and thus were not spurred to new hopes and activity when the fatal date had gone by. But this legend may have a foundation in truth or at least a symbolical value. The social and political conditions in Europe during the tenth century were terrible; for England the *Chronicle* is sufficient evidence of it: and on the Continent similar documents could easily be cited. The unceasing ravages which Normans, Arabs, and Hungarians inflicted upon Europe may well have aroused in men a blank feeling of despair no less crushing than the fabled expectation of the end of the world. After the year 1000 the political conditions did not suddenly improve, but the atmosphere became less disturbed: studies in particular were pursued in a manner more methodical owing to the activities of the Schoolmen and the other contemporary philosophers who cannot be classed, but must nevertheless be grouped with the Schoolmen.

Early in the Middle Ages there had been men of keen perception who realized, dimly at first and later more distinctly, that the barbarian invasions had brought about a serious decline in learning; and scholars who felt competent to impart any teaching became more or less clearly conscious of a task which they could not fail to undertake, the salvage of such fragments of knowledge as they had learned from the ancients. It is probably due to such impressions and intentions, that most of the authors seemed to renounce specialization, and wrote works of an encyclopaedic character. On the threshold of the Middle Ages Boëthius and Cassiodorus endeavoured to cram into their works large stores of information; later Isidore of Seville, Gregory of Tours, and the Venerable Bede wrote about all branches of learning.

Alcuin asserted that philosophy is 'naturarum inquisitio, rerum divinarum humanarumque cognitio quantum possibile est homini aestimare'; Alcuin's pupil and plagiarist, Rabanus Maurus, at the beginning of the ninth century compiled the great encyclopaedia of the earlier mediaeval centuries (*De Universo*). And let us note once more that all of them wrote in Latin and were only acquainted with Latin sources or with Greek works in Latin translations. There existed at that time some selections of Aristotle's *Organon* translated by Marius Victorinus and Boëthius, Plato's *Timaeus* translated and explained by Chalcidius in a way that rendered an accurate interpretation impossible; the outlines of other Platonic and Neo-Platonist works were known through the treatises of St. Augustine; there was also the *Isagoge* of Porphyrius translated by Marius Victorinus; and further Macrobius, Mamertus, Donatus, some of Cicero's works, Virgil, Ovid, Horace, Seneca, Juvenal, Lucan, Claudian, Vitruvius, Vegetius; a few rhetorical books, the Latin and some of the Greek Fathers in Latin renderings, and later the works of the Pseudo-Dionysius Areopagita, translated by John Scotus, Gregory the Great, Isidore, Bede, Marcianus Capella. A few additions, including a number of spurious books, would complete this list of the most common sources, the usefulness of which was further impaired by amazingly mistaken attributions.

It has been mentioned already that the intellectual activity of the tenth century was centred on single individuals and isolated schools: Odo at Cluny, Poppo at Fulda, and then Ratherius, Liutprand, Notker, Gunzo. Gunzo was among the most interesting figures, being a layman in the company of ecclesiastics and thus an outstanding representative of that lay education which amazed Otto of Freisingen; he showed a pugnacious punctiliousness that was later unfortunately to be the frequent heritage of the humanists. But Gerbert is by far the greatest of all his contemporaries. His intellect was so insatiable that he wished to know everything knowable; and so exceptionally powerful that he reached conclusions almost by divination, arguing from data that would have been insufficient for most men. At last, towards the end of the tenth and the beginning of the following century, there came on the stage another strange representative of lay scholarship, Anselm of Besate, and St. Anselm of Aosta whom De Wulf calls the first of the Schoolmen. The rise of Scholasticism renders the later process of transmission of the Roman heritage too simple to need explanation, for the philosophers who are described as Schoolmen have a common minimum of doctrine and knowledge, besides methods and tendencies of interpreting it which were proper to each ; but the Schoolmen were particularly linked to one another by a fundamental conception of culture. Truth, according to them, was not a personal possession discovered independently by each philosopher ; it was a treasure that had to be handed down from generation to generation, each generation increasing its preciousness by adding further discoveries. Thus the transmission of as much as had survived of ancient culture was understood by the Schoolmen to be the natural function of scholarship. They were no longer distressed, as were Jerome or Gregory of Tours, by a dramatic conflict between inborn love of learning and a conception of Christianity which rendered every profane knowledge abominable. The recurrence of such a contrast among the Schoolmen was rare and sporadic. No doubt the more important questions which were debated by them, concerned philosophy, such as the question of universals ; no doubt Scholastic philosophy tended in its development to identify itself with theology ; no doubt the Schoolmen did not abate the mediaeval claim to encyclopaedic knowledge ; but the great intellectual activity that was caused by Scholastic philosophy, and particularly the feverish search after truth, had a very great influence on all branches of learning.

John of Salisbury in the introduction of his *Metalogicus* inveighed against a typical reactionary who still contrasted religious duty with profane learning, but by his time this contest had already been won. Scholastic learning had reached its fullness ; it was incomparably broader in extent and deeper in appreciation than it had been for centuries. First the contact with the Arabic and Jewish schools of Spain, then the relations with the Byzantine and Oriental world coinciding with the Crusades and reaching their climax in 1204 with the capture of Constantinople, and lastly the intercourse with eastern philosophers which took place at the court of Frederick II, had been and were to be of invaluable assistance to progress.

The twelfth century prepared by tireless labours the triumph of Scholasticism in the thirteenth century. The first stimulus came from the discovery and translation into Latin of more works of Aristotle, who had been known so far merely as a dialectician; the ultimate perfection was rendered possible by Albertus Magnus and achieved by Thomas Aquinas. By then both the Dominican and the Franciscan orders had been founded, and they became, during the thirteenth century, the moving spirits of the oldest Universities, taking the lead which the Benedictines had held hitherto. It was in the thirteenth century that the very learned Robert Grosseteste showed that he had enough Greek to translate works written in that language at a time when few knew any Greek outside the Byzantine Empire and Basilian monasteries. It was then also that Roger Bacon forestalled later discoveries by his miraculous intuitions of the principles of science, and Meister Eckhart inaugurated German mysticism. Philosophy began at that epoch to acquire national characteristics, just as arts were becoming nationalized; the legacy had been passed down to the modern world.

Modern thought, however, did not succeed for a long time, and then in part only, in freeing itself from mediaeval influences. Already during the eleventh century the discovery of some forgotten classical works had rendered more complex the relations with ancient thought, and they soon acquired entirely new forms. Gunzo's pride and pugnacity, John of Salisbury's admiration for and imitation of Cicero's style, the almost humanistic tendencies of the Paduan group of poets who called Lovato their master, had all been indications of a new spirit which was arising. It was not many years before Richard of Bury started to collect books with the ardour of a bibliomaniac, and Petrarch led the way in a venturesome rediscovery of ancient thought; thus laying the foundations of Italian philosophy, as Meister Eckhart forecast the German and Roger Bacon the English philosophical tendencies.

The moderns were no longer satisfied with what ancient learning had been assimilated and elaborated by mediaeval thought; they endeavoured to establish a direct connexion with the classics by ignoring the Middle Ages. The direct Roman heritage, however small it was, which had been a powerful stimulus, became almost oppressive when it had grown larger, and proved a mixed blessing by stunting originality in those countries where the movement of the Renaissance was strongest.

There is a sign by which the attitude of scholars and groups of scholars towards the ancient world may be most surely traced. With a few exceptions the learned literature of the Middle Ages was all written in Latin. And mediaeval men of letters availed themselves of that language with a maximum of freedom; it was a spoken language for them, they used it in teaching and debating; they thought in Latin, and thus adapted Latin to all the requirements of their thoughts, feeling free from all puristic preoccupations. Only those scholars need be excepted who lived far from Roman centres, such as the Venerable Bede, and were more readily attracted to imitating the classical style. More often polish was understood as complexity or obscurity, and mostly it was not sought at all. There developed as a result a κοινὴ διάλεκτος, a kind of *lingua franca* of mediaeval thought, the best example of which may be recognized in the remarkably perspicuous language which was used by Thomas Aquinas. These scholars wrote just as they thought, being only preoccupied with the object of making their meaning intelligible; when one of them imitated the style of a favourite Latin author, it may be assumed either that he was a solitary exception or that he was influenced by some of the circumstances which brought about the refinement of the Renaissance. But such exceptions are rare, for there were but few who recognized their own inferiority in writing Latin or who compared the κοινὴ διάλεκτος to Augustan models and found it wanting as a means of expression. These were purists for whom Latin was no longer a language of common usage as it was for their contemporaries, a common and thus almost a living language; but an artificial means of cultivated thought, a dead language which could be imitated from classical models but could no longer be enlivened by new developments.

Modern nations were formed while the direct influence of Roman thought was exercised without interference. The humanistic return to the ancient sources took place when the structure of modern nations had already hardened. Each of them took to herself that portion of the new discoveries which she wished or was able to take. But the direct heritage was not apportioned in the same manner. All the peoples of Western Europe, whatever their political vicissitudes happened to be, between the fifth and ninth century formed, by degrees, a cultural unit, which remained one and inseparable up to the thirteenth century. To such a development all races contributed their share until the Schoolmen of Paris gave the absolute leadership to France.

Later the different nations ceased to have an instinctive feeling of the common origins of their civilization; other influences and particularly national tendencies were at work; so that there came a time when it was possible to mistake the movement of the Renaissance for the principal cause of Latin influence.

But if one wishes to have a ready standard by which to evaluate the importance of the heritage, or a test by means of which to trace the different processes of transmission and their relative efficiency, one needs only to ask a few simple questions. What would have been the fate of European thought if the Romans had not existed and had not become masters of the world? How great would have been the disaster if the barbaric peoples had been allowed to begin their devastations five or six centuries earlier, and if they had not met on their way the enormous and massive structure of Roman civilization ?

Such questions open out possibilities so terrifying that one dares not venture to press them ; but we might find another question less difficult to answer : What would have been the course of western civilization if the men of the Renaissance had not endeavoured to suppress mediaeval culture by superimposing upon it the revived culture of the ancients ? Perhaps some would be found to reply that those nations that appear to have been more fortunate in the modern age experienced less deeply the influence of the Renaissance.

It would be an unpardonable overstatement to affirm that the modern age has received a larger share of the legacy of Rome by natural transmission, than it has acquired from the Renaissance ; but it would be no less inaccurate to fail to recognize that a considerable portion of that which the men of the Renaissance did find and accept had already reached them, however modified, by direct transmission, and that they were enabled to carry out their own discoveries thanks to that which had been taught to them by the Middle Ages.

CESARE FOLIGNO.

BOOKS RECOMMENDED.

MIGNE, *Patrol. cursus completus*, *Patr. lat.*, lxxxiv–xcv, c–ci.

DÜMMLER, *Poetae lat. Aevi Carolini* in 'Mon. Germ. Hist.'

J. E. SANDYS, *A Hist. of Class. Scholarship*. Cambridge, 1903.

A. EBERT, *Allgem. Gesch. d. Lit. des Mittelalters im Abendlande*. Leipzig.

G. GRÖBER, *Grundriss der rom. Phil.*, vol. ii.

M. MANITIUS, *Gesch. d. latein. Liter. d. Mittelalters*, vol. i. München, 1911.

L. TRAUBE, *Vorlesungen u. Abhandlungen*, vol. ii. München, 1911.

R. L. POOLE, *Illustrations to the Hist. of Med. Thought and Learning*. S.P.C.K., 1920.

M. DE WULF, *Hist. of Med. Scholastics* (Engl. Transl.). London, 1909.

A. Graf, *Roma nella Memoria e nella Immaginazione del Medio Evo.* Turin, 1882.

D. Comparetti, *Virgil in the Middle Ages* (Engl. transl.) London, 1895.

The Cambridge History of Engl. Lit., vol. i, 1920.

F. Novati, *Le Origini* in 'St. lett. d'Italia'. Milan, no date (1899-).

J. B. Bury, *Hist. of the Later Rom. Empire.* London, 1889.

J. Bryce, *The Holy Rom. Empire.* London, 1905.

T. Hodgkin, *Italy and her Invaders.* Oxford, 1880–1899.

THE CONCEPTION OF EMPIRE

§ 1. The Roman Empire was born in the Eastern Mediterranean; and it was in the Eastern Mediterranean, in the city of Constantinople, that it died. We may almost say that it was Oriental in its origin: we may at any rate affirm that it was Hellenistic; and Hellenistic means the fusion of Greek and Oriental. The process of political development which prepared its birth began in the West, in a city on the Tiber which looked across the Tyrrhenian Sea to the setting sun; and it was the legal genius of Roman citizens—with their conceptions of *imperium* and *provincia*, *potestas* and *maiestas*—which gave to the Empire the framework and structure of its institutions. But the ideas on which it rested—the ideas which made it more than a structure, and gave it a root in the minds of men—were ideas which had germinated in the East. Any permanent society must rest on a body of belief and on the social will which such a body of belief creates. It was in the East that men had learned to believe in a single universal society, and in the government of that society by a king who was 'as a god among men', and indeed was a very god; and it was there, in the feeling of loyalty for the person of such a monarch, and even of 'adoration' of his divinity, that a corresponding social will had found its expression. If *imperium* was a Latin word, the idea of an empire and the idea of an emperor were not of Latin origin. We must recognize in the Roman Empire the result of the fusion of Roman political development and Roman institutional structure with Hellenistic ideas.

But it would be a grave error to magnify the Hellenistic element in this fusion at the expense of the Roman; and paradox would be wearing cap and bells if it proceeded to the proposition that the Roman Empire, if it was an empire, was not fundamentally Roman. While it was the Greek genius which, in its latter days, rose to conceptions of the unity of humanity, it was the Roman genius which translated those conceptions, in themselves unsubstantial and unbodied, into an organized system of life. But the word 'translation' fails to do justice to Rome. It implies that the Greeks first wrote an original text, of which the Romans afterwards issued an authorized version. It would be truer to say that the Romans built first—or at any rate built independently—a *de facto* empire, on which the Greeks afterwards looked, and as they looked exclaimed, '*τοῦτ' ἐκεῖνο*: this is the unity of humanity of which we have been thinking all along'. From this point of view we may almost say that Hellenistic conceptions settled upon and clustered round a Roman achievement; adorned and even modified that achievement; but left the solid core of achievement Roman still. It is hard to weigh men of action against men of thought: it is no less difficult to weigh a people of action against a people of thought. Perhaps it is unnecessary, as it is certainly thankless, to do either; perhaps we may avoid contention, without shirking difficulties, if we conclude by saying that Rome built an empire in a world permeated by the preparatory thought of Greece, and that Greek thought continued to permeate, and even came to cement, the empire which Rome had built.

There were empires before that of Alexander. There was the Egyptian Empire, which extended to the Euphrates, of Thutmos III (*c.* 1500 B.C.) and his successors; there were the Semitic Empires of Sargon of Accad (*c.* 2750) and Hammurabi of Babylon (*c.* 2100), of the Assyrians of Nineveh (750–606) and the Chaldeans of Babylon (606–539); there was the Persian Empire (organized like the Roman in provinces, and traversed like the Roman by excellent roads) which lasted from 539 to 330 B.C. The Empire of Alexander was founded upon the ruin—and also upon the tradition—of the Persian, as the Persian had been founded upon the Chaldean and the Chaldean upon the Assyrian. Whatever the inspiration of Greek ideas under which Alexander began; whatever his original conception of a 'crusade' and the reduction of the 'barbarians' under the Greeks—it is certain that he came under the sway of older traditions, and embraced a different policy. Rejecting the advice offered by Aristotle in a treatise 'On Kingship', that 'he should distinguish between Greeks and barbarians, dealing with the former as ἡγεμών and the latter as δεσπότης', he sought to unite East and West in a common equality. He fostered intermarriage between Greeks and Persians: he received Persians into his army; he adopted the ceremonial of the Persian court and the Persian system of provincial government. His policy was perhaps premature; and his successors reserved the higher offices of state for Greeks and Macedonians. But the spread of a common culture achieved what policy could not at once effect; and in the next century Eratosthenes could declare the unity of mankind, 'refusing to agree with those, who divided mankind into Greeks and barbarians and advised Alexander to treat the former as friends and the latter as foes, and declaring that it was better to divide men simply into the good and the bad'.

This meant a great revolution in thought—a revolution which was the necessary precursor of any imperial system in the Western world. Alexander had united the known world of his time (save Italy and the confines of the West) in a single society; and he had assumed the equality of all the members of that society. He had contradicted the two axioms hitherto current in the political thought of the Greeks—that a multiplicity of separate self-governing and self-sufficing cities was the best constitution of politics, and that differences and inequalities between the members (enfranchised and disfranchised, citizen and alien) were inevitably implied by the very genius of the city. His conquests and his policy had implied two opposite conceptions—that of a single cosmopolis of the inhabited earth, transcending cities as it transcended tribes and nations; and that of the equality of all men, or at any rate all free men, in the life of a common humanity. These are the two fundamental conceptions which inaugurate a new epoch—an epoch which succeeds to that of the πόλις, and precedes that of the national state; an epoch which covers the centuries that lie between Aristotle and Alexander at one end and Luther and Henry VIII at the other, and embraces in its scope the three empires of Macedon and Rome and Charlemagne. They are again the two conceptions which we find in the teaching of St. Paul, who believed in one Church of all Christians which should cover the world, and held that in that Church there was 'neither Greek nor Jew . . . barbarian, Scythian, bond nor free'.

Implicit in the achievement of Alexander there is thus the idea of the union in a single society of the peoples both of the East and the West, who had hitherto either developed in isolation, or, if they had met, had met in conflict. He united the Eastern Mediterranean with Western Asia: it remained for Rome to add the Western Mediterranean to the amalgam which he had created. But a unity such as that which Alexander had founded needed a cohesive principle: it needed a common centre of personal attachment and loyalty; and we must therefore proceed to examine the nature of the cohesive principle which he gave to his empire, and which Rome afterwards inherited from his successors. That principle, in a word, was the deification of the ruler. The deified king could claim the universality, and receive the universal worship, of a manifest god. On this ground Greek cities and Oriental nations could unite; and with the throne thus elevated to an altar loyalty could become a religion. However foreign it may seem to the Greek idea of the state as a free association of citizens, the conception of the deified ruler was none the less rooted in Greek habits of thought; and the actual deification of Alexander may be traced among the Ionian Greeks in the beginning of his campaign, before he touched the soil of Egypt or of Persia. Unlike the Semites, who fixed a great gulf between God and man, the Greeks conceived gods in the likeness of men, and elevated men to the rank of gods.[1] It was their common practice to promote founders of cities at death to the rank of hero, and to offer them 'hero-worship'; and it was only an extension of this practice when Alexander, the first leader of a united Greece and the greatest of all the founders of Greek cities, was even in life conceived to be not only a hero, but a god. But if the deification of Alexander was in accordance with Greek conceptions and practice, it was also aided by the conceptions and practice of the East. The Egyptian kings were regarded, if not as gods in themselves, at any rate as incarnations of the god Ammon or Re; and the Persian kings claimed 'adoration' in virtue of the *Hvareno*, a nimbus 'conceived . . . as emanating from the sun, but also as a token of supernatural grace'.[2] It was in the Eastern dominions of Alexander that the worship of the deified ruler became—what it had never

[1] Goethe's poem, *Das Göttliche*, expresses the Greek conception.

Und wir verehren
Die Unsterblichen,
Als wären sie Menschen,
Thäten im Grossen,
Was der Beste im Kleinen
Thut oder möchte.

Der edle Mensch
Sei hülfreich und gut!
Unermüdet schaff' er
Das Nützliche, Rechte;
Sei uns ein Vorbild
Jener geahneten Wesen!

[2] See H. Stuart Jones, *The Roman Empire*, p. 217. In this fascinating matter of the deification of rulers I have followed A. Bauer, *Vom Griechentum zum Christentum*, pp. 53–92, and P. Wendland, *Die hellenistisch-römische Kultur*, vi. 4 and vii. 3. See also W. Ferguson's *Greek Imperialism*; and Professor Murray's *Four Stages of Greek Religion*, pp. 133–41.

been formally made by Alexander himself—an institution of State. The kings of Macedonia never pretended to divinity; and indeed as they were the kings of a single nation there was no necessity that they should. It was otherwise with Egypt and Asia Minor, where there was no national feeling, and where traditions of supernatural monarchy were strong. Possibly in their lifetime, and certainly after their death, Ptolemy I and Berenice were the objects of a cult: Philadelphos and Arsinoe were worshipped as θεοὶ ἀδελφοί by 270 B.C.; and we may still read the inscription in which Ptolemy V is celebrated as 'living for ever, beloved of Ptah, God Manifest . . . son of God and Goddess, like unto Horus, son of Isis and Osiris'. In the Seleucid kingdom the two first rulers were only canonized after death; but Antiochus II is already θεός during his life.

It would be wrong to treat these swelling titles in any cavalier spirit. In their inception, whatever they may have become where they were staled by custom, they were more than adulation. They expressed a real gratitude of the subject for peace and good governance; they implied a serious policy of the monarch, who knew no other way of consolidating his throne or uniting his dominions. And as they accorded with old Greek conceptions, so they also agreed with the contemporary movement of religious thought. It was the age of Euhemerism, in which gods were explained as great human 'benefactors' and 'saviours' who had won canonization; and it was easy to turn a living benefactor and saviour into a present and manifest god. After all, empires have their legends. And the legend of divinity need not fear comparison with the Napoleonic legend.

§ 2. Greek philosophy was a more potent force in its decline than it was in the great days of Plato and Aristotle; and Stoicism exerted a greater influence on the lives of men and the development of States than the Academy or the Lyceum.

There is much in the philosophy of Stoicism which reflects the era of Alexander; and it was perhaps powerful because it marched with the times. The era was one of uprooting and emigration and the mixture of peoples, in which the West moved eastwards on a steady tide, and an ebb sometimes set from the East to the West. The early Stoics came from the East, and though they might inherit Greek physics and metaphysics, they were free from the prepossessions and prejudices of Greek political thought. Zeno, the founder of the school, was a hellenized Phoenician from Cyprus: he came from that region of the Cilician gulf, fertile in its contribution to human thought, which afterwards gave to the world the hellenized Syrian, Posidonius of Apamea, and the hellenized Hebrew, Paul of Tarsus. He came to Athens at the end of the fourth century, and lived there as a resident alien. It is difficult not to believe that he was influenced in his thought by the achievement of Alexander, which must have begun its course in the days of his youth in Cyprus; nor is it any licence of conjecture to suggest that the philosophy which he taught at Athens, at any rate on its social side, was the translation into an explicit theory of the principle implicit in that achievement.

In Stoic philosophy the whole universe is conceived as a single intelligible unity, pervaded by reason; and the Stoic belief in a World-State is simply the political aspect of this general philosophic conception. 'The whole Universe was only one Substance, one *Physis*, in various states, and that one Substance was Reason, was God.' Reason, God, Nature (φύσις) were all synonyms—synonyms for the intelligible and homogeneous essence of the Universe. Physically, that essence was regarded as a form of matter—fire or a fiery ether—'pure and most subtil' (as it is written in the Book of Wisdom), 'more moving than any motion', which 'passeth and goeth through all things . . . the breath of the power of God, and a pure influence flowing from the glory of the Almighty'. In God this essential Reason was whole and pure: in man it was a fragment (ἀπόσπασμα); but that fragment was 'the ruling principle' in man, which determined the way of his life. By it, in the first place, he was knit to God and knit to his fellows; in its virtue he was a ζῷον κοινωνικόν; and because it was universal, the κοινωνία was universal. From it, in the second place, he derived the law of this universal κοινωνία; for since reason was the ruling principle in each, it was the ruling principle of the society of all, and since, again, reason was the same as nature, the law of the universal society based on reason was the same as the law of nature. One universal society, one state of the whole world; one law of nature, with which all its members must live in conformity—these are the two great tenets of Stoicism. 'He taught'—so it is recorded by Plutarch of Zeno—'that we should not live in cities and demes, each distinguished by separate rules of justice, but should regard *all* men as fellow-demesmen and fellow-citizens; and there should be one life and order (κόσμος) as of a single flock feeding together on a common pasture (νόμος).'[1]

The teaching of Zeno had necessarily its negative aspects. He was the iconoclast of the πόλις, as he was the prophet of the World-State; and a criticism of the institutions of the πόλις, somewhat in the vein of his predecessors the Cynics, appears more strongly in the records of his views than it does in those of his successors, who modified his asperities. We are told that he refused to admit to his 'republic' (like Plato, he wrote a *Republic*) either temples or courts of law or currency or marriage or gymnasia or the ordinary system of education. These were perhaps the extremities of an early radicalism. More essential in his teaching was his insistence on equality. If all human beings had reason, there was a fundamental human equality; and though one might divide the wise man from the foolish, there was no argument for distinguishing between the status of men and that of women, and little argument for

[1] Plutarch, *de Alex. Fort.* i. 6. The word κόσμος means both 'order' and 'world'; the word νόμος both 'law' and 'pasture'.

distinguishing between the position of masters and that of slaves. Stoicism was thus an influence in favour of the equality of the sexes; and if it did not make for the legal abolition of slavery, it issued in the view that slavery was an artificial institution of human law, and that in the region of the spirit all men were, or might be, equal. The graded inequality of the city disappears before the solvent of this teaching; and in it we may see the emergence of a tenet, to which the Roman lawyers gave universal currency, that 'before the law of nature all men have an equal status' (*omnes homines natura aequales sunt*).

The vogue which Stoic philosophy came to enjoy at Rome, from the days of the Scipios to the days of Marcus Aurelius, is a matter known to every scholar. It imbued the Roman lawyers with their tenets of a universal law of nature and the equality of all men before that law. It carried its conception of the State of the whole world to Marcus Aurelius; and the classical text for that conception may be found in a sentence of his *Meditations*: 'the poet saith, Dear city of Cecrops; but thou—wilt thou not say, Dear city of God?' The thought on which the best of the Romans fed was a thought of the World-State, the universal law of nature, the brotherhood and the equality of men; and thought of this nature inevitably penetrated and determined the general conception which they entertained of their empire. It is of peculiar importance, therefore, that we should understand the stage of development which Stoicism had reached, and the form of presentation which it had found, in the days of the establishment of the Roman Empire—the days, we may also add, of the beginnings of the Christian Church, which also claimed to be a universal society, and also came under the influence of Stoicism. Here we touch the name of Posidonius of Apamea, who taught in the University of Rhodes (Cicero, among others, was one of his pupils) in the last century before Christ. He was not an original thinker: he was an eclectic, who wedded Stoicism to

Platonism and (it has even been held) to the religious doctrines of the East. It is his peculiar importance that 'the great body of his writings expressed with unique completeness the general mind of the Greek world at the Christian era',[1] and that, as such a synthesis, they formed, as it were, the *textus receptus* of philosophic thought on which Cicero, Virgil, and many others drew.

It has been suggested by Mr. Bevan that the formula for the activity of Posidonius may be found in a simple phrase—'to make men at home in the Universe'. In his philosophy the universe became companionable and comfortable. Above was the fiery ether; below the world of men. At death the fiery particle of the human soul sought to rejoin its own element, and was encouraged in its upward way by the disembodied souls who had found their goal. All was 'one great city, of which gods and men were citizens . . . a compact and knowable whole'. With the whole universe thus made a companionable society, it was natural to conceive of a human society here on earth, living in sympathy with itself as it lived in sympathy with Heaven. And if the dead thus moved upward to the ether and to God, it was also natural to think of the deification of the dead. Here Posidonius found room in his philosophy for that deification of rulers which was current in the Hellenistic East. The great dead had gone home to God and joined the Godhead; and even the great living might be regarded as sent by 'Providence' or 'the eternal and immortal Nature of the Universe' to be 'saviours of the community of the human race'.[2]

The philosophy of Posidonius is really of the nature of a religion: if it is based on Stoicism, it contains elements

[1] E. Bevan, *Stoics and Sceptics*, iii. See also P. Wendland, op. cit., pp. 60 ff. and 134 ff.

[2] These terms may be found in two Greek inscriptions of the time of Augustus quoted in Wendland, op. cit., pp. 409–10. The language is Stoic: the reference is to Augustus himself.

drawn, through Plato and the Pythagoreans, from the Greek mysteries; and it may also contain elements derived from the religions of the East. It has even been suggested that Caesar may have found in the religious system of Posidonius, with its union of philosophic speculation and popular belief, the model of a religion suited to the universal empire which he would fain have built on the lines of the absolute monarchies of the East. It is at any rate probable that Caesar knew the system of Posidonius; and without subscribing to any theory of connexion between the political ambitions of Caesar and the philosophic religion of Posidonius, we may certainly believe in a connexion between the religious development and the political evolution of the last three centuries before the Christian era. We have to remember that the ancient State was also a Church. The City had its civic religion, of which the civic magistrates were priests: 'the real religion of the fifth century', Professor Murray writes, 'was a devotion to the City itself'. In the same way the great monarchies of the third century had their monarchical religion; and their real religion, as we have seen, was a devotion to the deified king. With politics and religion so closely connected that they were one, it was inevitable that, just as political movements produced religious consequences, so religious movements should involve political results. Now the religious movement of the latter centuries before the birth of Christ was towards a fusion of cults and a general belief in a single God of the Universe. It would be irrelevant, and it is impossible, to describe that movement here. It is apposite, and it is necessary, to draw attention to its political consequences. A world with one religion will also tend to be a world of a single State. Granted the general conceptions of the ancient world, we may say that the growth of monotheism encouraged the growth of a universal monarchy.

§ 3. Meanwhile the political development of Rome itself was moving to meet the system of thought implicit in the

Hellenistic monarchies, in the philosophy of Stoicism, and in the religious trend. The original City-State of Rome, with its municipal system of magistrates, town-council (*senatus*), and town-meeting (*comitia*), had grown to the dimensions of a State greater than even the empire of Alexander. By a process of agricultural expansion, which sowed her peasant townsmen up and down Italy, Rome had become the mistress of the peninsula at the beginning of the third century. By a process of commercial expansion, which gave her trading citizens the monopoly of Mediterranean trade at the expense of Carthage in the West and of Corinth and other centres in the East, she had become the virtual mistress of the Mediterranean littoral in the middle of the second century. There ensued a century of troubles, from the tribunate of Tiberius Gracchus to the battle of Actium, in which the municipal constitution of Rome showed itself inadequate to solve the problems or secure the allegiance of the territories which had come under its sway. Even in Rome itself, governed under an unwritten constitution which rested on understandings, the actual supremacy acquired by an aristocratic senate in the period of expansion was challenged by a popular party in the name of the formal rights of the general body of citizens. In Italy at large the inequality between allies who were really subjects and Roman citizens who acted as sovereigns produced a second and even more menacing cleavage; and though after the Social War a remedy was sought in the grant of Roman citizenship to the allies (88 B.C.), it is obvious that a grant of citizenship which only meant inclusion in a civic assembly that they could not attend was no real bond of union between the Italians and the city of Rome, and only proved the inability of a City-State, which, with the world in its hands, remained in the sphere of civic ideas, to form even an Italian State. But it was neither the struggles in Rome nor the cleavage in Italy which in the issue subverted the civic constitution: it was the condition and the problems of the provinces of the Mediterranean littoral.

Nominally protected by regulations passed by the Senate, the provinces were actually the prey of Roman governors, who in their short term of office sought to exploit their riches, and whom the constitution provided no effective means of controlling. The result was disastrous alike to the provincials, who found that their lot was not protection but pillage, and to Rome itself, where the returned governor, with his wealth, his ambitions, and his experience of absolute power, was a menace to civic ideas. And the provinces also entailed problems of defence—problems of the frontier—which could only be solved by methods which constituted a still graver menace. Armies were necessary to face the Berber tribes in the south, the Celts and Germans in the north, the kings of Pontus and Parthia in the east. The danger was constantly recurrent: the armies accordingly became standing armies, composed of professional troops, alien in spirit from the republican constitution, and a ready instrument for monarchical ambitions. With a professional army came the professional general; and men emerged of the type of Marius and Sulla, Pompey and Caesar—masters of legions, and masters, if they would, of Rome. The dissensions in the city between the aristocratic party of the Senate and the *populares* who appealed to the masses were the opportunity of the professional generals. They threw their swords into the scale and arbitrated; and finally the greatest and the boldest, Julius Caesar, took the sword into his hands and ruled. He had enjoyed ten years' experience of absolute power in Gaul: he was master of the finest legions of the day; he was allied with the popular cause; he had a genius for men and affairs.

We may define Caesarism as a form of autocracy, backed by an army, which rests formally on some manner of plebiscite and actually—so long, at any rate, as it is successful—on a measure of popular support. So defined Caesarism is identical with Bonapartism. But there is a fundamental difference. Bonapartism showed itself personal and transitory, an ephemeral chase of flying glory: Caesarism became a permanent institution. Modified and veiled at first by the policy of Augustus, but showing itself clearly as it grew firmer and stronger, it controlled the Mediterranean world for centuries. The reasons for its permanence were partly negative, but largely positive. There was no nationalism abroad to oppose a non-national State: there were only dying City-States which had lost the instinct for autonomy, and tribal formations which had not learned to cherish political ambitions. There was no democratic spirit in the air to wither an absolute government: the temper of the times was one of acquiescence, and even of gratitude. Religion and philosophy were the occupation of stirring minds: the only opposition to the Caesars came from a group of aristocratic *frondeurs*, who accumulated memories but were barren of achievements. While there was little to oppose Caesarism, there was much to support its cause. The provinces enjoyed peace: their frontiers were defended; their governors were supervised. Their taxes were not diminished: they were even increased in order to meet the expenses of the new system of government; but extortion ceased, and it is significant that in the new security the rate of interest sank to one-third of what it had been under the Republic. The domestic factions of Rome died. In Italy the Romans and the Italians were equally subjects of Caesar. With the head of the army at the head of the State, the peril that the army might thrust its sword into the issues of the civil State was, if not removed, at any rate diminished. A professional soldiery might still by a *coup d'épée* depose or elect a Caesar: in the third century it dominated politics for fifty troubled years; and the military basis of the Empire was always a weakness of the emperors. But of the first two hundred years of the Empire, at any rate, we may safely say that they were years in which the civilian power was the master of the State.

If we would understand the feelings towards the Empire which were general among its subjects in the days of its foundation, we must turn to the literature and inscriptions in which they are recorded. What Rome and the Empire owed to Augustus is testified in Virgil and Horace; and their poetry is no adulation, but the expression of a feeling as genuine as that of Tennyson for Victoria and the Victorian Age. The language of inscriptions is even more instructive testimony, because it is more direct and more naïve. We may deduct a liberal discount on the ground of conventional flattery from some of the Greek inscriptions: they still remain significant. Augustus is 'the Saviour sent to make wars cease and to order all things'; 'through him have come good tidings' (εὐαγγέλια); 'in him Providence has not only fulfilled, but even exceeded, the prayers of all: sea and land are at peace: cities flourish in order, harmony, and prosperity: there is a height and abundance of all good things: men are filled with hopes for the future and gladness in the present'. It is impossible to doubt, as one reads these words, that the feeling of a new and better order lies behind them. A century of war, of extortion, of insecurity, of misery has come to an end. A new era is dawning. The Empire begins in hope, and continues in comfort.

> Magnus ab integro saeclorum nascitur ordo.
> iam redit et Virgo, redeunt Saturnia regna,
> iam nova progenies caelo demittitur alto.
> . . . .
> ipsae lacte domum referent distenta capellae
> ubera, nec magnos metuent armenta leones.
> . . . .
> aspice venturo laetentur ut omnia saeclo!

§ 4. The Empire was the solution of a problem: it was even more—it was a 'salvation'. Religious feelings supported its institution and continuance; and that religious feeling was one of adoration for a present god, sent by Providence for the ending of war and the saving of the community of the human race. Here we meet once more that idea of the deified ruler, which the Hellenistic East had known since the days of Alexander and his first successors, and which had already been moving westwards for many years before the reign of Augustus. Flamininus, the victor of Cynoscephalae, was greeted by the Greeks as deliverer and 'Saviour'; Chalcis decreed him divine honours; and like the deified rulers of the East, he struck coins with his own image and superscription. This was a first burst of feeling, natural in the first formal contact of the Greeks with a grave Roman commander; but as they realized that the Roman State had no permanent personal sovereign, they contented themselves for years to come with the worship of *Roma*. *Roma* was, however, a pale goddess: instinct, the stronger because it was now a habit, craved a personal object of devotion; and in the first century B.C. we find provincial governors worshipped as gods in the East. As great leaders of armies rose to new eminence in Roman politics, the monarchical instinct rose to greater heights, and found a still more swelling expression. Pompey, who had given security to the Eastern Mediterranean by his campaigns against the pirates and the King of Pontus, was not only celebrated in inscriptions as the saviour who had given peace to the world: the Athenians themselves declared him a god, and joined with the 'Pompeiasts' of Delos (the term indicates a formal cult established in his honour) in dedicating his statue to Apollo. The type and the genius of the absolute monarchies of the East became familiar to ambitious Romans; and when they received the shadow of divine consecration, they could not but covet the substance of absolute power which cast the shadow. The foundations of imperialism are being laid when the great leaders of the standing armies of the West begin to meet in the East the type of institution and the temper of spirit which can give a concrete body to their dreams and a definite goal to their ambitions. A Roman development meets a Greek conception. That is the genesis of the conception of the Roman Empire.

It was not Pompey, in spite of his Eastern experience and

honours, who was destined to Empire: it was Julius Caesar—who, if he had studied in Rhodes and heard Posidonius, had spent his political career in the West as governor first of Spain and afterwards of the two Gauls. Caesar was a scholar and a man of genius; and he could apprehend with a rapidity and seize with a vigour denied to Pompey the chances of a fateful hour and the opportunity for founding a 'new monarchy', which, new as it was to the West, was an ancient pattern in the East. It was not the 'restoration' of an archaic and half-legendary municipal monarchy which Caesar planned: it was the 'translation' to the West of that tradition of the divine monarch of a great State which lived in the East. Like Pompey, he received divine honours in the day of his success from the Greeks of the Eastern Mediterranean; but it was a new and significant thing that he received the same honours in Rome from the Roman authorities. After the battle of Thapsus, his statue was erected by the Senate in the temple of Jupiter with the inscription *Semideo*; after the battle of Munda, a second statue was erected, in the temple of Quirinus, with the dedication *Deo invicto.* A cult arose in his honour, with its college of *Luperci Iuliani* and its *flamen*: his image appeared on coins in token of his divinity; his admirers crowned his statue with the white woollen fillet once worn by the Persian kings, and afterwards by Alexander and his successors; and Shakespeare has made us all familiar with the story of Antony thrice offering him a kingly crown—which was in effect an Eastern diadem—on the feast of the Lupercalia.

The open and frank policy of translating to Rome an Eastern type of monarchy failed. It was not so much a passion for liberty, as a clinging to Roman ways and traditions in the face of a policy tending to the substitution of Oriental forms and conceptions, that inspired the opposition and dictated the murder of Caesar. Refusing to learn by the lesson of his failure, Antony—the confidant of his plans—repeated his master's attempt: taking the East for his province, and allying himself with Cleopatra, the one living representative of the divine monarchies of the East, he pretended to divinity and played the part of Hellenistic monarch. Octavian was more cautious and more ready to profit by the teaching of experience. He disarmed the opposition in Rome by disavowing any policy of adopting Oriental forms, and by professing to base his power on old Roman conceptions of consular *imperium* and tribunician *potestas*. On this basis, which from one point of view we may almost call nationalist, as from another we may call it antiquarian, he was able to gather the Latin West to his cause, uniting under his banner both the friends and the foes of Caesar; to discredit Antony as a representative of eastern enormities; and, defeating his rival, to unite the East and the West under a form of government which professed to be a partnership between the first magistrate of Rome and its ancient Senate.

But it was an absolutism none the less; and it was an absolutism which from the first contained the conception and the cult of the deified ruler. At the time of the formation of the triumvirate of Octavian, Antony, and Lepidus, at the end of 43 B.C., a temple was consecrated, on the place on which his dead body had been burned, 'to the genius of *divus Iulius, pater patriae*, whom the Senate and people of Rome have received into the ranks of the Gods'. This is the worship of the dead ruler; but, as in the Hellenistic kingdoms, the progress to a regular worship of the living ruler was rapid. Augustus, as the inscriptions which have already been quoted show, was being worshipped in the East as 'a saviour . . . through whom have come good tidings', by the year 9 B.C.; and even earlier (17–12 B.C.) he is described in another Greek inscription as 'God the son of God, Augustus, the Benefactor'. In Egypt he enters into the style of the Ptolemies: he is 'autocrat, Son of the Sun, Lord of the Diadem, Caesar, living for ever, beloved of Ptah and Isis'.[1] The language and practice

[1] The influence of Ptolemaic Egypt on the development of the Empire

of the East were transferred, in a modified form, to the West. Provincial *concilia*, analogous to the *κοινά* of Asia Minor, were associated with the imperial cult; and in Gaul (as in Spain and also on the Rhine) representatives chosen by the different tribes annually elected a priest for the service of the *Ara Romae et Augusti*. In Rome and in Italy the worship of Augustus was nominally forbidden; but in many of the Italian towns we may trace a cult of the emperor, with *Augustales* devoted to its service; and in the *vici* of Rome itself we find the worship of the *Lares Compitales* combined with that of the *genius* of Augustus.[1] The house of Augustus on the Palatine Hill was united with the temple of his patron Apollo; in his house were treasured the Sibylline oracles; to his house was transferred the cult of Vesta. 'The *Penates* of the *gens Iulia* were united with those of the State; and the future and fortunes of the Roman people were now placed in the house of Augustus.'

We must not emphasize the imperial cult unduly. Augustus never allowed himself to be entitled openly a very god in Rome itself, as Caesar had done: he assumed no crown: he claimed no form of divine honour. The poets of his age—Propertius, Virgil, Horace, and Ovid (especially Ovid)—may term him *Deus*: he acts as a plain Roman citizen. The religion which he would foster, and in the service of which he would enlist that feeling of mingled gratitude and hope which marks his age—as of men escaped from shipwreck, eager to dedicate their dripping garments to a saving deity—is the ancient religion of his country. He closes the temple of Janus

deserves notice. It had developed a remarkable system of administration (see Bauer, op. cit., pp. 33 ff.), as well as an advanced form of divine monarchy; and both of these developments influenced the Roman emperors, the more as they treated Egypt differently from all other provinces, ruling there in their own right as successors of the Ptolemies, and not as representatives of the city of Rome. The Egyptian system of taxation influenced the financial policy of Augustus; and it was when he became successor to the Ptolemies that he necessarily became a God.

[1] H. Stuart Jones, op. cit., p. 28; Wendland, op. cit., pp. 146–7.

in token of peace: he celebrates *Ludi Saeculares* to purge away the sins of the past: he dedicates an *Ara Pacis Augustae*, the crowning achievement of Augustan art. He would associate a religious revival with the nascent empire, and consecrate his power by the association: he would cast round the new system a halo, if not of the personal worship of his own divinity (though he never frowned upon such worship), at any rate of the religious awakening which the peace of the new system had brought and the policy of the new monarch had fostered. There is policy, after all, even in the religious policy which seems least political.

The general religious reformation of the Augustan age inspired Virgil: it had little abiding result in the mass. But the worship of the deified ruler continued and grew. Caligula and Nero pretended to a present divinity; but generally the emperor was elevated to the rank of *divus*, and made the object of a cult, after his death; and during his life it was his *genius* which was held to be sacred. Here was found the basis of allegiance. The oath of officials and soldiers was associated with the *genius* of the present emperor and the *divi Caesares* of the past. When the new dynasty of the Flavii succeeded to the Julian dynasty in 70 A.D., it sought to prove its legitimacy by assuming a similar divinity. Magistrates of Roman towns in the provinces took an oath to the divinity of Augustus, Claudius, Vespasian, and Titus: Domitian made the residence of the Flavian family (much as Augustus had done with his house on the Palatine) into a shrine served by a college of *Flaviales*; and, as in Egypt under the Ptolemies,[1] the women of the family received consecration along with the men. The deification of the emperor, and the allegiance which he receives in virtue of his divinity, are obviously the foundation, or at any rate the cement, of the empire. 'In this cult,' writes

[1] Vespasian was first proclaimed Emperor at Alexandria, while he was in Judaea. His first act as Emperor was to occupy Egypt; and here he wrought a supposed miracle of healing by the royal touch.

Wendland, 'with its peculiar mixture of patriotic and religious feeling, there was found a common expression, which served as a bond of union, for that membership of the empire which was shared by parts so different in nationality and in religion: it was the token and symbol of imperial unity.' The empire was, in effect, a politico-ecclesiastical institution. It was a Church as well as a State: if it had not been both, it would have been alien from the ideas of the ancient world. A City-State entailed a civic worship: an Empire-State entailed an empire-worship; and an empire-worship in turn—granted the existence of a personal emperor, and granted, too, the need for a personal symbol in a State so much larger and so much less tangible than a City-State which could be personalized itself—entailed the worship of an emperor. It is not irrelevant or disproportionate to linger over this aspect of the Roman Empire. If it had not shown this aspect to its subjects, it would not have been an empire; for it would not have been a coherent society united by a common will.

§ 5. But the empire was not only a religion: it was also a citizenship; and we have now to inquire into the development of a common imperial citizenship, with its corollary of a common imperial law. By the end of the Republic the municipal citizenship of Rome had already developed into a State-citizenship of Italy. Under this system, as it was inherited and developed by the early emperors, Italy was separated from and privileged above the rest of the empire; and in other respects (no troops, for instance, were quartered in Italy, but, on the other hand, only Italians could serve in the *corps d'élite* of the praetorian cohorts) Italy enjoyed an exceptional position. But the State-citizenship of Italy was gradually widened as colonies of Roman citizens were founded in the provinces, or provincials were admitted to Roman citizenship. Here the army played a large part: military service conferred Roman citizenship; and as troops were recruited mainly in the provinces, a broad highway was opened for the enfranchisement of provincials.[1] When the Emperor Claudius (who introduced Gaulish chieftains to the *cursus honorum* and the ranks of Senate) revived the office of censor and took a census, he found that the number of citizens had increased by more than a million since the end of the reign of Augustus. The civic body had become a new thing: if it included provincials as well as Italians, it also included freedmen as well as the free-born. It contained different nationalities and different classes; and its growth tended to abolish both differences.

The abolition of different nationalities meant the emergence of what we may almost call a Mediterranean nationality. We may date the emergence of this new nationality from the reign of Hadrian. He was the first emperor to diminish the peculiar privileges of Italy: he visited and adorned with buildings almost every province of the empire: he showed his cosmopolitan temper by recruiting special bodies of Oriental troops and by giving to a Greek the command of a frontier province; and, as his predecessor Trajan had done on a still grander scale (especially in Dacia), he spread Roman colonies over the empire.[2] Half a century after the death of Hadrian the Emperor Septimius Severus, an African by birth, destitute of Hadrian's ideal of a new nationality, but practically impatient

[1] From the time of Vespasian the Italians were excused from service in the legions; and legionaries were recruited entirely from the provinces—the eastern provinces providing troops for the East and for Africa, and the western provinces for the West. From the time of Hadrian the legions were recruited from the various areas in which they were quartered, and recruits were thus left to serve in their native country. Under this system a Briton recruited in Britain for service with one of the three British legions would receive Roman citizenship without leaving the island.

[2] Hadrian, like his cousin Trajan, was a provincial from Spain. The Julian emperors were all Roman: the Flavians were Italian, of a Sabine stock. Severus, whose family spoke Punic, and who married a Syrian wife, marks a new epoch in the principate.

of any anomaly which interfered with military efficiency or ease of administration, abolished the military privileges of Italy and granted citizenship to many provincial towns, especially in his own native province. It was the culmination of the policy of Hadrian and Severus, and at the same time the result of a tendency implicit in the very conception of the empire, when in 212 A.D. Caracalla promulgated the *Constitutio Antonina*, by which all free-born members of the communities of the empire were granted Roman citizenship. With one emperor and one allegiance—an allegiance shared by all, and shared equally by all—a common citizenship naturally followed.

The edict of Caracalla not only meant the blending of nationalities in one nationality: it also meant the blending of differences of status in a common equality. The empire had been from the first a levelling force. Augustus had already followed the policy of opening a career to all talents: as he opened the Senate to knights, so he opened the ranks of the knights for the admission of members of the *plebs*. This is the natural policy of any absolute government: it would fain enrich its service by drawing freely on all classes, and it would set the dignity of its service, which it proclaims a dignity of desert, above any dignity based on descent. In its passion for equality—which was quite compatible with a marked preference for its own confidential servants—imperialism came close to Stoicism, which proclaimed the equality of citizen and alien, man and woman, bondman and free, while it cherished a peculiar regard for the *sapiens* who had attained to high rank in the service of Reason. It may have been in the logic of principles other than those of Stoicism that the Roman emperors realized the Stoic ideal of a universal society in which all the members were equal; but we must remember that Stoicism influenced the Roman lawyers' conception of a law of nature, which knew no difference of status, and that the conceptions of the Roman lawyers influenced the policy of the Roman emperors.

The development of a common law for the empire accompanied, as it helped to promote, the development of a common citizenship. From early days, far back in the history of the Republic, the praetors had been gradually formulating in their edict a new procedure and system of law, which should be generally applicable to cases in which others than Roman citizens were concerned. If we look at the origin of this system, we shall call it the praetor's law, or *ius praetorium*: if we look at the area of its application, we shall call it the general law, or *ius gentium.* Commercial reasons dictated the growth of the new jurisprudence: a law was needed for commercial cases, in which foreign traders were concerned, and which grew more and more frequent as Rome became more and more a commercial city. The *ius civile* of Rome, even if it had not been, as it was, the prerogative of the Roman *civis*, was too archaic, and too much the law of a limited agricultural community, to suit these cases; and the law which the praetors began to apply, and which was thus the foundation of the *ius gentium*,[1] was the more modern merchant law which had come into being, and attained a general validity, in the Mediterranean area. Building on this foundation, and adding to this borrowed material a native legal genius and grasp of legal principle, the praetors formulated in their edict a system of law which had at once the simplicity and the absence of archaic formalism necessary for commercial cases, and the universality of application which would suit the conditions of general Mediterranean trade. This simple and universal law, thus formulated by the praetors, became connected with the conception of a law of nature. It is quite possible that the

[1] In this passage it has been assumed that the *ius* enunciated by the praetors in their edict was practically equivalent to the *ius gentium*; and it has been further assumed that the original basis on which the praetors worked, in shaping the procedure and system of law which they administered, was a merchant law generally current in the Mediterranean. In regard to both assumptions the reader is referred to the chapter on the Science of Law, § IV and § VII.

Roman lawyers realized the 'natural' character of the *ius gentium* even before they were imbued with Stoic philosophy: it is certain that, as they came to understand the Stoic conception of a universal law of nature, they came to regard the *ius gentium* as a close approximation to that conception; and though it was never universally or completely identified with the law of nature, it was at any rate regarded as the concrete expression of such a law in actual human society—less perfect, in that it denied equality and recognized slavery; but more serviceable, because it was actually formulated and administered in courts. As a school of jurisconsults arose at Rome, the practical application of the *ius gentium* in the praetor's court was supplemented by scientific inquiry; and from the second century B.C. a body of trained jurists applied their skill to elucidate and develop its implications. The majesty of the *ius gentium* was recognized—and at the same time its growth was stopped—when Hadrian realized a plan which is said to have been entertained by Julius Caesar, and caused the jurist Salvius Julianus to codify the praetorian edict in a fixed and final form. By this time the work had been done: the city-law of Rome had been expanded to meet the needs of the new Mediterranean state: a *ius gentium*, regarded as valid for all free men *everywhere* (this is the meaning of *gentium*), and assuming an ideal aspect by its close connexion with the law of nature—a connexion which helped to ameliorate the lot even of the slave—was co-extensive with the whole empire. And if the expansion of this *ius gentium* was stopped by its codification, there was another source ready and able to provide a law no less universal. The emperors had the power of issuing 'rescripts' in answer to any inquiry or petition; and these rescripts, if they dealt largely with matter of administration, were also concerned with matter of law. The Antonines used their power to advance the emancipation of slaves and to maintain the principle that all accused persons must be held to be innocent until they were proved to be guilty; and the *constitutiones principum*—the generic name applied to imperial rescripts, edicts, and decrees—became a great agent of legal progress down to the days of Justinian. Valid for the whole empire in virtue of their origin, they continued and completed the formation of a single law for the Mediterranean world.[1]

Along with the growth of unity in citizenship and unity in law there went also a unification of government. We can hardly say that the early empire possessed a unified government. The policy of Augustus was a policy of dovetailing the new into the old and uniting the new monarchy with the ancient Republic; and it resulted in a partnership, or 'dyarchy', under which the prince divided authority with the Senate and People—which meant, in effect, the Senate. This dualism is most obvious in the system which gave to the prince the frontier provinces and to the Senate the rest; but it is implicit in the whole structure. Dualism could hardly have worked under any conditions: it certainly could not work when the Senate was unable to govern, and imperfectly qualified even to oppose. The emperors, with their trained staff of officials and their supreme command of the army, were from the first the superior partners; and a zest for efficiency as well as a love of power drove them ultimately to rule in isolation. The process of development is slow: the struggle of the emperors and the Senate is for long years the real content of the political history of the empire. It is a proof of the legal genius of the Romans and their instinctive respect for precedent and constitutional tradition, that even the deified Caesars, masters of all the legions, should have respected for centuries the impotent

[1] It should be remarked that, great as was the legal genius of the Romans, the development of their law owes something to Hellenistic law, which we are gradually coming to know from papyri. We cannot, indeed, speak of Graeco-Roman law as we speak of Graeco-Roman civilization. But we may safely say that the Hellenistic kingdoms, with their high civilization and intricate commerce, had developed a common jurisprudence, which affected the Roman law of mortgage and other branches of the Roman law of contract.

majesty of republican forms. It may be that they were not without a suspicion that even the form of constitutionalism was better than the naked fact of a military autocracy, which might reveal to the legions only too clearly the fatal secret of their power. Whatever the reason, the fact remains that the structure of Augustus, doomed from the first to failure by its inherent flaws, was none the less slow in failing utterly. It is not until three centuries have run, and we reach the days of Aurelian and Diocletian, that we can finally detect a logical and thorough-going absolutism. To this day Roman Law preserves traces of the old dualism. If it can pronounce the emperor 'a living law on earth', and declare him 'free from all laws', it can also proclaim that 'it is a saying worthy of the ruler's majesty that a prince should profess himself bound by the laws'. If Ulpian enunciates the absolutist dictum, that 'the will of the prince has the force of law', he adds at once the democratic explanation, 'because the People confers upon him and into his hands all its own sovereignty and power'. We may argue with almost equal cogency that Roman Law implies absolutism, and that it implies constitutionalism.

If the transference of plenary sovereignty to the emperor is a slow process, the process may already be traced in the reign of Hadrian. As he sought to deprive Italy of its primacy, so he began to divest the Senate of its partnership. He gave an additional importance to the knights, who constituted the civil service: it was a knight who held the only considerable command which he gave to a subject; and knights were admitted to his *consilium* along with senators. Septimius Severus, even more inimical than Hadrian to the primacy of Italy, encroached still further on the prerogatives of the Senate. In his reign senators could no longer propose decrees: when treason was in question, their dignity no longer protected them from torture; and the Senate ceased to exercise an influence in the apportioning of provinces or the appointing of magistrates. The system of dyarchy is dying when the Senate loses even its patronage; but the death of the system belongs to a later epoch, and it is connected with a new ascendancy of the East and a fresh movement in the sphere of religion.

§ 6. From the first the Roman Empire had been divided into two parts—the Hellenized East and the Roman West; the one an amalgam of Oriental nationalities and religions, united by a general diffusion of Hellenic speech and culture, which was sometimes a veneer and sometimes a deep and genuine thing; the other a collection of Celtic cantons, Berber tribes, and Italian townsfolk, imbued with Latin speech and pervaded by Latin traditions. It is a division which history has proved to be deep: it is a division which led to the parting of the empire into Eastern and Western halves, as it led to the schism of Christianity between Eastern and Western churches. If Julius Caesar had perhaps inclined to the East, the policy of Augustus, with its strong Latin trend, had emphasized the West, and from the beginning of his principate to the accession of Vespasian we may trace, in literature as in other directions, a dominance of Latin culture.[1] From the reign of Vespasian Greek literature begins to flourish again; after the reign of Hadrian the centre of gravity begins to shift to the East, and the process begins which Constantine sealed by the foundation of Constantinople. What is ominous for the future is that as the East becomes more preponderant in the empire, it also becomes less Hellenic. Oriental nationalities and religions, dormant under Hellenism, but influencing Hellenism even while they were dormant, quicken to a new life; and the Roman emperors, drawn more and more eastward by the problems of eastern turbulence and eastern frontiers, fall under the fascination of eastern institutions and cults.

[1] Latin was the official language of the Greek East, and the Greeks used the services of interpreters. Public documents (such as the famous inscription termed the *Monumentum Ancyranum*) were bilingual; and the imperial chancery had both a Greek and a Latin department.

Early in the third century (227 A.D.) the Sassanids established a new Persian Empire with its capital at Ctesiphon; and under the rule of the new dynasty, Zoroastrianism—with its cult of Ahura-mazda, the 'wise lord', the god of heaven, who fights against Ahriman and the powers of darkness—became an official religion.[1] A form or a derivative of that religion was Mithraism. In the pure Zoroastrian faith Mithra was the god of light, the messenger of Ahura-mazda, the leader of his hosts; but as Mithraism became an independent cult he became the supreme god, the very sun, the vivifying, penetrating, conquering ruler of the universe. Greek elements entered into Mithraism: the symbol of the god slaughtering a bull, which appears in representations of Mithra, may well be such an element. As a fusion of Persian and Hellenic elements the Mithraic religion attained a great vogue, especially in the Roman army, and commanded the fervent allegiance of millions. The diffusion of Mithraism through the whole Roman Empire was prior to the third century; but the rise of the Sassanid dynasty, the ardent champion of pure Zoroastrianism, and the dominance of the Roman army, with its cult of Mithra, in the troubled politics of that century, may both have contributed to the primary importance which sun-worship now assumes.

The deification of the emperor, in the form inherited by the Romans from the Hellenistic monarchies, had by the third century become a lifeless and exhausted thing. It had no longer the glamour of a new thing from the East; and the feeling of hope and gratitude, which had inspired the worship of Augustus in the early days of the empire, was irretrievably gone. The period of the fifty tyrants (235–70 A.D.) had seen the name of emperor cheapened: it had combined civil war with foreign invasion, and exceeded the horrors of the period of slaughter which preceded the principate of Augustus. Some

[1] The compilation of the Zend-avesta belongs to the period of the Sassanid dynasty.

new system of government was once more needed, as it had been needed at the end of the first century B.C.: some new consecration, which would take the place of the cult of the *divi Caesares* as a bond of union and basis of allegiance, must support that system and gain it a general acceptance. Aurelian began and Diocletian completed the introduction of a new system of Oriental absolutism; and Aurelian made an Oriental cult the religion of the empire, and bade his subjects regard him as the earthly vicar and emanation of the Unconquered Sun.

The cult of the Sun introduced by Aurelian was not in itself Mithraism, though it had its connexions with the worship of Mithra, and was calculated to attract the ready allegiance of all his worshippers. It was a Syrian form of religion, which he had come to adopt in his eastern campaigns: it was a nature-cult, directed indeed to the worship of the brightest of the heavenly bodies, but not different in kind—except in its monotheism—from the worship of the planets and other forms of 'astral religion' which were current in the East. What it was in itself is perhaps no great matter, and at any rate does not greatly concern us here. The fact and the consequences of the adoption of an Oriental cult are of profound importance. That adoption meant a revolution in the position of the emperor; and it meant a revolution in the conception of the empire.

The revolution in the position of the emperor consisted in the change to an Oriental despotism. The old worship of the emperor as a god in himself may appear to us servile; but it had been compatible with the spirit of liberty and the forms of constitutionalism. After all, the conception of the deified ruler was fundamentally Hellenic, and not Oriental; and that conception could exist by the side of Hellenic and Roman ideas of the self-respect of the subject and the freedom of the commonwealth. When Aurelian claimed a new worship, not as a god in himself but as the incarnation or emanation of a god, he may seem to have claimed less, but he was really exacting more. He was moving in the sphere of Oriental ideas: he was asking for a blind prostration before a radiant divinity. He asserted a divine right, which could not be shared in any partnership: the Senate now lost even the formal privileges which it hitherto retained.[1] The purple, Aurelian told his troops, was the gift of God, who alone could limit his gift:

> The breath of worldly men cannot depose
> The deputy elected of the Lord.

But the emperor was more than a 'deputy': he was the image and epiphany of *Sol Invictus*. His was the nimbus emanating from the sun, which conferred a supernatural grace; and if he left to the sun the title of 'Lord of the Roman Empire', he might yet claim to be himself both 'Lord and God' (*dominus et deus*). He wore the diadem and the great jewel-embroidered robe copied from the Sassanids: he adopted the throne and foot-stool, before which all subjects must prostrate themselves in adoration. All this means a new and eastern empire; and all this passes into the system of Diocletian, which shows in the clear light of midday the results of the tendencies which dawn in the reign of Aurelian.

It was the work of Diocletian to exhibit with an exact logic the administrative consequences of the revolution in the position of the emperor which marked the end of the third and the beginning of the fourth century. He has been compared with Jeremy Bentham; and he was certainly no less impatient of survivals and anomalies, and no less anxious to make a clean sweep and establish a new system. He made no particular profession of divinity, if he maintained the solemn state of robe and diadem and adoration; but he pruned with a radical utilitarianism all the dead branches of the Roman past. The last trace of dyarchy disappeared, when the Senate became the

[1] Its members were excluded from military commands: it lost the old right of issuing bronze coins: the formula *Senatus Consulto* disappeared.

municipal council of the city of Rome and its suburbs, and a new division and regrouping obliterated any distinction between imperial and senatorial provinces. The empire became an intricate bureaucratic state, organized on a new basis of division, under which the military arm was independent of civil control, and one set of civil officials was jealously pitted against another. At the centre of the great cobweb, its 'universal spider', the emperor held the threads and spun the filaments in a lonely absolutism. Italy ceased to enjoy any primacy, and was taxed like any other area: Rome ceased to be a capital, and the centre was shifted eastwards to Nicomedia. Losing its roots in the past, the empire became a new autocracy: severing its connexion with Rome and Italy, it found a fresh basis in the East, where it might at once feel more at home in sentiment and sit closer to its work in the details of administration.

In the conception of Diocletian the empire was still a unity: in the actual process of history the deserted West tended more and more to become a unit on its own account. Diocletian implicitly recognized, as he definitely hastened, this tendency, when he divided the empire, for convenience of administration, into an eastern and a western half by a line drawn through Illyria. The old Graeco-Roman civilization, pivoted on the middle Mediterranean, and organized on the basis of a single political community, had shown signs of fissure for the last two hundred years. After the reign of Diocletian it cracked and split. The East fell away into Byzantinism: the West broke away into Latin Christianity. This meant a double change. The world became two instead of one (though men still clung for centuries to the conception of the one universal society); and in one of the two halves the Church became the basis of life in place of the State. It is the latter change which demands our attention; for it is here that we may see a fundamental revolution in the very conception of the empire —a revolution already implied in the reign of Aurelian, but first explicit in the policy of Constantine.

§ 7. When Aurelian made the worship of the Sun into the religion of the empire, and himself into the earthly emanation of the Sun, he was unconsciously acknowledging a great transference in the balance of human interest. The world in which the Unconquered Sun is proclaimed 'the Lord of the Roman Empire'—in which a temple is dedicated to his majesty upon his 'birthday'[1]—is not the world of Pericles or Alexander, of Cicero, or even of Hadrian. For many centuries—for the thousand years, we may say, from 700 B.C. to 300 A.D.—the basis of political life had been found in the political interest, and men had thought and acted as ζῷα πολιτικά. The State was the unit of life: religion was an attribute or dependency of the State. The State might be a small city—an Athens, worshipping Athene as the incarnation of itself: it might be a 'great society'—an empire, worshipping a deified emperor as the incarnate 'genius' of its imperialism: the dominant motive in either was political, secular—a motive of this world and the life of this world. This is the essence of Graeco-Roman civilization. By the third century A.D. there comes a transfer of interest. Human life seems to swing round on a pivot: the religious motive—long growing in strength; long spreading westward from its home in the East—acquires the dominance. For many centuries to come—for the next thousand years, we may almost say, down to 1300 A.D., when the great Church of the Middle Ages began to totter in the pontificate of Boniface VIII—the basis of human organization is the religious motive, and human society is ecclesiastical in its primary inspiration. There are still states: there is indeed still an empire. But it is the Church which counts; and kings who are kings by the grace of God are in the last resort kings by the grace of the Church. We cannot indeed assert the proposition of the whole Mediterranean world; but we may

[1] The birthday of the Sun was fixed on December 25, at the time of the winter solstice. Constantius vindicated the day for Christianity, and made it Christmas Day—the birthday of our Lord.

assert it at any rate of the West. And here we touch a paradox. The East, which gave religion and the Church to the West, fell under the control of the State. The West, which gave politics and the State to the East, came under the sovereignty of the Church. We may almost say that there was an interchange of gifts and of rôles. The western State moved into the East, to Constantinople, and subjugating the Church produced Byzantinism. The Church which arose in the East moved into the West, to Rome, and enthroning the Papacy produced Latin Christianity.

A religion which was an attribute or dependency of the State, and in the last resort a worship of the State, could never satisfy the religious instinct. The achievements of an Alexander, or the pacific triumphs of an Augustus, might create a gratitude and an adoration for the head of a State, which might last beyond the lifetime of their creator. But the State has its defeats as well as its victories; and the abiding religious instinct, with its own aspirations towards a society and its own hope of controlling human life by its principles, stood ready to take advantage of its defeats. The religious appeal became ever stronger in the ancient world, as the process of syncretism developed and monotheism moved to victory. Christianity grew to an irresistible volume. The worship of Mithra and of Isis, the worship of the Unconquered Sun and of the great mother Cybele—with their intimate societies, their arresting rites, their consolation and their passion—all drew their votaries and kindled a deep devotion. By the time of Diocletian the State had lost its appeal and become a structure based upon fear. It was a cobweb of suspicion: its activity was an activity of extraction of taxes, relentless, remorseless, to support an army and a mass of officials: it tied the artisan to his guild, the serf to his plot, the councillor to his town, in order that each, duly penned in his place, might do his State-service and pay his State-dues. There was no spontaneous social cohesion to constitute a political community: there was no voluntary social will to support a government. In this conjuncture the religious motive entered into the foreground of life, and swung forward to its triumph. The State, if it was to survive at all, could only survive by making the Church its ally, or, to speak more exactly, by becoming the ally of the Church. Thus the Roman Empire was driven in its last days by the mere instinct of self-preservation to adopt a religious creed as the basis—the only basis—on which it could still remain in existence. It sought to survive as an empire by becoming also, and indeed primarily, a Church. In the new religious temper of the times this was the only solution.

But why was the Christian Church in the issue the chosen ally of the pagan State? The State had persecuted the Church: the Church had regarded the State as anti-Christ: on what ground could they unite? We may meet these questions by the answer that, whatever the previous relations of the Christian Church and the Roman Empire, the peculiar conditions of the fourth century, as they have just been delineated, were such as to make an entirely new relation possible. The conflict between the two had depended on conditions which had ceased to exist. In the days in which the empire had found its basis in the worship of a deified emperor, the government had persecuted Christians because they had refused to participate in that worship; and in the Book of Revelation the Church had shown itself stung by such persecution to a passion of rebellion against the city of 'Babylon' and the worship of the 'dragon'. But Christianity, if it protested against the persecuting State, was not in its essence opposed to the State in any of its forms or activities. St. Paul recognizes that the powers that be are ordained of God; and prayers for the emperor and those in authority were customary among the early Christian communities. Christianity could recognize the State: what it could not recognize was the doctrine that religion was an attribute or dependency of the State; and as long as that doctrine lasted, in the form of emperor-worship and the enforcement of emperor-worship as an essential article of citizenship, there could be no alliance between Christianity and the empire. By the end of the third century emperor-worship had passed: the empire was feeling its way towards a new form in which political unity would no longer involve a form of political religion, but community of religion would create, or at any rate sustain, political unity. If the empire was to be united on this basis, Christianity, with its aspiration towards the Gentiles and its vision of an œcumenical Church, was ready to constitute the basis. It offered itself as a world-religion to hold together on the ground of religious unity an empire which was doomed to dissolution if it sought to remain on the ground of political unity. The emperors accepted the offer. They became the powers ordained of God for the guidance of things temporal in a new empire now conceived as a Christian society. They did not realize, nor did the Church itself realize, that as the Christian society elaborated its own principle of life, a new ecclesiastical emperor would arise in the Pope, and a new struggle of Church and State would ensue in which secular emperors and kings would seek to vindicate an independent political sphere against the claims of a theocracy. These results lay in the future. What happened in the reign of Constantine and his successors was that the autocratic emperors, remaining autocrats, agreed that the essential unity of the empire should henceforward be found in a common allegiance to the Christian creed. A bureaucratic machine controlled by an Orientalized emperor was united with a religious community based on the love of God and the brethren.

It was in 312 A.D. that Constantine, about to join battle with the legions of Maxentius, fighting under the banner of the Unconquered Sun, adopted a Christian symbol as his badge and marched to victory at the battle of the Mulvian bridge. He would oppose to the Unconquered Sun, deep-seated in the allegiance of Roman legionaries, the unconquerable Christ whose votaries no persecutions could daunt, and whose coming triumph he already recognized. His victory over the army of Maxentius was the victory of Christianity (as it were in the ordeal of battle) over Sun-worship and Mithraism and all the pagan cults. But it did not result in the immediate establishment of Christianity as the religion of the State. Constantine was content to recognize Christianity as one of the public worships of the empire. For the next seventy years the old pagan rites were officially performed in Rome; and the emperor, even while he was a Christian, and presided in Christian synods, was also the *Pontifex maximus*. But with the emperors confessing the Christian faith, and, still more, with the pressing need for a unification of the empire on a common religious basis, the establishment of Christianity as the one acknowledged religion of the empire was inevitable. The Emperor Gratian (375–83 A. D.) refused to wear the robes of the *Pontifex maximus*, and abolished the official recognition of pagan rites. The Emperor Theodosius I (379–95 A. D.), the last creative emperor, first as the colleague and then as the successor of Gratian completed the work. He summoned in 381 A. D. the synod of Constantinople, which ended the Arian heresy in the empire and defined the Christian creed; and he prohibited pagan profession as he proscribed heretical opinion. Behind the figures of both emperors stands Ambrose, Bishop of Milan, who inspired the weak Gratian as he curbed the stormy Theodosius. When in 390 A. D. Theodosius, solemnly rebuked and excluded for months from the Church on the ground of a massacre committed by his troops at Thessalonica, divested himself at last of the purple in Ambrose's cathedral at Milan, and after public penance was restored to the Christian communion, he showed not only that the empire had become a Christian society, but also that in that society (at any rate in the West) the officers of the Church might become the censors of the acts of the State.

§ 8. Historians have proclaimed the fall of the empire, or at any rate of the 'Western Empire', in the year 476 A. D.; and we may thus be led to conclude that the empire collapsed when it became a Christian society. Here we must make a distinction. In one sense the empire did not and could not fall, because it was one with Christian society, and Christian society still stood, and grew even firmer and stronger, as it absorbed into its life the barbarian invaders from the north. It may be urged, indeed, that what remained was a Christian Church, and not a Roman Empire; that the old universal State had gone, if a new universal Church had come; that in place of the old universal Graeco-Roman State there were now barbaric *regna*, hardly worthy to be called states, and only loosely united by a common profession of Christianity. Such a contention rests on a false antithesis—the antithesis between Church and State, conceived as separate societies. The Christian Church had fused with the Roman State in a single society, a Christian commonwealth, which was an empire as well as a Church and a Church as well as an empire. The continuity of the Christian Church involved the continuity of the empire, because the Church and the empire were not two societies, but two aspects of a single society. It may be urged again that, if this be so, the empire only survived as an 'aspect'—that is to say, as a mental conception—and that in the tangible world of institutions and administration it had no body and no existence. We may well admit that there is a large measure of truth in such a contention—though we may also urge that a conception which influenced the political development of Western Europe for many centuries was more than a ghost—and we must accordingly turn to consider the sense in which the empire, after all, 'fell' in 476 A.D.

In the first place the empire fell asunder into the two divisions of East and West. The cleavage was indeed far from being absolute, and the idea and even the form of unity long survived. So long as men cherished the idea of a single

Christian society, they could hardly admit to themselves the existence of two separate societies and two separate empires. The Church of the East, though it diverged more and more from the West, especially in the days of the iconoclastic controversy (*c.* 700 A.D.), was not repudiated by the West as schismatic until the eleventh century; and the Byzantine emperors were recognized as emperors even in the West until the coronation of Charlemagne, alike by barbarian kings and by the Bishop of Rome. None the less the East had finally diverged from the West; and we may, if we will, date that divergence in 476 A.D. It is a matter of choice. We may equally well date it earlier, from Diocletian's administrative division of the empire, or from Constantine's foundation of Constantinople, or from the dynastic division of Theodosius I; or later, from the coronation of Charlemagne or the final schism of the Churches. What matters is the fact that the East had steadily withdrawn itself into its own life from the second century of the Christian era, and that it gradually built a polity of its own fundamentally different from that of the West—a polity in which there was no Papacy, but the emperor was himself the head of the Church, and the Church was a department of the administration of the State. This is Byzantinism; and the essential conceptions of Byzantinism were inherited on the one hand by the Russian Tsars,[1] successors of the Caesars by marriage and governors of their Church through the Holy Synod, and on the other by the Turkish Sultan, at once Keisar-i-Rum in virtue of Constantinople and Commander of the Faithful in virtue of succession

[1] Ivan III, who married Sophia Palaeologus, used the title of Tsar (in old Slavonic *tsésar*) on documents and on coins: he termed himself *samodérzhets*, or autocrat of the Russias, in translation of the Byzantine *αὐτοκράτωρ*: he adopted the Byzantine crest of the double-headed eagle. Ivan IV was the first Russian sovereign to have himself crowned Tsar (1547 A.D.). It was Peter the Great who finally subdued the Russian Church to the State, and abolishing the patriarchate instituted a layman as procurator general of the Holy Synod to govern the Church.

to the Prophet. Augustus had strange successors. But Augustus was of the West; and Aurelian, son of a Pannonian peasant, and Diocletian, son of an Illyrian freedman, both of the East and both absolute rulers, might have recognized a closer kinship with an Ivan or a Selim.

In the second place, the empire in the West after 476 A. D. was in abeyance for some hundreds of years, so far as a visible emperor, or a capital, or a system of administration was concerned. There was no emperor to be seen, whether at Rome or Milan or Ravenna, and there was no imperial system of administration.[1] The splendour of the emperor at Constantinople might cast a shadow westwards, and men might feel, as long as they saw the shadow, that there was somewhere a substance of empire; but the substance was not in the West. If empire means an emperor, a capital, an administration, then Count Marcellinus was right when he wrote of the year 476 A. D., *Hesperium gentis Romanae imperium . . . cum hoc Augustulo periit.* But if empire means a society and a community, then we can only say that the empire survived in the West; and the whole of mediaeval history would be unintelligible if we did not realize that it survived. It survived as a *respublica Christiana*, a Christian commonwealth recognizing the formal suzerainty of the Byzantine successors of Constantine, but gradually developing a spiritual ruler of its own in the Bishop of Rome.

§ 9. In the *De Civitate Dei* St. Augustine faced the question whether the empire collapsed when it became a Christian society. He wrote before 476 A. D., but he wrote under the impression of the sack of Rome by Alaric; and he sought to meet the pagan argument that the adoption of Christianity was the ruin of Rome. Rome, he replies, had known vicissitudes and

[1] Justinian reconquered Italy, and it was under Byzantine government until 568 A. D. Even after that date there was a Byzantine exarch at Ravenna until 752 A. D. But that was all.

misery even under paganism. But this is only a negative answer; and Augustine quickly rises to the height of the true Christian argument. The love and enjoyment of God, which Christianity alone can give, are the true happiness of humanity; and they stand triumphant above all the chances and calamities of temporal events. Along this line Augustine moves to the theme of the Two Cities, which had already been handled by Marcus Aurelius—the City of Rome and the City of God; he sets one form of social life against another, and pits the heavenly against the earthly. He is far from identifying the heavenly city with the community gathered in the Roman Empire; and we may even doubt whether he identified the *Civitas Dei* with the visible and organized Christian Church. Scholars are divided on the issue: some have held that his city of God was 'a real institution with a definite organization'; others have thought that it was an unseen society, not built with hands, a spiritual society of the predestined faithful, distinct from the visible communion of baptized Christians. But we are probably justified in believing that even in the thought of St. Augustine himself, and certainly in the interpretation of later generations, the mantle of the city of God descended upon the visible Church. 'The conception of the Church as a social entity wielding governing powers', wrote Dr. Figgis, 'owes much to St. Augustine. He did much to strengthen the Church as an imperial force.' [1]

The Church which could thus be conceived as a social entity and an imperial force gradually acquired an imperial organization. The genius and the structure of the old imperial system passed into the organization of the Church. Residence in Rome, with the emperor far removed in distant Constantinople, contributed to establish the Bishop of Rome as the successor of the Caesars in the West; and the habit of looking to Rome for political guidance was continued in the tendency, which we may trace in the Church as early as the second century,

[1] *The Political Aspects of St. Augustine's City of God*, pp. 71–2.

to turn to Rome, as the guardian of the pure apostolic tradition, for guidance in all religious controversies. Hobbes wrote of the Papacy as 'the ghost of the deceased Roman Empire, sitting crowned on the grave thereof'. The author of the forged Donation of Constantine (perhaps compiled in Italy, in the latter part of the eighth century) expressed the same idea when he made Constantine give to Sylvester I his palace, diadem, and robes, 'with the city of Rome and all provinces, places, and cities of Italy or the western regions'. We must not exaggerate the inheritance, or conclude that the position of the Papacy was simply and solely the continuance in the religious sphere of the power previously wielded by the emperor in the political. A sacramental and sacerdotal Church, such as the Latin Church of the West, demanded in its own inner logic, and apart from any inheritance, a central fountain, abounding in a *plenitudo potestatis*, from which there might emanate to the bishops, and through the bishops to their clergy, the dignity of their office, the sacramental power, and the substance of the tradition they were set to teach. But if papalism, with its sovereignty and its infallibility, was inherent in the essence of such a Church, we may still believe that tradition and environment fostered the growth of what was innate.

A city of God conceived as a visible Church, and organized as a spiritual empire, may seem to leave little room for any *terrena civitas*. But it was many centuries before the claim of ecclesiastical dominance, if it was already implicit in the Church at the end of the fourth and in the fifth century, was finally asserted. Ambrose of Milan subdued Theodosius to penitence in 390 A. D.: it was not until 1077 A. D. that Henry IV knelt in penitence before Gregory VII at Canossa. In a world of barbaric German chieftains the times were not ripe for the sway of the Church; and during the long interval a theory of what we may call parallelism was held. There was indeed one society, men thought, and one only; but there were two governments, each with separate powers. This is the theory expressed by Gelasius I (and scholars have accordingly termed it Gelasian) in a letter to Anastasius, the eastern emperor: ‘ there are two things by which this world is principally ruled—the sacred authority of the Popes and the royal power.’ The one is set over things spiritual, and the other over things temporal; but the burden of the Popes is the heavier, as they must answer even for kings at the divine judgement. Two parallel sovereigns of one society, the Pope at Rome and the Emperor at Constantinople—this is the theory which is held in the West till the coronation of Charlemagne in 800 A. D. By that event a change was made, not in the relations of the two powers, but in the residence of the temporal power. There was a ‘ translation of the empire from the Greeks to the Germans ’ (not, we may note, a division, but a transference of a single and undivided empire); and henceforth, till the pontificate of Gregory VII, the Pope at Rome and the Emperor at Aix-la-Chapelle are parallel rulers of the society of the western world. The East is recalcitrant. The empire has been ‘translated’; but an East Roman Empire persists in remaining among the Greeks.

In the pontificate of Gregory VII we reach the days of ecclesiastical dominance. The system of parallelism—we may almost call it a new dyarchy, of a very different type from that devised by Augustus—is abandoned: the Church Universal, through its universal bishop, seeks to control the whole of human life: universal in extension, it would also be universal in its intensity of action. Society was recovering from the time of barbaric dispersion: trade was bringing the whole of Western Europe together: the Crusades and the spread of international orders were beginning to cement the unity. Gregorianism succeeds to Gelasianism; and Gregorianism means a gallant attempt of the Church, through its Papacy, to bring a united Christian commonwealth, in its every reach, under the control of Christian principle. In politics and in social life, in economics and in the studies of universities, the Church would be dominant: it would control kings in their government; by its canon law of marriage and of wills, as by its penitentiary system, it would guide the social life of the family and the individual; it would regulate prices and prohibit usury; it would build a great body of scholastic knowledge to satisfy every student. Gregorianism as an ideal (it could never be realized) means one universal society, which is a Church, based utterly on the law of Christ and controlled ultimately by Christ's vicar. Here the new development of the human spirit, the new trend to the religious life, which first found recognition at the end of the third and the beginning of the fourth century, attains its zenith. The combination of a religious society with an autocratic political society which we find under Constantine; the modified form of that combination preached by Gelasius, in which the religious society acquires a religious as well as a political government—both disappear. The religious society attempts its logical complement in a theocracy.

But the political instinct of humanity is not readily quenched. The Holy Roman Empire, against which Gregorianism was pitted, was not, it is true, a strong embodiment of that instinct. A Charlemagne might have the force of a Frankish Empire at his back: the German emperors from Otto I onwards (962 A.D.) were only kings of Germany and Italy; and while Germany was divided by tribalism and distracted by feudalism, Italy was the home of practically independent cities. Even Charlemagne, though his coins bear the inscription *Renovatio Romani Imperii*, had no tradition; and his successors were equally destitute of any connexion with antiquity. With no root in their own realms, and no tradition for their support, the German emperors of the Middle Ages were not adequate to the struggle with the Church; and though they might seek to vindicate an independent political sphere, they were worsted in argument and defeated in policy by the papalist forces. It was when a lay sentiment, fostered by the lawyers, arose in France, and associated itself with national feeling, that the Church found a stubborn enemy, and Boniface VIII at last met with defeat (1303 A. D.). A lay society, founded on a national basis, vanquished the conception of a universal empire in the form which that conception had more and more assumed during the thousand years since the death of Aurelian—the form of an ecclesiastical society. And the Reformation, in which the lay State, alike in England and in Germany, asserted the priority of the political motive and the supremacy of its king over all persons and in all causes as well ecclesiastical as temporal, marks the final defeat and disappearance of the conception of the Roman Empire.

ERNEST BARKER.

BOOKS RECOMMENDED.

J. H. BREASTED, *Ancient Times.*
W. FERGUSON, *Greek Imperialism.*
E. BEVAN, *Stoics and Sceptics.*
H. F. PELHAM, *Outlines of Roman History.*
J. B. BURY, *The Students' Roman Empire* (27 B.C.–180 A.D.).
——, *The Later Roman Empire* (from 395 A.D. onwards).
H. S. JONES, *The Roman Empire.*
E. GIBBON, *The Decline and Fall of the Roman Empire* (in Bury's edition).
Cambridge Mediaeval History. Volume I.
SIR HENRY MAINE, *Ancient Law.*
LORD BRYCE, *Studies in History and Jurisprudence.*
SIR W. M. RAMSAY, *The Church in the Roman Empire.*
C. BIGG, *The Church's Task in the Roman Empire.*
L. DUCHESNE, *History of the Christian Church* (translated).
J. N. FIGGIS, *The Political Aspects of St. Augustine's City of God.*

ADMINISTRATION

The title of this chapter reminds us that the art of government draws many of its terms from the stock bequeathed to us by the Romans, some of them with picturesque associations of which their modern users are not even dimly conscious. The civil servant who draws his *salary* does not, we may be sure, connect the name with the 'salt-money' which the Romans took as typical of the subsistence-allowances paid to their officials; the politician who advocates a change in *fiscal* policy never travels back in thought to the sealed baskets (*fisci*) in which the treasure of the provinces was conveyed to Rome: nor does the holder of *municipal* office reflect that his title recalls those half-assimilated subjects of Rome who shouldered the burdens of citizenship (*munus*, *capere*) but were as yet debarred from its higher privileges.

These, however, are verbal curiosities. The question to which we seek an answer is: In what sense are the bureaucratic States of to-day the inheritors of a tradition having its fount and origin in the Roman Empire? It is evident that there can be no question of direct continuity. The Germanic kingdoms which overspread Western Europe after the fall of the Empire at first borrowed some of the titles and offices of the monarchy which they replaced; but feudal states could not be subjected to the rigid centralization which formed the last term in the evolution of Roman institutions; and from New Rome the modern world has never desired nor attempted to draw inspiration. The Catholic Church is the one permanent institution which overlaps the ancient and the modern, and we may allow that in its chancery it kept alive the traditions of the later Roman bureaucracy in the Dark Ages; but it had nothing to teach in the matter of civil administration.

The establishment of the Roman dominion in the Mediterranean basin, which to the Roman seemed to include all that was worthy to be named the world (*imperium orbis terrarum*), was one of those truly great events in history which can happen but once. Its real meaning was that in the main stream of human progress the City-state was merged in the Great State, and its institutions were adapted to the new conditions. This adaptation was so far from perfect that the huge fabric tottered and in the end collapsed under the weight of its own superstructure; but the idea of an ordered empire, with a fully articulated system both of central and local administration, was a permanent legacy to political man.

The Romans were peculiarly fitted to be the instrument by which this great change was brought about. They had not the keen critical instinct of the Greek, which enabled him to lay bare by victorious analysis the organic structure of human society. We do not go to Roman thinkers for our definition of the citizen as the man who 'is able to rule and be ruled', or of law as 'Reason without Appetite'. Nor were they as ingenious as Greek statesmen in devising elegant political machinery such as that which was elaborated at Athens between the time of Clisthenes (end of the sixth century B.C.) and the date when Aristotle wrote his *Constitution of the Athenians* (328–325 B.C.). If we assume, not merely that the Aristotelian citizen is correctly defined, but that the type was in fact embodied in the average Athenian, then the assignment of offices by lot and the system of rotation which in a small community ensures that administrative experience shall be widely diffused, the representation of such a community by a Grand Committee or 'Council' (βουλή) with its monthly Sub-Committees (πρυτανεῖαι), the various Boards of Inspectors, the law-courts which are in effect representative bodies drawn by lot from the ranks of the sovereign people, fall into their places as parts of a coherent and rigidly logical scheme to which the Roman state can show no parallel. But this scheme is only applicable under conditions which were not in fact realized even in Athens, and to the modern statesman it must appear in the light of a mechanical toy.

It was not, then, from the Greek philosophers nor from the Athenian legislators that the Romans took their lessons in the art of administration. But they did learn much—perhaps too much—from the bureaucratic governments set up by the successors of Alexander in the Near East, and in particular from the monarchy of the Ptolemies in Egypt. Here the territorial state, with a docile subject population enjoying scarcely any measure of local self-government, presented itself to its rulers as an estate to be exploited by 'scientific management', and to this end the services of talented Greeks, whether exiled by faction or dislodged by economic pressure from their native cities, were fully utilized. The sands of the Nile valley have preserved for us records which are lacking for the other Hellenistic monarchies, and we must often be content to leave in doubt the source from which Roman officialdom borrowed or adapted its organs and methods. We must also bear in mind that the congeries of city-communities which still flourished on the fringe of the monarchical states, while frequently falling under the suzerainty or protection of one or another of them, though they had nothing to teach on the higher questions of politics, did much to elaborate the machinery of commerce, banking, and so forth, and to develop a system of legal conceptions applicable to such matters which were ready to hand when Rome became the dominant Mediterranean power and was compelled to study the technique of Imperial administration.

It was late in her history when these problems were forced upon her attention. The earlier stages in the growth of her institutions are for us largely a field for guess-work. It is possible to exhibit the developed constitution, after the manner of Mommsen, as a more or less coherent and articulated system of public law, but this is only because the work had already been done by the antiquarians and lawyers of the last century of the pre-Christian era, and the lacunae in their very imperfectly preserved remains can be restored in great part like the text of a mutilated inscription. But historical criticism has undermined the foundations upon which their construction was raised by destroying the credit of the narratives which profess to supply an authentic record of the events of Rome's early history, but are relatively late in origin, tainted with the suspicion of family falsification, coloured by Greek political ideas, and inconsistent with respect to essential matters. Fortunately we are not here concerned with historical details, but may confine ourselves to pointing out where the strength and weakness of Roman statesmanship lay.

In the first place, there were certain cardinal conceptions clearly grasped and firmly held, which must be assumed as the fundamental principles of the Roman republican State.[1] These were, on the one hand, the sovereignty of the people (*populus Romanus*) as the sole ultimate source of right, privilege, and authority, and on the other, the 'power of command' (*imperium*) vested by its decree in the magistrate. Early Rome was, above all things, a nation in arms, and its chief assembly was an ordered host, a 'town army' (*exercitus urbanus*) as it is called by the great antiquarian Varro. This accounts for the fact that voting in the Roman *comitia*, and therefore in the municipal assemblies which conformed to their type, was always by groups, each of which cast a single suffrage, and also for the rule that the assembled host must remain standing in soldierly fashion; Cicero, in his defence of Flaccus, a governor accused of extortion by the Greek communities of the province of Asia, contrasts the discipline and marshalling of the Roman assemblies with 'the heedlessness of a seated gathering' by means of

[1] It would be out of place to discuss the primitive monarchy, the existence of which is more convincingly proved by the survival of the priest-king (*rex sacrorum*) and the name of the *regia* given to the residence of the *pontifex maximus* than by the current legends.

which a Greek city transacted the business of State. In these matters the Romans failed to adapt their primitive institutions to the needs of a national and imperial State, and we have nothing to learn from them so far as regards the means by which the popular will finds expression. To the end the *populus Romanus*, in theory an absolute sovereign, can only give expression to its commands in response to a question put to it by the magistrate who has convened it. Its utterance is 'law' (*lex*)—the word means 'that which is laid down' and is applied, for example, to the terms of a contract or the conditions formulated by the diviner (*augur*) in seeking an omen from heaven—but it is *lex rogata*, 'law made by question and answer', like the formal acts of early legal procedure which consisted in the exchange of set phrases by the parties to a suit. Hence the right so to elicit a binding expression of the people's will was jealously restricted to those upon whom it had itself conferred the *imperium*. This 'authority' was remarkable both for the plenitude of its powers and the nature of its limitations in Law and Custom.

The *imperium* of the magistrate, the tenure of which was limited to one year, was in theory one and indivisible, military, judicial, and executive, and the specialization of functions which was gradually brought about 'at home' (*domi*, i.e. in the city of Rome) did not apply 'in the theatre of war' (*militiae*) from which Rome alone was excluded. It was possessed in all its fullness by each of its holders, and any of its inherent powers, though dormant in the developed constitution, might be revived if the occasion demanded its exercise. But it was just this fact which imposed upon it its most significant limitation. For each of its holders could paralyse the action of a colleague of equal (or *a fortiori* of lower) rank by the counter-stroke of *intercessio*, or the power of veto. Such a power may be (and was) so exercised as to provide the 'checks and balances' which are necessary to secure stability in government; but it may also create deadlocks and drive men to seek violent issues. The generic term for the holder of the *imperium* is *praetor* (the 'leader'), and the Greeks recognized it as a military title when they translated it by στρατηγός. The Romans adopted the simple expedient of providing for the growing needs of the community by increasing the number of these officials. To the two chief magistrates established on the fall of the monarchy the special name of *consules* ('those who take counsel') was given; but the constitutional lawyers distinguished them as 'senior magistrates' (*praetores maximi*) from the members added in later times to the supreme college of those 'with authority' (*cum imperio*), viz. the *praetor* 'who lays down law as between citizens', usually called the 'city praetor' (366 B.C.), the praetor 'who lays down law as between foreigners' (242 B.C., called for short *praetor peregrinus*), and the varying number of those appointed to govern Rome's oversea possessions or to preside in special courts as these were set up. Besides concurrent authority or 'collegiality', there was an important limitation of the power of the magistrate in the right of appeal to the people (*provocatio ad populum*) against a sentence, pronounced in Rome, which threatened the citizen with the loss of his life or civil personality. Tradition placed the assertion of this right in the first year of the Republic, and the earliest Code of Law expressly provided that no judgement should be pronounced in a capital cause save by the 'greatest assembly', i.e. the nation in arms.

From this stock of primitive institutions grew the Roman Republic. It was not the work of a legislator, such as many Greek constitutions were, or were alleged to be, but that of a people with a deep respect for tradition (*mos maiorum*), which led them to supplement rather than discard the out-worn organs of the body politic, leaving the new to find its *modus vivendi* with the old, and often to adapt old structures to new purposes, especially by the use of those convenient fictions which serve to disguise changes, to smooth transitions, and to economize thinking. The issue of the first great internal struggle which shook the growing fabric of the State is typical of Roman methods. We have no trustworthy account of the origin of the distinction between the 'fathers' (*patres*) and the 'multitude' (*plebs*). The most that we can say is that the Roman tradition lends no countenance to the views put forward in various forms by modern scholars, that the distinction was one of race, or that the object of the *plebs* was to secure admission to a citizen-body which did not include it. In primitive communities aristocracies spring from economic distinctions and fortify themselves by an appeal to religion, and this was so at Rome, where a limited group of families monopolized social and political privileges, and above all that of representing the Roman State in its strictly regulated transactions with the gods. The members of this group were the *patricii*, and the struggle which they waged with the unprivileged majority fills the first two centuries of Republican history. The essential features of the final settlement were the establishment of a State within the State, to wit, the corporation formed by the *plebs*, which at some date early in the fifth century had set up its own organization under its own officers (*tribuni*), and the grant to this corporation, by an enactment of the *populus*, of a concurrent right of legislation binding on all Romans. Henceforward there were two sovereigns in Rome, related as whole to part, yet practically equal in power; and in all legal texts and formulae they were carefully kept apart. The people assembled in *comitia*, the *plebs* in a *concilium*. The people issued 'commands' (*iubere* is the technical term) which alone were 'laws'; the *plebs* passed 'resolutions' (*scita*, from *sciscere*) which derived their binding force from the people's recognition. The people in *comitia* could alone elect to *magistratus*, and by a fiction these were termed (in lawyer's language) 'patrician magistracies', though they had long been thrown open to the *plebs*, which had besides its own 'officers' (*tribuni plebis*) and 'wardens' (*aediles plebis*), but could not invest them with the true *imperium*. In the later Republic such distinctions had no practical interest. The assembly of the *plebs* naturally adopted the group-vote (using the non-military unit of the tribe) and the restriction of initiative to the official convener (in this case the tribune or aedile), and the *populus* in turn came to hold assembly by tribes, so that the average citizen, and even the historian, except in technically expressed passages, applied the word *comitia* indifferently to meetings of the Whole and the Part. Yet it was not forgotten that the tribunes had been instituted to give protection (*auxilium*) to the *plebs* against the arbitrary action of the patrician magistrate, and that the free exercise of this function, which developed into a power of veto (*intercessio*) exercised by each member of the college of ten, was secured by the oath of the *plebs* to punish resistance with death.

Long before the final adjustment of the relations between *populus* and *plebs* was made, other questions, and those more important for the subject of administration, had begun to ripen. Tradition places in the fifth century the origins of an office which held an anomalous position in the Roman system. This was the censorship, the original function of which was the 'numbering of the host' and the performance of the rite of purification (*lustrum*) which followed it; this was repeated after an interval fixed in course of time at five years. The censors were of course obliged to keep a register of the citizens and their possessions, in order to determine their liability to taxation and military service, and it was natural that they should also be called upon to deal with the properties of the State and to enter into contracts on its behalf, the earliest of which no doubt were those which in historical times they farmed out before all others—for a fresh coat of red paint on the statue of Jupiter the Best and Greatest, and for the feeding of his sacred geese.

In the course of the fourth century B.C. they were entrusted with a yet more important function. It was the unwritten law of Rome that a person invested with executive powers should take counsel before action with a *consilium* or body of advisers. The general in the field had his staff, the judge on the bench his assessors, and the head of the State summoned the 'fathers' or the 'council of elders' (*Senatus*) to assist him in his deliberations, although he was not bound by any formal statute to follow their advice. According to tradition he had at first been free to choose his own advisers, but at some date prior to 312 B.C. the selection was transferred to the censors, and they in turn became gradually limited in their choice by constitutional custom, the effect of which was that ex-magistrates became entitled to a summons, unless passed over for conduct unworthy of a Roman. In this matter the censors enjoyed an unfettered discretion, with the result that they gradually set up a code of civil honour, breaches of which entailed *infamia*; and this code served as a model to the praetors, in whose court a similar set of rules was enforced by the deprivation of certain civil rights and privileges.

By the time, then, that Rome's internal strife was finally composed and she had not only acquired a dominant position in Italy but had been victorious in her first clash with an extra-Italian power, the Epirote monarchy of Pyrrhus, there had been superimposed upon the rudimentary institutions of the primitive soldier-state an organ of government none the less powerful because its authority was based upon Custom and not upon positive Law. The new problems which crowded upon the Romans in ever-increasing complexity were the result of external factors—the great struggle with Carthage and continuous territorial expansion. Their solution called for long views and settled methods in the handling of Rome's foreign relations, an improved and developed administrative system, and a progressive assimilation of fresh elements into the citizen-body. These are all affairs of high policy; and in such matters an official, however powerful in theory, if he only holds office for a year, will generally defer to the opinion of a body of which he is to remain an ordinary member for the rest of his life. Thus it came about that in the third and second centuries B.C. the Senate governed, but did not reign, whilst the People reigned, but did not govern. Writing in the latter part of the second century, Polybius, who was himself a practical statesman, noted that the Senate had the power of the purse, was responsible for the maintenance of order in Italy, and controlled the foreign relations of Rome. This, then, was the body which was called upon to adapt Roman institutions to the needs of a growing empire. It can scarcely be said to have succeeded in the task.

As the territory of Rome expanded, it became her duty to develop the machinery of administration and bring into being a trained official class. This was never seriously attempted. In the fourth century the annual *imperium* of the magistrate had, as an emergency measure, been extended in time to meet military needs by an act of the People (*prorogatio*). But custom soon established the rule that a decree of the Senate was a necessary preliminary; and this became the normal method of providing administrators for overseas territories, for the consuls (in time of peace) spent their year of office in Rome as heads of the executive, and the increase which was made from time to time in the number of praetors lagged behind the number of posts to be allotted. These posts were called *provinciae*, a name more familiar in its application to the regions placed under a military governor than in the more general sense of 'department'. It was the Senate which fixed the limits of *provinciae*, voted the contingent of troops to be placed under the governor's orders and the necessary supplies, and appointed his staff-officers or *legati* (though in this matter the commander's wishes were naturally consulted) and, on occasion, special commissioners (also called *legati*) to assist in the conclusion of a peace or the settlement of a newly-conquered territory. Such a settlement, whether framed in consultation with a senatorial advisory body or not, was imposed by and with the authority of the general and was known as a *lex* or charter bearing his name. We would gladly know more of these Provincial Settlements, such as the *Lex Rupilia* issued for Sicily in 132 B.C., to which Cicero appeals in his indictment of Verres for misgovernment, and the *Lex Pompeia* which Pompey drew up for Bithynia and which was still in force when Pliny was sent by Trajan as High Commissioner to that province in 111 A.D. In general we may confidently say that Rome cared more for security than for efficiency, that she interfered as little as she could with pre-existing arrangements, and that she recognized no unit save the *civitas*, which in the East was usually the city-state. The relations of such *civitates* to Rome were of three main kinds—either regulated by a treaty (*foederatae civitates*), or based on a unilateral and revocable grant of self-government (*liberae civitates*), or dependent on the pleasure of the Roman people and in effect on that of the magistrate; cities of this last class were generally known as 'tax-paying communities' (*stipendiariae civitates*). The Provincial Settlement regulated the rights and duties of the subject communities, and especially the process of law as between their members, and also where Roman citizens were parties to a suit. Where no special privileges were granted by treaty or charter, the governor administered that form of the 'law merchant' of the Mediterranean world which was recognized in the court of the *praetor peregrinus* at Rome: but though a corrupt official might often turn this to his own profit, the local courts were no doubt largely left to try the suits arising in each *civitas*. There was little direct interference with internal political conditions; but Rome looked askance on Greek democracy. Cicero, for instance, lays it down as the duty of a governor to see that the *civitates* are administered by the upper class (*optimates*), and an inscription from Dyme in Achaea records a peremptory order from a Roman magistrate requiring the infliction of the capital penalty upon an agitator who had proposed legislation 'contrary to the constitution bestowed by Rome on the Achaeans'. The Roman Government was essentially military, not civil, as the Greeks recognized when they translated the general term for 'governor' (*praetor*) by *στρατηγός* (army-commander), and of municipal institutions as cog-wheels in the machine of government there could naturally as yet be no question.

In Rome and Italy, too, progress was slow and interrupted. Instead of creating new offices, the Romans preferred to allot fresh functions to those which had existed from early times, so that the old titles became strangely inappropriate. The treasury was placed in the charge of the *quaestores*, who (as their name shows) had been created to assist the consuls in the detection and punishment of crime; the care of public sites, buildings, markets, festivals, and so forth was assigned to the *aediles*, in origin the two 'temple-wardens' appointed by the *plebs* to keep its archives, to whom a second pair, representing the *populus*, was afterwards added. Even the tribunes, whose rôle was political rather than administrative, seem to have played a certain part in the procedure of the civil courts, since their veto could be applied to the orders of the presiding magistrate and could thus be used to modify the issue referred to the jury for decision.[1] A few minor offices were set up for special purposes, but the little that we know of them does not suggest that they formed part of an ordered system. There were, for example, Masters of the Mint, whose full title was *tresviri auro argento aeri flando feriundo*, but an examination of the Republican coinage proves that even if they were appointed annually (which is doubtful) they were not the only officials who struck coins, since we find censors, aediles, and quaestors performing this function at various dates, while in the last century of the Republic the needs of the Roman armies in the field were met by issues of coin struck by the orders of the generals in command. From time to time the

[1] The defendant in an action in which Cicero appeared for the plaintiff adopted this means of bringing pressure to bear on the *praetor* in order to secure an amendment of the *formula* which would enable him to raise the plea of self-defence in justification of his use of force.

people issued special commissions (*curae*), the holders of which, not being annual magistrates with *imperium*, were free from some of the limitations inherent in such offices; thus the great military highways of Italy were constructed either by censors or by magistrates commanding in the field, but their maintenance and restoration was apparently entrusted to Highway Commissioners (*curatores viarum*) appointed from time to time. The great scheme for the settlement of Roman citizens on the public lands, associated with the names of the Gracchi, was executed by a permanent Land Commission of three members, to which, as originally constituted by the Sempronian law of 133 B.C., judicial powers were assigned. As Rome grew to be the capital city of a Mediterranean empire, the problem of its food-supply became urgent, and Gaius Gracchus, following a practice common in the cities of the Greek East,[1] inaugurated the supply of a corn-ration at less than cost price to the urban proletariat, without at the same time creating an efficient department to ensure the smooth working of the system, and it was not until 57 B.C. that a Department of Food Control (*cura annonae*) was set up; and even then the office created was but a pretext for giving wide political and even military powers to Pompey.

In no department was the failure of the Republican government to grapple with the problems of public administration more conspicuous than in the field of finance. Since war was the national industry of Republican Rome, there seemed to be no need to face the economic problems of peace. Direct taxation was an extraordinary measure, and the 'assessment' (*tributum*) levied upon the property of citizens came to be regarded as a War Loan, which might be and sometimes was repaid to the contributors. The immense acquisition of wealth which accrued to Rome through the conquests of the second century B.C. brought direct taxation to an end in 167 B.C.,

[1] The nearest parallel is to be found in the inscription from Samos, Dittenberger, *Sylloge Inscriptionum Graecarum* (ed. 3), 976.

and the expense of the armies of occupation which were maintained in the conquered provinces became chargeable to their inhabitants. Nor was the citizen of the Republic heavily burdened with indirect taxation. Harbour-dues (*portoria*) were imposed at the Italian ports, but the conception of a protective tariff was beyond the horizon of the Romans, and the dues themselves were abolished for a time in 60 B.C. Apart from these, the only indirect tax was one of 5 per cent. on the value of manumitted slaves, and the proceeds of this were not treated as revenue, but accumulated as a Special Reserve in the 'inner treasury' (*aerarium sanctius*). The State-chest itself was placed in charge of the quaestors, that is to say, of young men about to embark on a political career; their functions were limited to those of receiving moneys due to the State, keeping account and custody thereof, and making payments on the order of a magistrate.[1] They naturally fell into the hands of their subordinates, the *scribae* or clerks of the Treasury, and exercised no effective control over public finance, as Cato the Younger discovered; nor were they in any way concerned with financial policy. There was in short no official or department to which such questions might be referred, for the censors, as we have seen, were appointed at intervals and for short periods to deal with State-property and enter into contracts, the terms of which were fixed and might be varied by the Senate. This body was in short the supreme authority (subject to a possible appeal to the sovereign people) in financial matters, and though no doubt it was not lacking in advisers of experience and ability, it showed the defects of all deliberative bodies when called upon to deal with administrative questions. While taxation was light, the property of the State was large, especially as the conquest of Italy brought a considerable part

[1] The *Lex Acilia Repetundarum*, for example, prescribes that the moneys recovered from corrupt officials convicted under the law shall be deposited in sealed baskets (*fisci*) with the *quaestores*, and paid out to successful claimants on an order from the presiding judge.

of the soil of the peninsula under the ownership of the Roman people as *ager publicus*. Some portions of this were alienated by sale or allotment, whether to individual settlers or to the 'colonies' which served as outposts of Rome and centres for the diffusion of Roman ideas and customs. But much land remained in the hands of the State, and of this the greater part was undeveloped. To create a Department of Agriculture or of Public Lands lay beyond the range of Roman ideas. The City-State was careful to exact service from its members, but averse from furnishing them with permanent and remunerative employment, and preferred to raise revenue from its properties by farming out the collection of dues to a private speculator. The title of the State remained indefeasible, but the tenure of the occupier was protected by law against third parties; and custom at any rate prescribed that he should not suffer disturbance so long as his dues were paid. Whether, or to what extent, lands were also leased directly to State-tenants has been a matter of much dispute. This may have been done in some highly cultivated districts, but the general practice was for the censors to contract with tax-farmers (*publicani*) and not with the occupier, who had to furnish a fixed quota of the produce of land or a fee per head of cattle grazed on public pasture. Properly supervised, this system might have produced a large and fairly constant revenue; but there was no effective control by public officials, and the interest of the governing order lay in conniving at the absorption into what was practically private ownership of the huge tracts of land held in occupation (*possessio*) by Senators, far exceeding in extent the limits which had been set by law to such tenures. The social and political crisis brought about in 133 B.C. by the failure of the Roman State to administer its properties on sound principles found no peaceful solution; and the Gracchi were driven to challenge the validity of the existing constitutional usages and to initiate a revolutionary agitation which only ended with the fall of the Republic.

It was natural that the Senate, in administering the extra-Italian possessions of the State, should likewise follow the line of least resistance. The simplest plan was to impose a fixed tribute (*stipendium*) upon conquered nations. This was assessed upon the several communities (*civitates*) recognized by Rome, and the quotas were paid to the *quaestor* attached to the staff of the governor and served to defray the expenses of the occupation, any surplus being remitted to Rome. This system prevailed in the West; but the Eastern monarchies, adapting to their ends the practice of the city-state, had found it profitable to farm the revenues derived from the lands of their subjects. The classic example is the tithe-farming of Sicily, elaborated by the tyrant of Syracuse, Hiero II, in the third century B.C., who may possibly have learnt some of his methods from the Ptolemies.[1] The Romans, when the island fell into their hands after the First Punic War, incorporated the 'Law of Hiero' in their settlement of the province, and had its terms been scrupulously observed the tax-payer would have had little ground for complaint; but the third speech of Cicero against Verres (Actio II. iii) shows that where there was collusion between the Roman governor and the Sicilian tax-farmer the plight of the cultivators of the soil was a sorry one. Still graver were the evils which sprang from the practice of contracting, not with local collectors, but with companies having their seat in Rome, for the ingathering of provincial revenues. Such bodies of *publicani* worked on five-year contracts made with the censors at Rome, and their operations in all the fields of enterprise open to them were so highly organized that something very like the modern system of investment and shareholding came into being. The political consequences were important. Even in the Hannibalic period we find the 'order of public contractors' banded together in defence of

[1] The parallel drawn between the *Lex Hieronica* and the *Revenue Laws* of Ptolemy Philadelphus, partly preserved in a papyrus, by M. Carcopino (*La loi de Hiéron et les Romains*) is instructive.

one of its members when involved in a serious scandal; and this body was regarded with such suspicion and dislike by the Senate that, after the conquest of the Macedonian kingdom in 167 B.C., the gold and silver mines and forests which had belonged to the royal domain were allowed to remain unproductive rather than to fall into the hands of *publicani*. But the capitalist waited and won; and Gaius Gracchus secured the support of the wealthy investor by enacting that the contract for the collection of the tithes of the Kingdom of Pergamon, which on the extinction of the royal line had become the Province of Asia, should be put up to auction in Rome. The result was to exhibit on a large scale the patent vices of the Republican system—or lack of system; in other words, government by the unpaid aristocrat and exploitation by the irresponsible profiteer.

There is not much evidence that any serious effort was made, during the last century of Republican history, to devise schemes of administrative reform. Sulla is credited with the abolition (in any case only temporary) of the tax-farming system in Asia; the facts are obscure, and his measure may have applied only to a forced contribution levied by assessment on the several communities and treated as pre-payment of five years' taxation. His domestic reforms no doubt tended to make the existing system more workable. The number of magistrates was increased—a measure long overdue. The quaestors, for example, were raised in number to twenty, and by this means the Senate was automatically recruited without the intervention of the censors. The higher magistrates—so long as the system of Sulla remained in force—normally served their year's term of office in Rome, followed by a second year in an overseas province. But there was no attempt to secure more efficient government or to enforce responsibility to a central authority.

Nor does it seem that much was done to solve the chief problem which faced the Romans in Italy—the provision of an ordered system of local government for the scores of communities from the Alps to the straits of Messina whose inhabitants had become citizens of Rome. For Italy had now ceased to be a confederation. Rome had brought about the unification of the peninsula as much by policy as by arms. Variety of status, in an ascending scale leading up to full citizenship, had been the rule since Rome had made herself head of the 'Latin name' and dissolved the league of cities in which she was *prima inter pares*. The members of this federation had enjoyed reciprocal rights in private law, and this status, divorced from its ethnic significance, was conferred by the Romans on the garrison-colonies planted at nodal points on the military highways of Italy. By a curious survival, these artificially created 'Latin' communities remained in the technical position of independent and nominally sovereign allies of Rome. Other communities received the private rights, and shared the burdens, of Roman citizenship, and were therefore called *municipia*, but the political franchise was withheld from them until they had served their apprenticeship in public affairs. Some of them were not permitted to enjoy full self-government, but ranked as 'assize-towns' (*praefecturae*), to which Rome sent judges to administer her law. Then there were the colonies of Roman citizens, in which the institutions of the mother-city were copied on a small scale. But the great majority of Italian towns were in name allies of Rome (*socii*), in fact, as the terms of their pact with her became increasingly onerous, her subjects. The illiberal policy of the later Republic, and the closing of the avenues to citizenship hitherto open,[1] turned them into enemies, and it needed the Great Rebellion of 90 B.C. and the internecine strife of parties in Rome, each of which strove to outbid the other, to force the door.

[1] In the early part of the second century B.C. the reciprocal rights of 'Latin' citizens, and especially that of acquiring Roman citizenship, were limited, and a form of *Latinitas* was created in which the office-holders of a 'Latin colony', and no others, were admitted to full citizenship.

The political question was thus solved, so far as it could be solved without representative institutions; it remained to provide for the administration of United Italy, and to decentralize, so far as was practicable, the functions of government. This was done by the extension to all towns of Roman or Latin right of a form of municipal constitution which, though it was no 'sealed pattern', was stamped by certain salient features. The chief magistrates were four in number, two for the administration of justice, and two for the supervision of material interests. It was usual in colonies (whether Roman or Latin) to distinguish the former pair as *duouiri* (whose position was like that of the Roman consuls) from their junior colleagues, the *aediles*; but in the newly enfranchised towns, to which the old name of *municipia* was applied, a College of Four (*quattuorviri*) was the rule. There was a local Senate and assembly, and the group-vote, so typical of the Latin race, was introduced. We know little of the steps by which these institutions were perfected and diffused. There had been much copying of Roman methods in Italy before its enfranchisement; an inscription from the Oscan town of Bantia, written in the local dialect and dating from the time of the Gracchi, shows that censors and even tribunes were among the local magistrates. The Great Rebellion was not, it seems, followed by the enactment of any Local Government statute of general application, but charters were issued by special commissioners dispatched to organize (*constituere*) the several communities. From Tarentum comes a fragment of the local charter which, though not free from the tokens of careless drafting so common in Roman laws, shows how a common type was being evolved. The local senate is the final authority in matters financial, and the magistrates must render account to it; each of its members must, as a guarantee of his social standing, furnish proof that he is the *bona fide* owner of a house 'roofed with not less than 1,500 tiles'. It seems that Julius Caesar, throughout his public career, took a special interest in municipal affairs, and initiated general legislation in this matter. As consul in 59 B.C. he passed an 'agrarian law' relating to the foundation of colonies, and containing provisions which were copied into later statutes; ten years later, on becoming master of Rome within a few weeks of his crossing of the Rubicon, he enfranchised the inhabitants of all urban communities between the Po and the Alps in fulfilment of a promise which conservative obstruction had hitherto prevented him from making good,[1] and almost at once a law was passed of which a few clauses are preserved in an inscription, and are highly important as providing for the decision of civil suits, within certain limits, in the local courts, sometimes with and sometimes without an appeal to Rome. In the last year of his life Caesar, as it appears, passed a Local Government Act for all Italy. Our knowledge of this comes from an inscription found at Heraclea, one of the Greek colonies in South Italy, which had been reluctant to accept the gift of Roman citizenship in 89 B.C. and to surrender its sovereign status secured by treaty. This document seems to contain a series of excerpts from one or more laws rather than a continuous text, but it is clear that the important clauses which relate to the qualifications and disqualifications for the membership of the local senate are of Caesar's time. It is also provided that in the years in which the census is held in Rome, a register of Roman citizens and their property shall be made by the local magistrates and returns forwarded to Rome. Thus we see that the foundations of that municipal system which was,

[1] The case of the Transpadanes is interesting. The region north of the Po, including the plains of Lombardy and Venetia and the Alpine valleys, had not been included in the settlement of 89 B.C., but by a *Lex Pompeia*, bearing the name of the father of Pompey the Great, the urban communities had all received the later Latin right, while the backward Alpine tribes had been 'assigned' (*attributi*) to adjacent towns as being unripe for self-government. Their Romanization had so far advanced in half a century that, when the Latin towns became Roman, they were in turn promoted to *Latinitas*.

next to her system of law, the greatest creation of Rome were well and truly laid by her most brilliant statesman. Nor was he content with bringing greater order and unity into the local administration of Italy. Viewing the Empire as a whole, he made it his aim to implant germs of Roman life in the dominions overseas. His re-settlement of Corinth and Carthage, whose desolate sites cried shame upon the brutal and selfish methods of the oligarchy, was an object-lesson too plain to escape notice; and we are fortunate in possessing large portions of the charter issued on the foundation of a colony at Urso (Osuña) in Southern Spain, planned by Caesar, 'dictator and imperator', but not established until after his death. This document, which in its drafting shows signs of the feverish haste with which the work of the urban departments was carried on under Caesar's rule, is one of the most valuable sources of our knowledge of Roman municipal organization. We observe that the highest offices are thrown open to freedmen, as in the similar colonies founded by Caesar in Africa. He had a robust faith in the power of Roman civilization to assimilate foreign elements.[1]

The dictatorship of Caesar shattered the machinery of Republican government, as he intended that it should. The history of the century of revolution had shown that the strong central authority which was needed to transform the institutions of the City-State into those of a Mediterranean Empire must be wielded by a ruler either exalted above the Republican constitution or invested with special powers not inconsistent with its principles and precedents. Had Pompey been as great a statesman as a captain, he might have satisfied the latter condition. As it was, the extraordinary commands with which he was invested in order to meet the challenge of the pirates

[1] The Laws and Charters referred to above, together with those issued to two Spanish communities in pursuance of Vespasian's grant of the Latin right to all non-Roman towns in Spain, are excellently translated and edited by Dr. E. G. Hardy (*Roman Laws and Charters*, Oxford, 1912).

and Mithradates to Roman supremacy furnished examples of the method by which the limitations of the *imperium* could be transcended and the lack of co-ordination between its several holders could be remedied. Abroad, the grouping of provinces under a High Command, the extension of the *imperium* for a term of years, and government by means of a staff of *legati* responsible to the *imperator*, came to stay. But at home it was hard to find a place for the personal ruler within the old framework, and Caesar, in his hour of victory, felt no scruple in converting the dictatorship, which was nothing if not an emergency measure, and had been treated even by Sulla (who revived it after a long lapse) as a temporary expedient for carrying through constitutional reforms, into a permanent instrument of government. He showed his contempt for the Republican magistracies by allowing them to remain vacant for a year and more, and ruling through his 'deputies' (*praefecti*), upon whom their *insignia* were conferred; but he had taken no steps to reorganize the public services on a permanent basis when his career was cut short.

It was left for Caesar's heir to set about the task which he had failed to accomplish on more promising lines. We need not discuss the fictions and adaptations by which Augustus built up for himself an authority whose limitations, though in practice illusory, were formally consistent with the traditional sovereignty of the *Senatus populusque Romanus*. Our business is to exhibit in outline his most permanent creation, an administrative system under which an Empire of many races could live in peace and prosperity and could be welded together without haste or violence in an ever-growing unity.

It has been maintained that the bureaucratic régime elaborated by Augustus was more or less closely copied from the system in force in the Hellenistic monarchies, and particularly in Egypt, where the emperor was not at pains to disguise his true position and ruled, in the eyes of the native population, as the successor of the Ptolemies. There is some exaggeration here. It would be hard to point to any institutions of which we can certainly say that they are directly borrowed from those of Ptolemaic Egypt. Alexandria had a night-watch under a military officer (*νυκτερινὸς στρατηγός*) and Augustus, in his later years, provided the capital which he had done so much to beautify with a fire-brigade (*vigiles*) under a military organization.[1] In order to finance a scheme of army pensions, for which a special Treasury (*aerarium militare*) was created in 6 A.D., a succession duty (*vicesima hereditatum*) was imposed upon Roman citizens; such a tax is thought by some to have been levied in Egypt, but the question is open to doubt. On the other hand, Augustus seems to have dealt freely with the institutions which he found in Egypt: we possess extracts from the new Code of Regulations (*γνώμων*) which he issued for one of the financial departments which he found already in existence, the *ἴδιος λόγος* or Department of Special Revenues derived from fines, escheats, and confiscations. Nevertheless, it is true in a broad sense that Augustus, realizing the need of a permanent and professional service to administer his Empire, also realized that this must take the form of personal service rendered to a superior, as in the great monarchies. From the same source springs the blurring of the line between public and private affairs, and especially between the property of the State and that of the ruler, with which we shall have to deal. But it must be remembered that the great fortunes accumulated by the Senatorial aristocracy in the period of conquest and exploitation, especially in the Near East, had been invested either in land or in the lucrative enterprises of finance, and that a great house was also a great business concern with an army of agents and clerks, a private posting-service, and so forth; so that Romans were already familiar with large-scale management and, although they made free use

[1] From the pails which they carried they received the nickname of *sparteoli*, which we might render 'Bucketeers'.

of Greek ability in subordinate positions, were fully capable of far-sighted direction. As for the second order in the State, of which the *publicani* formed the nucleus and marrow, they were naturally conversant with all that concerned the collection of revenue.

Now Augustus knew well that the smooth working of a system depends upon assigning to each part its appropriate function. The Senatorial order, in virtue of its traditions, would tolerate no subordination other than that of military service; but as his staff-officers, Senators could and did govern the provinces in which standing garrisons were maintained. The urban magistracies of Rome, though their existence gave historical continuity to the government and distinction to the career of individuals, could not be of great use in the routine administration of a world-capital; but useful work could be found for that estimable and indeed invaluable person, the professional Committee-man, on the various Commissions (*curae*) which were set up by Augustus, as his biographer tells us, 'in order to increase the number of those taking part in public administration'. Let us take a typical example. Rome was supplied with water by the great aqueducts, which bore the names of their builders, but were not entrusted to any permanent department or official for maintenance and fell into disrepair. Augustus himself undertook their restoration at his own expense—a work of many years; and his trusted minister, Agrippa, besides adding two to their number, got together a staff of 240 slaves (his private property) and compiled a register of persons entitled to receive supplies of water. He died in 12 B.C., and bequeathed his slaves to Augustus, who took the matter in hand in consultation with the Senate. A Water Board was set up, with powers conferred by a statute passed in the assembly of the people, and regulations were made for it by decree of the Senate, which conferred upon the Commissioners the *insignia* of a Roman magistracy. The first Chairman of this Board was one of the great courtiers of the reign,

M. Valerius Messalla Corvinus.[1] There was also a Highway Board (though here the work of supervision seems to have been distributed), a Board of Public Works, a Tiber Conservancy, the main object of which was to prevent floods by regulating the bank and dredging the stream, and a Board for the distribution of corn-doles. The last case is instructive. The Control of Food Supply (*cura annonae*) was too important a function to be let slip by the Emperor, and by the close of his reign (as we shall find) he had placed it in the hands of a controller appointed by and responsible to himself. The Senatorial officials were concerned only with the administration of the dole. As time went on, Augustus found it possible to institute offices more directly dependent upon himself which a Senator could hold without derogation to his dignity, such as the Treasurership of the Military Pension Chest and, above all, the great post of Prefect of the City; this officer was responsible for order in the capital and had a military force of three regiments at his disposal.

For the administration of the Empire at large Augustus relied on the second order. They had always been known as 'Knights' (*equites*), because, even after the actual service of Roman citizens in the cavalry had ceased, the property-qualification required therefor was still noted in the census-registers; and Augustus employed those upon whom he bestowed the 'public horse' as officers in his army, especially in command of the 'auxiliary' regiments of non-Romans, as the first step in their career of public service, and held a brilliant annual parade of the corps on the 15th of July. From this class he chose those who showed military ability to govern frontier districts—for example, in the Alpine regions—but above all, he drew from its ranks the Financial Agents (*procuratores*) who were the backbone of the administration. By the Act of Settlement

[1] Our knowledge of the procedure comes from the tract *On the Aqueducts* written by Sex. Julius Frontinus, Governor of Britain A.D. 74–7, and afterwards Chairman of the Board.

on which the constitutional monarchy was based, Augustus was placed in command of a specified group of provinces, including all those garrisoned by the legions.[1] For the maintenance of the army, the defence of the frontiers, and the general administration of these provinces, he was wholly and solely responsible, and their revenues were placed at his disposal. Here was an ample training-ground for a new public service, which was at the same time the household of the Emperor. This service had its civil and military branches, but the time had not yet come when the two careers could be differentiated, and the Emperor's servants passed freely from one to the other. There were prizes, too, to be won in this profession. Highest of all were the vice-royalty of Egypt (*Praefectura Aegypti*) and the command of the Household Brigade (*Praefectura praetorii*) ; next to them came the posts of Corn Controller (*Praefectus annonae*) and Chief of the Fire Brigade (*Praefectus vigilum*). In course of time the *procuratores*, though properly financial officials (and strictly speaking 'personal agents' of the Emperor), came to be entrusted with the governorships of the smaller provinces, a process which probably began in the lifetime of Augustus. The rendering of Roman terms in Greek writers is at first liable to variation, but it seems that when Archelaus, the successor of Herod the Great in the kingdom of Judaea, was deposed in 6 A.D., his territory was placed under a *procurator* 'with the power to kill', as Josephus puts it ; and the system was freely extended to newly annexed districts. The Emperor was of course not confined, in his choice of subordinates, to free-born Romans ; and by the employment of manumitted slaves he infused new blood into the official class, though in this matter he walked more warily than his successors.

The machinery was thus created by which a much-needed survey of the resources of the Empire could be made and a

[1] Except that of Africa, i.e. Tunis, where one legion remained under the *imperium* of a Senatorial proconsul until the reign of Caligula.

balance of receipts and outgoings struck. The 'decree' that 'went out from Caesar Augustus that all the world should be taxed' shows us how this work was regarded in Judaea, where it appears that a system of periodical assessments was introduced, of a type found in the adjacent kingdom of Egypt. But the *census* in the Western provinces was a much more elaborate undertaking, begun in 27 B.C. and continued for many years. At the close of his life, Augustus was able to bequeath to his successor an 'Abstract of the whole Empire', which, besides the 'states' of the Armies, recorded the sums in the Treasury and the several chests (*fisci*) and the outstanding payments due on account of indirect taxes (*vectigalia*): to this were appended the names of the freedmen and slaves who could be held to account for these sums.[1] The plural *fisci* implies the keeping of separate accounts for the various provinces and departments under Imperial control; but it was not long before the singular term *fiscus* came to be used of the Imperial treasury as a unit; and the language which writers such as Seneca and Tacitus use of it shows that it was regarded as being, if not the Emperor's private and personal property, at any rate at his free disposal so long as he maintained the public services and the defences of the Empire.

The establishment of a central financial authority with a trained *personnel* made it possible to substitute direct collection of revenues for the wasteful and oppressive system of tax-farming. It must not be thought that so far-reaching a change was carried through by Augustus. But the two great taxes imposed upon the provinces of the Empire, *tributum soli* or land-tax and *tributum capitis*, levied on personal property, were collected by Imperial officials.[2] To dislodge the *publicanus* from the collection of indirect taxes was a much slower process, and we read of abuses in this matter which Nero, in a mood of

[1] Julius Caesar had, as Suetonius tells us, placed the administration of the public Treasury in the hands of his private slaves.

[2] The tithe-system had already been abolished by Julius Caesar.

generous impulse, proposed to extirpate by the abolition of all *vectigalia*. But the operations of the tax-farmer were closely supervised by Imperial agents, and private profit was gradually reduced until the time was ripe for the elimination of the middleman. This system was introduced by Augustus in connexion with his new Succession Duty, and the revenue officials of this department have left abundant traces of their activity in inscriptions from all parts of the Empire. In Egypt the grip of the bureaucrat was quickly tightened, and the farming of taxes (or of State lands) was converted from a source of profit into an onerous burden. In an edict of 68 A.D. the Viceroy of Egypt, Tiberius Julius Alexander, an able and liberal-minded administrator of Jewish origin, speaks of the compulsion exerted in order to provide for the farming of revenues as a growing abuse, and promises to satisfy the petitioners who protested against it by maintaining the voluntary principle, which (he adds) 'is better for the finances of our Lord' and accords with 'the common practice of the provinces'; but the bureaucratic spirit prevailed against breadth of view, and Egypt became an object-lesson in the methods of the servile State.

Augustus had a clear intuition of the two complementary tasks which a creative statesman is called upon to perform: the first, to trace with firm outline a programme of administration, the details of which may be left to his successors to fill in; the second, to foster in his subordinates the growth of a tradition of loyal service and a code of professional honour. His long reign, exceeding forty years from the Act of Settlement of 27 B.C., gave him the time he needed; and he had a discerning eye for men and their capacities. In his later years a certain C. Turranius, who had been Viceroy of Egypt, was recalled in order to organize the new Imperial Department of the Corn Supply of Rome, which depended very largely on the Egyptian tribute in kind. He was among the first to swear allegiance to Augustus's successor, and thirty-four years

Fig. 1. TIMGAD IN ALGERIA, A ROMAN COLONIAL CITY

The Forum, looking west, with the columns of the Temple of Victory

Fig. 2. HARDKNOT CASTLE AND THE SCAFELL RANGE

From a drawing by W. G. Collingwood, F.S.A.

later we find him still in office, sitting as a judicial assessor in the Emperor's court and, on account of his great age, consulted in priority to the Prefect of the Guard, who was his senior in the official hierarchy. Some years earlier, as we are told by Seneca, he had received permission to lay down his office from Caligula, but after a short experience of enforced leisure, petitioned the Emperor to reinstate him in his office. The story is doubtless true, though Turranius can hardly have been ninety years old at the time, as Seneca would have us believe; and it shows that Augustus knew where to look for the stuff of which great civil servants are made. That he left a political testament we know, and that he indicated the lines which his successors were to follow in perfecting his administrative system we cannot doubt. Tiberius held that what was policy for Augustus was law for himself. In the early years of his reign Strabo, expressing no doubt the view of the Greek world, wrote: 'It is hard to administer so great an Empire save by committing it to the care of one man, as of a father: never, in fact, has it fallen to the lot of the Romans and their allies to enjoy such abundance of peace and plenty as that which Augustus bestowed on them from the day when he assumed sovereign power, and which his son and successor Tiberius continues to bestow, *taking him for the standard of his administration and his ordinances.*' Unfortunately we know little of Tiberius's influence on administration, save the bare fact that he retained his subordinates for long terms in offices or dignities for which they seemed to him to be well fitted; but it must have been during this period that the household and entourage of the Emperor developed into the highly centralized bureaucracy which stands revealed in the reign of Claudius. The clerical staff employed by the Emperors was made up of freedmen and slaves; and we are not to think of these latter as mere drudges or chattels. In the reign of Tiberius one Musicus Scurranus, an Imperial slave, cashier in that branch of the Treasury which received the revenues of Gaul, died in

Rome, and an inscription was set up in his honour by his *vicarii*, that is the slaves whom he was permitted by legal fictions to own. They comprised his 'man of business', his controller of expenses, three secretaries, a doctor, a keeper of the wardrobe, two keepers of the plate, two chamberlains, two lackeys, two cooks, and a lady with no specific title!

Out of such elements was built up an organization which, without ceasing to be the Imperial household, became the Whitehall of Ancient Rome. The accountancy of the *domus Caesaris* was supervised by a freedman with the title *a rationibus*. We meet with this expression in inscriptions of Tiberius's reign, but it was not until the accession of Claudius that the office, in the hands of an able Greek, M. Antonius Pallas, whose name shows that he had been the slave of the Emperor's mother, gave to the financial secretaryship a position, corresponding with that of a modern Minister of State. We possess a poem addressed by Statius to the son of his successor, Claudius Etruscus, a Smyrniote Greek by origin, manumitted by Tiberius and promoted by Claudius. The poet speaks of the 'world's expense' as defrayed by the revenues which poured into the Imperial treasury, both from the taxes of the subject peoples and the ever-growing domain of the Emperors. The pay of the army, the corn-ration of Rome, the various public works and services of Italy and the issue of coinage are among the items of his balance-sheet. Next, if not equal in importance, was the principal private secretary of the Emperor, known as *ab epistulis*. The functions of this official were manifold. His principal duty (as we see from another poem of Statius) was to deal with the reports from provincial governors—and the correspondence of Pliny with Trajan shows that this can have been no light task; he also issued commissions and warrants of promotion in the Army, and grants of personal privilege, such as Roman citizenship or the Latin right, not only to individuals, but to communities. And we must not forget that Imperial letters had the force of law and were included among the *constitutiones* which made up the corpus of Imperial legislation. The third department of first-class rank was that of the Clerk of Petitions (*a libellis*), the importance of which lay in the fact that the 'rescript' appended to the petition might convey a far-reaching decision on a point of law or administration referred to the Emperor. The holders of these posts might have been slow to acquire importance but for the fact that Claudius, by nature and upbringing, was amenable to the influence of inferiors. He has often been compared with James I, and a 'wise fool' he certainly was; but an instructive parallel might also be drawn between his reign and that of Edward II, which, as recent researches have shown, was of considerable importance in the development of the royal household into a public service. In England the place of the Imperial freedmen, always in close dependence on their patron, was taken by the 'clerks' in the narrower sense of that word, who, being unable to found noble families, were obliged to seek advancement in a career where the prizes were bishoprics conferred by the King.[1]

It was natural that under such a ruler the new civil service should encroach upon the functions of the Republican magistracies. We hear that Claudius transferred certain duties hitherto imposed upon the quaestors, who as young men on the threshold of the senatorial career lacked experience, to his own subordinates. The control of the harbour of Ostia, where the corn-fleet discharged its cargo, was one of those functions. Claudius constructed a new harbour, the *portus Augusti*, and the quaestor gave place to an Imperial agent. Moreover, the Emperor's servants were assimilated in dignity and even in constitutional powers to the magistrates of the Roman people. It was no new thing to grant the insignia of the magistracy to the great prefects of equestrian rank; Tiberius had given the *ornamenta praetoria* to the

[1] The Chancellorship traces its origin to the office of the King's chaplain, who wrote his master's letters in the intervals of divine service.

commanders of the Guard and the quaestorian insignia to the chief of the Fire Brigade; but Claudius was more lavish in the distribution of such decorations. The *ornamenta consularia* were bestowed on provincial agents, and a subservient Senate was induced to vote the insignia of the praetorship to Pallas when he laid down the Financial Secretaryship and 'squared accounts with the State'. Claudius also secured the Senate's consent to an enactment conferring upon his procurators the right of jurisdiction in fiscal suits. The effect of this was to make the tax-gatherer a judge as well as a party in such causes, and there is reason for thinking that more enlightened rulers suspended this provision; but in the long run the paramount interest of the Treasury asserted itself, and it is instructive to note that Ulpian, writing at the close of the second century on the duties of a proconsul, says: 'There is no business in the province which may not be transacted in his court: but if the case be one which involves the pecuniary interest of the Treasury and concerns an agent of the Emperor, he will be wise if he refrains from trying it.'[1] The *Moral Epistles* of Seneca, written to his friend Lucilius, Imperial agent in Sicily under Nero, show us how important a personage, even in a Senatorial province, the procurator had by this time become.

Order was maintained in the new official hierarchy by a graduated scale of salaries and a system of promotion based thereon. The highest grade which can be shown to have existed in the first century was that of the *ducenarii*, or procurators receiving a salary of 200,000 sesterces (£2,000 a year). To this belonged the Agents-general in the greater provinces, whether governed by Imperial *legati* of consular rank or by Senatorial proconsuls, and in a few districts formed by the grouping of minor provinces.[2] In the same class we find

[1] *Digest*, i. 16. 9.

[2] It is noteworthy that for convenience of administration the distinction between Imperial and Senatorial provinces was neglected. Thus the Sena-

the procurators enjoying independent commands in important frontier regions or recently annexed States, the principal administrative officials in Egypt, and the heads of the central departments in Rome such as that for the collection of the Succession Duty and the management of the Emperor's private domain (*patrimonium*). Next in order came the *centenarii*, who received a yearly salary of 100,000 sesterces (£1,000). These included the agents in Imperial and Senatorial provinces whose governors were of praetorian standing, the administrators of some small districts, chiefly in the Alps, and the holders of certain posts in Rome subordinate to the great equestrian *praefecti* mentioned above or to the Senatorial commissioners such as those for the water-supply and public works. The same salary was given to a certain number of the agents who administered the Imperial domains in the provinces, gold and silver mines and so forth. Minor posts were filled by the *sexagenarii*, who drew 60,000 sesterces (£600 a year).[1] It is not until the second century that we meet with *trecenarii* (receiving 300,000 sesterces or £3,000 a year), and the number of such posts was probably very small, if not confined to the chief financial secretaryship.

The policy of Claudius naturally met with disapproval among the Conservative elements in Roman society, especially in those aspects which appear to us most enlightened. Claudius took a more liberal view of the Empire and its destiny than Augustus, who jealously maintained the privileged position of the Italian race. Reverting to Caesar's conception of the Senate as a representative council of the Empire, he admitted Gaulish chieftains to its ranks on the occasion of his revival of the censorship ; we possess an edict by which he confirmed the

torial province of Narbonensis (Provence) and the Imperial province of Aquitania (SW. France) formed a single district for the collection of Succession Duty.

[1] The system is worked out with full details by Domaszewski, *Rangordnung des römischen Heeres.*

very doubtful title to the Roman *civitas* of certain Alpine tribes in the valley of the Upper Adige; and in the bitter but instructive satire penned, according to tradition, by Seneca for the amusement of Nero's court we read that 'he had made up his mind to see every Gaul, German, and Spaniard wearing the toga'. In provinces where Romanization was in progress, such as Noricum (Tyrol) and the Mauretanias (Algeria and Morocco) he furthered the extension of the municipal system. A recently discovered inscription from Volubilis, about half-way from Fez to the Atlantic seaboard, records the grant of citizenship and certain material privileges to the inhabitants of a Punic settlement; this was in response to a petition presented in person by the enfranchised son of a Punic father who had rendered good service in suppressing a serious revolt.

The reign of Nero marks no real reaction. On his accession a high-sounding programme was drafted by Seneca and delivered to an enthusiastic Senate, whose rule (within the limits of Augustus's 'dyarchy') it professed to restore. There was some attempt to keep the two spheres of administration separate whilst Seneca's influence lasted, but in his later years Nero darkly threatened to 'remove the Senatorial order from the State and entrust the provinces and armies to knights and freedmen'; and this doubtless helped to hasten his fall.

Before we leave the Julio-Claudian dynasty a few words may be said of the system of government through client-princes, which the Republic had adopted as a means of evading responsibility and shelving awkward questions, and Augustus had adapted with great skill to his own ends. Under the later Republic the 'friends and allies' of Rome became her tenants-at-will in respect of their ancestral kingdoms, and on the demise of the crown it lay with the Senate to grant or withhold recognition of the monarch's successor. In practice this meant that on the extinction of the native dynasties the kingdoms ceased to be protectorates and were absorbed into the Empire, though it was usual to base the claim of Rome upon a bequest, real or fictitious, by the last of the line: it was thus that Pergamon, Bithynia, Cyrene, and Cyprus were annexed, and Egypt only escaped the same fate through the mutual jealousy of the parties at Rome which competed for the right to exploit so rich an estate. Augustus found in this system an instrument ready to his hand. He flattered the *amour propre* of the Senate by allowing it to sit as a High Court of Justice to try a client-prince for a crime which was also an insult to the majesty of Rome; but Strabo, who knew the Greek East intimately, after drawing the distinction between Imperial and Senatorial provinces and the methods by which each group was administered, continues: 'But kings and dynasts and tetrarchs are and always have been his.' In his system of administration these protected princes were called upon to fulfil an important, though not a permanent, function, by introducing into their territories Roman methods of government and paving the way for eventual annexation; the mediatized sovereigns of the first class were encouraged to form marriage-connexions which made them almost a single family, and their children were often educated in Rome with the Imperial princes and thus fitted for the duties of their station. Nor were the petty chiefs of frontier tribes or outlying regions neglected in the Imperial scheme. An inscription found at Chichester mentions one Cogidubnus, who is described as 'King and Imperial Commissioner' (*legatus Augusti*, the title of provincial governors) in Britain; and Tacitus, in his life of Agricola, mentions that some native communities were placed under his rule by Claudius; the conjunction of titles (which is without parallel) illustrates the hybrid nature of the institution. At Susa in the Alpine valley of the Dora Baltea there stands an arch adorned with quaint, uncouth reliefs, set up in 9 B.C. by one, M. Julius Cottius, military governor of the tribes in that region; he was the son of 'King Donnus', and there is reason to think that the title was temporarily restored to his family; but the reliefs show that it was as a Roman officer in command of Roman troops that he wished to be remembered. This system of protectorates, having done its work well, was brought to an end (save in outlying districts in the East) by the Flavian dynasty.

With Nero ended the Julian line and the first chapter in the story of the Empire. The links with the aristocratic Republic as well as with the Caesarian monarchy were severed, and it could no longer be said, *c'est toujours le beau monde qui gouverne le monde.* Vespasian represented the *bourgeoisie*, and it was time that they were called to govern, for they had been thoroughly trained for the task. The dynastic policy of the Flavians, forced upon them by the circumstances of their rise to power, need not concern us; what we have to note is the fact that the administration of the Empire passed into the hands of an able and in the main conscientious official class, representative not only of Italy but of the provinces, and constantly recruited by fresh elements, which found their way into the Senate through the avenue of the Emperor's service. Agricola, probably descended from a Gaul enfranchised by Caesar, was the son of a senator, but the grandson of two Imperial agents, and this, as his son-in-law Tacitus says, is 'the knight's patent of nobility'; and the history of the next two centuries records no set-back in the rise of the second order. With the old régime there vanished the reluctance of free-born Romans to fill the household posts which gathered up the threads of the Imperial bureaucracy. Otho appointed as his Secretary of State Julius Secundus, a brilliant young barrister from Gaul, one of the 'leading lights of our bar', as his pupil Tacitus calls him; Vitellius, says Suetonius, gave to knights the places in the household service formerly held by freedmen; the Secretaryship was held by a Greek librarian under Domitian; the Ministries of Finance and Petitions were entrusted to knights under Trajan; and Hadrian definitely made these posts the prizes of the civil service.

Under Domitian, again, we find knights sitting with senators in the Imperial *consilium* or Privy Council, and salaried law officers became an important element in that body; the *noblesse de robe* was indeed no new thing among a people which had chosen Law as its peculiar science, and Domitian's successor, Nerva, represented it on the throne. It was the Flavians, too, who gave to the Greeks of the Eastern provinces a share in the honours as well as in the hard work of government: concealed under Roman names we find Celsus of Ephesus (whose Memorial Library has been brought to light by recent excavation) and Quadratus, seemingly a Pergamene, advanced to the highest places in the Empire, though not (as yet) entrusted with the government of Latin provinces.

Vespasian, the son of a tax-farmer and grandson of a debt-collector, for whom money 'had no offensive taint', stood for Peace and Economy at least as whole-heartedly as the politicians who play with those counters in modern democracies. Except for a brief spell of extravagance under Domitian, leading to the appointment by his successor of an Economy Committee of five members, which wielded not the axe in vain, there was a long period of conscious and fairly successful effort to develop the resources of the Empire by careful husbandry, and especially to place its economy on a broad base by the encouragement of agriculture. An experiment begun by Nerva and extended by Trajan and his successors deserves mention here. Public-spirited citizens were wont to create rent-charges on their estates for the benefit of their native towns, which they thus endowed with revenues to be applied for the maintenance of poor children. The central government took up the idea, but made the system subserve a further purpose. Capital was lent to landowners on the security of their estates at moderate rates of interest (usually 5 per cent.) and the income was placed at the disposal of the Local Authority in order to provide subsistence (*alimenta*) for the children of the poor. Stress was publicly laid on the charitable object of these foundations, but it is obvious that their economic importance was great. There was no such free market in liquid capital in the ancient world as we enjoy to-day, and the State was performing, in relation to the greatest industry of the Empire, to wit, agriculture, the function which is now left to the private enterprise of the banker. But besides this there was much to be done in the settlement of vacant lands, to which cultivators were attracted by offers of low rents and remission of taxation. It was not quite a new idea. Nero had appointed to the Viceroyalty of Egypt one Vestinus, a Romanized Gaul from Vienne, whom Claudius described in his famous speech delivered on the admission of Gauls to the Senate as 'my man of business and one of my best friends', and he endeavoured by offering favourable terms to bring into cultivation waste or derelict areas in the Nile valley. The land policy especially associated with Vespasian, Trajan, and Hadrian was directed to the development of the State's resources in land (or, which came to the same thing, the Imperial patrimony) in other parts of the Empire, especially in Africa, from which we have a number of all too fragmentary inscriptions recording the ordinances made by Imperial domains for the great estates (*saltus*), grouped in districts administered by agents at Carthage or Hadrumetum, and generally let to middlemen (*conductores*) who collected dues from the small holders or *coloni* and were also entitled to exact *corvée* (fixed in one example at two days' ploughing, two days' labour at seed-time, and two at harvest) for the cultivation of their own demesne. It may well be that some features of the system were modelled on the institutions of the Eastern monarchies to which Rome was heir; but the Roman administrators must be credited with very considerable success in adapting these methods to the needs of a great territorial State. The mineral wealth of the Empire, too, was scientifically exploited. From Aljustrel in Southern Portugal comes a bronze tablet inscribed with an official letter, presumably from the procurator of the province, to the agent entrusted with the management of a local silver mine, giving the regulations made by Hadrian for the acquisition of mining claims by private contractors, who paid a price based on the assumption that one-half of the value of the ore belonged to the *fiscus*, and were then obliged to begin operations within twenty-five days and forfeited their right if work were intermitted for six months. A second and more interesting tablet found in the same place shows the care taken by the government to regulate the details of life in the mining village which was of course its property. The local shopkeepers worked, it seems, under contract with the State. The keeper of the public baths has to supply hot water every day, clean his boilers once a month, admit women from daybreak till one p.m. and men from two till eight, and exclude soldiers, children, and the freedmen and slaves employed by the Imperial procurator. The shoemaker must provide footwear of all kinds and sell hob-nails 'according to the regulations of the iron-works'. The licensed barber has a monopoly, except that private slaves may shave their masters or fellows. There is but one redeeming feature in this paternally regulated community: *schoolmasters pay no rates.*

What room, we must now ask, was left in this all-embracing bureaucracy for the free play of local and regional forces? We saw how the Republican statesmen and Julius Caesar created a type of municipal constitution capable of diffusion in those provinces which were fitted for urban life. With the grant of a local charter went the bestowal either of full Roman citizenship or the status of 'Latinity' which was the half-way house to the *civitas*. The privileged position of Italy was no interest of the Emperors, least of all of those who, like Trajan and his successors, came of families domiciled in provincial towns; and the Western world was rapidly Romanized. Vespasian granted the Latin right to all towns in Spain which did not yet possess it; and the complementary fragments of two of the scores of charters issued in pursuance of his edict, which were discovered at Malaga, furnish us with some of our most valuable evidence concerning ancient Local Government. In these communities only the magistrates and their nearest relations became citizens of Rome; an extension of the franchise to all members of the local Senate probably belongs to the second century, where this 'greater Latinity' is bestowed on African towns; and the path was gradually made plain for the famous Edict of Caracalla, which conferred Roman citizenship on all the subjects of the Empire except certain 'depressed classes' such as the Egyptian *fellahîn*. Rome was wise enough not to interfere drastically with the government of the Greek πόλεις but to leave them to assimilate their institutions to the Roman model; and in the Celtic provinces the cantonal system was slowly but surely municipalized, as may be illustrated from our own island by the inscription from Caerwent set up in pursuance of 'the decree of the council' by the *respublica* of the community of the Silures.

It was a great achievement to have sown the soil of Western Europe thick with the seeds of civic life, and to have provided the subjects of the Empire with a school in which they might learn to command and to obey. From the towns of every province came a succession of fit persons to serve the higher offices of state; and within the protective shell of the military monarchy material prosperity grew and local and Imperial benefactions increased the amenities of social life. But the germs of decay were present in the system. The interests of the several communities could find no representation in the central government; nor was there any really effective means of expressing the common will of a region or province. There were, it is true, certain Provincial Assemblies (*concilia*), modelled on the κοινά or city-leagues of the Greek world. It may be doubted whether Augustus, who founded the most important of these, the 'Council of the Three Gauls', intended them to pave the way for the extension of provincial self-government. In the first instance their function was the maintenance of the new State-religion, the cult of Rome and the deified Emperors with impressive ceremonial, attended by popular amusements, and the passing of loyal or congratulatory resolutions. The dignity of the annual high-priest of the cult, who was also President of the Provincial Council, was no doubt highly prized for its social distinction. The 'rulers of Asia' of whom we read in the Acts hold an important position in Ephesus in virtue of their office; and throughout the East we find similar titles—Armeniarch, Pontarch, Thrakarch, and so forth. The assemblies could of course pass complimentary votes in honour of a governor, and they could also—which was of much greater importance—institute proceedings against him for maladministration; but this was the only substantial privilege which they enjoyed. There is no evidence that they had a voice in matters of finance or administration. The burdens of the President's office, especially the expense of the gladiatorial shows celebrated at the festivals, became too heavy to be borne. We possess, in an inscription found near Seville, the text of a speech delivered in the Senate, which refers to the action of Marcus Aurelius and his co-regent in cutting down these expenses and describes the unconcealed delight of 'the priests of the faithful Gauls' on hearing the good news.

In the towns, too, the ruling class paid dearly for their social pre-eminence. Even in the Flavian charters it was provided that compulsion might be exerted to secure candidates for the chief municipal offices if none such offered themselves for election. Nor was the central government satisfied with the management of municipal finance, and as early as the reign of Trajan, Imperial inspectors were appointed, with the title of *curator reipublicae*, to check defalcations and extravagance and to supervise expenditure on public works. The earliest examples of this institution in the West came from Italy and the Senatorial province of Narbonensis (Provence); in the East its nature was more clearly expressed by the Greek equivalent λογιστής ('Auditor'). These officials are drawn, sometimes from the Senate, sometimes from the equestrian order. At first exceptional, this institution soon became prevalent, if not universal, especially in the Eastern provinces; and the *curatores* came to exercise wider functions than that of examining the local accounts, and to act as supreme magistrates nominated by the central government, thus depriving the communities at once of initiative and of responsibility. Another and more drastic measure of interference with local autonomy was also initiated by Trajan, who sent 'Reformers' (*correctores*, διορθωταί) to Senatorial provinces. His commissioner in Greece, Sex. Quinctilius Maximus, was instructed to set in order the affairs of the 'free cities' only; but Pliny the younger was put in charge of the whole province of Bithynia (one of those reserved to the Senate in the settlement of Augustus) and his correspondence with Trajan, consisting of more than fifty letters, to which are appended the Emperor's replies, shows that an honest attempt was made to check the extravagance and corruption of the local authorities. It also proves that the Emperor's method of dealing with the varieties of local law, custom, and institutions was cautious and conservative; though the Imperial edicts and the decrees of the Senate are of general application and go to the making of an ever-growing body of municipal law, the government is loth to abandon the conception of an Empire formed by a federation of independent communities, each with its own history and traditions. But we also see the unmistakable signs of failing vigour in the life of the towns—reluctance to shoulder the burdens of local office, and the restriction of such offices to a defined class, sharply separated from a parasitic populace. Pliny was not the last of the High Commissioners appointed for Bithynia. It is significant that under Hadrian the post was conferred upon a Romanized

Greek, whose name—Gaius Julius Severus—would certainly not suggest that he was a descendant of Pergamene kings and Galatian tetrarchs, and possibly connected with the dynasty of the Herods. Almost a century later, the historian Dio Cassius, himself a native of the province, writes that his beneficent rule was fresh in the memory of the Bithynians.

The reign of Hadrian supplies the next landmark in the history of the Imperial administration. It is a mistake to regard him as primarily a scholar, a connoisseur, and a cosmopolitan. He was much more than these. His journeys throughout the Empire were undertaken in order that he might acquire a knowledge of its needs. His biographer tells us that 'he examined diligently the receipts from the provinces, in order that he might make good any local deficiency', and that 'he had as all-embracing a knowledge of the public finances as any careful householder possesses of his private affairs'.[1] He looked upon the Empire as a whole, not as a congeries of *civitates* under Italian rule, and took the first step towards the equalization of Italy with the provinces by appointing four judges of assize to try cases in the peninsula. He broke with the idea that the citizen must be equally qualified to render service in peace and war, and definitely established a Civil Administrative Service drawn from the equestrian order. This official hierarchy, already (as we have seen) graded according to salary, soon acquired titles indicative of rank (*vir egregius*, *perfectissimus*, *eminentissimus*), and its sphere of activity grew at the expense of those of the Senate and the Imperial freedmen. This bureaucracy no doubt had the defects which are common to such governments; but at any rate it had the qualities of those defects, and kept the solid framework of the Empire intact through all the strains and stresses of the third century after Christ.

[1] The *Ara legis Hadrianae*, found in North Africa, which speaks of 'the unwearying diligence with which he watches over the interests of mankind', illustrates his encouragement of agriculture.

In the meanwhile a decisive step had been taken by Septimius Severus and his successor in the direction of undisguised absolutism and at the same time in that of the unification of the Empire and the simplification of the machinery of government. For the first time since the foundation of the Principate a legion was permanently encamped in Italy, almost at the gates of Rome,[1] and it was commanded not by a Senatorial *legatus*, but by an equestrian *praefectus*. The Edict of Caracalla was inspired by the conception, which must have been present to the minds of the great lawyers of the time, that the elaborate gradation of privilege, leading up to the jealously prized *civitas Romana*, was an antiquated anomaly in the days when all were subjects of a ruler 'whose will was law'.[2] On the other hand, the institution of municipal councils in the centres of population in Egypt (hitherto directly governed by Imperial officials) swept away a distinction which had become meaningless and even cumbersome. The chief financial measure taken by Severus has often been misunderstood. This was the creation of the *res privata principis*, which has been very naturally explained as the Emperor's Privy Purse. There is good reason for thinking that it was much more than this, and that in fact a central treasury came into being which received the consolidated revenues of the enormous domains assigned to the *fiscus*, swollen by the great confiscation of private estates belonging to the supporters of Severus's rivals, Albinus and Niger. The *fiscus* was openly claimed by the Emperor as his own; the *aerarium*, still named the 'Treasury of the Roman people', was now little more than the municipal chest of Rome.

We possess a document of great interest as showing the impression made by the Imperial bureaucracy on a capable administrator. The historian Dio Cassius, himself a senator of the highest rank, who had held the consulship as the colleague

[1] The *legio secunda Parthica*, quartered at Albano.

[2] *Quod principi placuit legis habet vigorem* (Ulpian, cited in *Digest*, i. 4. 1).

of an emperor, inserted in his history of Rome, which he wrote in retirement in the second quarter of the third century of our era, two speeches professedly delivered by Augustus's chief advisers, Maecenas and Agrippa, when consulted by him as to the constitutional settlement to be made after his final victory. The speech of Agrippa, recommending a genuine restoration of Republican government, is a mere rhetorical exercise, intended as a foil to that put into the mouth of Maecenas, which advocates a centralized monarchical government.[1] This is worthy of careful study. Generally speaking, it gives a survey, not of the institutions of Augustus, but of the system formed by 250 years of gradual growth on the lines which were traced by the inevitable logic of history. But it also contains features suggested without doubt by Dio himself, which are the more remarkable since they tend to curtail the power of the Senate of which their author was a member and to which the reigning Emperor, Severus Alexander, professed a deference in strong contrast to the ruthless despotism of the founder of his dynasty. Dio is jealous of the personal privileges of his order, especially of the precious right of the senator to be tried by his peers ; [2] but in matters of administration he is the perfect bureaucrat. The Republican magistracies are to be maintained for the sake of historical continuity, but they are to be purely urban, to enjoy distinction without practical influence, and to be dispensed wholly as a matter of Imperial favour. The heads of the bureaucracy, the prefect of Rome and the two prefects of the guard, are to be appointed for life ; the two latter are to have deputies with jurisdiction over the Emperor's servants. It is proposed that the properties of the State shall be sold and that the sums thus realized shall be lent at moderate rates of interest, especially to landowners—a development of the system of *alimenta* above mentioned with

[1] Dio Cassius, lii. 14 ff.

[2] When sitting as a High Court of Justice for the trial of peers, the Senate was to be represented by ex-consuls as 'Law Lords'.

a more far-reaching aim. A tight hold is to be kept on the municipal bodies, and there are to be no popular assemblies in the cities of the Empire.[1] A ban is placed on foreign religions, and the Emperor is warned against the pretensions of philosophers, who 'use their profession as a cloak to work infinite harm to peoples and individuals'. The provinces are to be subdivided in order to be of manageable size, and civil and military administration are to be kept separate.

Dio had an eye for the future as well as for the past. The course of events in the half-century which followed led to the realization, in a broad sense, of his characteristic ideas. Gallienus, in the throes of apparent dissolution endured by the Empire, removed the control of the legions, and with it the government of the more important provinces, from the Senate and gave it to Imperial *praefecti*, after the example set by Augustus in Egypt, and followed (as regards his newly created corps) by Septimius Severus. Aurelian, who asserted the divine right of absolutism and made Rome familiar with the Oriental conception of a ruler who represents on earth the Unconquered Sun supreme in the Universe, carried the 'provincialization' of Italy a step farther by instituting *correctores* (cf. p. 132) for its several regions. It was left for Diocletian to bring to a logical conclusion the process of the time, to separate finally civil and military administration, to subdivide and re-group the provinces, to reorganize both the central departments and the staffs of the provincial governors,[2] creating a horde of officials so monstrously swollen in number that, as the so-called Lactantius tells us, 'there were more receivers than contributors' in the Empire. He and his successor,

[1] There is evidence from inscriptions that *comitia* still met in the second century.

[2] The term for a 'staff' or 'department' was *officium*, from which 'office' is directly descended. In the New Monarchy all 'officers' formed a quasi-military hierarchy and wore the *cingulum militiae*; but in the Civil Departments this was merely formal.

Constantine the Great, also put the final touches to the new social order based on hereditary status. This system was of gradual growth. The Empire had been slow to break with the ancient practice of leaving public services to private enterprise. Just as the collection of taxes by private farmers subsisted for a century and more under increasingly stringent supervision by state-officials, so (for example) the supply of food to Rome, though under the control of a department of State, was actually carried out by private guilds of corn merchants and shippers, who were granted special privileges and immunities from public burdens by Claudius and incorporated by charter in the second century. But State-aid meant then (as always) State-control; and the 'blessed word compulsion' soon found its way into the vocabulary of government. The writings of the great jurists of the Severan period, embodied in the Digest, still put in the forefront the privileges enjoyed by the guilds; a century later, the enactments included in the Theodosian Code show that all services of importance to the State are rendered by hereditary corporations from which there is no escape save by entry into the ranks of the bureaucracy. More than this, the cultivators of the soil were reduced to the position of hereditary serfs, legally free citizens of Rome, but deprived of all freedom of movement and bound to the estates whose owners were held responsible to the Government for the payment of taxes in kind, now rendered necessary by the collapse of the currency, and for the provision of recruits for the army.

The government of the *municipia*, too, was drawn into the net of caste. The municipal senators, who were responsible for the taxes and arrears due from the territory of their cities, eagerly sought avenues of escape from the ever-increasing burden laid upon their shoulders. Those who were fortunate enough to secure a place in the *officia* might hope to rise to Senatorial rank, which was attached to certain grades in the hierarchy, and carried with it exemption from municipal burdens. Others enrolled themselves in the legions; while their places were taken by the sons of veterans who sought to evade hereditary military service by self-mutilation and were pressed into the *curia*!

Thus the Roman Empire bequeathed to mankind an example and a warning. It was not the 'violent and vulgar fraud' which a modern writer has named it: neither, perhaps, if we knew it better, should we regard the epoch of the Antonines as the golden age which others have descried in it. In Haverfield's judgement, 'the believer in human nature can now feel confident that, whatever their limitations, the men of the Empire wrought for the betterment and the happiness of the world'; and he finds the greatest work of the Imperial age in its provincial administration. That means that Augustus and the best and ablest of his successors patiently built up, for an Empire consisting in part of small town-territories with traditions of particularism and in part of wide spaces tenanted by tribes of many races and cultures, a framework within which men could, on the whole, work out their own salvation, could be drawn together in mutual understanding, and could acquire a wholly new patriotism, linked with the great traditions of Rome, and a new spirit of public service. This achievement was due to the practical genius of the Romans, who excelled in the adaptation of old means to new ends. But their very success dug the pitfall which entrapped them. They mistook the means for the end, and forgot (as the best of administrators are prone to do) that the State was made for man and not man for the State. The modern world has a more difficult problem to solve—the transformation of the congeries of States administered after the pattern first traced in outline by the Romans into a body-politic embracing the human race. We cannot foresee the method by which the solution will be found, still less can we estimate the period within which the task will be accomplished; but we shall be fortunate if the builders of the new order bring to it the tact and patience of Augustus and his infinite capacity for taking pains in framing provisional institutions so as to provide for orderly development.

H. Stuart Jones.

Books Recommended.

Mommsen, *Provinces of the Roman Empire*, ed. 2.

W. T. Arnold, *Roman Provincial Administration*, ed. 3; and *Studies in Roman Imperialism.*

Lord Cromer, *Ancient and Modern Imperialism.*

Sir Charles Lucas, *Greater Rome and Greater Britain.*

Lord Bryce, *Studies in History and Jurisprudence.*

F. Haverfield, *Some Roman Conceptions of Empire.*

T. Frank, *Roman Imperialism.*

A. H. J. Greenidge, *Roman Public Life.*

H. Mattingly, *The Imperial Civil Service of Rome.*

COMMUNICATIONS AND COMMERCE

Although history never repeats itself exactly, and the problems of one age are never identical with those of another, it can scarcely be denied that at the present time it is well worth while to study the lessons of the past. The task of evolving order out of chaos which confronts modern statesmen in the field of foreign policy is no new one. Roman history provides an obvious parallel, and the bewilderment with which the men of to-day regard the present state of Europe recalls the feelings which were awakened in the contemporaries of Cicero by the collapse of the political system under which Rome had risen to greatness. But this collapse was only apparent; Roman statesmanship was not yet bankrupt; a better system replaced the old, and the darkest period was succeeded by several centuries of orderly government. Thus the study of the methods employed by Augustus and those who collaborated with him in re-founding the Roman State may well give confidence to those who are now attempting to build a new Europe on the ruins of the old, and may furnish them with valuable suggestions. It is with one of the most significant aspects of this great constructive achievement that this chapter is concerned.

The writer well remembers the impression which was made on his imagination when on his first visit to the Continent he saw a railway carriage labelled Ostende–Constanza, and realized how closely far-distant countries were linked together by the railway system of Europe. This early experience was later recalled to his mind when in a road-book of the Roman Empire he studied the lines followed by the great trunk roads which traversed it from end to end—the road from Milan to Boulogne by the Cottian Alps, Lyons, and Rheims, or the road which ran from the same city to Alexandria by way of Aquileia, Sirmium,

Constantinople, Nicomedeia, and Antioch. There is indeed no doubt that until the nineteenth century communication between one part of Europe and another was never so rapid and so safe as during the early centuries of the Christian era, when the whole civilized world was united under one beneficent government. Those who at the present time feel that the only hope for the survival of European civilization lies in a gradual breaking-down of the barriers which separate nation from nation should fully appreciate the consequences which this fact involved. Rome did not consciously aim at imposing a uniform civilization on her subjects, but the admirable system of communications which she developed, in the first instance for military purposes, had its inevitable result. All that was best in Italian culture soon penetrated to the farthest limits of the empire, and in return the provinces contributed to the common stock not merely goods but men and ideas. Many of the greatest figures in the Latin literature of the first century A.D. were Spaniards, and before the end of the century a Spanish emperor was at the head of the State. As has been well said, 'Christianity spread first directly along the great roads that led to Rome, as every free and natural current of thought necessarily did owing to the circumstances of the period, and from the centre was redistributed to the outlying parts of the empire',[1] or again, 'To establish in anything like completeness the scheme of roads in a Roman province is to apprehend the physical basis upon which reposed that old centralized imperial power to which the desperate survival of Europe clung; is, farther, to comprehend the relationship of town with town, of garrison with garrison, and of bishopric with bishopric. It is an explanation of the passage of armies, of commerce, and of ideas for just over one thousand years.'[2]

As early as 70 A.D. it was possible for a Roman general, addressing Gallic tribes which had revolted from Rome, to use the words: 'All is common between us. You often command

[1] Sir W. M. Ramsay. [2] Mr. H. Belloc.

our legions, you govern these and other provinces. There is no privilege, no exclusion.' A Greek orator of the second century expresses himself as follows: 'You have made Rome to be the name not of a city but of a nation (γένος) of which we all are members, a nation which includes all others in itself. You have shown the truth of the proverb that the earth is the mother of all, and the country to which all men belong; now Greek and Barbarian can go easily whither they will as though from one homeland to another; for the Cilician Gates, the sandy approaches to Egypt, trackless mountains, wide rivers, uncivilized peoples present no dangers, but we are safe whether we are your fellow citizens or merely your subjects.' The various Roman provinces preserved their own characteristics, Greek remained throughout the language of the East, and Celtic lingered among the lower classes of Gaul and Britain; but in the best days of the Roman Empire men were able to move freely, seeking their fortunes, from one province to another, whether as public servants or as traders. To be a provincial soon ceased to be a disqualification. The visitor to a Roman post in the north of England who remarked 'How cold the Romans must have found it here!' evidently imagined that the officials and soldiers of the Roman Government in the provinces were men of Italian birth. But the fact is that it was only at the very beginning of the principate that the governing and official class, whether civil or military, was predominantly Italian. From about 70 A.D. Italian soldiers were rare, and to an increasing extent the military units were recruited from the provinces in which they were stationed. Even Agricola ventured to employ British soldiers in his war against the Caledonians.

No attempt was made to exclude foreigners from Rome itself, which is gloomily described by Tacitus as 'the cesspool of the world', while Juvenal complains that the Syrian Orontes had flowed into the Tiber. It has been established that throughout Italy a large proportion of the shopkeeper class consisted of men of Greek or Oriental origin. The trade of the Roman Empire was to a large extent in the hands of easterners, whose presence in the western provinces is attested not merely by tombstones but by the rapid diffusion of the Oriental religions which prepared the way for Christianity. When St. Paul refused to regard the Church as a Jewish sect, and decided to preach his faith in other provinces as far west as Spain, he showed himself well worthy of his Roman citizenship.

The excellence of the communications between the districts administered from Rome was an important cause of this rapid dissemination throughout the Empire of a homogeneous civilization. In our own country the improvement in the means of transport which has taken place in recent times is the chief cause of the gradual disappearance of local peculiarities. 'When the lord of a Lincolnshire or Shropshire manor appeared in Fleet Street' during the reign of Charles II, 'he was as easily distinguished from the resident population as a Turk or a Lascar. His dress, his gait, his accent, the manner in which he gazed at the shops, stumbled into the gutters, ran against the porters, and slid under the waterspouts, marked him out as an excellent subject for the operations of swindlers and banterers.' This was at a time when 'the inhabitants of London were, for almost every practical purpose, farther from Reading than they are now from Edinburgh, and farther from Edinburgh than they are now from Vienna'.[1] It is the 'broad highroad that leads to England' which has transformed the Scotsman from an enemy into an ally of the Englishman in the task of spreading British civilization. Ease of communication has made the world an economic whole. A financial crisis in America produces its effect in England before many hours are over, and every British householder suffers from a bad harvest in Canada. Probably at no time in history can a parallel to these phenomena be found except in the days when Rome

[1] Macaulay.

was supreme. 'The credit of the Roman money-market', says Cicero, 'is intimately bound up with the prosperity of Asia; a disaster cannot occur there without shaking our credit to its foundations.'

This parallel is sufficiently close to make very obvious the difference between ancient and modern conditions. Under Roman rule the world was not only economically but politically one. No barriers of race or language prevented free intercourse. No protective tariffs hindered interchange of goods. Of course, it was a small world, surrounded by a ring of barbarians, and the problem which has now to be faced is on a much larger scale. But the example of Rome provides hints for its solution. The claim made by some that Western civilization is still essentially Roman is difficult to substantiate at a time when the political condition of much of Europe reminds us rather of Gaul before the coming of Caesar, or of Germany as described by Tacitus. Though Rome learned much from Greece, the ideal of complete autonomy for small States was not one that appealed to her.

The problem of communications has to be considered by every imperial power, and indeed by every power which desires commercial intercourse with its neighbours, and it is only right to point out that in certain parts of the world the task of Rome was greatly simplified by the work of earlier rulers. Only in recent years have we come fully to realize the debt which the Romans owed to the States of the eastern Mediterranean, where she inherited the achievements of men who in their turn had taken over much from the old Persian Empire which Alexander overthrew. The conventional view of the Persian Empire as a typical Oriental tyranny, derived as it is from a superficial reading of Herodotus, who was full of Greek prejudices, is in many respects misleading, and writers of later antiquity, in their desire to glorify Rome, were apt to do less than justice to her predecessor. An unprejudiced study of Persian institutions shows that Darius possessed many of the qualities which are rightly admired in Augustus, and, in particular, was conscious of the need of combining central control with a due regard for the variations of local conditions. The Persian system of satrapies presents many parallels to the Roman provincial system, as developed under the principate. Such knowledge as we have of the internal communications of the Persian Empire reminds us of Rome. Every reader of Herodotus is familiar with his account of the ' Royal Road ' which connected Ephesus with Susa, and of the postal system, which can be applied almost verbally to the Roman *cursus publicus*. Many other Persian roads have been identified—the road from Babylon by Ecbatana (Hamadan) to Bactria and India, the road across Asia Minor from the Gulf of Issus to Sinope, and the main road through Phoenicia which led from Mesopotamia to Egypt. Of course, most of these roads followed older lines, determined by geography, but so did many Roman roads, and the Persian Government deserves credit for keeping them in such a condition that rapid transit was possible. An army could advance along the ' Royal Road ' at the rate of nearly 20 miles a day, and the ease with which Alexander overthrew the Persian power is partly to be explained by the excellent system of communications which was available for his advancing army.

There is every reason to suppose that the work done by Persia in opening up the lands of western Asia was continued by the Hellenistic states, into which the unwieldy empire of Alexander was divided. The roads along which St. Paul moved so easily on his missionary journeys were probably only to a small extent the work of Rome. When Rome annexed the kingdom of Pergamum, transforming it into the province of Asia, she at once got to work on the roads, and many milestones dated 129 B.C. are still extant; but if the milestones were an innovation, it is improbable that the roads themselves were new, though their surface was no doubt greatly improved by the Roman engineers.

Cicero, writing in 60 B.C., contrasts the Africans, Spaniards, and Gauls as 'immanes et barbarae nationes' with the civilized Greeks, and, although he exaggerates, it is true that in the north and west of Europe Rome was more of a pioneer than in the east. West of Sicily and the Bay of Naples the only important centre of Hellenic influence was Marseilles, a town with which Rome stood in friendly relations from an early date. To the Romans, Greeks were natural allies, while Carthaginians and Etruscans were foreigners. When they annexed the African possessions of Carthage they may have dimly felt, as their French successors undoubtedly feel, that they were winning for Mediterranean civilization a region which geographically belongs to Europe.

Long before Roman times northern and western Europe had been connected with the Mediterranean by ancient trade routes, following more or less beaten tracks. Herodotus had heard of a great river, the Eridanus (probably the Vistula) flowing into the northern ocean, from which amber came to the Greeks, and of 'Tin Islands', which were in all probability the Scillies, and although he denies the existence alike of the river and of the islands, he admits that amber, tin, and gold come to Greece from the ends of the earth. Carnuntum on the Danube, well known as a Roman military station, owed its importance in early times to its position on an 'amber route' from the Baltic. Mysterious sacred objects wrapped in straw reached Delos from the Hyperboreans; they were handed on by one Scythian tribe to another till they arrived at the head of the Adriatic, whence they were brought overland to Greece via Dodona. Greek traders from the settlements near the Crimea penetrated Russia as far as the Urals, and the enterprising Phocaeans who founded Marseilles about 600 B.C. pushed up the Rhone valley to central France and the Rhine.

The actual lines along which men have communicated with each other by land have been largely determined by geography, and have varied little throughout the course of history; one age differs from another more as regards the volume of its land communications than as regards their direction. If the railways of modern Italy follow almost everywhere the lines of Roman roads, this is due to the fact that the Apennines can only be crossed easily at certain points. In France at all periods there must have been movement of men and goods along the valleys of the Rhone, the Saône, the Loire, the Moselle, and the Seine, and through the gaps of Belfort and Carcassonne. 'If the Roman system of roads has had so long a life', says M. Jullian, the historian of Gaul, 'if it has had such success in history, this is not because it was the scientific work of a conquering people, but because it accepted the directions of nature and the experience of earlier peoples.' The pre-Roman roads of Gaul cannot have been very bad; Caesar was able to move his troops with great rapidity during his Gallic campaigns, and Hannibal's army sometimes advanced 24 miles a day.

If stress has been laid on the existence of tolerable roads in the Roman provinces before their annexation, it is with no desire to minimize the greatness of Rome's achievement. It was one of her most admirable characteristics to take things as she found them and modify them gradually to suit her needs. If it was convenient, she made her roads follow old lines, but she was not the slave of geography, and was quite prepared to cut through mountains and build great bridges over rivers if it was really necessary. The network of roads in a province was remodelled to serve her ends, and a glance at a map of the roads within an area makes clear the principles under which it was administered. A brief account of the roads of Gaul will explain what is meant.

Lyons (Lugdunum) was given the status of a Roman 'colony' soon after the death of Caesar, and when the territory which he had acquired for Rome was organized by Agrippa in the reign of Augustus, this town was made the meeting-place of four important roads leading (1) in a westerly direction towards Bordeaux and Aquitania, (2) to Belgica and the Rhine, (3) to the English Channel and the crossing to Britain, (4) down the Rhone to Marseilles. A fifth road, constructed a little later,

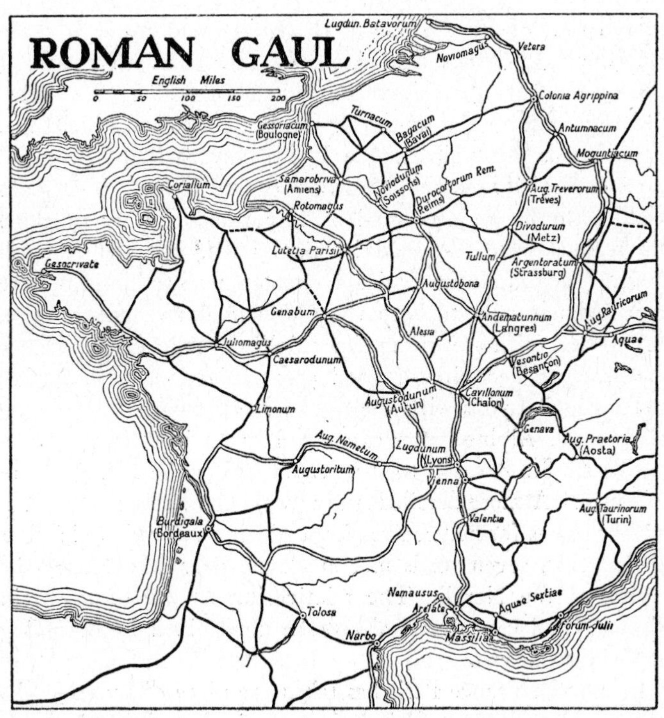

FIG. 3.

crossed from Lyons to the upper waters of the Loire near Roanne, and followed that stream all down its course. The roads running north of Lyons followed the valley of the Saône as far as Chalon, where they diverged. (1) The road for 'Upper Germany' ran in a north-westerly direction along the Doubs toward Besançon, and through the gap of Belfort to

Strassburg. (2) The road for 'Lower Germany' ran due north through Dijon and Langres till it reached the upper Moselle, and then followed that stream through Metz and Trèves to the Rhine. (3) The road for Boulogne and Britain probably followed the last-mentioned road as far as Langres, whence, guided roughly by the line of the Marne and Aisne, it made for Rheims, Soissons, and Amiens. (4) A fourth road left Chalon for Autun and Auxerre, and then ran along the Yonne and the Seine to the mouth of the latter river at Lillebonne. These roads must have made Lyons very accessible from all parts of the 'Three Gauls', whose capital it was. The roads leading to the Rhine served an important military purpose. No legions were stationed in Gaul itself, but the Rhenish troops ('commune in Gallos Germanosque subsidium') were expected not only to keep the Germans out of the Empire, but to deal with any rising that might occur in Gaul. Hence the absolute necessity of good communications with Lyons, and through Lyons with the rest of the province. Two good roads across Alpine passes connected Lyons with Italy, (1) by the Little St. Bernard to Aosta, and (2) by the Mt. Genèvre to Turin. A more detailed study would show that many much smaller towns formed centres from which roads radiated: thus no less than seven roads met at Bavai, near Maubeuge, the capital of the Nervii. The relative importance of towns in Roman Gaul can almost always be determined by observing how the roads ran.

In modern France Paris has taken the place of Lyons as the seat of government, and it is from Paris that the main roads radiate, but it is not fantastic to see in the great network of 'routes nationales' which now covers France a symbol of that ideal of centralized government which she has inherited from Rome. Again, great stretches of modern highway follow Roman lines, the cause of any divergence being usually the need of serving some town which has gained importance since Roman times. Chalon and Langres are still the meeting-points of important roads. French roads follow the Roman example in running straight from point to point, and this is a familiar feature of those English highways which still coincide with Roman roads, such as Watling Street running from London to St. Albans, Dunstable, and Towcester. There is no more fascinating occupation than to speculate on the reasons which have led modern highways and railways to coincide with or diverge from tracks laid down by the Romans.

To travel by road in winter is even now apt to be a rather uncomfortable experience, so it is not surprising that records of disagreeable winter journeys have come down to us from antiquity. The best known of these accounts is written by the rhetorician Aelius Aristides, who travelled from Asia Minor to Rome in the winter of 155–6 A. D., taking 100 days on the way, along the north coast of the Aegean and by the Via Egnatia to Dyrrhachium. He tells us that the fields along the road were flooded, the inns bad, and the inhabitants surly. But at the same time he states that he travelled as fast as the couriers who were taking dispatches to Rome for the provincial governors, whose average speed is supposed to have been 50 miles a day. Allowance, too, must be made for the fact that he was in bad health, and had to undergo an operation in Rome when he arrived, so that he was unusually sensitive to discomfort. On the whole it seems probable that at all seasons of the year travelling by land was easier in Roman times than at any period before the days of railroads. 'The roads of the Middle Ages', says Jusserand,[1] 'were sometimes like those of the modern East. During the rainy season immense pools of water cut off the usual track; they increase little by little, and at length overflow and form true rivers. A road is often nothing else than a place along which men customarily pass.' In 1339 Parliament could not meet on the day fixed, as the majority of members could not reach London because 'they were so troubled by the bad weather'. It was

[1] *English Wayfaring Life in the Middle Ages*, pp. 81 f.

no better three hundred years later. In 1668 Pepys lost his way on the road near Salisbury, and again between Newbury and Reading; the same thing happened to Thoresby on the great north road between Doncaster and York in 1680.[1] Sometimes when the floods were out travellers had to swim for their lives. Such experiences must have been indeed rare in the best days of Roman rule. The roads along which Caesar was able to travel 800 miles in eight days cannot have been frequently flooded. A messenger bringing the news of Nero's death to Galba in Spain covered 332 miles along a Spanish road in thirty-six hours. Of course these speeds were exceptional, but a good authority has calculated that an average rate of five miles an hour could be maintained by ordinary travellers.

We have said above that Roman rule secured not only speed but safety for those who moved along the roads, but unfortunately the experience of the man who 'fell among thieves' on the road from Jerusalem to Jericho was not unique. We possess many tombstones of men, and even of women and children, who were killed by robbers. The main roads of Italy itself were not perfectly safe. In the time of the younger Pliny a wealthy knight disappeared from the Via Flaminia not far north of Rome, and Juvenal mentions brigands on the Via Appia. It was easy to organize robber bands among the barbarous slaves on the great estates. Robbers figure in the pages of Appuleius, and a character of Lucian draws an imaginary picture of a chief of brigands whose little band of thirty men expanded into an army of 50,000 with which he conquered the world. Tiberius sent 4,000 freedmen 'infected with Jewish and Egyptian superstition' to Sardinia to put down robbers. In justice to Rome, however, we must remember that the security which is now enjoyed on the high roads of the more civilized countries of Europe is of very recent date. Though St. Paul complains of 'perils of robbers', his

[1] Macaulay, *History of England*, ch. 3.

journeys in Asia Minor were considerably safer than those of travellers in those parts at the present day. Erasmus consoles himself for the discomforts of a winter journey in the north of France about the year 1500 by the thought that he will not be troubled by robbers, and was relieved to reach Louvain from Cologne without encountering any. It was still dangerous to travel from London to Dover at the beginning of the nineteenth century, and more recent instances of brigandage could be quoted from other European countries.[1]

The Roman Government was well aware of its duty in this matter. Though the greater part of the army was during the first three centuries of the Christian era permanently stationed on the frontiers, a very large number of soldiers was employed on the duty of keeping order both in Italy and in the so-called 'unarmed' provinces. Augustus and Tiberius posted bodies of troops along the main roads of Italy, and there is some evidence that a line of these *stationes* was a permanent feature of the Via Appia. In the provinces it was the duty of the governor 'to hunt out plunderers of temples, highwaymen, kidnappers, and thieves, and to punish them in accordance with their offence'[2]—an order which implies that they were provided with means of carrying it out. Pliny, when Governor of Bithynia under Trajan, was provided with troops to protect the important road which connected Byzantium with the legions on the Euphrates. A cohort of what corresponded to 'metropolitan police' was stationed in Lyons, and another in Carthage, members of which were no doubt available for service in any part of Gaul or Africa where the safety of the communications was threatened. Inscriptions prove the presence of military posts at points where important roads met. If need arose, the magistrates of municipal towns were probably authorized to raise a militia among the inhabitants, who went out against

[1] Allen, *Selections from Erasmus*, pp. 22, 74; *The Times* of 30 May 1822 records the condemnation to death of various highwaymen.

[2] *Digest*, i. 18. 13.

thieves 'with swords and with staves'. The police system of the Roman Empire had a distinctly military character; but in Asia Minor, as we often read in the accounts of the martyrdom of Christians, there was a civil official styled Irenarch, entrusted with the task of dealing with robbers and other evildoers, and commanding a body of non-military subordinates. In Egypt, again, Rome inherited from the Ptolemies an elaborate police force, quite distinct from the troops of occupation.

The evidence which has been summarized is enough to justify the view that in this matter things were better under the Roman Empire than they were until quite recently.

A few words must now be said on the Roman solution of a problem which is still an anxiety to modern governments. From what sources was the money raised which was expended on the construction and repair of the roads? To speak generally, there seem to be four ways in which this problem can be met. The expenses may fall either on the owners of the land through which a road runs, or on the actual users of the roads, or on local authorities, when such exist, or on the central government. Experience in every country has shown that to make the upkeep of roads a burden on adjoining landowners is both unfair and unsatisfactory; important highways often traverse thinly populated country which derives little benefit from them. This method was employed in England in the Middle Ages with lamentable results, although to keep the roads in repair was regarded as a religious duty. Later the burden fell on the parish, which was too small a unit for the purpose. The present policy of making county councils responsible for the roads is open to criticism, and considerable grants have to be made by the Road Board from public funds. In France a sharp distinction is drawn between 'routes nationales', which are kept up by the central government, and 'routes départementales', which are the affair of the separate departments. The policy of keeping the roads in repair by means of tolls levied on the users, though it has sometimes been regarded as the wisest, is now discredited, and it does not seem to have been employed by the Romans.

What their actual policy was in this matter it is not easy to say, and it probably varied at different periods. Under the Republic the actual construction of Italian roads, such as the Via Flaminia, must have been paid for by the State, which required them for its armies, and not by the magistrates who supervised the work and gave their name to the roads; but there is some evidence that the cost of upkeep was met from the proceeds of a charge made on the so-called *viarii vicani*, who occupied what was treated as public land along the line of the roads, while the actual work was done by contractors employed by the Government. Even in Republican times we encounter *curatores* of the Italian roads, who were responsible to the Government for their upkeep, and under the principate, when the emperor had undertaken the *cura viarum*, the office was held by senators of high rank, who were entrusted with public money, and were expected to contract for any work which required to be done. It is almost certain that from the reign of Augustus the imperial treasury bore the expense of the construction and upkeep at least of the main roads, the work on which was often done by soldiers. An arch still standing at Rimini records the thanks of the Senate and People to Augustus for repairing the most frequented roads of Italy at his own expense. Under Domitian the officer in charge of the imperial *fiscus* had to calculate the demands of the 'far stretched line of roads'.[1] Numerous milestones both in Italy and the provinces mention the expenditure of money by emperors on roads. On the other hand, contributions were certainly made for this purpose by towns and individuals; thus, when under Hadrian a new road was made between Constantine (Cirta) and Philippeville in Tunis, the track itself

[1] Statius, *Silvae*, iii. 3. 102.

was paid for by the former town, and the cost of the bridges fell on the *possessores territorii Cirtensium.* We even find the emperor and the neighbouring landowners sharing the expense of repairing a strip of the Appian Way. In spite of this last instance the evidence seems to support the view that the central government not only made itself responsible for what were described as *viae publicae* or *consulares* or, occasionally, *regiae,* as opposed to *viae privatae* or *vicinales,* but exercised a general supervision over the roads of the empire even when it did not pay for them, as is indicated by the frequent occurrence on inscriptions of the phrase *ex auctoritate imperatoris.* It seems, then, that the Roman method of dealing with the problem closely resembles that which has been adopted in modern France.

What has been said on this question illustrates the great value of the information which can be derived from Roman milestones, of which about 4,000 have fortunately been preserved. Milestones can fairly be claimed as a Roman invention: though uninscribed stones were placed at fixed intervals along the roads of Ptolemaic Egypt, it is unnecessary to suppose that the Romans derived this particular idea from that country, as inscribed milestones have been found in Italy dating from a time when Rome was not yet in contact with Egypt. The date at which a milestone was set up can often be exactly fixed, as under the Republic they bear the name of a magistrate and under the principate the name and titles of an emperor. Augustus erected in Rome a 'golden milestone' from which the roads of Italy radiated. Milestones on the main roads of Italy generally give the distance from Rome, but this is rare in the provinces, where the distance is as a rule given from the main town of the district, so that scholars are enabled to reach valuable conclusions about the relative importance of towns in Roman times. Where roads met, pillars were set up giving the distance from several towns. Some silver vases have been discovered in Italy in the shape of milestones, recording the main distances between points on the road from Cadiz to Rome, possibly reproductions of a monument in the former town. On milestones there is as a rule only one number, but occasionally they mention the distance both from the starting-point and the end of the road. 'When one is walking along a road', says Quintilian, 'it relieves one's weariness to read the distances on the milestones. It is a pleasure to measure the weary way one has come, and to know how far one has to go makes one foot it more courageously.'

It is fortunate for the historian that Roman milestones contained more than a bare record of distances. Often the date which they establish is of great importance, e.g. the dates of the roads made by Popillius (consul of 132 B.C.) from Capua to the Straits of Messina, and by Trajan in 111 A.D. from Syria to the Red Sea. The discovery of a milestone on a road leading from Strassburg through Offenburg into Germany is an important piece of evidence for the policy of the Flavian emperors on the Rhine. Milestones establish a fact which Tacitus does not deign to mention, that Tiberius attempted to open up to civilization the wild country which lies behind the coast of Dalmatia. In fact, no study of the provincial policy of the emperors which fails to lay stress on the evidence of milestones is satisfactory. It is from this source, for instance, that we know that Claudius interested himself specially in Gaul, and Hadrian in Africa and the eastern provinces. A most significant fact is that from the time of Trajan the milestones of Gaul reckon distances in leagues (the native unit of measurement) and not, as is usual, in miles. In the East, though the inscriptions are generally in Latin, the figures and the names of places are usually given in Greek.

A result of the systematic measurements which have been described must have been the accumulation of a vast amount of accurate geographical information, and the question now arises to what extent this was available for general use. What maps and road-books were at the disposal of a Roman traveller?

Poets did not hesitate to refer to distant regions, and passages such as

> Sive per Syrtes iter aestuosas
> Sive facturus per inhospitalem
> Caucasum vel quae loca fabulosus
> Lambit Hydaspes

imply a fair amount of geographical knowledge in Horace's readers. There is, indeed, evidence that private persons possessed maps to an extent probably unparalleled till quite recent times. A girl in Propertius whose lover was at the wars consoled herself in her loneliness by studying a map of the 'eastern front'.

> Et disco qua parte fluat vincendus Araxes,
> Quot sine aqua Parthus milia currat equus;
> Cogor et e tabula pictos ediscere mundos.

Under Domitian a certain Mettius Pompusianus got into trouble with the suspicious emperor for having a map of the world on the walls of his house and for carrying about a copy of it. A writer of the late third century pleads on patriotic grounds for the teaching of geography by means of maps in the schools of Autun.

An official map of the known world, not merely of the Roman Empire, was prepared by Agrippa for Augustus, and displayed in the Porticus Vipsania at Rome. In addition to the outlines of the various countries it seems to have contained, possibly on the parts representing the sea, notes of the exact measurements of certain areas from north to south and from east to west—measurements which have been reproduced by Pliny. No doubt copies of this map were made and had a wide circulation. No conclusion as to its appearance can be drawn from the only surviving copy of a Roman map, the so-called Tabula Peutingeriana, now in Vienna. This is a long strip, 21 feet by 1, and gives a very distorted view of the shape of countries; it evidently had the practical object of giving the line of roads, and was possibly accompanied by a road-book.

In a sermon of St. Ambrose the follower of Christ is compared to a soldier on the march who receives from his general a road-book (*itinerarium*) which will guide him safely along the road to his destination, ' donec ad eam urbem perveniatur, quae quasi regalis eligitur, in qua fessis exercitibus requies ministretur '.[1] These Roman road-books were either *adnotata* or *picta*, i. e. they contained either mere notes of distances and other similar information, or in addition maps and diagrams. The chief surviving example, the so-called Itinerarium Antonini, useful as it is, is a very inferior production, containing nothing but distances between points on certain roads. It is generally agreed that it is based on a map, and that it is not an official publication but the work of an amateur without scientific training.

The Romans approached the work of map-making in a highly practical spirit. As has been said: 'The immense difference between an Eratosthenes, who read the size of the earth in the stars, and an Agrippa, who calculated from the numbers on milestones the length and breadth of each province, is typical of the contrast between the Greek and the Roman character.' It would indeed be foolish to pretend that a Roman traveller was provided with the guidance which is available in modern maps, but it is not too much to say that it was his own fault if he lost his way on any of the main lines of communication. The geographical knowledge of the Middle Ages was ludicrously inferior to that possessed by the Romans,[2] and the rediscovery of Ptolemy in the fifteenth century marks the beginning of modern cartographical science.

In order that the network of roads should fully carry out its purpose of serving the military and administrative needs of the government, the creation of some form of public post was absolutely necessary. Under the Republic officials in the pro-

[1] I owe this reference to Kubitschek in Pauly-Wissowa, *Real-Encyclopädie*, s.v. ' Itinerarien '.

[2] See the mediaeval maps reproduced in *Encycl. Brit.* vol. xvii, pp. 637f.

vinces had their own *tabellarii*, but no systematic attempt was made to facilitate the rapid transmission of dispatches to and from Rome till the reign of Augustus, who, as we saw, was possibly influenced by Persian methods. The correspondence of Pliny with Trajan shows that the efficient system which existed under the early principate enabled a provincial governor to keep in very close touch with the authorities at home. At most periods, if a message was not particularly urgent, it was carried by couriers who travelled on foot, but messengers who were provided with a *diploma* by the emperor or a provincial governor were entitled to requisition carriages from the towns which lay on or near the road along which they passed. This duty of providing vehicles for government service was one of the heaviest burdens which Roman towns had to bear, and in spite of attempts to lighten it made by Claudius, Nerva, Hadrian, and other emperors, the old system always returned. Imperial couriers attained considerable speeds. Sir William Ramsay considers that those of them who were provided with a *diploma* covered on the average 50 miles a day, so that Constantinople could be reached from Rome in twenty-four days, and Alexandria in fifty-four. Thus Pliny could get an answer from Trajan in less than two months. Couriers travelled as a rule by land, but not always; the news of Galba's accession could hardly have arrived in Alexandria within twenty-seven days if it had not been brought by a ship running before a favouring breeze. Such speeds would probably have been considered good in England in the seventeenth century, for in 1635 two months passed before an answer was received in London to a letter to Scotland or Ireland.

It must not, however, be imagined that private correspondence was forwarded by the imperial postal service. When Pliny provided his wife with a *diploma* in order that she might use the machinery of the post to hasten her journey to the side of a bereaved relative, he confesses to Trajan that he has done so in a tone which shows that such action was quite irregular. There was never any question of providing the general public with facilities for rapid travel or rapid delivery of letters. As Hirschfeld remarks: 'The Roman public post, created by Augustus entirely for public purposes, always retained, in spite of reforms in detail, this one-sided character, and was not, like the modern post, a benefit to the subjects, but rather a grievous burden.' The letters addressed by St. Paul and other Christian leaders to the churches of the Empire[1] were no doubt put into the charge of some convert who happened to be travelling in the right direction, and under the principate, as in the days of Cicero, commercial companies and wealthy men had their own staff of *tabellarii*. It must be admitted that the Romans did less to facilitate the carriage of private correspondence than has been done by modern governments since, at any rate, the fifteenth century.

This summary of certain aspects of the Roman road-system will have served its purpose if it has succeeded in making clear that on the one hand the roads were one of the most potent means whereby the Roman government created a citizenship transcending barriers of language, nationality, and colour, and that on the other hand the solutions given by the Romans to certain very modern problems are still worthy of study. It remains to consider briefly what use was made in Roman times of communications by sea, and to show that by means of a highly developed trade the world was united economically as well as politically.

The original Romans were an agricultural rather than a sea-faring people, and, when naval warfare was thrust upon them, it was to their Greek allies in the south of Italy that they turned for assistance. Commerce, too, seems to have interested the Roman State but little until the last century of the Republic, and to have remained throughout very largely in the hands of Greeks and hellenized Orientals. But it must be remembered

[1] For a list of such letters see Harnack, *Mission and Expansion of Christianity*, vol. i, pp. 372 f.

that after the Social War, at least, the Greeks of Italy were Romans politically, and that we have here a good example of the benefits conferred by the spread of Roman rule. By securing safe communications the government enabled every class and every race to exercise that form of activity which it found most congenial. To an enterprising Greek merchant of Puteoli or Smyrna or Alexandria Roman rule brought nothing but advantages. No barriers except moderate customs-dues, which were not protective in character, hindered the free movement of goods from one end of the Empire to the other.

The anonymous writer of an interesting pamphlet written during the Peloponnesian War notes the influence of sea-power on Athenian culture. Athens, he says, can obtain the choicest products of Sicily, Italy, Cyprus, and Egypt, and thus, while other Greek states are 'provincial' in their language and ways, Athens has a civilization which derives something from all Greeks and Barbarians. This feature appears on a still larger scale in imperial Rome, but, while Athens was inclined to monopolize the advantages which her sea-power produced, Rome put them at the disposal of her subjects. The cosmopolitan character of Roman civilization was a result of freedom of trade: the ships which brought to Rome the products of the whole world brought also administrators, philosophers, and preachers of new religions.

Roman literature is full of references to the risks which traders took in search of gain.

> Impiger extremos curris mercator ad Indos,
> Per mare pauperiem fugiens, per saxa, per ignes,

says Horace, and again:

> si neque fervidis
> Pars inclusa caloribus
> Mundi, nec Boreae finitimum latus
> Durataeque solo nives
> Mercatorem abigunt; horrida callidi
> Vincunt aequora navitae.

Juvenal declares that the sea is more peopled than the land. Trimalchio, the rich and vulgar freedman of whom Petronius gives so amusing an account, boasts that he made ten million sesterces from one voyage of a ship laden with wine, pork, beans, perfumes, and slaves. An inscription tells us that a Phrygian merchant made seventy-two voyages round the Peloponnese to Italy.

Ancient ships were indeed very much at the mercy of winds and waves. Tartessus, in the south of Spain, was 'discovered', says Herodotus, by a Samian vessel which was making for Egypt, but was carried by the east wind through the Pillars of Hercules. This is an extreme instance, but the story of St. Paul's voyage to Rome is enough to show how difficult it was for a ship to follow a well-defined route or to foresee the length of a journey. The Mediterranean was practically closed to navigation between November and March, and it was only between the end of May and the middle of September that sailing was considered safe. The corn required for the populace of Rome during the winter had to reach the city by the autumn. It is true that under favourable conditions very rapid journeys were possible. Thus King Herod Agrippa, who, on the recommendation of Caligula, travelled home by Alexandria, reached Egypt 'in a few days' from Puteoli, and a ship is said to have sailed from the south of France to Egypt in seven days. As a rule, however, voyages were much slower. Rapid travel by sea from Italy to Alexandria was only possible in the height of summer, when ships ran before the north-west Etesian winds, and the return voyage was always a more serious affair. Lucian vividly describes a leviathan merchantman which put into the Peiraeus seventy days after leaving Alexandria. After tacking against the Etesian winds it was driven into the Aegean; with better fortune it would have reached Italy by the south coast of Crete in the same time. The best authorities think that the average duration of the voyage from Alexandria to Puteoli was fifty days even in summer. The trading vessels of Roman times were not very small; St. Paul's ship carried 276 persons, as well as a large quantity of grain, and we read of a ship which held 600 passengers. Lucian's ship was 180 feet long and 45 broad.

In spite of the difficulties and dangers of seafaring, Horace is not exaggerating when he says that every part of the world was visited by traders. Though we hear little of the activities of the Roman fleet, it seems to have kept the seas free of pirates, who are scarcely mentioned after the days of Pompey. The dangers which attended navigation came from nature far more than from man.

Long before the arrival of Caesar in Gaul the way had been prepared for him by the activities of Roman merchants, a large number of whom were massacred at Orleans at the time of the rising of Vercingetorix. Their chief object of merchandise seems to have been wine, which with other luxuries was excluded from the territory of the Nervii, who believed that 'courage was enfeebled by these indulgences and manly vigour enervated'. The Germans, too, forbade the importation of wine into their country. But under the principate this ascetic regulation was relaxed, and the products of southern industry found a market in North Germany and even in Scandinavia, where large quantities of Roman glass and metal-work have been found along with many coins. Mention has been made above of the trade in amber from the Baltic coast. Though the frontiers of the Roman Empire were well marked and carefully guarded, no attempt was made to confine trade to the regions under Roman rule. The German word *kaufen* 'to buy' is supposed to be connected with the Latin *caupo*.

While trade with northern Europe was conducted mainly by land, the commercial intercourse with the East, which developed with extraordinary rapidity under the early principate, was almost entirely in the hands of sailors, as the land routes were blocked by the powerful Parthian kingdom. The annexation of Egypt by Rome after the battle of Actium must have been an unmixed blessing to that country, which became the starting-point of a vigorous trade with Arabia and India. As early as 25 B.C. 120 ships left the single port of Myos Hormos annually for India, six times as many as had sailed from the Red Sea for the same destination under the former government. There was a steady demand in the luxurious cities round the Mediterranean for ivory, perfumes, pepper, pearls, tortoise-shell, and other luxuries which only the East could supply. The rapid development of this trade under the early principate is reflected in the writings of geographers. While Strabo, who wrote under Tiberius, has little detailed knowledge of Arabia and India, the author of the so-called *Periplus Maris Erythraei*, which is commonly dated fifty years later, shows a personal acquaintance with both coasts of the Red Sea, with the Gulf of Aden as far as Cape Guardafui, and with India as far as Cape Comorin, and has something to say of Africa as far as Zanzibar and of Asia as far the Malay Peninsula. A century later the writings of Ptolemy show that the information available about these remote regions had gained in accuracy; some identify his Cattigara with Hanoi in French Cochin China. Chinese silk reached the Mediterranean both by sea and by overland routes. After the discovery by a certain Hippalus of the facts about the monsoons ships sailed direct, when the wind was favourable, from the south of Arabia to the mouth of the Indus. The journey from Alexandria to India and back occupied six or seven months—from the summer solstice till the following February. Native rulers put no obstacles in the way of trade; ambassadors came to Augustus from India, and to Claudius from Ceylon, and we learn from Chinese sources of an 'embassy' from Marcus Aurelius which visited China in 166 A.D., though it is doubtful whether this was more than a band of merchants masquerading as representatives of the emperor.

The objects imported into the Roman Empire from regions which lay outside were mainly luxuries, small in bulk and unprocurable elsewhere, for which there was a constant demand at almost any price. When we turn to consider the internal trade of the Empire we are faced with difficult questions, to which very various answers have been given, regarding the general character of industry at the period with which we are concerned. Some writers have supposed that large-scale production was then nearly as common as it is now, while others maintain that it was almost unknown, and object to the use of such terms as 'factory' and 'industrial capitalist' with reference to the Roman Empire. The truth undoubtedly lies between these two extreme views. It must on the one hand be remembered that the transport of bulky objects for long distances by road or in ships which we should now regard as small, must have been an expensive affair. Surprise, for example, has often been expressed at the absence of any measures to protect home-grown Italian corn against foreign competition, but this can be easily explained if we realize that foreign grain 'long before it reached its destination would have risen to a price far outside the competition of home-grown wheat, which was thus much better protected by the expense of transport than by any duty'.[1] Under these conditions goods produced close at hand would be preferred to similar objects brought from a distance; nor is there any reason to think that the economic factors which are now so unfavourable to the small producer were operative in Roman times. 'The Roman producer was much nearer to the consumer than he is to-day. . . . A full-fledged factory system of production emerged only in certain favourable circumstances.'[2] Production was only on a large scale when its objects were, for whatever reason, unprocurable except from a few sources.

Yet in spite of the cost of transport there was undoubtedly a very considerable movement of commodities from one part

[1] Ferrero, *Greatness and Decline of Rome*, vol. ii, p. 324.

[2] Frank, *Economic History of Rome* (1920), p. 166. This book contains a full and valuable discussion of the problems touched on in the text.

of the Roman Empire to another. Natural products, however heavy, were exported to the countries where there existed an effective demand. Thus Italy imported grain in the form of tribute from Egypt and Africa, metals from Spain and the Danube, and marble from Greece, and exported large quantities of wine and some olive-oil. The manufacture, too, of certain kinds of goods was for one reason or another localized. Most of the fine metal-work which has been found inside and outside the Empire is supposed to have been produced in the neighbourhood of Capua. Egypt had almost a monopoly of the manufacture of carpets and fine linen, and Spain and the north of France of coarser varieties of clothing. The extent to which the ordinary necessities of life were imported into Italy is well illustrated by an inscription in which a shopkeeper of Reate described himself as 'Mercator omnis generis mercium transmarinarum'.

Of all the objects in common demand the one whose production was most definitely localized was high-class pottery. Every visitor to a Roman museum is familiar with a reddish-brown highly glazed ware known as 'Samian' or *terra sigillata*. Pottery of this character was originally made in Italy, mainly at Arezzo, whence it was exported in large quantities to the provinces. In the first century of the principate, however, rival factories were established in Gaul, which soon succeeded in ousting the Italian ware even from the markets of Italy itself: a box of red pottery which had arrived at Pompeii just before its destruction in 79 A.D. contained more Gallic than Italian vessels.[1] At Lezoux in the Auvergne near Clermont many furnaces and storehouses have been discovered, and it is thought that here alone a population of 25,000–30,000 was engaged on the production of *terra sigillata* for the world market. A study of the stamps which the makers fortunately impressed on their wares justifies the view that this industry was not only centralized in a few places but was in the hands

[1] *Journal of Roman Studies*, iv. 27.

of a quite small number of employers, whose wealth is established by the size of the houses which they occupied. As time passed this business extended to the Rhine, but it was always a monopoly of a few well-marked centres and probably of a few large firms, about whose organization we would gladly know more than we do. Very similar conditions prevailed in the manufacture of glass and fine metal-work, which called for skilled workmen and expert knowledge of processes. It seems indeed probable that factory towns like Lezoux were not so uncommon as some writers have maintained, though when the objects produced were perishable and we have not the assistance of makers' stamps it is obviously much less easy to reach definite conclusions.

From an early period in their history the Romans showed themselves fully aware of the advantages of a uniform system of currency. In the fourth century B.C. they issued a common coinage for the whole of their Italian dominions, and under the principate, though in the eastern provinces local currencies were not absolutely forbidden, their circulation was restricted, and coins issued from government mints were alone employed in interprovincial trade. Many of these mints were in the provinces, but the standard was determined by the central government, and it was only when the central government was weak, as in the third century A.D., that variations occurred. The *argentarii*, who originally had been changers of money, developed before the time of Cicero into something very like modern bankers; they not only received money on deposit, paid it out on receipt of a written order, and lent it at interest, but they made arrangements with their correspondents in other parts of the empire for the provision of money to their clients. Without any transfer of cash it was thus possible for an Italian to make payments in a province, or for a provincial to satisfy his Italian creditor. The problem was a more difficult one when it was necessary to make payments outside the Roman dominions. The discovery of Roman coins in such regions as

Scandinavia and Ceylon proves that imported luxuries were often paid for in money, and this export of coins was an important cause of the depreciation of the currency within the empire, as the supply of the precious metals was strictly limited. On the whole, however, Roman trade was little hampered by such monetary difficulties as those of which Europe is at present acutely conscious.

The account which has been given of the facilities which existed in Roman times for the movement of men, of commodities, and of ideas from one end of the known world to the other will have failed of its purpose if it has not established that the modern world has still much to learn from the study of Roman institutions. It is, of course, foolish to minimize the differences between ancient and modern conditions, and no attempt has been made to do so. Travel by land in the Roman Empire was slow, if judged by the standards which have prevailed since the introduction of railways. The invention of telegraphy has revolutionized the process of disseminating news. Ancient ships could not carry great quantities of heavy goods, could only sail at certain seasons, and cannot be compared for speed and comfort with modern steamers. But these obvious considerations should not blind us to the permanent significance of that aspect of Roman civilization which has been considered in this chapter. Free communication was only rendered possible by the *pax Romana*, and the *pax Romana* is an ideal which the modern world has not yet been able to realize. Only those who know what it meant in the early centuries of the Christian era can understand the fascination once exercised by the idea of the Holy Roman Empire and the appeal which the Roman Catholic Church still makes to many who cannot fully accept her tenets. Those who hope that the hatreds and jealousies which now prevent European nations from freely co-operating in the work of civilization can best be overcome by intercourse between men of different races and languages, and who see in social and economic ties the most potent means of averting the horrors of war cannot but be encouraged by the thought that at one time their ideal was a reality. Though there is no Latin word for 'nationality', the Roman government had to face problems similar to those which have in more recent times confronted the rulers of Ireland or Poland, and displayed a tact which is well worthy of imitation. Rome's Italian allies were so much impressed by the excellence of her rule that they actually went to war to secure incorporation in the Roman state. Rome did not indeed encourage *tribal* patriotism, but she liked her citizens to be loyal members of the *city* to which they belonged. Cicero, as has been well said,[1] forgot that he was a Volscian, though he was proud of his connexion with Arpinum. In certain provinces Rome may almost be said to have created nationalities. When Caesar went to Gaul he found it inhabited by mutually hostile tribes, but though no direct steps were taken by Rome to put an end to the tribal system, which has left its trace on the names of the towns of France, as the centuries passed, Gauls, like Sidonius Apollinaris, thought more of their province and of the Empire and less of their tribe. They almost forgot that they belonged to the Aedui or the Remi, and developed a provincial patriotism in which it is not fantastic to see the origin of French national feeling.

The Romans did not like fine phrases, and talked little of their 'imperial mission'. The benefits which they conferred on humanity were the indirect results of an enlightened self-interest. Roads were originally constructed for the convenience of Italian armies, and the franchise was extended because it suited Rome's interest to attach some of her subjects closely to herself. It took some time before it became clear that a liberal provincial policy benefited equally both rulers and subjects. Gaius Gracchus and Caesar were in advance of their contemporaries in pressing for a rapid extension of the franchise, but experience soon convinced even conservatives of the

[1] Strachan-Davidson, *Cicero*, p. 6.

soundness of their views. The Roman state could indeed, as the Emperor Claudius said, only perform its task 'transferendo huc quod usque egregium fuerit'. The inevitable result of intercourse between rulers and subjects was the disappearance of the distinction between them, and the creation of a world-citizenship.

The study of Roman history provides the modern world with warnings as well as with instruction. Though, as has been frequently pointed out, Rome did not lay excessive stress on uniformity, dangers were undoubtedly latent in her centralized system of administration. If the Republic had too few officials, the later Empire had far too many, and it is from the history of Rome under Constantine and his successors that opponents of bureaucracy can draw their most cogent arguments. But this centralization was in the first instance an unmixed blessing, and in the centuries with which this chapter has been mainly concerned the dangers which it involved were scarcely apparent. The first two centuries of the Christian era were one of the few really great periods of human history. To Augustus and the best of his successors can be justly applied the words used by a famous scholar of Pericles: 'The statesman who in the ghastly succession of barren and bloodstained centuries which constitute the world's history has created a moment to which we may apply the words

Verweile doch! du bist so schön!

may rightly be regarded as a great magician.' [1]

If a Thucydides had written the history of the Roman Empire he would have noted in its leading figures an Athenian tolerance and liberality combined with a Spartan regard for law and order. Even Tacitus, who devotes so much space to the personal vices of emperors, realized that these scarcely affected the provinces, and that a Nero and a Domitian accepted and applied the general principles laid down by

[1] Wilamowitz, *Aristoteles und Athen*, ii, p. 102.

Caesar and Augustus. Of the work done by Rome no part was of greater significance and none of more lasting value to mankind than her encouragement of free intercourse.

G. H. Stevenson.

Books Recommended.

L. Friedlaender, *Roman Life and Manners under the Early Empire* (Routledge, 1909), vol. i, p. 268 f.

H. Stuart Jones, *Companion to Roman History* (Oxford, 1912), pp. 40–51, 316–37.

R. C. Bosanquet in *Companion to Latin Studies* (Cambridge, 1910), pp. 409–35.

Sir W. Ramsay, *Roads and Travel in the New Testament* (Hastings's Dictionary of the Bible. Extra volume).

T. Codrington, *Roman Roads in Britain* (Third edition, S.P.C.K., 1918).

H. Belloc, *The Stane Street* (1913).

W. Warde Fowler, *Social Life at Rome* (Macmillan, 1908), chap. 3.

THE SCIENCE OF LAW

I

How we have inherited Roman Law. Reasons for an inquiry into its value. The verdict of Christianity. The present inquiry does not deal with the fundamental notions. The two grounds on which the study of Roman Law is important.

WE have come into our heritage of Roman Law by two distinct successions. To a great extent we are the *heredes necessarii* of Roman Law: we never had the power to prevent Roman Law from being a prime element in the formation of modern Western civilization. This is because the breach of continuity caused by the disintegration of the Western Roman Empire was far from complete. The invaders themselves had already long been subject to the influence of Roman civilization, and, of course, existing provincial institutions and law entered into the social system of the new barbarian kingdoms. It has been shown that even in England, where the conquest was most thorough, the economic organization of the conquerors was affected by what they found. And in provinces where large masses of romanized population and the Catholic Church survived there is a patent, though disjointed, continuity. In this way we are *heredes necessarii* of Roman Law.

But the law books which for centuries have been venerated as the Civil Law, the *Corpus Iuris* of Justinian, were compiled in the East after the West had been lost to the Empire. They were thus not the law encountered by the barbarians in the provinces detached by them in the fifth century, and, except in the portions of Italy recovered by the Eastern Empire in the sixth, are not a survival, but a discovery made and enthusiastically embraced by Western Europe. At the end of the eleventh century there was an acceptance of this heritage; there began then a deliberately chosen study of the *Corpus Iuris* which has continued ever since, with far-reaching effects upon the formation of modern European law and upon the history of thought. This influence is distinct from the influence by continuity, but, of course, not independent of it. The older influence prepared the way for the later.

'Once heir, always heir', is a Roman maxim. We cannot alter the fact that by necessity and by choice the law of the Roman Empire has played a great part in the formation of our civilization. It is too late to repudiate the *hereditas*, even if it has proved *damnosa*. What, then, is to be gained by appraising its value?

The answer is that history demands the valuation of cultural elements. A valuation of the legacy of Roman Law has a practical bearing on the limited question, how far it is worth preserving as a subject of academic study; but it has also a wider interest. Roman Law is, or is not, one of the great achievements of the human mind. It has been used by later ages well or badly. We are either the heirs of a great tradition or the dupes of a professional superstition. This part of our spiritual heritage should be jealously guarded and cultivated, or as far as possible eliminated.

It may be said that these questions have to a great extent already been answered by the course of history. Christian civilization has not accepted Roman Law as a whole. Portions of it, notably the law of slavery and marriage, have been rejected. We are thereby warned not to regard Roman Law as the perfect expression of the natural law, as *ratio scripta.* And equally we are entitled to infer that the fundamental institutions of Roman Law, the family, private property, and the sanctity of contracts, which Christian civilization has made its own, are truly human and natural.

This is an argument from authority, which will carry no weight with those who do not accept the authority. And even those who admit the argument must not exaggerate the ground which it covers. The process of selecting from the mass of existing custom and law those institutions which are consistent with Christianity has been gradual, and may be still continuing. Not that the Church's ethical teaching has ever been defective, but merely that, because a society is predominantly Christian, it does not follow that its positive law is wholly Christian. We must allow for the possible survival even yet of institutions which a thoroughly Christian civilization should, or could rightly, abandon.

Thus, Christianity did not make away with slavery for many centuries, and has never, by any authoritative pronouncement of which I am aware, condemned it as *per se* wrong in all circumstances. Simply, in the course of years, slavery was found to be incompatible with the dignity of the human soul, asserted by Christianity for the first time with effective force. Again, the marriage law of that scrupulously religious legislator Justinian is very far from the Christian law, as it existed from the first days of the Church.

I do not think that this consideration destroys the Christian authority for those institutions which are the very fabric of our society. But in any case I must assume these institutions as being the only ones upon which a legal system can be based. A society which rejects them will certainly not need to trouble itself with the Roman, nor indeed with any, jurisprudence. It will have substituted for law the administrative decrees of those who have captured the machinery of government.

The matter to be examined here is, thus, not the fundamental sanity of Roman Law, but the merits of its technical elaboration. Its continued study is justified on two grounds. First, its history affords a unique example of the juristic method of legal development, of law not simply positive, but existing of right and co-ordinated and developed by reason. We can observe the method in which the fundamental ideas of family, property, and contract, expressed at first in a rude collection of customs, were by a process extending over many centuries developed into a consistent body of reasoned doctrine, essentially not created by the State, though sanctioned by its protection. On this first ground the study of Roman Law is valuable not only as a preparation for professional work, but as inculcating the true conception of law and of legal progress. Secondly, Roman Law in its final state, as it stands in the *Corpus Iuris* of Justinian, became by revival the basis of modern European law. This is a mere statement of fact, true whatever we may think of the mediaeval veneration of the Civil Law. It makes Roman Law a subject of the first importance for mediaeval and modern history. We begin with a rapid survey of the revival of Roman Law.[1]

II

The Revival of Roman Law. Canon and International Law. Glossators, Bartolists, Humanists, Natural Law School, Historical School. Relation of England to the revived study. Modern significance of Roman Law.

As we began by saying, the influence of Roman Law upon modern Europe has been exercised both by continuity and by deliberate revival. It would be wrong to regard the influence by continuity as accidental, a mere result of the political ascendancy of Rome, because the excellence of Roman Law is itself a large part of the explanation of that ascendancy. It explains why conquered peoples were content with their dependence, and how inclusion in the Roman Empire came to be regarded as a blessing. The continuity of Roman Law after the break-up of the Empire is a very large subject. A great deal of it survived, but necessarily in a debased and adulterated form. Doubtless the barbarians brought new elements of value into our civilization, but they destroyed Roman Law as a technical system, whilst absorbing the memory of a civilized

[1] For further details see Vinogradoff, *Roman Law in Mediaeval Europe*; Sohm, *Institutes of Roman Law*, translated by Ledlie.

world united in the Empire under one law, as in the Church by one faith.

The later influence of Roman Law by study and adoption carries us on to more legal ground. To the Middle Ages the Roman or Civil Law was nothing vague, but the law of a definite point of time, the death of Justinian (565 A. D.), stated in a definite set of law-books, the *Corpus Iuris Civilis*. The Roman Law which the *Corpus Iuris* displaced was naturally derived from an earlier period, namely that preceding the destruction of the Western Empire. If we except the portions of Italy recovered by the Eastern Empire and make some allowance for infiltration, we may say that the *Corpus Iuris* was discovered to the West by Irnerius, who at the end of the eleventh century founded at Bologna the famous school of the Glossators.

The new study spread like wildfire through the nascent universities of Europe, indeed was often a cause of their foundation. It has continued ever since in the principal intellectual centres of Europe, restoring and preserving the science of law. But for it the laws of Europe might have been a medley of local customs. It upheld the conception of law as a reasoned systematic whole, to be developed by scientific interpretation. It supplied a common ground upon which rival theories of jurisprudence could meet. It became, as Maine puts it, the *lingua franca* of jurisprudence. And it affected political no less than legal theory. A more material aspect of its influence is that by being incorporated, to a greater or less extent, in all European legal systems it enabled centuries of legal advance to be overtaken in one stride.

The general influence exercised upon jurisprudence and political theory by the Civil Law is illustrated by the two international systems, Canon Law and modern International Law. It is no coincidence that Canon Law as a science begins with the publication at Bologna, 'the head-quarters of the new secular jurisprudence,' about the year 1140 by a monk named Gratian, of a treatise entitled *Conçordia discordantium canonum*, better known as the *Decretum Gratiani*.[1] Of the edifice which was built up on this foundation large parts were but a mediaeval version of Roman Law. So again it was inevitable that the foundations of modern International Law should be laid by civilians (as students of Roman Law are properly called) and by moral theologians, who drew their materials very largely from Roman Law. This second development has a special interest for us owing to the prominent part played in it by English civilians. Their history from the sixteenth century has not yet been systematically studied.

The particular influence of the Civil Law upon the municipal systems of the West varies from country to country. At its highest it culminated in a general 'reception', that is, in its adoption as the common law of the country; so in Italy, so by Germany from the end of the fifteenth century and by Scotland somewhat later. This adoption was necessarily accompanied by the evolution of a mediaeval Roman Law. Even in Italy, in which Roman Law had existed in some sort without interruption, a considerable work of adaptation was necessary in order to bring the *Corpus Iuris* into practice. Its immense materials had to undergo processes of selection and rejection, and of combination with elements from other sources. This was not the point of view of the earliest civilians, the Glossators of the twelfth and thirteenth centuries, who studied the *Corpus Iuris* in its entirety, not historically but as a system, and not loosely but in unrivalled detail. They were essentially theorists, in spite of their great effect upon the practice both of their own and later times. Their subsequent influence was exercised through the great gloss (*glossa ordinaria*) in which Accursius summed up their work at the end of the first half of the thirteenth century. The adaptation of Roman Law to actual

[1] See the article 'Canon Law', reprinted from Renton's *Encyclopaedia of the Laws of England* in Maitland's *Collected Papers*, iii. 65 ff.

needs was performed by their successors, the post-Glossators or Bartolists (Bartolus of Sassoferrato, 1314–57). This necessarily involved a deformation of pure Roman Law, and was bitterly criticized by the brilliant humanistic school of the sixteenth and seventeenth centuries, whose own methods and intention were historical and therefore really inconsistent with the practical application of the texts.

The humanistic point of view was impossible for lawyers who had to put the *Corpus Iuris* into practice, and accordingly the Bartolist tradition was not broken by its criticism. But from the end of the seventeenth century, when humanism was waning, political and legal speculation was governed by a new doctrine of Natural Law. The Natural Law School appealed to reason, and not, as had the Glossators and Bartolists, to Roman Law (*ratio scripta*), for the discovery of natural law. There followed a widespread movement to substitute modern codes for Roman Law, but it is observable that to the codifications of municipal law, as to the elaboration of International Law, the contribution of Roman Law was very great.

The final blow to Roman Law as a living system came from the German historical school which dominated the scientific legal studies of the nineteenth century. Its cardinal doctrine was that law is essentially the product of the national legal genius, from which it followed that the reception of an alien system is against the very nature of law. This doctrine led on the one hand to an intensive study of Germanic legal conceptions as being those suitable for Germany, and on the other hand to a revived humanism in Roman Law, which under the leadership of Savigny was studied as the law of a particular people in its historical setting. The ultimate result was the displacement of Roman Law in Germany by the Civil Code, which came into force in 1900. Nevertheless old methods of exposition die very hard, and the effects of the older points of view lingered on in the academic tradition of Roman Law till quite modern times. A purely historical study of the subject hardly dates from before the closing years of the nineteenth century.

From this European movement towards Roman Law England stands comparatively apart, because the early efficiency of her political institutions provided her with a native Common Law, strongly centralized in the royal courts. We had, indeed, an Anglo-Norman school of Glossators; its founder was one Vacarius, who came to England before 1150 and spent here the rest of his long life. There is good evidence that he founded a school at Oxford; considerable manuscript remains suggest that its influence extended to Normandy and possibly to Cambridge. But the school was true to type. What strikes one in the glosses of Vacarius and his followers is their complete aloofness from the law of the country in which they were teaching. They exhibit the purest Romanism of the early Glossators, among whom they deserve an honourable place. But Bologna retained the leadership of the movement, and it was not English professors, but the Bolognese Azo (died *c.* 1230) who supplied the Roman elements in Bracton's fundamental work on the laws and customs of England (*c.* 1250). If we can boast of a post-Glossator, it is Bracton, and his work is summed up by Maitland as Romanesque in form, English in substance. After him there was no further reception of Roman Law in England.

That is not to say that the influence of the Civil Law upon English Law ended with Bracton. We have to remember the large departments administered by special courts, which did not apply the Common Law, but Canon and Merchant Law, into which the Civil Law had entered much more largely. Again, both Canon and Civil Law have contributed to the branch of law known as Equity, which has long been an essential part of our system. We have also to remember that in every age many an Englishman has studied the Civil Law in an English or foreign university, as ancillary to the Canon Law, as an introduction to diplomacy, or as a sort of cosmopolitan jurisprudence. Even in judicial decisions of the nineteenth century one can detect the effects of acquaintance with current Romanistic learning. But there has been no wholesale reception; our law has a unique independence which, with its wide diffusion and technical merits, makes it the only equal rival of the law of imperial Rome.

The underlying cause of the extraordinary revival which we have glanced at has been the belief that Roman Law is the Natural Law. This identification we can no longer accept, but neither can we accept the exaggerated nationalism of the nineteenth-century historical school which at once in effect denies the universal in human nature and overlooks the all-pervading influence of international cultural relations. More simply, we shall say that law must vary with social conditions, and that these never recur. Exceptional circumstances may have made the revival of Roman Law on the whole beneficial, but it must have caused much injustice and much unhappiness. At any rate there can be no question of repeating or continuing the experiment. We have to do for ourselves what the Romans did for themselves, produce a law adapted to our own needs.

The unique experiment would not, however, have been possible but for the supernational character which Roman Law had attained in its last stage. It was anything but merely national, it was the law of an international civilization, and relatively universal. Hence its veneration in the Middle Ages as Natural Law was not entirely unjustified. But this point of view we have now left behind, and, though the material rules of Roman Law can never be a matter of indifference, its most important lesson for us lies in its method. That method is also what is most truly Roman in a legal system which, so far as its actual institutions are concerned, might almost be called Graeco-Roman or Byzantine.

III

In the universalization of Roman Law how much is due to Greek culture? The *Corpus Iuris* as a system is Byzantine, but its most valuable part is the Digest. The Digest is substantially classical, but was the classical law itself truly Roman? Discussion of Greek influence. The method of Roman Law comes from the Republic, and is national in origin.

The history of Roman Law shows us a very remarkable evolution. We see not only a crude primitive system brought to civilized maturity, but the law of a small peasant City-State transformed into the law of an international Empire. To this process the Roman character gave continuity: between the Twelve Tables (450 B.C.) and Justinian (527–65 A.D.) there are no revolutions in the tradition of private law. The history of a purely national system for a thousand years would be interesting enough, but it would convey no universal message. The Roman Empire, as it developed, created the idea of a supernational State, which since has never wholly left men's hearts. The creation of that idea would have been impossible without the creation of a supernational law, and neither creation would have been possible without the Roman character, the national *gravitas*, which enabled the Roman jurists to take reason, with its witness, the common customs of mankind, as the principle of their expansive interpretation, without indulging in the construction of speculative Utopias.

The tenacity of the national tradition was severely tested. There was a time when the new wine of Greek philosophy and rhetoric might have turned the lawyers' heads; they carried it like men, and were refreshed. Not much later came a time when public liberties were destroyed, and it might have seemed a natural corollary to make private rights the creatures of the State. Actually the development of private law proceeded almost undisturbed, gaining by the peace which the empire brought and losing nothing of its essential independence. There came a time when external pressure and, still more, internal dissension produced so profound a decay of the State and, as its remedy, so autocratic a concentration of powers that the secular tradition was wellnigh broken. But by that time the work of the jurist was an acquired good, a valued heritage, to be preserved, as far as might be, in the eastern surroundings to which the empire was more and more confined. The fourth and fifth centuries are a dark age for Roman Law, but at their close, just when the western provinces were being finally severed from the empire, we come upon an as yet unexplained revival of jurisprudence centred in the law-school of Berytus, which seems to have furnished the intellectual preparation for the compilation of Justinian's *Corpus Iuris* (527–65 A.D.).

Thus for a period of a thousand years there was both stability and progress. There was progress, by which is meant not that the law was always being improved materially, still less technically, but that a reasoned adaptation of existing rules to changing social environment was constantly at work. And there was stability; the work of adaptation was done within the limits of one continuous tradition.

There have been many conquerors, but there has been only one Roman Empire. The question arises which, one imagines, must recur elsewhere in this book, whether the explanation lies in the political genius of the Romans, or in the culture of one of the conquered peoples. How far was the construction of a supernational law, in response to the need created by the success of Roman arms, the work of mature Greek world-philosophy? Were the Roman jurists creators or only transmitters? An examination of this question leads to the conclusion that, while Greek culture, and to a less extent and at a later stage Christianity, were great factors in the evolution of the Civil Law, more particularly in its universalization, the juristic method which is its peculiar glory was a purely national creation of the Romans, having become a fixed tradition before the end of the Republic. This conclusion will direct us to the period in the history of the Civil Law which has most significance for us.

What has been known and venerated for centuries as the Civil Law, namely the *Corpus Iuris* of Justinian, is as a whole Byzantine work. This is clearly undeniable in regard to the Novels and so much of the Code as was originated by Justinian or his Byzantine predecessors, but equally in regard to the numerous alterations of classical materials tacitly made by the compilers of the Digest and the Code, undeniable in fact in regard to the *Corpus* taken as a system. If one had to apply it as such, one would doubtless start from the Code; that at least was the book upon which the mediaeval Glossators based their systematic *Summae*. But it is certain that they would not have troubled so much about the Code had it not been accompanied by the Digest. For it is the Digest which gives to the *Corpus Iuris* its special excellence and explains its continued influence.

The root of the matter lies in the Digest, which is a collection of excerpts or fragments from the works of the jurists of the classical period, that is, with a few exceptions, from writers of the first three centuries of the empire. Each fragment is prefaced by the name of the author and of the work from which it comes. But we are expressly warned by the introductory constitutions of the Digest that numerous alterations have been made in the classical texts. Since authentic classical texts independent of the Digest are extremely scanty, exactly how much was altered by Justinian's compilers is a delicate question, in fact the most debated question in the modern study of the Digest. The problem is of great interest, and might well receive more attention in this country, but it hardly arises in the present connexion, when we are speaking of spirit and method, and not of the detail of particular legal institutions. A great deal in the Digest is certainly due to Justinian, but there would have been no sense in his choice of this historical form if the substance were not classical. We may, then, take the Digest as fundamentally classical, without denying that Justinian undertook a colossal task when he set out to bring even selected classical passages into harmony with the law and ideas of sixth-century Constantinople.

The *Corpus Iuris* was a work of great merit. It carried much further the work of universalizing Roman Law which had been begun by the classical jurists. The pure classical law, had it been preserved, could not have influenced the Middle Ages as did the hybrid *Corpus Iuris.* An old-fashioned, but crushingly sensible, work, Troplong's *L'Influence du Christianisme sur le droit civil des Romains*, disposes of any inclination to exalt the pagan jurists at the expense of the Christian emperors. Except from one point of view : the really lawyerly contribution to the *Corpus Iuris* comes from the classical lawyers, as any one who has dipped into the Digest and the Code is aware. One of the merits of the Byzantine compilers, and that which secured the immortality of their work, was that they had the discernment to cling to the classical tradition, so far as the lapse of centuries seemed to permit.

The specially legal excellence of the Civil Law is therefore derived from the classical period, and it matters not that its transmission is Byzantine. But the influence of Greece upon Rome dates from even before the classical period. How far is the classical law itself truly Roman ? It is certainly surprising that the Romans should have produced a jurisprudence incomparably superior to that of the Greeks, who were far ahead of them in every other department of thought. Yet, even in their first enthusiasm for Greek culture, the Romans were as conscious of their superiority in law as they were of their inferiority in other spheres. This superiority, as we are now being taught,[1] was not due to any incompetence of the Greek mind in jurisprudence. They were rich in legal ideas, which were not just bright ideas, but formed a common and persistent racial stock. These ideas make a unity, but one which,

[1] Vinogradoff, *Greek Jurisprudence.*

though extraordinarily interesting to the comparative jurist, is not a legal unity. To hold and develop their ideas in a stout framework of tradition the Greeks lacked the political conditions and the character. Thus they enter the legal history of Europe only by their contribution to the cosmopolitan jurisprudence of Rome. It may then be asked whether what they lacked was not simply political unity and stability, and whether what we call Roman Law is not largely the product of Greek culture working inside the solid Roman organization?

The answer to these questions must distinguish periods. It is obviously true that in no historical period was Roman culture independent of Greek, and that as Roman Law advances Greek influence must be more and more taken into account. When we get to the empire national civilizations are disappearing. We are in the presence of an international civilization which is quite as much Greek as Roman. But lawyers are highly conservative, and of all traditions a legal is the most tenacious. The framework and technical method of the classical jurists descended to them in essentials from the Republic. They were a tradition that had been formed in a distinctly national period. Similarly, scholars have observed that it was in the language of the jurists that classical Latin survived longest.

Of course, even if we go back to the earliest firm standing-ground, we do not escape from the Greeks. The actual copying of Greek rules by the Twelve Tables (*c.* 450 B.C.) is insignificant, but, in insisting that the latitude which the vagueness of customary law left to the magistrate must be diminished by the enactment of a written code, the Roman *plebs* was but repeating, one may think imitating, a democratic claim that had been made in Greece and in *Magna Graecia*. The borrowing of a fundamental idea of this kind is more important than the adoption of concrete rules and institutions. In the obscure period between the Twelve Tables and the end of the Punic Wars, the institution, under treaties, of tribunals of *recuperatores* for *peregrini* immediately suggests Greek parallels, and the introduction of the formulary procedure towards the end of this period has been attributed with some probability to the influence of Rome's Hellenistic provinces. We need not here seek further verification of the hypothesis, *a priori* almost necessary, that during the period in which Rome became mistress first of Italy and then of the Mediterranean world, Greek institutions were affecting the development of Roman Law. But if Greece is to claim Roman Law, something more must be proved than that the Romans were ready to take individual ideas, even very important and in some number, from Greece.

The crucial period is the last century of the Republic, when a very great expansion of law coincided with the wholesale reception of Greek culture by the Roman upper classes. Since the human mind does not live in compartments, the domination of Roman education by Greek teachers and Greek thought had necessarily a powerful effect upon the one native intellectual pursuit of the Roman noble, jurisprudence. But here we encounter the fact that at this date the Romans were perfectly conscious that in law they were the masters of the Greeks. Some well-known lines of Virgil need not be recalled, but Cicero writes: 'incredibile est . . . quam sit omne ius civile praeter hoc nostrum inconditum ac paene ridiculum: de quo multa soleo in sermonibus cotidianis dicere, cum hominum nostrorum prudentiam ceteris omnibus et maxime Graecis antepono.' [1] While it is true that in their philosophy and to some extent in their method of presentation the late Republican and imperial *prudentes* were governed by their Greek teachers, in their fundamental method of juristic development they were independent, simply because it was a method that had already been formed and embodied in a professional tradition. The highly technical and national science originated by the old *pontifices*, who were the earliest lawyers, and elaborated by their

[1] *De Orat.* i. 44. 197.

successors, was able to absorb and digest Greek culture without loss of identity. The new learning, the *doctrina transmarina atque adventicia*, which worked in many directions as an anarchical solvent, proved for the law a wholesome food, necessary for its due growth in correspondence with supernational needs.

IV

Classical Roman Law a product of jurisprudence rather than of legislation. The Edict belongs to jurisprudence. Its importance under the later Republic in connexion with the formulary system. *Ius civile* and *ius praetorium*. Theory and practice of the *ius edicendi*.

THE result of what has just been said is that it is to the Republican period that we must give first attention, as being the period in which Roman Law acquired its specific quality. Moreover we may put legislation aside and concentrate upon jurisprudence because, like our own law, Roman Law was not in the main developed by legislation. Of course there were very important statutes. The Twelve Tables (*c.* 450 B.C.) in particular were so fundamental that Livy, doubtless exaggerating, could call them still the fount of all public and private law. The Republic and early Empire produced other less comprehensive, but important, statutes; still, in the whole pre-Byzantine period we can say that the development of the private law was in the main not by enactment, but by progressive interpretation and by the gradual formulation of custom.

The unenacted law was not a confused mass of shifting customs, but the steady tradition of a learned class, a tradition which at first sight appears rigid, but which in fact was ever expanding and absorbing, and becoming at the same time more scientific and systematic. In the creative period of the late Republic the praetor's Edict, an organ which on a strict analysis might be considered legislative, appears to compete with the *prudentes* in the work of development. But, apart from the fact that, like other formal sources, the Edict required interpretation, we shall see that both in its authorship and in its nature it belongs itself to jurisprudence rather than to legislation. Nothing can disguise the fact that the Republican law was the creation of a class of practising lawyers.

The Edict, however, deserves special consideration. It was an indispensable instrument of progress during the decisive period, and its peculiar operation imprinted indelibly upon Roman Law a technical characteristic, the antithesis *ius civile* and *ius praetorium*, which offers an interesting parallel to our own antithesis law and equity.

It cannot be understood without some reference to Roman procedure. Two kinds of civil procedure are found under the Republic, the archaic procedure *per legis actionem* and the classical procedure *per formulam*, the latter introduced about 150 B.C. They have in common the division of the action into a first stage before the magistrate (*in iure*) when the issue or point in dispute was defined, and a second stage before the private juror (*in iudicio*, normally before a single *iudex privatus*) when the issue was decided.

The difference between the earlier system and the later lay in the first stage, *in iure*. Speaking by way of general contrast with the formulary procedure, one may describe the *legis actiones* as highly technical rites in which the praetor and parties played parts fixed by law. In spite of the qualification *legis* it is clear that even after the Twelve Tables the appropriate formularies were left to jurisprudence; they were to be found at first in the archives of the *pontifices*. And, in spite of the inexpansibility of the *legis actiones*, which led to their supersession, new formularies were composed by a jurist as late as Sextus Aelius Paetus (consul 198 B.C.). The knowledge of the procedural precedents and the power of developing them gave the early lawyers control of the law at a vital point.

The later system was more elastic. The issue was reached

by informal debate before the magistrate (*in iure*), and was embodied in a written instruction to the *iudex*, called the *formula*, which ordered him to condemn or absolve the defendant according to the answer found by him to the question therein raised. Technically the parties had to agree to it (*accipere*), but practically they were governed by the magistrate's Edict, which announced what remedies the magistrate was willing to grant and, where necessary, the conditions of their being granted. It was in the Edict that one found the *formulae* of actions and the supplementary clauses, such as special defences, which might be added to them.

Without supposing the praetor to have been powerless under the system of *legis actiones* we can have no doubt that in this later procedure his powers were far greater. The Edict as we know it is bound up with the formulary system. The praetor's primary duty was to carry out the civil law; hence a large part of the Edict simply announced *formulae* raising a question of civil law. But it contained also, to take the most obvious examples, *formulae* raising either a question of civil law upon the basis of assumed fictitious facts, or simply a question of fact. The law resulting from these latter remedies and others was *ius praetorium*, as opposed to *ius civile*.

This opposition worked quite differently from our own opposition of law and equity, for the reason that there was no Roman court independently administering the *ius civile*. Hence, where the *ius praetorium* overrode the *ius civile* or granted a remedy unknown to it, the *ius civile* simply suffered a virtual extinction. In the English system the common law was administered by separate courts, and the legal rights which they recognized were the basis of the equitable rights enforced by the Chancellor.

No theoretical limits can be set to the changes which the praetor might introduce by his Edict as *ius praetorium*. Of course under the empire, like the other magistrates, he became dependent on the emperor and lost initiative, but, until the

Edict was stereotyped by Hadrian, each praetor in theory made his Edict for himself at the beginning of his year of office. It was simply a programme in which he announced how he intended to use his official discretion. But this is theory; practice was quite different. Though the office of *praetor urbanus* was not a professional prize falling regularly, like an English judgeship, to a highly skilled practising lawyer, the praetor invariably came from a close governing class, whose tradition of statesmanship included jurisprudence. He might of course be *prudens*, as a recognized legal authority was termed; in any case he could hardly escape knowing a good deal of law. Above all he was bound, like all Roman magistrates, to take advice, and in the drafting of his Edict he would be advised by the jurists of his *consilium*. Quite inevitably the Edict became traditional. The incoming praetor took over his predecessor's Edict in bulk, sometimes the experiment of a new clause would be tried, sometimes an old clause would be dropped as a failure. In this way the standing parts of the Edict were clauses which had stood the test of practice, and thus were combined the advantages of statutory and of customary law. There were certainty and definition, but also close touch with realities, constant testing by forensic and commercial practice.

In the last century of the Republic the Edict was the main instrument of the great advance in the law. In particular it introduced principles of fair dealing which were capable of indefinite expansion by later jurisprudence. Almost every progressive legal idea of this period may be brought under the rubric *ius gentium*, but we have purposely avoided identifying the *ius praetorium* with the *ius gentium* because, from the technical point of view, to do so involves a misconception both of the contents of the Edict and of the idea of *ius gentium* (see VII). We have also abstained from mentioning the edicts of the other magistrates who at Rome and in the provinces had a jurisdiction parallel to that of the *praetor urbanus*. What we have sought to make clear is that the urban Edict even in this its most creative period was an organ of jurisprudence rather than of legislation.

V

Republican jurisprudence a department of statesmanship, the *prudentes* representing the specialized ability of the governing class. The system of precedents. The beginnings of abstraction. The *responsum* system. Legal literature of the Republic and early Empire.

COMING to the jurisprudence of the Republic, we must first explain who the jurists were. A profession is to us a more or less organized corporation, usually endowed by the State with monopolistic privileges, the exercise of which is regarded as an honourable means of livelihood. Membership of the corporation is attained by definite steps, such as election or examination. In Republican Rome the *prudentes* were just a few men designated as such by a peculiar social tradition, to whom the exercise of their craft was not a means of livelihood, but part of a public career. In the earliest times jurisprudence was the preserve of the holders of priestly offices : *ius civile reconditum in penetralibus pontificum.* But from 300 B.C. onwards the priestly colleges were open to all, and moreover the practice of making a mystery of the law, which the Twelve Tables had failed to abolish, ceased. Any Roman youth who wished to become *prudens* could now attend the consultations, discussions, and instruction of some one who possessed the tradition. But Roman society was essentially aristocratic ; recognition as *prudens* was accorded by a public opinion which was governed by an intensely conservative and aristocratic tradition, so that the position was no more open to the talented under the Republic than was the *cursus honorum.* The names of the great *prudentes* of that period betray the freemasonry of the governing class, and even show a *de facto* maintenance of the ancient connexion between the science of law and the priesthood. Of course the Republican *nobilitas* was never absolutely closed, and the genius of a *novus homo* might extort recognition in the law courts as on the field of battle. But the *prudentes*, as a class, stood a little apart and distinct from the advocates; thus Cicero, though a good lawyer, was not *prudens*. There was no doubt as to who they were, and they were not numerous in any age.

This aristocratic tradition may seem a bad thing, but it was precisely what gave to Roman Law its exceptional combination of continuity and elasticity. One can imagine forms of class monopoly that would be simply harmful, the monopoly of a priestly caste or of bureaux of pettifogging scribes. But the republican *prudentes* merely represent the specialized ability of a great governing class, whose instinct was too sagacious to allow the science of law to slip into the hands of underlings. To this class jurisprudence was a branch of the art of government; it was the 'urbana militia respondendi, cavendi, scribendi'.[1] The class that created the Roman Empire produced the men to direct the national legal tradition and form it into a science. These men were not mere specialists; they were by their family position and careers too much in touch with the realities of government to be enslaved to technicalities. They developed Roman Law *pari passu* with the needs of the Roman State.

Just enough is known of the jurists before the closing years of the Republic to give an idea of their work. They were practical men, whose activity as jurists took the usual practical forms: they drafted a will, a contract or a release, they arranged a compromise, they advised on questions of law, particularly, though they were not ordinarily the actual pleaders, on the technical conduct of an action. That these activities were regarded as a high public service is illustrated by Pomponius' statement[2] that a Scipio Nasica was given a house in the *Via Sacra* close to the law courts for the convenience of his

[1] Cicero, *Pro Murena*, 9. 19. Cp. *de Oratore* i. 48. 212.

[2] *D.* i. 2. 2. 37.

consultants. Their method was a method of precedents, which Englishmen should be the last to underrate. A jurist who seeks to determine a present case from precedents must evidently proceed through a general principle, though he may not make it explicit. The older juristic literature, compiled before the effects of Greek influence began to be felt, seems to have consisted of commentaries on the Twelve Tables, of collections of formularies, especially procedural, and of *responsa* (to be explained hereafter). To Cato the Censor's son (died 152 B.C.) can probably be traced the first conscious abstraction of the general from the particular, by the formulation of *regulae iuris* which expressed general principles in maxims. It is significant that we know him to have been imbued with Greek rhetoric. From his works, says Pomponius, *ceteri oriuntur.*[1] But the process of abstraction was already implicit in the system of precedents. The essential difference lies between the man who, basing himself on actual decisions, proceeds to apply the principles they involve to a further case, and one who constructs a system of abstract principles derived from his philosophy. The former is the true juristic method, and it remained the fundamental method of Roman Law in spite of the increased power of abstraction and systematization which Greek culture bestowed.

The *communis opinio* of the *prudentes* in the last resort settled the law. It was elicited in practical forms, of which the most characteristic is that of the well-known *responsa*. The *iudex*, to whom fell the decision of a lawsuit, would, as a Roman of the upper classes, generally know some law; indeed we hear of learned lawyers whose services as *iudex* were much sought after. Like the praetor he had a *consilium*, and this might include legal experts. The *auctoritas rerum perpetuo similiter iudicatarum* is stated by one classical jurist [2] to possess *vim legis*, and another [3] writes that, in a disputed question of local

[1] *D.* i. 2. 2. 38.

[2] Callistratus, *D.* i. 3. 38.

[3] Ulpian, *D.* i. 3. 34.

custom, the first matter to consider is 'an etiam contradicto aliquo iudicio consuetudo firmata sit'. But the authority of *iudices privati* in making binding precedents could not be that of professional judges, still less that of the judges of our own central courts. Authority of this sort belonged to the *prudentes* owing to a peculiarly Roman practice.

It was common for the *iudex* or a party in a case to lay a statement of the facts before a *prudens*, who, on the hypothesis that the facts were correctly stated, gave a *responsum*. This was just the solution of its giver, and its authority depended on his position in public opinion. The whole thing, one can hardly call it system, was curiously unofficial, but in practice the *responsa prudentium* had a binding authority, both in the actual case and as precedents, equivalent to that of an English judgement. This method of legal development by precedents is a striking similarity between the two greatest legal systems, and it remained to the close of the classical period the fundamental method of Roman jurisprudence. If a *responsum* was theoretically only persuasive, it was persuasive by authority rather than by argument. 'Iurisconsultorum valent responsa etiamsi ratio non redditur.'[1] It does not seem to have occurred to any one to question them.

In the last half century of the Republic Greek influence on the jurists becomes plain, and the resulting advance is great. It was accompanied by a great growth of literature, which continued under the Empire. The first systematic treatise on the civil law comes from Q. Mucius Scaevola (consul 95 B.C.). It seems to have been much concerned with the definition and classification of legal concepts according to Aristotelian logic. Some of its discussions about *genera* and *species* reported by Gaius look like the immaturities of neophytes. Still it was a great step forward when by the side of collections of precedents and isolated *regulae* appeared a scheme of law conceived as a logically connected whole. The ground gained was con-

[1] Seneca, *Epist.* xv. 94. 27.

solidated by Cicero's friend, Servius Sulpicius Rufus, whose numerous disciples close the republican and begin the imperial period.

Practically nothing survives of the republican literature; what the Digest has preserved of the imperial, though but a fragment, is too much for more than summary review. It comprises collections of *responsa* and of casuistical discussions (*quaestiones*, *disputationes*) and monographs, but also systematic works in the shape both of elementary manuals (*institutiones*) and of treatises on a large scale. System, however, except in the sense of internal coherence, was not a virtue or a vice of the Roman lawyer. Thus the large treatises on the *ius civile* were based on a traditional order settled by Massurius Sabinus (middle of first century after Christ), and those on the *ius praetorium* on the order of the Edict, which itself, even in the stereotyped form given to it by Salvius Julianus under the instructions of Hadrian, is only very loosely systematic. The method of the jurists remained fundamentally casuistic and practical. It is true that there are occasional traces of scholasticism; what seem to be purely academic questions are at times unduly prominent; over certain topics Greek metaphysics appear to be exercising a bad influence. The very growth in bulk of literature necessarily tended to substitute learning and compilation for origination. It is to be remembered that we owe both our selection and the present form of the classical literature to a later age of scholasticism; nevertheless the impression that it makes is overwhelmingly practical.

VI

The effect of the change from republican to imperial government upon jurisprudence. Effect on the Edict and on the *responsa*. The *ius respondendi*. Growth of autocracy. Effect of the removal to Constantinople.

The displacement of republican by imperial government was necessary for the evolution of the City-State into the empire. A consequent extension of autocracy into the sphere of private law was to some extent unavoidable, and in itself was likewise favourable to the process of universalizing Roman Law. But there was no revolution. The destruction of public liberties so bitterly described by Tacitus had not its counterpart in a conception of private rights as emanating from the emperor. On the contrary, jurisprudence reached its zenith in the comparative peace of the first two centuries. The credit for this result belongs in part to the emperors themselves, who had the wit to see that their rule depended on the greater security it afforded to the ordinary man in his person, family, and property. But chiefly it belongs to the national respect for law, to the conception of law which the republican jurists had established. Law to the Roman was not simply something positive and enacted, but existed in its own right in order to satisfy human needs. The early emperors themselves adopted this point of view, and though naturally their rescripts struck a more legislative note than the old *responsa*, in substance they identified themselves with the professional tradition of the jurists.

Nevertheless things could not be quite what they had been, but then the work that remained to be done was one rather of detailed development than of creation. The *ius civile* was already pretty well settled, and the chief *negotia iuris gentium* had already emerged; the distinction will be explained below (§ VII). The effect of autocracy upon the Edict itself, as distinguished from its interpretation, is well marked; it became less creative under the imperial control which was secured by the fact that the whole magistracy had become dependent. The position of the *prudentes*, that deeply-rooted source of aristocratic power, required more delicate handling. Essentially it was respected. Augustus merely brought the *responsa* to some extent within the imperial influence by giving to certain jurists the *ius respondendi ex auctoritate eius*, an institution which existed as late as Diocletian.

We may best judge of the nature of this innovation by the

answer given by Hadrian to certain petitioners for the privilege a century after it had been instituted. Roughly it was this [1]: 'I am delighted that any one who has confidence in his powers should offer his *responsa* to the public, but the privilege of giving them on my authority is one which I grant of my own motion, not in answer to petitions.' In effect the emperor tells the petitioners that there is nothing to prevent them from giving *responsa*, with such authority as their own professional reputation may confer. But one suspects that Hadrian, *more suo*, had his tongue in his cheek, and that here, as elsewhere, his name marks a definite stage in the movement towards centralization. The days when without the imperial *ius respondendi* a man could hold the independent position of a Labeo under Augustus were past.

Inevitably the authority of the *prudentes* must have come to depend more and more upon designation by the emperor, less and less upon public opinion; a gradual transition which respected the traditional conception and science of law. The old connexion between jurisprudence and a public career was not broken. From the time of Hadrian the leading lawyers exercised much of their influence as members of the imperial *consilium*; their handiwork is visible in the drafting of rescripts, one class of which took the form of the old *responsum*. In fact, in the decay of legal science witnessed by the third century, the old traditions appear to have died hardest in the imperial Chancery; the last words of the true Roman tradition are to be read in the rescripts of Diocletian, which remain classical in form and substance.

The transfer of the real centre of government to Constantinople was accompanied by the fall of this last stronghold. Some continuity with the tradition of the *prudentes* was doubtless preserved in the higher tribunals and in the law schools of the East, but the Law of Citations (426 A.D.) and the character of the constitutions of the fourth and fifth centuries are

[1] Pomponius, *D.* i. 2. 2. 49.

witness how feeble. Yet there were pressing legal tasks ahead, and in the absence of science they were accomplished chiefly by imperial legislation which, unsatisfactory as it was, did much to prepare the later history of Roman Law by carrying its denationalization a stage further. By it the national peculiarities, not to say archaisms, which lingered in all departments of the classical law, but especially in the family law, were smoothed away. The formulary procedure disappeared, and a system of a more modern type took its place. Moreover the acceptance of Christianity involved the creation of an entirely new branch of public law dealing with the Church, which proved not the least important contribution of the *Corpus Iuris* to mediaeval jurisprudence. But, apart from certain reforms which are demonstrably due to the new Christian ethic, it is not clear that the change of religion affected the private law to any great extent. On general considerations one would expect a reaction to it in all departments, and it has been maintained that a softening of the hard individualistic lines of the classical masterpiece which can be detected in the Digest is due to its influence. But, apart from the question how far the classical law has indeed been modified in this sense, the difficulty is to show that the equitable tendency is specifically Christian and not simply Hellenistic.

VII

The universalization of Roman Law. The two stages in the process. The *Constitutio Antonina.* The second stage by legislation, the first by jurisprudence. In the first stage the doctrines of *ius gentium* and *ius naturale.* The liberalism of classical law. Equity and legality.

We have just observed that the denationalization or universalization of Roman Law was only completed, and in a technically inferior manner, by the autocratic legislation of the eastern empire. The *Corpus Iuris* of Justinian is commonly treated as the ultimate term in a continuous evolution. There is truth in this view, but it obscures a change in the nature of the process. In the classical period the evolution can be attributed to liberal and equitable principles working organically, in the later period it is mainly a result of the external circumstance that the stream of Roman Law was gradually confined to its eastern channel, where applied to various oriental populations it was bound by simply practical exigencies to lose its remaining national characteristics.

The change in the nature of the evolution may, from this point of view, be fixed at the passing of the famous *Constitutio Antonina* (212 A.D.), by which Roman citizenship was, with exceptions not relevant here, granted to all *peregrini*. To this measure, although it was but the culmination of a gradual extension of citizenship, there were strong objections from the juristic point of view. In Roman Law, especially, but not only, in the departments of family law and the law of succession, there still remained a core of purely national institutions. These now became applicable to masses of new citizens who did not understand them, and at the same time, particularly in the civilized East, strongly-rooted native institutions were abolished. To take a standard illustration, the *Constitutio Antonina* not only threw open to the Greek provincials the Roman contract of *sponsio*, but also closed to them their own native custom of written contracts.

The result was that native custom persisted, and Roman Law was garbled in the attempt to adopt it. We have thenceforward to distinguish between the law which the central government held to be valid and the law actually in force in various provinces. The former is Roman Law, the latter a number of versions of it adulterated by local traditions. It is an idle question whether jurisprudence, if it had not at this period undergone a rapid decline, could have unravelled this tangle. Without the sword of legislation it probably could not have done so. At any rate, the situation was actually dealt with by hand-to-mouth legislation, culminating in the great synthesis of Justinian.

It would be desirable, in conclusion, to speak in more concrete terms of the process of denationalization or universalization than has been done hitherto. To attempt to do so for the later period would, however, result in a catalogue of legislative reforms connected mainly by the practical need of accommodation to Hellenistic custom. But substantially the same problem had been proposed to Roman legal statesmanship by the existence of the Roman Empire in a much earlier period, though before the *Constitutio Antonina* it could be largely shelved by leaving the provincials to their own law. There had long been the question what law a Roman tribunal was to apply to a *peregrinus.* The classical answer was found in a partial denationalization of Roman Law, which was reached by doctrinal methods and does admit of a short characterization.

Roman Law began by being *ius civile*, applicable only to Roman citizens, but in quite early days the *ius civile* was to some extent simply thrown open by grants of *ius conubii* or of *ius commercii.* These grants remained exceptional, because not generally suitable, and other solutions had to be sought. To some extent the Romans adopted a system comparable to modern private international law, consisting of rules referring questions of marriage, status, and succession now to the Roman and now to the foreign law. But the most general solution was found in the idea of *ius gentium.*

The *ius gentium* may be defined[1] as the universal element, in antithesis to the national peculiarities (*ius civile*), to be found in the positive law of every state, a philosophical distinction with no obvious practical bearing. As applied by the Romans to their own classical law the *ius gentium* in this sense covers a great deal; not much of family law or of the law of succession, though certain praetorian principles were referred to it; certain parts of the law of property; nothing, curiously enough, of the law of civil wrongs, but almost the whole of the law of

[1] Cf. Gaius, I. I.

contract. This very enumeration, however, suggests that the *ius gentium* bore two different senses. The philosophical sense covers what we have enumerated, but means no more than that an institution said to be *iuris gentium* is found in principle at Rome as elsewhere; for instance, slavery is said to be *iuris gentium*, but its detailed regulation is *iuris civilis*. But when, on the other hand, Gaius (about 160 A.D.) states that he is speaking of that kind of partnership (*societas*) which is *iuris gentium*, he implies a point of practical law, namely that a Roman court will enforce such a partnership regardless of whether the parties are *cives* or *peregrini*. In this practical sense the *ius gentium* covered only those rules, institutions, and principles of actual Roman Law which, owing to their simplicity and correspondence with the general practice of mankind, were applied to *cives* and *peregrini* indifferently, the *ius civile* describing, in this antithesis, those not so extended. Under the *ius gentium* in this practical sense fell almost the whole classical law of contract and little else.

From the practical lawyer's point of view this narrower sense is more important than the philosophical. Involving as it did the recognition of a common law of contract throughout the empire, it must be reckoned one of the greatest achievements of classical jurisprudence. At the same time, to represent the *ius gentium* as simply a dogmatic juristic construction is from the historical point of view one-sided. It expresses very well the extension to *peregrini* of such specifically national practices as the stipulatory form of contract and release by question and answer, but with regard to the greater part of the law of contract, which is what *ius gentium* in the practical sense amounts to, what has to be explained is its very existence and its application to Roman citizens. For example, the so-called consensual contracts (sale, hire, partnership, mandate) are not institutions of the original *ius civile*, found on reflection to be *iuris gentium* and therefore extended to *peregrini*, but are evidently alien to the original Roman system.

For historical explanation we have to turn to the jurisdictions established at Rome from an early date to deal with cases in which *peregrini* were concerned. About these we have little information. We know that they were at first regulated by international treaties, and that from 242 B.C. there was a special praetor, 'qui inter peregrinos ius dicit'—(*praetor peregrinus* as opposed to *praetor urbanus*). We must infer that the only rules which these courts could apply were derived from the customs generally observed in the commercial intercourse of the Mediterranean peoples. The body of custom so formulated by Roman magistrates (Edict of *praetor peregrinus*) must have contained a strong tincture of Romanism, but is nevertheless the most probable beginning of that decisive departure from the formalism of the ancient civil law which is the characteristic of later Roman Law.

Thus the practical needs of intercourse with and between *peregrini* caused the definition and enforcement of a body of customs roughly coinciding with what was afterwards, and perhaps already, called the *ius gentium*. The penetration of the law as between citizens by this younger body was in historical times most visibly promoted by the semi-legislative power of the (urban) praetor's Edict. But that is not the whole story, for on that showing the *ius gentium* ought to have been mainly *ius praetorium*, whereas in fact transactions belonging to the *ius gentium* so important as the consensual contracts were sanctioned by full civil law actions. These must therefore have been incorporated in the civil law by custom, at first extra-judicial and therefore inconspicuous, taking shape as the recognized practice of honest folk and not merely of *peregrini*, then perhaps asserted in the unrecorded arbitrations of forgotten *boni viri*, and ultimately crystallized in actions granted by the urban praetor at dates when the sharp distinction between civil and praetorian law had not developed.

Later the edictal development of new civil law actions in response to custom remained a possibility, but the main edictal innovations took the form of *ius praetorium*. To what extent the urban praetor borrowed directly from his peregrine brother our ignorance of the early history of the Edicts makes it impossible to say. For the mere fact that an institution is said to be *iuris gentium* tells us nothing on this point, because once the philosophical conception of *ius gentium* had been formed under the influence of Greek theory and in connexion with the doctrine of *ius naturale*, innovations adopted because reasonable would in general fall of themselves under this head. Thus the sum total of the *ius gentium* in Roman Law came to include all that was progressive in that law; it was that increasingly large part which could be developed by reason unfettered by the archaic and stereotyped traditions of the old *ius civile*. Its distinguishing feature was its departure from the formalism of the old *ius civile*. But a tough core of *ius civile* survived, chiefly in family law and the law of property, until after the end of the classical period, and was not thoroughly expelled before Justinian's legislation.

Greek philosophy introduced before the end of the Republic the kindred conception, *ius naturale*, which meant, apart from special views, the law imposed on mankind by common human nature, that is by reason in response to human needs and instincts. The two ideas were identified as early as Cicero, though there is a theoretical distinction and some jurists distinguished. There remains in any case the difference of appeal. Still the virtual identity shows the fundamental harmony of Greek and Roman views of life.

The doctrine of *ius naturale* has often been regarded as the dominant force in the juristic development of the early empire, but in modern times a different view has prevailed. Like that of *ius gentium*, it was in itself only a reflection upon existing law, gave in itself no legal sanction to what was not otherwise law, and was overruled in cases of conflict by what was law. Cicero [1] preaches its superiority to positive law, but we look

[1] *De Repub.* iii. 22. 33 (Lactantius).

in vain for a Roman jurist who asserts that principle of subordination of positive to natural law with which later ages have been too familiar. The principle is, in fact, anarchic, and confuses the functions of legislation and interpretation. The greatest influence of the idea of *ius naturale* was exercised centuries later, but there is a danger of underrating its importance in Roman Law itself.

In our own law such notions as reasonableness, *boni mores*, public policy and convenience, equity and good conscience play a considerable part. They provide a wide margin for juristic development, and we have been taught [1] to appreciate the influence which a theory of ethics, by dominating educated opinion, has exercised upon our case-law, and not merely upon our legislation. Similarly, Roman Law made use of common-sense standards such as *aequitas*, *bona fides*, *aequum et bonum*, *bonus paterfamilias*, *dolus*, and, though there was no attempt to deduce the law from an imaginary state of nature, the philosophy of law held by the jurists gave to their handling of these humbler notions a breadth and freedom which they might otherwise have lacked. Besides giving a deeper meaning to the practical idea of *ius gentium*, the idea of *ius naturale* provided the judgements of common sense and common morality with a philosophically based claim to universality and with a theoretical consistency which chaotic goodwill can never afford.

The older Roman jurisprudence had been highly formalistic and literal. *Summum ius summa iniuria*, and yet formalism and literalness are necessary as checks upon the vague equity known as 'doing justice between man and man', which commonly ends in generosity at the expense of justice. Classical jurisprudence managed to combine a liberal spirit of equity with the steadying element of legality. Equity, in the strict technical sense, peculiar to English Law, of *ius praetorium*, was not altogether arrested by the fixing of the Edict, for the

[1] Dicey, *Law and Opinion*.

later interpretation of the Edict by the jurists was extremely bold. Further, a new source of equity, approximating it is true to legislation, had arisen in the development of law by imperial rescript. More important, because all-pervading, is equity in the broader sense of humane interpretation. It would be impossible here to study the concrete solutions of the great jurists from which their method has in the main to be derived, and of direct discussion of method there is little in the Digest, which is a practical law book. Still, its third title is devoted to the methods of interpretation, though with primary reference to statute law. Brief and pithy, this model of classical elegance should be read ; it cannot be summarized. On the one hand are the immortal canons of equitable and benignant interpretation : 'Scire leges non hoc est verba earum tenere, sed vim ac potestatem', and again : 'Benignius leges interpretandae sunt quo voluntas earum servetur' [1] ; on the other hand insistence on respect for the interpretation settled by practice and custom : 'Minime sunt mutanda ea quae interpretationem certam semper habuerunt',[2] and again : 'Optima est legum interpres consuetudo'.[3]

Doubtless it is to the new spirit which Hellenistic culture breathed into the traditional methods of the republican jurists that we should attribute much of the liberalism of the later law. To it we must refer the clear formulation of the moral purpose of law and of the sublimity of the jurist's vocation which appears in the definitions of jurisprudence as *iusti atque iniusti scientia* and as *ars boni et aequi*, and in the picture of the jurist as the priest of justice.[4] Fine phrases, expressing an ideal which the Roman lawyer-statesmen, *veram nisi fallor philosophiam non simulatam affectantes*,[5] had for centuries made real.

F. DE ZULUETA.

[1] Celsus, *D.* i. 3. 17, 18.

[2] Paul, *D.* i. 3. 23.

[3] Paul, *D.* i. 3. 37.

[4] Ulpian, *D.* i. 1. 1 ; 10. 2.

[5] Ulpian, *D.* i. 1. 1. 1.

TEXTS AND ENGLISH LITERATURE ON ROMAN PRIVATE LAW

1. Texts. Those outside the *Corpus Iuris* are collected in Girard's *Textes de droit romain* and in Riccobono's *Fontes iuris Romani.* Add Part II of Bruns's *Fontes iuris Romani antiqui.* Editions of special works with translation and commentary: Moyle's *Institutes of Justinian*, Poste's *Institutes of Gaius*, and Muirhead's *Institutes of Gaius* and *Rules of Ulpian.* The best edition of the *Corpus Iuris* is the Berlin stereotype edition in three volumes.

2. Literature.

(*a*) *Elementary.* Chapter 44 of Gibbon's *Decline and Fall*, of course out of date. Murison's new edition of *Hunter's Introduction to Roman Law.*

(*b*) *More advanced.* Sohm's *Institutes of Roman Law* translated by Ledlie (historical; brilliant and readable). Buckland's *Elementary Principles of Roman Private Law.* Muirhead's *Historical Introduction to Roman Private Law* (ed. Goudy).

(*c*) *Advanced.* Buckland's *Text-book of Roman Law.* Roby's *Roman Private Law in the Times of Cicero and the Antonines.* Greenidge's *The Legal Procedure of Cicero's Time.*

FAMILY AND SOCIAL LIFE

Of all the vehicles by which the Legacy of Rome has been conveyed to later ages the most important by far is Roman Law, but it is not from the dry rulings of the lawyers alone that the legacy can be understood. The lawyers were not the creators of what is most valuable in their legal system. Roman Law, so far at least as it enshrines a legacy of culture, is rather an expression of Roman character—a deposit of Roman common sense working through the centuries on problems as they successively arose—than the creation of any outstanding men of genius. What we have most need to study is not the work of Papinian or Paulus or Ulpian, of whom two at least were not Romans at all, but the outlook on life implied in the principles which it was their business to set in order and elaborate. And if in Roman Law it is not the famous names which matter so much as the spirit behind the whole, the same is true of Roman history in general. Herein lies one of the many differences between Rome and Greece. The permanent contribution of Greece to mankind is concentrated in the monuments left as a possession for all time by its poets, historians, philosophers, and craftsmen—a comparatively small number of great men who themselves were the highest achievement and consummation of their race. But with Rome it is otherwise. Figures, it is true, like Lucretius and Virgil, Julius Caesar and Augustus, stand out far above the heads of their contemporaries: but it is not in men such as these, nor in any small number of individuals, that we can find expressed the whole character of the people. To grasp not only how Rome came to be successful in the task of building up an empire greater in every sense than the world had known before, but also why her success was deserved, we have to look deep down into the lives of humble men and women in the back-street and the village whose virtues and whose failings made Rome what she was. These are the people who were Rome: their spirit is the spirit of Roman Law. It is they whom we want to know; and to find them as they really were, still uncontaminated by foreign influence, we must go back to early days and begin with the Republic.

The social history of Rome down to the reorganization set on foot by Augustus in the time of Christ falls into two periods, between which the division lies near the middle of the second century B. C. In the former Rome was not seriously affected by the Hellenistic East: in the latter the oriental influence became so strong that there was serious danger of the old Roman traditions being lost. How far the Romans had to sacrifice the ideals of their fathers the sequel will show; but the interest lies rather in the extent to which, thanks to their extraordinary tenacity of what was good, they managed to preserve their treasure against the alluring blandishments of eastern depravity.

The ancient world differed from the world with which we are familiar in many ways, and particularly in one which it is not altogether easy to appreciate. Nowadays we find morality, less definitely perhaps than in the past but still quite plainly, bound up with religion, and it is from religion at least indirectly that for the average man morality still gets its sanction. But in Greece and Rome, where ideas of a future life were elusive and uncertain and where the gods of the popular belief were remarkable least of all for either the care or the practice of morality, this was not the case. In both, though of course there were more esoteric cults of which it is not true, public religion was an affair of contract between man and God in which the obligation on the human side was for no more than the due performance of the proper rites at their appointed times. Save for the half-hearted attempt, made by Philo of Alexandria at the beginning of our era, to fire decaying Hellenism with the moral zeal of the Jewish law, there is hardly a sign of religion coming to the aid of tottering morals until the great message of Christ conquered Greece and Rome alike. Till then morality fared as best it could alone. Greece, through licence and ill-discipline, had collapsed: the glory of Rome is that she did not do the same.

What religion on one side failed to provide was made good on another by the most interesting of all Roman institutions—the family. It was at home that the Roman acquired the virtues that he held in highest honour, and what these virtues were it is worth while to inquire in some detail. Virtue itself is a Latin word, but its meaning has somewhat changed since Roman times. To the Romans manliness was its connotation; but in the early days when its meaning was acquired, manliness was most prized in the form of courage on the field of battle, so that the chief association of *virtus* was always with physical bravery. More interesting to us are the other kinds of excellence which by degrees won for themselves a place by the side of courage as life grew gentler and the social structure developed in complexity. What they were we know from many sources: according to Cicero it was *gravitas*, *pietas*, and *simplicitas* that the influence of the home was expected to supply. And in these was expressed the genius of the Roman people. The first meant no more than the serious sense of responsibility which makes even the smallest affairs of life seem things too great to be trifled with, but only to be decided after long consideration of the result. *Gravitas* to-day is a Caledonian characteristic; and in the ancient world it was this peculiarly Roman quality which made Rome generally a stranger to the unthinking enthusiasms of the moment which produce a last state worse than the first. When Rome was induced to make a change, the change was usually a success. *Pietas* was the natural corollary to this—the attitude of proper submission which *gravitas* creates to all established institutions. When Virgil was embodying in Aeneas the qualities of the Roman race and made his hero above all things *pius*, it was no mere sanctimonious other-worldliness that he had in mind, nor indeed anything purely religious at all. *Pietas* to the Roman was only a general acceptance of the powers that were, both human and divine, so that in its widest sense it means little more than the expression of discipline in relation to authority. Finally there is *simplicitas*—the quality of the man who sees things clearly and sees them as they are. The Romans have often—and unjustly—been called unimaginative by critics content with an unsympathizing knowledge of the Roman mind from the outside alone; but though they never rose to the tremendous heights of Greek speculation, so long as Livy, Lucretius and Virgil survive there will not be wanting proof that the Romans had an imagination of their own. Their peculiarity was that it did not carry them away: they were saved from that by their *simplicitas*, which enabled them at need to keep their feet firmly planted on the ground. How fully this habit was developed, their success in terrestrial matters may be left to show.

Such were the virtues for which the Romans held themselves indebted to the family—the unit in the Roman social structure upon which depended the well-being of the whole. Our word 'family' itself is an inheritance from Rome; and in essence its meaning is still unchanged, even though the *familia* in Italy was not in all respects the same as a family to-day. Such difference as exists is due to the *familia* having been more than the parents and their offspring: it included not only these but their servants, their retainers and, what was more important, their household gods as well. In times even earlier than the dawn of Roman history the *familia* had its centre in a kind of wigwam, like those whose type is preserved in the hut-urns of the Early Iron Age in Latium which are familiar objects in Italian museums; and in the age of history this core survived in the *atrium* or central living-room of the later Roman house. But what matters is not the house itself so much as the fact that the house was at the same time a home in the fullest meaning of the word, and it is of the home that the Romans can claim to have been the creators. In earlier times and in other regions of the ancient world homes, as we understand them, were things unknown: all that the Greeks, for instance, could show was the house and nothing more, a place to eat in and to sleep in and to be used as a harbour for the holder's property. With the Romans it was different. What they felt about their homes we may gather from a speech delivered by Cicero in 57 B.C. After he had been forced into exile the year before, his political enemies had torn down his house and, what was worse, by a characteristic abuse of religion had tried to prevent its ever being rebuilt by dedicating the site to Liberty. On his return Cicero pleaded for its restoration, and on his side he had all the Roman prejudice against the destruction of a home. Even when allowance is made for rhetoric justified by the occasion, it is safe to say that his words, to have a point at all, must have expressed a sentiment which the audience would share. 'Is there anything', he asks, 'more hallowed, is there anything more closely hedged about with every kind of sanctity than the home of each individual citizen? Therein he has his altars, his hearth, his household gods, his private worships, his rites and ceremonies. For all of us this is a sanctuary so holy that to tear a man away therefrom is an outrage to the law of heaven.' This home life was an invention of the Romans, and an invention which had vast results.

Of the two kinds of denizens—divine and human—to be found in the Roman home, first for the divine. In the far-off days when thought was young the simple forbears of the Roman stock seem to have peopled with spirits the most prominent features of their environment. There were spirits of the fields and spirits of the woodland that lay beyond; but besides these there were spirits inside the house. There was Vesta of the hearth, the Penates of the store cupboard, the Lares, whether spirits of the dead ancestors or of the family estates does not matter now, and the Genius of the *pater-familias*—the power through whose presence he was enabled to perform the duties of his station. These were the forces—forces soon personified—with which the early Romans felt themselves surrounded in their homes; and though in course of time their nature changed and they no longer preserved so closely their primitive associations, they still remained to serve as symbols of the home belonging in all its independence to one family and to one alone. To the Romans, Lares and Penates always meant what the words still mean in English to-day; and it was the household cults which held out longest against all attack and survived when the State gods had been killed by the influence of Greece.

More important, however, and more interesting than the divine elements were the human. Here the core of the group was to be found in what we should call the family—the father, the mother, and the children; but round them clustered besides a number of other people, both bond and free, whose lives in one way or another were bound up with this particular centre. They were the slaves and retainers, but still they were entitled to inclusion in the *familia*. Over all the human beings whose place was in this little social world various degrees of power were wielded by the father at its head; and though there were certain limitations in its exercise which it was customary for him to observe, in reality to all alike he came near to being absolute master. His power even went so far as life and death—not in theory alone but in actual practice. So late as the age of Cicero there was a famous case in which a senator named Fulvius put his son to death for having taken part in Catiline's conspiracy against the State. Only in the second century A.D. was this kind of thing made a criminal offence; nor was it until the time of Constantine, when the influence of Christian ethics was being strongly felt, that any serious steps were taken to make illegal the action of a father who decided after the birth of a child that he would not bring it up himself, but expose it to die or meet any other fate it might come by at the hands of some chance finder.

Yet the rule of a father was no rule of mere savage brutality. His power was great; but had it been regularly abused, the power itself would never have survived. The reason why abuse was scarcely known in a system so full of danger is to be found in that respect for tradition which, as we have said, was one of the most familiar features of the Roman mind. Paternal authority, vast as it was, could never be exercised with impunity except in accordance with a law which lost nothing of its force because it was unwritten; and that law, whatever its severity, was always unswervingly just. In reality the father of a family held a position more like that of a judge than of a tyrant, but still of a judge whose authority to enforce his decisions once made was unchallenged. Such was the *patria potestas*, enduring because it was good, which above all was responsible for the discipline which made the Roman people.

This was the setting of Roman education; for in the healthy days of Rome education began at home, and at home, so far as it was of permanent value, it ended. The training of the later age, when among the rich at least discipline and duty were yielding their places as ideals to the ambition for personal success, is a subject which it is no loss to ignore. Notoriously, when two cultures meet, it is by the less laudable elements of the elder that the younger is attracted; and this was what happened to Rome when she came to know the Greeks. Along with much that was good Rome learned from Greece a great deal that was bad. Of the latter kind was the Greek training in rhetoric, which unfortunately found a soil well prepared for its reception among the governing class of Rome. Its results were almost wholly evil: by making persuasiveness its end instead of truth, by setting plausibility before honour, it produced an effect on Roman culture of a kind for which Rome had no reason to be grateful. But rhetoric was a thing alien to the Italian peoples, and it may be left. To see Roman education unaffected by the influence of the East one must go back to the second century B.C., when men were still to be found who clung tenaciously to the traditions of their ancestors. Such a one was the elder Cato. The tale is familiar of how in 155 B.C. the Athenians sent an embassy to Rome to beg for the reduction of a fine which had been laid upon their city. Naturally for this purpose they appointed three of the most famous rhetoricians at their command—Carneades, Diogenes, and Critolaus—although not one of the trio was an Athenian by birth: their eloquence was all that mattered. When they arrived in Rome, they began to use their spare time in giving not only displays of rhetoric but also instruction in their tricks to any one who cared to listen, and so great was their success that the young men of Rome, and even their elders too, were carried away by the charm of the new revelation. Then old Cato stood up and urged that these aliens should be sent home with all possible speed. It was for the youth of Greece to sit at the feet of men like these: the sons of Rome should give heed only to their rulers and their laws, as in the past. In a contrast like this the Roman ideal of education appears in all its strength and all its weakness. Discipline was the aim; but it was discipline unleavened by the culture which alone can make life more than a weary round of thankless toil. Roman devotion to duty is a high example to posterity; but it was an enthusiasm which too often fell short of complete success through its failure to stop and ask the reason for its own necessity.

It happens to be in connexion with the elder Cato that a considerable amount of our scanty information about early Roman training has been preserved. Besides a few scattered fragments from the works of Cato himself there is a chapter on this subject in his biography by Plutarch. From Cicero we know what the Romans thought were the ends to be achieved. Among people like them in their early days whose enemies were so many and so near, it was natural that physical courage should hold a foremost place from which it was only gradually deposed. Yet this was almost an easy thing to attain in comparison with other forms of virtue which by the time of

Cicero were recognized as more important. Mere reckless rashness may pass for the true courage which sees the dangers and is undismayed; but it was harder to counterfeit the virtues of a more peaceful age. Of these the chief were three. Self-control comes first; second is obedience to all authority from parents to the magistrates of the State; and third is *benevolentia* —something like charity or goodwill—to one's neighbours. So much may be gathered from Cicero; but to these must be added that self-respect which alone makes possible the moral life. Old Cato knew its value. A wife and a son, as he said, are the holiest of all holy things; and rather than degrade his boy by entrusting his education to a slave, he preferred to turn schoolmaster himself. It would be bad enough that the child should be rated by a slave, but worse by far that he should be in debt to a slave for so precious a thing as education. So Cato set to work. He trained his son in manliness by riding, boxing, swimming in the Tiber, and practice with the weapons of war—occupations which bore fruit when the boy won a name for courage at the battle of Pydna. Self-control and charity, as these were understood at Rome, he learnt above all from the example of his parents. The comfortable and corrupting habit of consigning children to the nursery was alien to Rome: it was more in accordance with Roman ways to do as Varro's parents did—to keep the children with them even at meals to wait upon their elders and to listen to their talk. But besides this there were the tales of early Rome—tales, we may guess, like those of Horatius and Coriolanus which each had a moral of its own. These were the reading-book, and the story goes that, rather than let the boy miss anything of the traditions of his race, Cato wrote them down in large letters with his own hand. In this it was the stories that mattered: reading and writing for their own sakes were an affair of small importance, picked up by degrees from father or mother without any sort of system. Of culture and refinement, of an attempt to develop individual gifts, there is nothing to be seen; not altogether because culture was despised, but also to some extent for the reason that men of Cato's stamp thought meddling with the Muses a too risky pastime. But already in the second century there were those who took another view. Hellenism by now was making its attractions felt among the richer class. Aemilius Paullus, conqueror of Macedon and father of four sons, entrusted the education of them all to philosophers and rhetoricians brought from Greece. Nor was he condemned by the result: one of his sons grew up to be Scipio Aemilianus.

In appearance the Roman training was no more than Cato gave; but in reality there were other influences as well. The mere belief, which everybody shared, that there were spirits peopling every feature of a boy's surroundings could not be without some effect. Their presence he was never allowed to forget. Not only were there the rites of the deities within the house to serve as a reminder, but in the farm as well there was a ceremonial to be performed over almost every operation in the yearly round. Of such a kind was the procession of the Ambarvalia which, towards the end of May when crops were ripening and harvest hopes were high, made a solemn circuit of the fields to fend off evil spirits from the corn. And such things did not happen on the countryside alone; cities too needed their protection and got it in the same way. The rite of the Ambarvalia was no more important in ancient times than many others; but it has a special interest in the modern world because it was adopted by the Christian Church and by the Church brought into England. It is to the Roman Ambarvalia that we owe Rogation-tide processions through the fields, and with the Roman practice too is connected our beating of the parish bounds. Christianity of course has changed the meaning of the ceremony: nowadays its purpose would presumably be called the invocation of a blessing from the deity. In Rome it was different—to keep away unholy powers, powers which were always very near. And when it is remembered that rites such as this happened in Roman times not once a year but almost every week, it is not difficult to realize how hard it was for a Roman to forget that he was always in the presence of beings greater than himself. All around him was an unseen world, and before its denizens he felt that awe which man must always feel when he is face to face with powers mysterious, inscrutable, and beyond control. That feeling is what the Romans called *religio*, and if a people may claim to be religious merely because it shows this attitude of mind, then no people in the world's history has been more religious than the early Romans.

If religion cannot be neglected in the formation of Roman character, hardly less important was the influence of the mother. From the time when the child ceased to be an infant right on until it was old enough to be the companion of its father it was the chief object of its mother's care, and in later centuries it was this devotion to their children which was thought the greatest glory of the early Roman matrons. The nature of the power they wielded was a result of the general position held by women in the Roman world, and it was here that the Romans made one of their most notable advances on their predecessors. It is an old tale which tells how Gaius Gracchus, even when he was a man and holding office as tribune of the *plebs*, bowed to his mother's judgement in affairs of state. At her request he is said to have withdrawn a bill wherewith he had intended to avenge the murder of his brother ten years before. And it was not her sons alone who knew how much they owed to their mother's care: Cornelia was honoured by the State itself when her statue was set up at public expense with the inscription 'Cornelia, mother of the Gracchi'. But in this the Gracchi were by no means unique: even within the range of our scanty information there are several others, and of these the most interesting, if only we could get at the facts, would be Julius Caesar the dictator. For how much he was indebted to his stern mother Aurelia we shall never know in detail; but of one thing we are as certain as in such a lack of evidence we can ever be—that until her death in 54 the influence of Aurelia was second only to that of Caesar himself in moulding his career.

In coming to women we have reached the very heart of Roman civilization. Home life, by its presence or its absence, can make or mar society, and it is on women that a healthy home life depends. It is not the occupation of the women that makes the difference, but rather the general attitude taken to them by the men; and this is just as important in societies like that of ancient Egypt, where the women seem sometimes to have gone out to work while the men stayed at home, as it is in those of the type with which the modern world is familiar. There have been many periods in history when passion has run wild and men have regularly had recourse to violence and outrage for the settlement of what we should regard as ordinary questions of the day. To some extent this was the case in Greece, where the worst curse of political life was the readiness with which men took up arms against their fellow citizens for the furtherance of party ends. What this faction and the struggles it produced meant in Hellas is familiar to every reader of the third book of Thucydides. This hardness of heart, this readiness to set smaller store by human life than by the most insignificant of causes, appeared again in the world of Rome at a time when Hellenism and Christianity were combining to produce a single effect—the reduction of women to a status far below that which had been theirs in the days when Roman ideals still retained their pristine purity. The Christians of the early church freely butchered their opponents or, what was meant for worse, did all that human malice could to consign them for eternity to the torments of the damned, merely for some difference of opinion on points which nowadays few men have heard of and fewer find it worth their while to understand. Against insanity such as this woman is no unfailing prophylactic; but still it remains true that in both these periods of history, and in others too where conduct of this kind is found, the cruelty characteristic of the age appeared in a society where the home was a thing of small account and women were regarded as definitely the inferiors of men. Of course it would be absurd to suggest that the influence of women is always humane; but that is not the point. What really matters is that women on the whole, when they are allowed to build up round themselves a proper home, seem somehow to have a sobering effect on their husbands' conduct in wider spheres. In the scraps of information which newspapers convey from the areas of industrial dispute to-day it is possible to see how this is so; and the history of the past suggests the thought that it would be seen more clearly still in a great loss of sanity among the men, if suddenly home life were brought back to the embryonic condition which we find, for instance, in some of the Hellenic states.

The position of women in Rome is not altogether easy to understand, because here, as with many other Roman institutions, theory and practice did not agree. The law at least was severe: in principle it allowed women no independent existence. In early days marriage always involved the husband's being invested with the power called *manus*, which gave him over his wife all the rights which he held over their children in virtue of his *patria potestas*. The meaning of this, as we have seen, was that he could even go so far as to put his wife to death; and this theory in fact survived, though perhaps in a somewhat mitigated form, at least so late as the first century of the Empire. Tacitus has a tale, interesting not for this reason alone, of an affair which caused some stir in Rome during the principate of Nero in 57 A.D. A senator named Aulus Plautius, who had been in command of the military force with which Claudius had invaded Britain fourteen years before, was married to a lady named Pomponia Graecina. In 57 this lady was charged with the acceptance of a 'foreign superstition', which means in all probability that she was suspected of being a proselyte to the Jews; and since the

Romans at this time commonly believed that Judaism was incompatible with marital obligations, it was not unnatural that the decision in this case should have been left to her husband. Whether this Pomponia was in reality one of them 'that be in Rome, beloved of God, called to be saints' whom St. Paul addresses, whether in fact the 'alien superstition' was not Judaism but Christianity, and whether or not Pomponia's burial place has actually been found in the Catacombs of Callistus, are questions which here need not be raised. Rather we should notice the way in which her husband with a council of the lady's relatives tried the case, obviously with power to pass some kind of sentence. It happened that Pomponia was acquitted, but we can guess what her fate would have been in the other event. Though at so late a period she would scarcely have been put to death, she might certainly have been banished by a punishment hardly less severe to some remote and perhaps pestilent island in the Mediterranean. This was the fate which, at the hands not of her husband but her father, had befallen an even more famous lady, Julia the only child of Augustus. Her morals approached modernity more closely than befitted the daughter of one whose policy was to restore what was best in the Republic, and finally after a scandal more shocking than the rest she was banished for life by Augustus, not as emperor but in virtue of his paternal power. For five years she was kept on the miserable rock of Ventotene, and even then the sentence was only modified so far as to let her end her days a prisoner at Reggio di Calabria.

Such were the lengths which theory allowed. Under ordinary circumstances the Roman practice towards women was very different. At the beginning of republican times traces are to be seen of a movement towards emancipation: already in the Twelve Tables women may hold property. In home life this tendency showed itself in a development of the forms of marriage ceremony. The ancient rite of *confarreatio*, which was the only kind of Roman marriage with a religious as well as a legal side, seems generally to have consisted of offering to Jupiter a cake of *far* which was afterwards administered sacramentally to bride and bridegroom in order to break down the *tapu* which otherwise would have been violated by their intercourse. The legal effect of this ceremony was to create in the husband complete marital authority over his wife, and the feature most interesting to us is that, so far as our imperfect knowledge goes, the form of service seems to have included nothing that set a limit to the wife's subjection. More advanced than this was the second method of marriage—by what was called coemption. Whatever the origin and meaning of this may have been—and the Romans themselves did not know—its effect, as Ulpian says, was to prevent the wife being regarded as a slave, to enable her in fact to use towards her husband the famous phrase 'Ubi tu Gaius, ego Gaia'—'Where you are master I am mistress'—a phrase which was the Roman way of expressing the partnership of man and woman which is typical of Roman marriage. Marriage by the third form—*usus*—was a simpler affair: when man and woman had lived together for a year, the state deemed marriage to have taken place and recognized the husband's marital authority. The interest, however, does not lie here so much as in a provision found already in the law of the Twelve Tables whereby the legal passage of the woman into the power of the man who was in fact her husband could be avoided. For this purpose it was enough for her to pass three nights a year outside her husband's house, and so long as no year was allowed to run without this *usurpatio trinoctii* the wife's legal position remained what it had been before her married life began.

The first impression which this arrangement gives is not the true one. Its purpose was not to license concubinage, but rather to avoid the legal consequences of marriage which, since they involved the wife's passing into the *manus* of her husband, were incompatible with the more developed attitude towards women. There was all the difference in the world between a mistress and a wife—even a wife of this latter kind who wilfully avoided the *manus* of her husband; and this difference was marked by the payment of a dowry, the visible indication that the parties concerned intended their union to be permanent. Divorce of course was easy—dangerously so indeed—but the risk of the social structure being undermined thereby was not so great as it might have been in other circumstances. One condition in particular was working for the preservation of a sound married life. What we call love-matches between boy and girl, whereby a pair scarcely yet come to years of discretion commit themselves to a pact which ought to last as long as life merely at the bidding of transient emotion, were not the Roman practice. And nowadays it is matches like these which are largely responsible for the laborious days of judges in our divorce courts. From this disruptive element the social life of Rome was free, because there love was supervenient—the effect rather than the cause of marriage. The Roman method was, while the parties were still no more than children, for the betrothal to be made not to suit their own opinions but in accordance with the judgement of their parents; and strange though it may seem to us the result was not to drive love from married life. It is true that in theory the consent of both parties to a marriage was required, but *patria potestas* at all times seems to have been so strong that it was scarcely possible to escape the parents' choice. In the letters of that many-sided mediocrity the younger Pliny there is a famous case of Roman match-making, interesting in particular because the groom at least was a grown man old enough to determine his own fate. Rusticus Arulenus and Junius Mauricus, both intimate friends of Pliny, were brothers, and when Arulenus was put to death by Domitian for having been rash enough to admire in public Paetus Thrasea and Helvidius Priscus, the two leading Stoics of the last generation, his brother Mauricus took over the guardianship of his family. When the time came to find a husband for the daughter, Pliny was consulted, and among his letters is one in which he runs his candidate. Just the man is providentially at hand, a certain Minicius Acilianus of Brescia, who was a senator and had already held the praetorship; and this with all his other virtues, his family, his income and even his complexion, Pliny trots out with the enthusiasm of a dealer selling horses. That was the Roman way—to make the choice as carefully as might be and leave the love to come later on. In their betrothals the Romans pinned their faith to the reason of fifty where we trust the emotions of twenty-two, and here as usual reason showed that it could hold its own against the rival.

Such was the development of marriage forms which accompanied the advance of Roman women to virtual equality with their husbands, and how real the companionship came to be may be seen from sepulchral monuments of every kind. When death came at length to one or other of the pair, the survivor honoured the memory of the friend who had gone by a stone on which were written words that still have a tale to tell. Praises vary, as of course they must; but the familiar abbreviation S·V·Q—'sine ulla querela', without a quarrel—to describe the relations which had been, are an indication of the frequency with which the Roman and his lady shared a single life often for nearly half a century. This is a small sign; but greater are not wanting. Most famous of all is a document preserved on stone from the time when Julius Caesar and Augustus were rescuing the world from chaos. It is a memorial, in the form of an address to the dead, set up to his wife by a Roman gentleman who had been in great danger for political reasons during the Civil Wars. The tale is one which has been told before, but it is one which will always bear re-telling. Lucretius Vespillo and the lady Turia—we may call them by these names though they are not known for certain—were betrothed in the years of war between Caesar and Pompeius, and even at this early time the bride was able to render her future husband some services which were the first of many benefactions for which his gratitude is recorded. After various vicissitudes the couple were married during the dictatorship of Caesar, but on his death a new peril befell Lucretius when he found his name in the fatal list of the proscribed. Then came a fresh series of adventures in which husband and wife were apart, nor did they meet again until Turia had passed through the ordeal of an interview with the brutal Lepidus for her husband's sake and Lucretius had finally been pardoned by Octavianus. Thenceforward they lived together in a happiness which would have been complete if there had been children in the house; but when on this account Turia proposed that she should leave her husband for him to take another wife, Lucretius cries out that he almost lost his reason at the thought of parting from the lady to whom he owed so much. For this was a case of love; and as he says when his wife had died and their forty-one years of married life were at an end, with her faithfulness and obedience, her gentle kindness, her care for the business of the house, and her simple piety unspoilt by new beliefs, Turia could claim all that a man could give—and all that Lucretius regrets is that he could give no more.

Yet this does not mean that the Romans were sentimental: they were not. 'Never kiss your wife unless it thunders' was a precept of old Cato's; but he of course tended towards severity. Indeed, apart from having taken a boat on one occasion when he might have walked and having lived intestate for a single day, he used to boast that his only regret in life was that once he had entrusted a secret to his wife. That was going too far: the ordinary Roman would not treat his wife like that. Even old Cato himself, as we have seen, knew that a wife and a son are the holiest of all holy things; and it was a daughter of the younger Cato who wounded herself to make her husband Brutus, the assassin of Julius Caesar, share with her his most private thoughts. But on the other hand in their appreciation of women, as in all things, the Romans retained their sanity. At Rome the freedom of women did not involve their pretending to be men, nor did they feel themselves aggrieved at exclusion from the few occupations for which by nature they are not equipped. Inevitably there were exceptions, but they were rare. We hear occasionally of lady doctors in the Roman world, and more often of women who essayed to practise at the bar. Valerius Maximus even gives a chapter to the female pleaders, among whom was one Afrania who 'harried the bench with her barking' in the last days of the Republic; but Valerius is very like a Roman when, after saying that she died in 48 B. C., he ends his account with the remark that 'it is better to record the death of such a creature than its birth'.

So far the picture has been bright; but as time went on there were developments which it is as unpleasant to dwell upon as dishonest to ignore. In the last century of the Republic there began a process which in the end was responsible for the most far-reaching results. The basis of the ancient economic system was slavery, and in course of time it became the custom to give slaves their liberty with a generosity which ever grew more free. In a generation or two, if not at once, the descendants of these freedmen achieved the full citizenship of Rome, and so, since the slaves themselves were in most cases Greeks or Orientals, the population of Italy and its neighbourhood became steadily more oriental in its composition. The Orontes flowed into the Tiber, and when Juvenal rises in his wrath thereat it is no mere influx of eastern creeds and eastern manners that he decries, but rather the spread of a new race over his native land. It was these people who brought with them the new cults from the East; but for our purpose what was more important was the eastern morality which they brought as well.

Though they were by no means rare on the countryside, the fact that these freedmen in the majority of cases had been domestic slaves and not slaves employed on the land was responsible for the tendency they showed, so soon as they had won their liberty, to congregate in the towns and particularly in Rome; and it was just there that during the first century the social structure was in no condition to absorb them without damage to itself. It is not to be suggested that their influence was wholly bad: indeed, both immediately and still more in the course of a few generations they were productive of much that was good. There can be no denying that at least from the time of Claudius to the end of the Flavian epoch the Greek freedmen were the most efficient body of administrators in the service of the empire; they had a *flair* for business which, for all his canniness, the Roman lacked. And again in justice it must be said that to a great extent these men were the ancestors of that free proletariate which from the beginning of the third century played a vital if unspectacular part as social ballast during the stormy history of the later Empire. But in spite of this, at the time of their first appearance they had an effect which cannot be admired. The mere fact that they had been slaves had ingrained in them a materialism which slowly grew more pronounced as time went on. Money is the one reward which a slave can appreciate, and money remained the god whom these slaves served even after their enfranchisement. For that they are not to be blamed: it was only their misfortune that they had not been bred in the tradition of free Romans to make not wealth but duty and honour the end for which a good man ought to live. And yet it was not without reason that the true Romans of the age loathed this freedman class with a detestation which finds uniform expression in the works of men so various as Martial and Tacitus, Juvenal and Pliny. From them, and still better from the *Satyricon* of Petronius, we can see the cause. In part it was jealousy at the sight of men vaunting what they chose to call success, but a still stronger spring of hatred was that disgust which is familiar in all ages at new-won wealth when it is concentrated in the hands of those who lack the culture to use it aright. Every time Pliny moved out of Rome by the *via Tiburtina* his wrath must have been roused, as we know it was, by the great monument of Pallas, the freedman whom Claudius made his minister of finance and who amassed a fortune three hundred times as great as the census of a senator. And all around there were displays of vulgar ostentation—palaces built with pillars of precious stone and baths with pipes and basins of solid silver—to arouse the envy and outrage the taste of Romans who had neither the desire nor the opportunity to acquire wealth on a scale such as this.

Yet mere vulgarity is a vice which is venial when it stands alone. The real danger of these freedmen to society lay deeper. Already in the last phase of the Republic the increase of wealth and its uneven distribution had created class-divisions within the state which boded no good for its welfare in the future, and it was by the advent of the freedmen that these divisions were hardened to a dangerous degree. Society split up into groups—groups hostile to one another—and when there is hostility of this kind the result is that men inevitably set loyalty to the group before loyalty to the State. Of this disruption jealousy and disgust at the egregious performances of the upstart were the immediate cause, but behind them lay that pride of race which at all times—and not without justice—was characteristic of the Romans. Popular opinion always regarded the Greeks as an inferior people, and there was even some taint attached to men who came from the country towns of Italy. Cicero was scoffed at by his enemies because he was a *municipalis eques* from Arpinum, and on one occasion the Emperor Gaius sought to do public insult to the memory of Livia herself, the wife of Augustus, by recalling that her maternal grandfather had been a local magistrate at Fundi. But in course of time the danger passed. Many of the Roman families died out, chiefly through their own selfishness in keeping down the birth-rate, and those that survived, even if they were strong enough to resist, were slowly reconciled to the new order when first a native of Reate, then an officer from Spain, and finally men from every quarter of the empire climbed on to the throne of Caesar. The old Rome at last was conquered by the races she despised.

For the nationalities which won the heritage of the conquering stock this was in many ways a gain, but a gain at the cost of great damage to the Roman ideal. In Rome itself and the larger cities the old tradition scarcely survived: only in Roman law and in the sheltered country parts of Italy, particularly in the north, did it find protection from the oriental attack. Life in the city of Rome under the empire is an unsavoury subject of which little need be said. That there was a general moral collapse there can be no denying. When the ruler of the Roman world first had his own mother assassinated and then set his subjects a lesson in behaviour by scouring the streets at night with a band of drunken friends to waylay and rob the passers-by, a puritanical atmosphere was not to be expected. With the example of their emperors on the one hand and the vagaries of freedmen *parvenus* on the other, with every kind of accepted religion called into doubt by the scepticism of Greece and with the old calls of duty lulled into silence by the seeming security of an age which was sinking into coma under the incubus of growing bureaucracy, the Romans found themselves surrounded by temptation without a guide to keep them on the path. They were left free to win themselves one new vice after another, urged thereto by forces too numerous to recount. Only one of these deserves a special mention. This was the unbounded increase in the number of slaves who, as always happens, brutalized and demoralized their owners in general and the womenfolk in particular. Like women in most ages, those of imperial Rome found it impossible to exercise aright an absolute power over their fellow creatures; and they grew cruel. It must never, of course, be forgotten that in the long run the tendency was clearly for the treatment of slaves to become more humane; but at the same time it must be confessed that during the first and second centuries of the Empire there was a great deal on which it would be unpleasant to dwell. There is much exaggeration in Juvenal's 'Legend of Bad Women'; but there is also much that is true. The wife who for a mere whim crucifies her husband's slaves is no invention, nor indeed is it likely that her husband would feel as much indignation thereat as was felt by Juvenal: for Juvenal, despite all his faults of judgement, had moral fervour enough to set him above the more revolting prejudices of his time. But about the brutality of the average inhabitant of Rome when he was writing there can be little doubt, and it is not a matter for surprise. Wealth was so great and slaves were so plentiful that there was no economic reason for kindness as there had been in earlier days; and besides this, predisposing men to violence, was the wide-spread fear that, had they only known it, Rome was really in the power of the vast hordes of slaves quartered in the house of every substantial citizen.

This attitude to slaves was only one sign of decaying morality. There were evils even more serious. The new ideals which had come in from the East where home life was hardly known, overlaid on the Roman reluctance to suppress the female sex, ended in the spread at Rome of a moral licence which finally destroyed its victims. The Greek view of woman was that she should be the silent servant of her husband, too far inferior because too little educated to share his life with him and under no responsibility save for the most ordinary domestic routine. When this ideal was brought to Rome, where such effacement of the women was impossible, the result was that they clung to the care-free life of the house that was not a home sanctioned by Greek tradition, without surrendering the claim to equality with their husbands justified by Rome. So there arose the race of unlovely women who bulk large in the history of the early empire—all unattractive, some repulsive for their attainments as intriguers, poisoners, adultresses and even worse—the destroyers of the Roman home, who taught every one with whom they came in contact to live for themselves alone. In the sordid picture which the age presents the only feature of encouragement is the promise of extinction which their selfishness contains. Already by the end of the Republic race-suicide had shown itself to be a threat full of danger, and social legislation aimed at an increase of the birth-rate was at once among the most important and the least successful undertakings of Augustus. But limitation of families went on with ever-increasing rigour until by the time of Hadrian there had ceased to exist all except one of the great houses which in the age of Cicero had formed the aristocracy of Rome.

It was against the licence of which such things were the result that at length there came a long-awaited protest from the Christians. In the apostolic age the Christian attitude to women was by no means severe; but though this generosity continued into later times, by the side of it there soon developed a movement in the opposite direction. When Christianity saw the effects on civilization of this unbridled liberty among women, it inevitably and rightly reacted towards a more stringent view—a view less liberal than the Roman, but still a view which circumstances made necessary. The Roman emancipation of women had to be annulled when woman was no longer able to use her freedom aright; and so the new tendency was in the direction of the Greek ideal whereby the wife was the humble servant of her husband and no more. Veiled as it is in sophistical quibbles about the sanctity of the married state, this seems to be the origin of the feeling which Tertullian was expressing in his famous outburst to the female sex—'Know that each one of you is an Eve. . . . You are the doorway of the devil: you are the unlocker of that forbidden tree: you are the first violator of the divine law. You it is who so easily destroyed man, the image of God.' The last charge is the most serious, and the implication is that the characteristics shown in the early days of Eden still survived.

If the upper classes in the city of Rome were corrupt, the

state of the common people as a whole was no better. At all periods in its history Rome has been peculiar among the great cities of the world in never having become industrialized. Though there was inevitably a population of small workers supplying their own wants and those of their neighbours, the great surplus which in the ordinary course would have been engaged in production for export was not only without employment but without any prospect thereof. These were the people who lived, if they were lucky, in the great blocks of tenements built in the style of a modern slum, where home life was a thing utterly unknown and where the chief interest was in bread and games provided free. Nor was it only the lower classes who lived like this. The poet Martial, who if he was not rich was at least not a pauper, had a third-floor flat, and in an earlier age so great an aristocrat as the dictator Sulla spent part of his youth in the top story of a lodging-house which he shared with a miserable freedman. It is a curious fact of history that in domestic architecture these cramped and top-heavy warrens, of whose type we know something from the excavations at Ostia, are the legacy of Rome, and not the Roman house with its *atrium* which was the embodiment of Roman family life. A life of indolence in conditions such as these did not make for a population of much value to the world, and unfortunately Rome was rich enough to keep these useless mouths in an idleness which ever claimed to grow more luxurious at other people's expense. It is an unpleasant thought that of the three most impressive material remains of ancient Rome—the Colosseum, the Pantheon, and the Baths of Caracalla—two were created to satisfy the class of whom Rome had least reason to be proud. Though men and women of every station thronged the great amphitheatres in a crowd far more frenzied than can be seen even at a football match to-day—and in a crowd that was bestial in its tastes as well—it was from the idle mob that the demand for these amusements had first been felt. And for the mob too were chiefly meant the great public baths whose ruins are still gruesome to every one who can picture the orgies of effeminacy run mad on which their walls looked down.

But as time went on Rome became less and less representative of the Roman world. Of the two great Roman towns which the spade has laid bare, Pompeii—the home of a degraded people who would have met no more than their deserts if all instead of a mere handful had perished in the ashes of Vesuvius—is a monument of the depth to which Rome and some other cities of Italy had sunk, while African Timgad is an enduring memorial to the undiminished vigour of the Roman ideal far and wide in the second and third centuries A. D. There in the bleak uplands of the Aurès the French excavators have exposed a town which flourished and was strong from the time of Trajan onwards, and it was in countless places like this that the traditions of Rome survived. In Italy itself there were regions where they were still vigorous, although the literary men of the time concentrate so much on Rome and the vices it contained that in their remains the healthier if less exciting people of the countryside are apt to be forgotten. Yet it was now that there occurred the wide extension of agricultural tenancy which is the aim of the wise landlord in the work of Columella; and when tenancy was spreading at the expense of slave-worked farms directly under the great landowner we have an indication that, though many of the tenants were not altogether prosperous, the state of country life on the whole was sound.

Nor were the richer people all without their virtues. At this period the better side of the educated class found expression in what may generally be called Stoicism, not in Stoicism as a body of doctrine—for as such it had many obvious defects—but in Stoicism as an attitude or an outlook on life. In an age when men were being carried off their feet by the wild rush for wealth, when in the race they baulked and jostled their competitors in an access of unbridled selfishness, it was all gain that there should be a great class which believed that virtue is its own reward, that virtue is the one end in life, that virtue is the only title to power and that in virtue even a slave may excel the highest in the land. To the brutal slave-drivers whom Juvenal depicts Epictetus has a word to say. 'Slave that you are yourself, will you not bear with your brother who is sprung from God, from the same seed and of the same heavenly descent as you ? . . . Remember what you are and whom you rule—that they are kinsmen, your brethren by nature, the offspring of God.' Men who could hold that doctrine were not likely to be quite devoid of charity to their neighbours. In their homes the Stoics applied their teaching and upheld the claims of decency and family life, but though their thought clothes itself in the garments of contemporary philosophy, the body within is really the ingrained tradition of Rome still vigorous and with its value unimpaired. Though they saw around them much that was vicious and disgusting, many men of the early empire whose writings have come down seem to have lived a life which old Cato might have praised. Seneca and Tacitus, Juvenal and Pliny all have a high view of woman as she ought to be, and with that before them their views on other things as well were worthy of their ancestors. Nor was it all a mere ideal. To this age belongs some of the purest family affection known in the ancient world; and if a single instance must be enough it is not because more are wanting. Arria, who stabbed herself to show her husband Caecina Paetus the way to death, may have been an abnormal woman, but Calpurnia, the third wife of the younger Pliny, was a more ordinary mortal. She was a woman who made it her business to share to the full her husband's interests, reading books because she thought he liked it, filled with hope for his success when he had to make a speech in court, setting his verses, such as they were, to music and listening in rapture behind a curtain when he was reciting his compositions to his friends. And all this, as Pliny says, she did for love. But the love was not on her side alone: Pliny's letters to her show that his own feeling was just as strong. When she was away he kept her portrait by his bed at night and wandered by force of habit to her empty room at the accustomed hour of the day; he implores her to write not once a day but twice; and when she is ill he is tortured with anxiety.

Pliny and Calpurnia were a pair in domestic life above reproach. But if their life in the second century A. D. had been unique, if with them and their contemporaries the force of a great ideal had died away, they would be the objects of a melancholy interest indeed. Fortunately they are not; and that is what the modern world should remember. They were not the last survivors of a bygone past, but belonged rather to a class which kept alight the torch of Roman tradition in the most stormy period and handed it on to a new generation in whose hands it burned bright again and shed its light over the age of the Antonines, the golden age of the ancient world. To the end the tradition was remembered. In Italy there were many Plinys, many in his own station and still more in the humbler walks of life, and in the provinces there were men like the sturdy burghers of Timgad, all guarding their inheritance. The inheritance was never lost, but preserved and handed on to posterity; and it is because of this preservation that the deeds of the Romans, in their failures no less than in their success, always bear the stamp of greatness which makes them seem worth while and raises them above the dead things of the past to be a possession precious in every age.

HUGH LAST.

BOOKS RECOMMENDED.

*W. WARDE FOWLER, *Social Life at Rome in the Age of Cicero* (Macmillan).

T. G. TUCKER, *Life in the Roman World of Nero and St. Paul* (Macmillan).

*SIR S. DILL, *Roman Society from Nero to Marcus Aurelius* (Macmillan).

W. E. H. LECKY, *History of European Morals from Augustus to Charlemagne* (Cap. ii).

J. DONALDSON, *Woman; Her Position and Influence in Ancient Greece and Rome, and among the Early Christians* (Longmans, Green & Co.).

* The works marked with an asterisk are of especial value.

RELIGION AND PHILOSOPHY

A MAN may leave as a legacy either wealth which he has inherited or wealth which he has himself made. And the former no less than the latter in passing through his hands is almost bound, if he is a man of character, to acquire some touch of his personality which transforms it into something new. The house which he has inherited from his ancestors will be modified or added to, it may be even rebuilt, and the park and gardens laid out afresh, so that they all bear the stamp of his character and generation and pass to his children with an aspect different from that which they wore in his father's day. Now our inheritance from Rome is of both kinds. In some fields, such as that of law and administration, the wealth we inherit was of Rome's making: the great fabric of laws was built up by her lawyers, and in the administration of her empire the work was of necessity her own, for the problem was without previous parallel.

In the sphere of religion and philosophy it might well be thought that Rome's work was that of transmission. If it were that alone, our debt to her would still be incalculable. That Greek philosophy was spread abroad, that it survived the gradual decay of Greek culture, was due to its conquest of the Roman educated mind. 'In the second Punic War,' says a characteristically prosaic early Roman versifier, who chronicled the literary history of his country, 'the Muse with winged feet' (like the god Hermes) 'made her entry into the savage, warlike race of Romulus', and from that moment the Muse was assured of immortality and universal acceptance. Still more indisputable is the debt of transmission which we owe to Rome in religion. Thanks to the 'paved ways' (*viae munitae*) of her empire Christianity was able to pass abroad from the little

Jewish community of Palestine to Asia Minor, to Greece, to Rome itself, and thence to be diffused again westwards and southwards; thanks to the Roman commerce in ideas Christianity was brought into touch with Greek thought and so strengthened in its theology; and it was owing to Rome's ultimate adoption of Christianity as the state religion that it became the accepted creed of the civilized world.

The debt to Rome as an intermediary is obvious and all-embracing: without her the religious and philosophic thought of modern Europe would be impossible. Yet if Rome were a mere intermediary, there would be little to chronicle: she might occupy the place of a great 'wireless' installation, which, receiving a message from abroad, radiates it out to the world; the world devours the message, but it is of little moment from what centre it is diffused. The purpose of this chapter is to ask the question whether Rome was indeed in religion and philosophy a mere receiver and transmitter, or whether she has not left on both a certain characteristic impress which has modified them and enriched them, the traces of which may still be found in modern modes of thought and practice. The answer will, I think, in the main be this: that Rome gave a practical turn to philosophic thought, which infused into it a new vitality and is a permanent element in the philosophy of Christianity and the modern world; that she created by a philosophic eclecticism, reacting on her own natural bias, a type of character which is the foundation of the accepted ideal to-day; and that she established for good or for ill the conception of an institutional religion.

The task is one of analysis: we must endeavour to disentangle from the complex mass of our Graeco-Roman inheritance that which is of really Roman origin. And the simplest and most satisfactory way to accomplish this is to take the advantage which history gives us, and watch the skein, as it were, in formation. If we can trace in a brief sketch the process which went to the making of current thought in imperial times—the thought which passed on into the Middle Ages or received new life at the Renaissance, and so became our inheritance—we shall be better able to detect what is characteristically Roman in it: for we can pause at each stage and ask what elements in it have been handed on to us. Nor need we attempt too strictly to keep apart the threads of religion and philosophy, for it will be found to be one of the characteristics of Roman thought—in this respect unlike the Greek, but nearer to our own—that the two were fused: when philosophy came to Rome, it was at once applied as the test of religion, and out of philosophy again sprang the religious thought of the empire.

The foundation is laid far back in the religion of the early Roman people—an agricultural community of united households. The nature of this religion is really a discovery of the last fifty years—the result of a patient digging beneath the surface of such works as the *Fasti* of Ovid, the remains of Varro, the history of Livy, and the garrulities of Macrobius and Aulus Gellius. But much has been written about it now—in England especially by Warde Fowler—and it is not necessary here to do more than recall very briefly its main features. It was a religion in the stage which anthropologists know as animism, the recognition, that is, of the presence of spirits, not of developed or anthropomorphic gods. To the Roman mind these spirits were localized: each had its sphere—a wood, a hill-top, a spring—and within that sphere it exercised its will. The characteristic word for such a spirit is *numen*, which, if it can be translated in a single English word, must be rendered 'will': 'the word suggests', says Warde Fowler, 'that the Roman divine beings were functional spirits with will-power, their functions being indicated by their adjectival names', such as Silvanus, Neptunus, Portunus, and many others. Now the Roman even in these early days was a practical man, and he thought in the concrete terms of his own daily life; although he could occasionally allow himself such a wide general conception as that of Iuppiter, the spirit of the sky, the main development of his religious thought lay about his life in the fields and his life in his home. Hence on the one hand the establishment of a great series of festivals marking the seasons of the agricultural year, such as the Saturnalia, or sowing, the Robigalia, for the aversion of mildew, the Consualia, for the storing of the harvest, and on the other the unique series of household deities which consecrated the various parts of the house—Ianus, spirit of the door; Vesta, spirit of the hearth; the Penates, spirits of the store-room; and the Lar familiaris, probably a field-spirit, brought indoors in the first instance as the tutelary spirit of the slaves of the household. In its sphere the 'functional will' is powerful: it must be approached with a sense of awe—for this is what *religio* appears at first to mean—but its normal relation to men is kindly, and its goodwill may be kept by the offering of appropriate gifts at the appropriate time.

This is no doubt a homely and primitive state of mind, but it is a 'pure religion breathing household' piety, if not household laws—for as yet its connexion with morality is slight—and it was capable of great developments. In Roman literature it was overwhelmed by Greek anthropomorphic mythology, which, sweeping away the natural Roman attitude of mind in the tide of its own preconceptions by a haughty assumption of similarity and a ruthless process of assimilation, almost obliterated its traces. Yet below the surface it was always there: Ovid, the most typical of Graeco-Romans, can yet in the exact spirit of the old religion speak of a sacred grove at the sight of which one must exclaim 'numen inest', and can describe Vesta just as a primitive Roman might, as 'the living flame'. The old piety must have persisted in many a household in Rome itself, and in the field-worship of the country. The last fight of Christianity was with the *pagani*, the people of the country-villages, clinging to their ancestral cults, and Augustine's attack was delivered not on the Graeco-Roman pantheon, but on the little *numina* of the pontifical litanies (*indigitamenta*).

Fig. 4. Lararium at Pompeii.

There was then a real continuity and persistence about this spirit-worship of the old Roman farmer. What has it left us or how has it affected the inheritance into which we have come? Its direct legacy is sufficiently marked but comparatively unimportant: it is a legacy of practice rather than of thought. When Christianity became the official creed of the Roman Empire, it was at pains in characteristically Roman fashion to let the new grow out of the old—just as Augustus had done in his religious reforms—and as far as possible, without compromising with paganism, to assimilate it. It is a matter of common knowledge that much of our association with the Christmas season—the holidays, the giving of presents and the general feeling of geniality—is but the inheritance from the Roman winter festival of the Saturnalia. An investigation of some of the strange rites which are still held at *Feste* in the small Italian towns would reveal many survivals of paganism: no one, for instance, who has seen the festival of the *Ceri* at Gubbio (Iguvium) can doubt that it descends from some pagan spring-time ritual or fail to suspect its connexion with Cerfus or Cerus Martius, the local deity of the Iguvian tablets. And indeed the cult of the saints in any fully Catholic country must have more than an accidental similarity with the old worship of the local *numina*.

But more important than such direct legacies of practice is the spiritual temper which underlies them; it was a rough and primitive, but genuine religious sense which had possession of the Roman mind, and in spite of the great weight of the Greek influence, guided it in the later development of religious and philosophic thought. And that primarily in three ways: first the Roman, even in the most sceptical days, never quite lost the sense of a spiritual presence which is the first essential of a religious consciousness, and later on, when Rome recreated her religion out of philosophy, this sense becomes prominent again; secondly, there is the conviction that religion must permeate all the little things of daily life; and thirdly, in spite of all the formalities which choked the ceremonial of the old religion, there remained a genuine desire for a direct relation between man and god: this again we shall see emerging in the imperial writers. And if this relation tended to express itself in legal terms, as something of a binding contract between man and god, it is only the more characteristically Roman. These things were enduring, and they had, I believe, their influence on the acceptance of Christianity, and even on the form of its theology and doctrine: the ultra-legal expression of the doctrine of the Atonement, for instance, owes much for better or worse to the juristic ideas of Rome.

The agricultural settlement became a City-State, and with a truly Roman admixture of conservatism and elasticity the old religion was adapted to the new needs. The ancient round of festivals, whose agricultural significance was now lost, was nevertheless preserved intact and still carried out in every detail: formalism increased, and in a while the very names of the *numina* in many instances became unintelligible. On the other hand the old rustic spirits took on new functions in their new surroundings: Iuppiter, the sky-spirit, and therefore the god of oaths sworn under the vault of heaven, becomes the deity of internal justice; Mars, in the main at any rate an agricultural deity in the earlier stage, becomes now the god of war. In this stage there are from our present point of view two features of special note. In the first place we have the gradual but unmistakable establishment of a State religion. The old cults had been in the hands of individual households: the State now takes them over and consecrates them to its own uses. A great temple is built on the Capitoline Hill—the centre of the new Rome—and in it is established the worship of a divine triad symbolizing the religious majesty of the State, at first Iuppiter, Quirinus, and Mars, symbol no doubt of the union of the two old settlements on the Palatine and Quirinal hills, and then, after Etruscan influence had made itself felt, Iuppiter, Iuno, and Minerva. A priestly hierarchy too was created, *flamines* for the principal deities, and the college of *pontifices*, associated with many of the minor rites, presided over by the *pontifex maximus*, who becomes the repository of sacred law and keeps the secret of the festival calendar, which he only reveals to the people month by month. The vague contract-notion in the earlier relation between god and man is embodied now in the juristic system of the State: the *ius divinum* becomes a department of the *ius civile*. Religious considerations in return govern the activities of the State: the calendar ordains days 'fast and nefast', and on the latter the senate cannot meet, the law-courts are closed, and public business cannot be transacted. So too the great functions of the State become clothed in religious significance: the victorious general ends his triumphal journey through the city by climbing the winding road up to the Capitol to consecrate his spoils in the temple of Iuppiter. This connexion of State and religion receives a new force on the introduction—probably from Etruria—of the auguries and auspices. The magistrate now must not hold his assemblies for elections or legislation unless the auguries are favourable, nor may the general take the field till he has first obtained the blessing of the auspices: the gate was opened to the political abuse of religion in the latter days of the Republic. This development must be of the greatest importance for those who are considering the history of the Christian Church. Here for the first time is a real institutional religion with its sacerdotal organization in the colleges of Pontiffs and Augurs: here too is the definite linking of 'Church and State'—Greece shows no real parallel to it, and the Hebrew ideal of a theocracy is different from this partnership—and we can contemplate in its history both the value of the consecration of public life and the possibilities which it involves of the degradation of religion.

The other feature is not perhaps so full of immediate significance to us, but is of great importance for the understanding of Rome's own subsequent religious development. The new City-State soon came into conflict with the other peoples of Italy, and Rome's gods were pitted against their gods. Sometimes Rome was temporarily defeated: should she forgo the religious advantages of her opponents? More often she was victorious and wished to assimilate the conquered population: should she absorb their religion? Her answer was invariably for assimilation in religion too, and during these years of struggle we see the gradual introduction into Rome of the deities of the Italian tribes. Minerva came probably from Etruscan Falerii to be the patroness of the trade-guilds: Castor and Pollux came from Tusculum after the battle of Lake Regillus (496 B.C.): Hercules Invictus—without doubt an Italianized form of the Greek Heracles—took up his abode at a famous altar in the Forum Boarium and there oddly enough presided over luck in commercial enterprise. This was the first-fruits of Rome's ever-ready adoption of foreign cults: in religious matters the Roman seems always to have craved for 'some new thing'. Some have attempted to explain this easy-going assimilation by the natural tendency of polytheism: if there are many gods, why not a few more? The more divine help one can have at one's command the better. I do not find this explanation convincing: certainly it was not so in polytheistic Greece, where the limits of the Olympian hierarchy were carefully guarded. So august a new-comer as Dionysus had a struggle to gain his place which has left its mark in many legends, and an outlandish deity like Sabazios never won full recognition. Rather I take it to be a trait in the Roman character, part of that toleration and adaptability which made them later such great colonizers and empire-builders. Be this as it may, this assimilation of religions had far-reaching results in Rome's later history. The cults of the Orient found their way to Rome by means of traders and soldiers, were welcomed, and ultimately assimilated by a process of syncretism into general religious thought. It was only when Christianity came, scorning any assimilation and refusing to 'bow the knee in the house of Rimmon' that there was collision and struggle: and when capitulation followed, it had to be whole-hearted, for the God of the Christians could make no compact with the deities of polytheism. Christianity is not so exclusive nowadays; perhaps it is almost too ready in a Roman spirit to welcome new ideas from other creeds and philosophies.

Rome was thus prepared to receive, and the contact with Greece, which followed the conquest of Italy, opened the flood-gates. As if conscious of her own lack of culture, Rome welcomed with open arms what Greece had to give her. Art, literature, philosophy, religion were eagerly accepted, and Rome set herself to imitate and adapt, and so in the end to create her own forms. In religion the work was rapid and characteristic: the old *numina* in the hands of the State had long been moving to a more concrete and anthropomorphic conception. Now the process was completed by their identification one by one with the gods of the Olympian hierarchy: Iuppiter becomes Zeus, Iuno his wife Hera, Mars Ares, Minerva Athena, while Bacchus is identified somewhat oddly with the old corn-spirit Liber, who now takes over the patronage of the vine from the sky-spirit, Iuppiter, to whom it naturally belonged. The process is pushed into the minutest detail, so that, for instance, the old dawn-spirit, Matuta, is linked up with the incongruous Greek deity Ino-Leucothea. The identification is wholesale: the Roman deities take over the outward representation of their Greek counterparts—even the Lares henceforth appear in the form of the Dioscuri—they inherit their personal characteristics, their family relationships, and their legends. In literature at any rate the old and truly Roman religion is henceforth drowned in the new Graeco-Roman mythology, which, before modern research had rediscovered the original strata, was taught to us as the religious belief of Rome. Not unnaturally it all rapidly became unreal and carried with it a profound religious scepticism. In the poetry of the Augustan age religion is little more than setting and machinery.

All this is degradation: it opened the gates wide for scepticism and superstition. The genuine Roman religion, if crude, was yet capable of developing into a truly spiritual conception of the universe and of human life: the Graeco-Roman religion was the plaything of the poets or the tool of the politicians. For our present purpose it may be disregarded: it has left us—except in literature—little or no direct legacy, and in the history of Rome's religious experience it is a back-water. But there were two elements which made for salvation. First there was the continued vitality in the country and among the common people of the old religious attitude. Greek culture was always in Rome the possession of the educated classes: it had throughout a struggle for existence; the Graeco-Roman drama practically died out because it could not get an audience, unless it could be so presented as to appear stocked with topical political allusions, and even—to take a more technical instance—the Greek method of scansion by quantity had the greatest difficulty in maintaining itself because it conflicted with the natural Roman pronunciation by stress-accent. So beneath the surface of the Graeco-Roman religion the old faith survived: in the houses at Pompeii we find small shrines peopled with statues not of the Graeco-Roman hierarchy but of little Lares and Penates, and the real religious affection of Virgil—the most truly Roman of the poets for all his Greek culture—lies not with the gods of Olympus, but with the *di agrestes* of the Roman countryside. And if the common people thus possessed their souls in the old faith, salvation came also to the educated from the source which at first sight seemed the most destructive influence of all—Greek philosophy.

The Roman was not naturally a philosopher. In the early days of her history Rome was no doubt too much engaged in the practical task of securing her position against her rivals to have much time for reflexion, but the true causes lie deeper than external circumstances. The Roman was a man of action and affairs: he could think deeply of the next step, but he did not often question himself about the ultimate goal or the nature of the world around him. Among the fragments of early Roman literature which have come down to us the nearest approach to philosophic reflexion which we find is certain general moral maxims of the type which later on were freely interspersed in drama. Some of these are attributed to the blind Appius Claudius, the famous censor of 312 B.C.: 'When you see a friend, forget your woes', 'Every man must forge his own fortune;' others to a mysterious personage known as Marcius the prophet, 'Be the last to speak, the first to hold your tongue', 'Though you stir up hatred, do not reject the good.' Such sayings show indeed a certain love of generalization on life, but they are not very deep, and they deal with practical life and life on the surface. For the first dawn of philosophic thought we have to wait till the influx of Greek culture had begun its work, and then in the unexpected setting of a tragedy of Pacuvius (*c.* 150 B.C.) we find a reproduction of Anaxagoras's scientific teaching of the 'fatherhood' of the sky and the 'motherhood' of the earth—and even this need not indicate any genuine interest, for it is a careful translation of Euripides.

About Pacuvius's time philosophers from Greece began to visit Rome, and in 155 B.C. a famous embassy from Athens included the heads of three of the chief philosophic schools—Diogenes the Stoic, Critolaus the Peripatetic, and Carneades the Academic. Shortly afterwards the first systematic study of philosophy was made by the 'Scipionic circle', the small literary coterie which gathered round the younger Scipio and included Terence the comedian, Lucilius the satirist, and C. Laelius the cultured Roman, who was afterwards to figure in Cicero's philosophic dialogues. Their object was at once to study Greek literature and, taking it as a model, to purify Latin style. Philosophy seems to have held a high place among them, and their teacher was Panaetius the Stoic, who had been brought up in the philosophic schools of Athens and became attached to Scipio soon after the middle of the century. Panaetius's successor as head of the Stoic school was Posidonius, and Posidonius was one of the masters of Cicero: the tradition of the Republican philosophers is clear.

We are apt to think of Greek philosophy in its classical period and to associate it with the names of Socrates, Plato, and Aristotle. Theirs was the philosophy of the City-State, for which in the moral sphere the good man was synonymous with the good citizen. But with the break up of the City-State under the rule of Macedon, an era of individualism had set in, and men now turned to philosophy to learn how to live their lives as independent individuals: it was even a matter of debate whether the good man would take part in public life or not. It is true that there still survived in Athens the two schools of the Peripatetics who regarded Aristotle as their founder and the Academics who looked back to Plato; but the former by this time had let themselves drift into little more than commentary on their founder's works, and the latter, especially under Carneades, the representative of the Academic school in Rome, had devoted themselves mainly to a sceptical and critical attitude, picking holes in the theories of their opponents, but offering little themselves of a constructive nature. The two schools with real vitality in the second century B. C. were the Stoic and the Epicurean, both of which made a strong claim to provide a way of life. Nor were their moral ideals in effect very widely separated: the Stoic putting before himself 'self-sufficiency' (*αὐτάρκεια*) as his ideal, to be attained by a life lived 'in accordance with nature', the latter aiming at 'tranquillity' (*ἀταραξία*), as the expression of the highest pleasure, which is the complete removal of pain, mental and bodily. But in their bases they differed greatly. The Stoic believed in a world-spirit (*anima mundi*), which pervaded and ruled all things, a spark of which in the individual life was at once inspiration and guide. The Epicurean held a material view of the world, banished the divine from all contact with perceptible things, and with man's life, which he regarded as controlled by a perishable soul, itself a compound of concrete material atoms. It might have been expected that Rome—a greater City-State than any in Greece—would have turned back to the older philosophy. Cicero indeed followed the example of Plato in the writing of a *De Re Publica*; in it he argued that the ideal constitution was a mixture of the three elements of monarchy, aristocracy, and democracy, such as was to be found in the Rome of the second century B. C. He also modelled on Plato his treatise *De Legibus*, another work of political philosophy, and would at all times have regarded himself as an adherent of the Academic school. But even Cicero is much tinged with Stoic ideals, and among his contemporaries the prominent men appear either as Stoics or Epicureans; Cato and Brutus were leaders of the Stoics, Cassius and Cicero's intimate friend Atticus of the Epicureans. The truth is that Rome as a City-State was herself breaking up: her imperial problems were too vast for the old republican machinery to grapple with them; the magistrates and the senate were the real rulers, and the average Roman citizen had little opportunity to manifest the qualities of the good citizen. It was too the teachers of Stoicism and Epicureanism who settled in Rome; a revival of Platonism or Aristotelianism would have involved research in books, and the Roman preferred the living teacher to the written word.

This is no place for an exposition of the tenets of the Stoics and Epicureans—that belongs moreover to the study of Greek philosophy—nor of the Academic criticisms of Cicero on both and his eclectic mediation between them. But there are some features in the general attitude of this first period of philosophic study in Rome which are of great significance in their general bearing and have not been, I believe, without effect in the inheritance of ancient thought which has passed to the modern world. Greek philosophy recognized the three departments of logic, physics, and ethics; Plato and Aristotle had dealt with them all: Zeno, the founder of Stoicism, had recognized the same division, and even Epicurus, though he professes to despise logic, had to lay down a *Canonica*, or method of procedure, and dealt at great length with physics as the foundation of his ethics. Rome with its characteristic dislike of abstract speculation, and its eager preoccupation with a 'way of life', showed from the first a marked preference for the problems of ethics. Panaetius appears to have paid little heed to logic, and though he wrote on physics, he light-heartedly abandoned the theory of his own Stoic school. Posidonius did more all-round work in philosophy, but, as we shall see, his real bias was religious. In the Epicurean school we have the greatest physical treatise in antiquity in Lucretius's *De Rerum Natura*, a systematic and magnificent exposition of the atomic theory; but even his interest is at bottom not in the physical system for its own sake, but in the freeing of men's minds from the superstitious terror of divine interference in this world and of the punishment of the soul in the after life. Cicero, omnivorous student and voluminous writer, endeavoured to cover all fields, and wrote both a tedious treatise called the *Academica* in which he expounded and refuted the Stoic logic, and on the physical side an account of the creation of the world in the *Timaeus*, an almost literal translation of Plato's dialogue of the same name, with no original contribution, a fact which in itself shows his comparative lack of interest. The great bulk of his philosophic work is ethical or religious.

Another notable feature in the Roman philosophy of this period is its eclecticism, a tendency to modify the tenets of any one school by the admixture of elements from others. The good Epicurean, it is true, is faithful to the words of the master and will not add to or detract from them a jot or a tittle: Epicurus is to him a 'god' and his 'divine discoveries' the one 'wisdom'. Lucretius shows a rare devotion to his 'father': ''tis thee I follow, bright star of the Greek race, and in thy deepset prints firmly now I plant my footsteps, not in eager emulation, but rather because for love I long to copy thee';

and nothing has emerged more clearly in the recent study of Epicurean sources than the exact faithfulness with which the doctrine has been expounded in the *De Rerum Natura*. Yet all Epicureans were not equally true, and the charred remains at Herculaneum have revealed Lucretius's contemporary Philodemus dealing with the forbidden topics of logic and rhetoric. In the Stoic school there seems to have been no such restriction. Panaetius deserts the Stoic physics for a theory of his own, based upon a combination of arguments from Peripatetics and Academics, and in his ethical theory he often abandons the strict doctrine for something more palatable to his Roman audience. Similarly Posidonius is largely influenced in his physical views by Plato and by the Alexandrian doctrine of the Logos, which lies also at the bottom of his logic. The normal form of a philosophic dialogue of Cicero is the exposition and counter-exposition of the Stoic and Epicurean views, followed by a rather unconvincing Academic summary with a leaning to the Stoic side. This may seem a small and rather technical point on which to lay emphasis, but it has, I believe, a wider significance. It was a movement towards greater freedom of speculation. The Roman philosopher, though no doubt he took his philosophy at second-hand, yet felt himself less bound than the Greek to follow the tradition of his school: he was, as Horace professes himself, a free-lance, 'nullius addictus iurare in verba magistri,' and who shall say that in this respect the modern world is not nearer to Rome than to Greece?

What then was the ethical attitude evolved by this eclectic process? It was not in the main—and this is characteristic again of Rome—an ethical theory, but a search for an ideal type of character. Here it is that Stoicism comes out supreme among its rivals. The critical Academic had little that was positive to teach in ethics, and Cicero, the professed Academic, tends in his works on morals to assimilate himself more and more to Stoicism. The Epicurean had indeed his traditional theory and his accepted ideal: 'the simple life' untroubled by the pains and desires of the body or the cares of public life or close personal relationships, a tranquil existence devoted to the study of philosophy; but it seems doubtful whether this ideal was ever pursued in practice by any Roman except Lucretius. Atticus was a man of the world and Cassius mingled freely in politics, and the Epicurean watchword 'pleasure' was soon interpreted in a baser sense. Cicero in the *In Pisonem* gives us a repulsive picture, doubtless much exaggerated, of Piso's friend the Epicurean philosopher, and in the next generation Horace half in jest can describe himself as 'a pig from Epicurus' sty'. The real Epicurean ideal was pitched too high for the Roman: it was capable of parody but not of modification. Roman Stoicism was equipped with all the traditional ethical philosophy, which is glibly repeated by its professors without much alteration: virtue is knowledge and the wise man therefore cannot err, 'rex eris,' as Horace makes the boys say in their game with an untranslateable pun, 'si recte sapias': virtue is to live in accordance with nature, to obey the divine instinct implanted in us at birth. The good man will exhibit the four cardinal virtues, wisdom, justice, courage, temperance: he will regard external goods with indifference, and disregard pain as being 'no evil'. Now this ethical theory was not indeed without its influence on Roman thought in general, and it has been noticed that 'the conception of an immutable law, emanating from God, guided Roman jurisprudence and through the praetor's edict influenced legislation': and if it guided Roman jurisprudence, then it guided that of modern Europe. Yet it was not the moral theory of Stoicism which gripped the Roman imagination so much as its practical outcome. If philosophy was to become a real force in Rome, it must be an effective 'way of life', and Stoicism became such largely because its ideal was exactly suited to the Roman temperament. 'The heroes of the early Republic', it has been said, 'were unconscious Stoics', and perhaps equally unconsciously the Roman thinker tended to assimilate the Stoic ideal to his own early heroes. For it contains in it characteristics closely akin to the old Roman virtues of *gravitas*, the sober self-restraint alike in prosperity and misfortune, and of *pietas*, the due observance of one's relations to family and friends, to the State, and to the gods. And so from the first we find, not indeed a warping of the Stoic ideal, but an adaptation of it to its Roman setting. Thus Panaetius, as Professor Arnold has observed, 'sets before us Stoicism as the school which will train the scholar, the gentleman, and the statesman', and does not hesitate to admit that external goods may be worthy of pursuit, so long as they do not conflict with virtue: he emphasizes temperance among the cardinal virtues, for it is temperance which the Roman particularly admires. So again Horace, professed Epicurean as he was, is holding before us a Romanized Stoic picture in the 'iustum et tenacem propositi virum' and in the famous portrait of the patriotic fortitude of Regulus. And Virgil has given us in Aeneas not merely the typical Roman but the typical Roman Stoic, with his sense of divine mission, his *pietas* to man and gods, his fortitude and his justice: 'iustitiaene prius mirer belline laborum?' In fact the ideal of the Roman Stoic cannot better be illustrated than in his traditional choice of heroes, in mythology Hercules and Aeneas, in history Scipio the younger and Cato of Utica. To the modern world this ideal has been conveyed above all by the Roman *Lives* of Plutarch, a book prominent in the educational system of Europe and the inspiration, as we know, of Shakespeare's Roman plays. In Seneca, the chief Stoic writer of the early empire, we find the culmination of this tendency: he cares but little on the whole for the theoretical foundation of morals, but will select traits and principles from almost any available philosopher in order to put together the picture of his ideal Roman.

Why, it may be asked, should we care for all this? It seems

a distortion and even a degradation of philosophy, and does not tend to exalt our notion of the thinking powers of the Roman. For two reasons: in the first place it is just this attitude of the Roman (as of the later Greek) thinkers which bridged the gulf between philosophy and practical life, which placed the attainment of a philosophical ideal within the capacity of the average man and made it a living power among individuals and in the State. Stoicism was, like Christianity itself, a 'way of life' for the humble and uninstructed as well as for the lofty and learned: think of the contrast between the social position of Epictetus and that of Marcus Aurelius. And secondly, the actual ideal so formed was one which was destined to last. A recent writer (Professor Arnold) has been at pains to show the Stoic element in Christianity. Paul was of Tarsus, a stronghold of Stoicism, and we may trace in his epistles the influence not only of Stoic theory but of the Stoic moral ideal: think of words like 'endurance' (*ὑπομονή*), 'temperance' (*ἐγκράτεια*) and of the picture of the Christian warrior armed with the 'whole armour of God'. Be this as it may, there can be no doubt that in the general thought of Europe the Stoic ideal has exercised a profound influence. The idea of fortitude and indifference to pain and sorrow, to take one trait alone, still sways men's minds; how often was a Stoic attitude commended during the War! The Roman Stoic ideal has certainly survived, and for this reason, if for no other, Seneca and Epictetus and Marcus Aurelius, its exponents in very different settings and attitudes, have still much to say to us.

There is one more feature of Roman philosophy which is of even greater importance for the present purpose—its close connexion with religion. 'Of course,' says Professor Burnet, 'philosophy may culminate in theology, and the best Greek philosophy certainly does so, but it begins with science and not with religion.' This dictum might not be accepted by all modern writers, but it is certainly true that Greek philosophy grew independently of the current religion, and even where, as in Plato, it culminated in an abstract theology, it had comparatively little to say on the everyday practice of religion. Rome did not construct her own philosophy, but received it ready-made from Greece, and it was perhaps her good fortune that she was thus enabled to apply it at once to the problems of religion, which, as we have seen, had been made more acute by the wholesale imposition of Greek anthropomorphism on the faded animism of her own native beliefs. The educated Roman was disturbed by the difficulties which surrounded orthodox practice, and from the first saw in philosophy an instrument of religious criticism: both Stoicism and Epicureanism were brought to bear at once. The influence of Epicureanism was in the main destructive. Epicurus himself had been anxious to free men from 'the myths about the gods', because he regarded them as fatal to the tranquillity of mind which he put before his disciples as their ideal. Lucretius seized upon this feature in his master's teaching with a fanatical enthusiasm: the gods, he argues, are our ideal of the tranquil life, they cannot be disturbed by the 'billows' of anger or affection; they live their blessed life in the spaces between the worlds and care nothing for the affairs of men. They will not then interfere in the life of men; they will not be moved to favour by our prayers, nor will they vent their indignation on us when we offend against them. The whole poem is a savage attack on *religio*, the spirit of cringing before the gods; Lucretius will turn aside again and again in his scientific argument to deny the theological view of the creation and government of the world, and indeed the purpose of that great argument itself, worked out in the minutest detail, is to establish the absolute supremacy in the world of the *foedera naturai*, 'natural law', as against divine interference. Yet it is noteworthy that even in Epicureanism a place was left for religion. Lucretius was no atheist, the gods exist and men can apprehend them by a kind of spiritual intuition, and so by means of these 'images' of the gods which visit his mind, something of their tranquillity can be conveyed to him in a kind of communion—a lofty idea but remote, no doubt, from the common practice of religion.

If the Epicurean thus appeared as the enemy of orthodox or popular religion, the Stoic was regarded as its champion. In the doctrines of the world-spirit providentially governing the universe, and the divine spirit in man implanting in him the sense of moral obligation, Stoicism had laid a theological foundation both for physics and for ethics. The question was how far this theological basis was capable of reconciliation with the ideas and practice of polytheism. Among the earlier Greek interpreters of Stoicism Chrysippus had already moved in this direction and had started the idea of the allegorical interpretation of myth. But as soon as the school got a hold in Rome, this side of its theory received great development. Though Panaetius had taken up a rather sceptical attitude towards divination, Posidonius whole-heartedly set himself to the work of adjustment. In treatises on the Gods and on Divination, which were the source of Cicero's exposition of the Stoic view in works of the same name, he elaborated a reconciliation of philosophical theology and popular belief. Though Cicero in his discussion opposes this view with the Epicurean denial, his own wavering conclusions seem to move in the Stoic direction. Seneca later on in his own discursive way supports the Stoic position, and, as we shall see later, takes a further step. The main contentions of this apologetic, as it almost is, are that the gods exist, which is upheld by the common consent of mankind, that they are immortal and benevolent towards men, that they govern the universe, and that they seek the good of men. This is really an elaboration of the fundamental idea of 'providence', but it still does not touch the crucial question, for the 'world-spirit' is one, but gods are many. The Stoic answer was given in an implicit movement towards monotheism: 'the gods' become 'God', and Iuppiter, already recognized in popular belief as *optimus maximus*, is exalted into a unique position, the other gods being either regarded as forms which Iuppiter assumes, or allegorically explained away as personifications of the powers of nature—Iuno the air, Apollo the sun, and so on. Now all this may not be very satisfactory as philosophy; but the point I wish to emphasize, and it is brought out again by the very existence among Cicero's philosophical works of the *De Natura Deorum*, *De Divinatione*, and *De Fato*, is the strong feeling that philosophy and religion could not be kept apart. They must be brought into relation, even if, as with the Epicureans, the relation should be one of hostility.

I have dwelt at some length on this first era of philosophic thought at Rome, because, though doubtless itself derived from Greek sources, it contains the gist of all that followed, and because it not only had an influence in forming the teaching of the Christian Church, but is also significant for us in even wider spheres. In philosophy it asserts the spirit of free speculation, not tied to the tenets of a particular set of dogmas; in ethics, brought now into greater prominence, it is a movement towards a practical rule of life and a definite moral ideal; above all, it insisted on the correlation of speculative philosophy and practical religion.

Of new elements in this strange compound of thought, whose growth we have been following, there is not much that remains to be chronicled; but in the early empire there were two prominent features, one of which had incidentally far-reaching consequences. 'Caesar-worship', as it is sometimes vaguely called, does not perhaps concern us much. Suggested no doubt by contact with the East, where the conception of the Man-God was firmly established, and grafting itself on a natural instinct in the Roman mind to exalt the heroes of the past into a kind of immortality, it was at first a natural expression of the popular gratitude and devotion towards those who had produced peace and order out of the chaos of civil disturbance, and later lost its meaning and became little more than a political convention. It certainly had nothing to do with Christology, whose root-idea was that of God becoming man and not man becoming God; and if its influence is to be traced at all in later history, it would be rather in the conception of the Holy Roman Empire and the theory of the divine right of kings.

The other new feature of this period was of far greater importance in its consequences—the reception of the religions of the East. This was not merely due to the characteristic Roman readiness to adopt and adapt, but in origin at any rate had a special motive. As the traditional state-religion became more and more a meaningless formality, frigid and unsatisfying, men's minds began to crave something more vital and emotional. The process had begun far back in Republican times: by the advice of the Sibylline Books as long ago as 204 B.C. at the end of the second Punic War, the cult of the Magna Mater of Phrygia had been brought to Rome, and her strange orgiastic ritual won such a popular influence that the senate was constrained to make controlling regulations. Later on in the Mithradatic wars the soldiers of the Roman army brought back the worship of the Cappadocian Mâ, with its curious initiation rite of the *taurobolium*, in which the novice, baptized in bull's blood, emerged, as we learn from many imperial inscriptions, *in aeternum renatus*. The conquest of Egypt brought the cult of Isis with its fastings and its festivals, at which was represented the resurrection-drama of Osiris. All these cults had a firm hold in Rome by the end of the Republic, and were threatening to supersede the outworn Graeco-Roman religion. Augustus, by his rebuilding of the temples and his attempt to attach the state-cult to the imperial household, endeavoured to stem the tide, but in vain. In spite of official disapproval the new worships gained an ever-growing influence, and their number was constantly increasing. By the third century A.D. we find such cults as that of the Syrian Atargatis, the Phrygian Sabazios, and the sun-god Baal pervading Rome and carried by the army to the distant provinces. But the greatest of these was the Persian Mithra. Brought home probably for the first time by the soldiers of Sulla's Eastern army, his cult seems then to have made little impression; but by the third century Mithra was the soldiers' god above all others, and his worship had been carried by the army into the remotest parts of the empire: there are traces of a Mithraic shrine on the Roman Wall in Northumberland. The appeal of this cult is not difficult to realize. Theologically Mithra was the god of light, and as such the 'mediator' (μεσίτης) between the one unknowable God and the race of men. Born upon earth of the 'generative rock', he performed a journey, full of struggle and pain, in which he vanquished many opponents, including even the great bull, the first-created living creature. He thus became at once the link between God and man, and the type of the suffering and struggling life of man. His worshippers were initiated with purifications and celebrated together the love-feast which Mithra himself had instituted. With this great and popular worship Christianity had to wage war: the superficial points of resemblance between the two religions are obvious, their differences in reality immense. Mithraism, to mention no other points, was founded on a myth with no historical background, and it was devoid of direct ethical teaching. Yet there was a moment when it almost seemed a question whether Mithra or Christ should conquer the world.

There can be no doubt that this influx of Oriental cults was a weakening of Rome's religious consciousness, a sign, as Professor Gilbert Murray has put it, of 'nerve-failure'. Ecstatic orgies and sensational symbolic dramas are an appeal to the emotions instead of to the intellect or the will: mystic initiations substitute a ceremonial purification for real purity of heart. And the secret of the widespread popularity of Mithraism is surely that it was on a far higher level than the rest: it offered a noble conception of God and implied a strong moral ideal which had marked affinity to that of Roman Stoicism. Mâ, Isis, Baal and the others were sapping the vitality of Rome and assisting in her social decay. But meanwhile what were the thinkers doing? They were not untouched by the general tendency, yet they clung tenaciously to the natural development of previous thought. More and more Stoicism became supreme over its rivals, yet the stronger its ascendancy the more willing it seemed, in its eclectic spirit, to seek good wherever it might find it and to incorporate it in its own teaching. And it is not fanciful to see the influence of the mystic cults. In the first place they affected the position of the teacher, who became, as Sir Samuel Dill has shown, both the personal 'director' initiating his pupil into the doctrine and keeping watch over his moral life, and then the 'missionary' to the masses, bringing them into the fold with all the proselytizing zeal of one who has found the truth. But more important than this, the rather cold philosophic religion of the Stoic becomes more personal and intimate. The general idea of a world-providence passes into a conception of the care of God for the individual, and prayer from formal petition into something like communion. Already in Seneca there are traces of this: he has 'a higher vision of the Creator, the pitiful and loving Guardian, the Giver of all good, the Power which draws us to Himself', and he recommends the practice of nightly self-examination as in the sight of God. More marked is this sense of personal relation in Marcus Aurelius and Epictetus: challenged as to the source of his knowledge of the gods, the emperor can reply more as the mystic than the philosopher, 'from my continual experience of their power I have the conviction that they exist', and Epictetus in a notable passage exclaims, 'Have courage to look up to God and say, "Deal with me hereafter as Thou wilt, I am as one with Thee, I am Thine. I flinch from nothing so long as Thou thinkest it good. Lead me where Thou wilt, put on me what raiment Thou wilt. Wouldst Thou have me hold office, or eschew it, stay or fly, be rich or poor? For all this I will defend Thee before men."' 'Natural religion' is here not far from revelation.

And if philosophy was in this way seeking for religion, so religion was striving for a unifying philosophy. The monotheism of the earlier Stoicism, which centred in Iuppiter, was a mediation between the claims of the various deities of the Graeco-Roman hierarchy. But now it was a matter of the reconciliation of all the creeds of the civilized and semi-civilized world, focused in Rome and each making absolute claims for its own supreme deity. This time it was an eclectic revival of Platonism which came to the rescue. In the works of Plutarch, written towards the end of the first century A. D., we find the monotheistic idea reasserted with a new strength. God is the one, supreme, eternal being, ' of whom it is impious to say that He was or shall be ' ; we may only say that ' He is '. And the gods of mythology and of the world-cults are not indeed forms or presentations of Him, but rather inferior beings, daemones, beings intermediate between God and the world, his messengers at times, at others powers striving to thwart his will. What an opening this gave for the subsequent attacks of Christianity on the pagan hierarchy it is easy to see, but for the time it seemed to solve the vexed contest of religions, and it was at least a new and nobler assertion of a monotheism standing out above them all. A century later the ideas are set out again in more popular form by the African Apuleius, who at the end of his fantastic novel tells of the initiation of his hero into the rites of Isis. But Isis is now the supreme deity ' of the thousand names ', and she greets her novice with the words ' Lo, I come to thee, the parent of all nature, mistress of the elements, origin of species, highest of holy spirits (*numinum*, the old word come to life again) . . . whose godhead, one beneath many forms, the whole world worships'. Philosophy has passed again into religion, and the long struggle of conflicting claims seems drawing to a close.

It was into a world of ideas such as these that Christianity came. It may be that Hellenism contributed most to the formation of its theology, but Rome gave it its opportunity. And that not merely because the world-wide commerce of ideas established by the Roman Empire enabled it to reach Rome and thence to be disseminated, but because the soil was uniquely ripe for its message. In it the craving of philosophy for a more intimate relation with God and the desire of the religious for a satisfying monotheism were alike satisfied. But it could not conquer the Roman world without a struggle, for it could not submit to its terms. Rome now as ever would have welcomed another religion which was content to take its place among many and submit to incorporation in the facile syncretism of a Plutarch or an Apuleius. But the claim of Christianity was absolute: it required an undivided allegiance and a complete rejection of its rivals. And so the early Christians were persecuted, not for their doctrine, not—though there was some pretence of this—for their practices, but because they refused to accept the state-religion and to swear by its deities: had they been prepared to do this, they might have held in private what opinions and beliefs they liked. But persecution strengthened the new creed and assured its final acceptance.

Beyond this matter of opportunity I would not make any extravagant claims for the contribution of Rome to Christianity. Much might of course be said on the side of ecclesiastical organization: the architecture of the Christian church was that of the Roman basilica; the organization of the new priesthood owed much to that of the old Roman religion—a new Pontifex Maximus at their head; Roman jurisprudence greatly influenced canon law, and the whole constitution of the Church was largely modelled on that of the Roman State. Ritual too owed something of its orderliness and sobriety to the ritual of the Roman cults, and as Warde Fowler has pointed out, it was Rome which contributed to the Christian vocabulary such words as 'piety', 'saint', 'sacrament', and 'religion' itself. Rome supplied in fact the conception and the setting of an institutional religion. But neither organization, nor ritual, nor terminology, are in themselves religion. To the thought of Christianity I believe that Rome contributed something of the moral ideal derived from the specifically Roman Stoicism: something too of the insistence on the correspondence of theology with religious experience which has always characterized Christianity at its best. And in the wider sphere of religious and philosophic thought in general, the modern world owes much to the influence of Rome.

If that influence is to be symbolized in any one figure, it is that of Virgil. The Middle Ages, on the ground of the

'Messianic' Eclogue, hailed him as the prophet of Christianity, and Dante made him his guide through the Inferno, deriving much of the general form and indeed of the details of his picture from Virgil's description of the lower world in the Sixth *Aeneid*. But it is in a wider sense that we now see Virgil as the epitome of the Roman attitude to life and in many respects the forerunner of modern thought. In Aeneas he has portrayed once and for all the ideal Roman, with the historic Roman's qualities of *pietas* and *gravitas* and the Stoic philosopher's conscience and fortitude. With his deep love of the old Italian religion he has combined a grave philosophic outlook, sober but never pessimistic, and unites a high religious sense of the divine government of the world with a conviction of the infinite value of little things. He is indeed a type of that fusion of religion and philosophy which I believe in this sphere is Rome's greatest legacy to modern thought.

But rather than attempt to draw out points of resemblance or to define the debt, I would leave this brief sketch to suggest its own application. After all, the greatest inheritance which one age or civilization can bequeath to another is its own experience: and the experience of a great people, naturally religious and by persuasion philosophical, cannot be without value for us, who find ourselves in many ways akin to them alike in character and in destiny.

C. BAILEY.

BOOKS RECOMMENDED.

W. WARDE FOWLER, *The Religious Experience of the Roman People* (Macmillan, 1911).

—— *Roman Ideas of Deity* (Macmillan, 1914).

E. V. ARNOLD, *Roman Stoicism* (Cam. Univ. Press, 1911).

R. D. HICKS, *Stoic and Epicurean* (Longmans, 1910).

EDWYN BEVAN, *Stoics and Sceptics* (Clarendon Press, 1913).

W. WALLACE, *Epicureanism* (S.P.C.K., 1880).

SIR S. DILL, *Roman Society from Nero to Marcus Aurelius* (Macmillan, 1919).

—— *Roman Society in the Last Century of the Western Empire* (Macmillan, 1898).

F. CUMONT, *The Mysteries of Mithra* (translated by T. J. McCormack: Kegan Paul, 1910).

T. R. GLOVER, *The Conflict of Religions in the Early Roman Empire* (Methuen, 8th ed. 1919).

SCIENCE

§ 1. *The Roman Attitude to Nature*

THE scientific idea, the conception of a reasonable universe, came to the peoples of Central Italy at a much later date than that at which it began to influence the Greeks of the Eastern Mediterranean and of Southern Italy. With the Romans pure science always remained somewhat of an exotic; it was applied science that attracted them. The determining factor in the development of science within the Empire was the absorption of the kingdom of the Ptolemies, whose capital, Alexandria, was and long remained the scientific head-quarters of the world. Yet despite the stimulus that followed on the contact with Alexandrian thought, Rome produced no great creative scientist. It is in the distribution and dissemination of the Greek wisdom rather than its development that we see the rôle of Rome.

Yet though Rome cannot be said to rival Greece in pure science, it must be allowed that in an allied department her achievements are remarkable. Among the Greeks art in its highest development excelled in idealistic representation—as did science in abstract reasoning. Man, the main theme of the Greek painter and sculptor, became godlike; the lower creation is less often represented, and when it is, the beauty of the animal is reflected from the nobility of its master. As for plants, they are practically omitted from Greek art save in connexion with ornament.

Now this contrasts profoundly with the development of art at Rome. The character of Augustan art was determined by the character of the Augustan country gentleman. The great Roman landowner, like his representative nearer home, was no great hand at philosophizing; least of all was he given to what would have seemed to him that useless spinning of arguments about the essential nature of things which provided a leading motive in Greek scientific literature. But if no philosopher, he was a lover of the countryside, an observer by temper in that field which the Greek had taken to investigating because he believed it to lie on the road to knowledge. He had it in him to become a shrewd and close-observing naturalist, one who paid attention to the habits of plants and animals perhaps more than to the minute details of their form, but seldom given to general ideas about them.

This Roman spirit, slow to acquire any appreciation of the scientific attitude, yielded little in the way of scientific results. Yet the art which Rome produced in the Augustan age is instinct with the study of bird and beast and flower and tree. Nature is treated as she had never been before. The affection of Virgil for his bees, his cattle, and his herbs recalls the power and faithfulness with which creatures and plants are represented in Augustan art. Thus panels of the tomb of the Haterii in the Lateran museum [Fig. 5] render to perfection the habit of a young wind-blown wild-rose. The buds are particularly natural, but the opened flowers strangely show four petals instead of five. At the top of one of the pillars three bees may be seen drinking from the hollow in the capital, while a fourth has been seized in the claw of a bird. Two other birds—perhaps 'Bee-eaters', *Merops apiaster*—pursue bees among the branches below. The scene might have been prepared to illustrate passages in Virgil's fourth *Georgic*.

There are many instances of the faithful imitation of nature in Augustan art. It would not be easy to find any parallel in Greek art of the best period to the treatment of plants in some of the metal work of Pompeii [Fig. 7]. Even the brutality of a Cato finds reflection in the procession of fatted sacrificial beasts on the altar of Domitius Ahenobarbus [Fig. 6]. Compare the ewe and her young of the well-head at Vienna [Fig. 9] with the noble head of the Parthenon steed, and you have the contrast epigrammatically set forth. The feeling of the Augustan artist is that of one studying nature

Fig. 5. PILASTERS IN LATERAN MUSEUM

Birds pursue bees among branches of wild rose
Cp. Virgil, *Georgics*, iv. ll. 8–29

Fig. 6. FROM THE ALTAR OF DOMITIUS AHENOBARBUS (LOUVRE)

as something quite outside man; it is the sheep herself who tends her young; her love is not a sentiment reflected from mankind. The Augustan artist has produced a nature study. The Greek has wrought a creature that sets forth the glory of the god.

When Hellenism first began to influence Roman thought, about the time of the second Punic war (*c.* 214 B.C.), Latin literature had as yet no scientific element. During the period between 200 and 189 B.C. Rome broke the power of Alexander's successors and established her protectorate throughout the Eastern Mediterranean. The influence of Greek ideas now grew rapidly. With the triumph after the battle of Pydna (168 B.C.) numerous Greek hostages, educated and of good family, came to Rome, and the library of the Macedonian king which was brought with them made a nucleus for the infiltration of Roman society by Greek wisdom.

FIG. 7. Silver bowl ornamented with vine-shoots from Pompeii, after Overbeck.

For long there were those who struggled against this development without being able to stem it. Among them was Marcus Porcius Cato (234–149 B.C.). He prepared a sort of encyclopaedia for the use of his son, in which he endeavoured to show that the old Roman literature could hold its own against this newfangled material from Greece. Of that treatise only fragments have survived, but in his book *De re rustica* we possess the oldest Latin prose work that has come down to us. Its contents are very miscellaneous, relating principally to rural economy, but dealing also with cookery receipts, magical formulae, medical prescriptions, and much other strange material which shows how little scientific was the traditional Roman attitude.

Although the relation to science improved as time went on and all educated men learned Greek and were affected by Hellenic philosophy, it is probable that the general scientific principles of the Greeks as expressed in the writings of the Hippocratic, Aristotelian, and Alexandrian schools were seldom understood even by educated Romans. The prevalent attitude towards nature among the Latin-speaking upper classes, whether Italian or provincial, was expressed by the Stoic creed. That system, based on a rigid conception of the interrelation of the different parts of the world, provided little stimulus for the acquisition of new knowledge or for anything in the way of research. Thus, in place of knowledge accumulating progressively on a basis of a wide and far-reaching theory, we get either a type of exact but intellectually motiveless observation or a rejection of all knowledge not of practical importance.

There have been various attempts to explain why the Romans did not continue the scientific work of the Greeks. It is a strange phenomenon, for the value of the experimental method was still being demonstrated by the achievements of the Alexandrians. That school continued its activities under Roman rule and was the ultimate source of the only important Latin medical work that has come down to us, the *De re medica* of Celsus. It has been said that the Roman mind could find no time from conquest and administration to attend to scientific matters, but this will not explain the whole matter, for there were those among the Romans who were able to answer the no less exacting claims of philosophy, of literature, and, above all, of rhetoric. Much too has been made of the view that regards the scientific pause as due to the lack of instruments of precision. This, however, hardly explains the facts, for scientific instruments are at least as much the result as the cause of the application of scientific method. The matter seems rather to have lain deep in the Roman character. It is wrapped up in the nature of the favourite Roman philosophy, Stoicism, it needs to be considered in general relation to the Roman psychology and is not improbably related to the Roman obsession for Rhetoric.

In general we may say that Roman science appears at its best in the department of ' Nature Study ' and at its weakest in ' Pure Mathematics '. The success or failure of the Romans in any scientific field may be roughly gauged by its nearness to one or other of these disciplines. The gauge must be biased, however, by the Roman desire for ' useful studies '. There was for instance, as we shall see, a special development in certain departments of Geography.

§ 2. *Latin works on general Science*

We have several works by Latins which deal with the implications of science in general. These, however, seldom involve any expert knowledge of natural phenomena, and are concerned rather with the philosophical relations of the science of their day than with science itself, as we understand that word to-day. Of such works the most striking and widely read is the *De rerum natura* of Lucretius (*c.* 95–55 B.C.). The man is aflame with his theme and exhibits a veritable missionary zeal. Yet, however magnificent as literature may be the work of Lucretius, and however important as our best representative of Epicurean views, it is too close an imitation of Greek philosophy to be of the highest value for our immediate purpose. It neither records first-hand observations nor does it represent an attitude of mind that can be considered as typically Roman. Lucretius, nevertheless, is interesting for us as the only Latin writer who gives us a complete and coherent scheme of natural knowledge.

The attention of the scientific reader of Lucretius will naturally be drawn to his atomic view of matter. The atomic conception was very ancient and had been taught by Leucippus (*fl. c.* 450 B.C.), Democritus (*fl. c.* 410 B.C.), and Epicurus (342–270 B.C.) among the Greeks. Lucretius, following these writers, explains the origin of the world as due to the interaction of atoms, and this interaction, he believes, is without the intervention of any creative intelligence. This is not the place to discuss the position of the gods in the Lucretian scheme, but we may note that even mental phenomena are for him of atomic origin and there is no real existence save atoms and 'the void' (*inane*). 'Nullam rem e nilo gigni divinitus unquam.' *Nothing is ever begotten of nothing by divine will.* Everything springs from 'semina certa', *determinate units.* The genesis of all things is typified by the generation of organic beings and the species of plants and animals give us models for all processes and natural laws. This conception of generation has its converse. 'Haud igitur possunt ad nilum quaeque reverti.' *Things cannot then ever be turned to naught.* Such an attitude involves that 'indestructibility of matter' which, despite the modern change in our conception, is the historical foundation on which our chemical and physical knowledge has been built.

The resemblance of the Lucretian theory to modern atomic views is, however, more apparent than real; not only are the atoms of Lucretius of different shapes and sizes but also he knows nothing of the definite laws by which they are held together as molecules, he has no inkling of the real nature of chemical combination, and he is without that 'doctrine of energy' that is so characteristic a feature in all modern physical theory. Moreover, his work had little direct influence on the development of the modern doctrine. Epicurean thought has not, in fact, historically been very favourable to scientific development. The atomic view of matter was practically lost during the Middle Ages, and Aristotelian philosophy, which involved the doctrine of the continuity of matter, was paramount for centuries. Atomic views, it is true, were known to a few 'Arabian' philosophers, e.g. Averroes (1126–98) and Maimonides (1135–1204), but their general standpoint was abhorrent to the scholastics. Lucretius was rediscovered by the scholar Poggio in 1418 and deeply affected the philosophy of the Renaissance. The influence of that philosophy waned with the great physical synthesis of the seventeenth century with which the name of Galileo (1564–1642) is associated. Atomic views continued to be held by a few isolated thinkers, but modern scientific atomism arose almost independent of the ancient sources. John Dalton (1766–1844), the father of modern atomism, was probably not directly influenced by Lucretius.

Yet there is one scientific department in which the influence of Lucretius on Renaissance philosophy may be said to have borne more direct fruit. Lucretius concludes his work with a description of the plague at Athens in 430 B. C., and in describing this visitation he follows very closely the account of Thucydides, and the Lucretian version is of interest as having contributed something to modern views of the nature of infection. In discussing the nature of the plague Lucretius demands 'What is its cause?' and he answers—working out his atomic theory here also—that 'just as there are seeds (*semina*) of things helpful to our life, so, for sure, others fly about that cause disease and death'. Now in the sixteenth century Lucretius, whose work had been printed as early as 1473, was studied by an eminent Veronese physician, Girolamo Fracastoro (1483–1553). That acute investigator had absorbed much from the ancient atomic philosophy. Pondering on the nature of epidemics—of which he was a close and accurate student—Fracastoro developed a theory that such diseases were due to *seminaria*, 'seed-stores', the separate *semina* or 'seeds' of which reproduced their like in infected victims to whose bodies they were carried by *fomites* or 'foci of infection'. These 'seeds of disease' of Fracastoro bore some analogy to the Lucretian atoms.

Fracastoro followed Lucretius in denying any essential distinction between the living and the non-living. For him vital phenomena were explained as a product of atomic activity. Such views became widely diffused in the sixteenth century, though they were seldom fully understood. As a result of misunderstanding 'atom' became a synonym for 'living mite' or 'animalcule' and is thus encountered in the writings of Shakespeare, for instance (see *As You Like It*, III. v. 13, and contrast with III. ii. 246). Much of Fracastoro's theory can be read into Lucretius, but the Renaissance physician developed it with newly acquired knowledge and with a skill peculiarly his own. The theory of infection remained much where Fracastoro left it until quite modern times when it assumed a new meaning at the magic touch of Louis Pasteur (1822–95).

Some have seen in Lucretius the beginnings of a theory of evolution. He certainly exhibits a *scala naturae*, a 'ladder of life' somewhat similar to that which may be discerned in the writings of Aristotle. The earth produces out of herself first plants and then animals of an ever higher and higher type. 'Even as down and hair and bristles are first formed on the limbs of beasts . . . so the newborn earth raised up herbage and shrubs first, and thereafter produced the races of mortal things.' This idea of 'spontaneous generation' was almost inevitable until the realm of minute invisible life had been explored by means of the microscope which was not invented until 1608. It is thus no wonder that Lucretius follows Aristotle and all antiquity in assuring us that 'even now many animals spring forth from the earth, formed by rains and the heat of the sun'.

Did Lucretius take the matter farther and did he have any conception of lower forms passing into higher forms? In a sense he certainly did. Moreover, he invoked for the process a mechanism for the clearer explanation of which the world had to await the arrival of Darwin. Yet notwithstanding our familiarity with the idea of 'survival of the fittest', the Lucretian view of the manner in which the more perfect creatures reached their present state must sound very strange to modern ears :—

'Many monsters earth then essayed to create, born with strange faces and strange limbs; the man-woman, between the two, yet not either, sundered from both sexes; things bereft of feet; things without hands; things dumb; things blind; things locked together by the clinging of the limbs so that they could not move nor avoid calamity nor take what they needed. Monsters and prodigies she would thus create, yet vainly, since nature forbade their increase, nor could they reach the bloom of age nor find food. . . . Many races of living creatures then perished nor could beget nor propagate, *for whatever animals now feed on the breath of life, either craft or courage or speed has preserved their kind from the beginning of their being.*'

When we turn to the phenomena which Lucretius has chosen for special description we cannot fail to be struck with the fact that he has been drawn to those which present something of the magnificent, dramatic, or cataclysmic. There is nothing of the quiet and minute observer about him. Thunder and lightning, water-spout, volcano and thunderbolt, suffocating vapours and great pestilences—these are the themes he selects for description. Almost the sole exception is his account of the magnet. This has a special interest because the passage drew the attention of William Gilbert (1540–1603), physician to Queen Elizabeth. Gilbert's *De magnete*, the first important work on experimental science to be printed in England, appeared in 1600. He quotes Lucretius on the magnet and exhibits Lucretian influence.

The remarkable composition of Lucretius takes an isolated place in Latin scientific literature. More characteristic are the *Rerum rusticarum libri III* of Varro and two works of the first Christian century, the *Naturalis historia* of Gaius Plinius Secundus (23–79 A.D.), the most complete and extensive work of its kind that has come down to us from antiquity, and the *Quaestiones naturales* of Lucius Annaeus Seneca (3 B.C.–65 A.D.).

Marcus Terentius Varro (116–27 B.C.) was born at Reate in the Sabine country, where the old Roman qualities are supposed to have lingered longest. He was educated by L. Aelius Stilo, the first systematic Latin philologist and antiquary. Later he went to Athens and came under Platonic influence ; he exhibits, however, throughout his works some Stoic leanings. Varro wrote encyclopaedically on the sciences, and his works were the prototype of the numerous mediaeval works on the 'liberal arts'. He distinguished *nine* of these studies, namely, grammar, dialectic, rhetoric, geometry, arithmetic, astronomy, music, medicine, and architecture. Of these the last two were not recognized by Cassiodorus (490–585 A. D.), Martianus Capella (*c.* 500 A. D.), and Isidore (560–636 A. D.) who handed down the tradition to the Middle Ages, and the number was thus reduced to seven.

Varro, like Cato, tried to collect Latin learning and set it over against the Greek. Of the works of Varro unfortunately only two have been preserved, the *Res rusticae* and a part of the *De lingua latina.* If Varro depends on Cato, he develops a surer judgement based on more experience and knowledge. As a friend of Julius Caesar, whose literary and scientific tastes he shared, we should expect from him this higher and more tolerant standard. He was employed by Caesar in arranging the great stores of Greek and Latin literature for the vast library which he intended to found.

The *Res rusticae* was written by Varro in his eightieth year. In the first book he devotes himself to the general theme of agriculture, in the second he discusses cattle and farm animals, and in the third bees, fish, and a number of wild creatures. The old scholar records, to some extent, his own experience, but has collected his material mainly from the writings of others. He thus already exhibits the derivative tendency which is so marked among later Latin writers on scientific topics. His interests are wider than might perhaps be expected, and he does not confine his discussion to his own country but makes comparisons with other districts and lands. The presentation is enlivened by humour and the scene does not lack animation, though the mechanism of the dialogue often works stiffly. He uses every opportunity to bring in etymology, and he rejoices in artificial separations and divisions, so that in general the work gives one very much the impression conveyed by many treatises of mediaeval origin. Yet his style is always lucid and is sometimes vigorous and racy.

Among the more pleasing of the pictures that Varro draws is that of the life of bees. This, however, is far inferior in accuracy to that set forth by Aristotle (384–322 B. C.) in the *Historia animalium*, and contains nothing that is not to be found in the poetic account of Varro's younger contemporary, Virgil (70–19 B.C.). Among the more remarkable passages in the work is one in which sanguine observers have perceived an anticipation of the modern discovery of the nature of malaria. 'In building houses', he says, 'you must avoid the neighbourhood of marshy places . . . because when the marshes begin to dry they engender a multitude of invisible insects which are introduced into the mouth and nostrils with the inhaled air and occasion serious illnesses.'

Varro, along with the other Latin agricultural writers, early drew the attention of the scholars of the Renaissance. His work was transcribed by some unknown Veronese humanist as early as 1329. Cato, Columella, and Palladius were soon added to form a collection *Scriptores rei rusticae*. After the invention of printing this collection was widely circulated. The first edition appeared at Venice in 1472, and many subsequent issues, bearing the names of distinguished scholars, poured from the presses during the hundred years which followed.

In the next writer we have to consider, the elder Pliny, the Greek leaven has worked further than in Varro. Pliny was born at Como in 23 A.D. and was educated by P. Pomponius Secundus, a poet and military man who inspired him with a love of learning. He studied botany in Rome in the garden of Antonius Castor. Coming under the influence of Seneca he studied philosophy and rhetoric, and practised as an advocate. Pliny saw military service in Germany, visited Gaul, and became a procurator in Spain. After a stay in Rome during which he completed his *Natural History*, dedicating it to Titus, he was appointed by Vespasian prefect of the fleet at Misenum. He was stationed there at the time of the eruption of Vesuvius which overwhelmed Pompeii and Herculaneum in 79 A.D., and he owed his death to his desire to observe that phenomenon more closely. Pliny's education, his career, his opinions, and his character are all typical of the Italian tradition of his day.

As a writer this erudite and much travelled man exhibits great industry and an interest in natural phenomena that is quite uncontrolled by any real scientific standards. Learned and curious, Pliny is entirely devoid of critical faculty. In his *Naturalis historia* he collected an enormous amount of material, entirely unsifted, and this work his nephew rightly spoke of as an 'opus diffusum, eruditum, nec minus varium quam ipsa natura'. By Gibbon it was described as 'that immense register where Pliny has deposited the discoveries, the arts and the errors of mankind'. It was drawn from about 2,000 works—most of them now lost—by 146 Roman and 326 Greek authors. The *Natural History* of Pliny, to which we shall frequently refer, may be divided into eight sections which are intended to cover the whole of physical knowledge. The character and relative length of these sections is significant. They are distributed thus:

(1)	Book	1.	Introductory.
(2)	,,	2.	Cosmology.
(3)	,,	3–6.	Geography.
(4)	,,	7.	Anthropology.
(5)	,,	8–11.	Zoology.
(6)	,,	12–19.	Botany.
(7)	,,	20–32.	Medicine.
(8)	,,	33–37.	Mineralogy and Art.

The main thought that goes through Pliny's book is that nature serves man. Natural objects are hardly described as such but only in relation to man. All things have their 'uses'. 'Nature and the earth', he says, 'fill us with admiration . . . as we contemplate the great variety of plants and find that they are created for the wants or enjoyment of mankind.' This world of wonder is, however, effectively without a God and works by rule—though it is a somewhat crazy rule which these disordered, credulous, wonder-loving volumes set before us. 'It is mere folly to inquire into the nature of God . . . ridiculous to suppose that the great head of all things regards human affairs.' Yet in this world in which he lives man himself occupies a quite peculiar and not always enviable position. ' While other animals ', he says, ' have an instinctive knowledge of their own powers . . . only man is helpless without instruction. He alone desires honours and possessions . . . he alone provides for his grave and even for his future after death . . . All other animals live at peace with their kind . . . but verily with man, most of his misfortunes are man's doings.'—Man the beast of prey! *Lupus est homo homini, non homo quom qualis sit non noscit*, ' A man is not human but vermin to a stranger '—so Plautus (died 184 B.C.) had written long ago.

Many of the matters on which Pliny expresses a judgement would have been impressed on him in the manifold life of Imperial Rome. Many of the animals he discusses were brought to the capital from the furthest ends of the earth, for the arena or for the kitchen. So too with plants; Pliny describes a botanic garden kept by a Roman for the purpose of ascertaining the medical and allied properties of herbs. In descriptions of living creatures Pliny goes back to Aristotle and Theophrastus, but there is no systematic building of the subject and he is scientifically far inferior to his sources. Medical plants are treated in greatest detail and he holds the view that all plants have their own special medical powers. The thought that nature exists for man constantly recurs. His philosophy, which accords in general with the Stoic scheme, is largely drowned and lost in his love of detail and is often submerged in rhetoric.

Seneca (3 B.C.–65 A.D.) has gone over to the Greeks more fully than Varro or Pliny. Lucius Annaeus Seneca was born at Cordova and his mother appears to have been a native Spanish lady. At an early age he came to Rome and there he spent practically all his life. He came under Stoic influence and made his mark as an advocate. Seneca became praetor and consul, acted as tutor to Nero, and is said to have amassed a colossal fortune. After his pupil's accession he showed himself subservient to that monster's designs. Nero ultimately turned against him, and Seneca, having been ordered to prepare for death, anticipated his sentence. His end is described in a powerful passage by Tacitus.

A provincial and a member of one of the newer families, a brilliant rhetorician with a passion for philosophy, of which he was an eloquent but unsystematic exponent, a man whose undoubted balance and judgement had been earned in affairs rather than in action, with an interest in nature rather in its cosmical than in its detailed aspects, Seneca provides in many respects an interesting contrast to his contemporary Pliny. If inferior in character, Seneca is the larger-minded of the two. His work is less typical perhaps of the Roman attitude, but it is the more philosophical and far more critical. Yet his *Quaestiones naturales*, even more than the *Naturalis historia* of Pliny, is borrowed material. The number of direct observations that it contains is small. Seneca is distinctly less credulous than Pliny, but just for this reason he fails to preserve so much interesting material. The chief importance of his work is that it exhibits the attitude to nature of the more philosophical—and, we would add, *rhetorical*—Romans of his day.

Seneca is a Stoic, but does not hesitate to criticize the opinions of the school to which it is evident he is but loosely attached. The subject of the *Quaestiones naturales* is a general account of natural phenomena, but as such it is ill arranged and imperfect. It deals chiefly with Astronomy and Meteorology together with Physical Geography, exhibiting a special interest in earthquakes and allied phenomena. Seneca fell into that trap which had caught so many Greeks before him, the confusion of philosophy with science. It was a habit of many ancient writers that they would only consider phenomena in relation to their conception of the world scheme as a whole. Even the medical system of antiquity suffered from this tendency, though Celsus assures us that it had been his master Hippocrates himself 'who first separated medicine from philosophy'. Our author, who was called by Dante 'Seneca morale', was especially interested in Ethics, a moralist first and physicist or scientist afterwards. Physics—which for him meant a general description of the Universe—led to a knowledge of man's destiny and through that to a consideration of man's duty. 'Some moral significance', he tells us, 'should be attached to all studies and all discussion. Whether we seek into the secrets of nature or treat of divine things, the soul must be delivered from its errors and from time to time reassured.'

At the end of each book Seneca sums up the moral to be derived from the phenomena investigated. This is often of the most distant and strained character. Thus, terminating his discussion of the phenomena of light, he asks, 'What was nature's purpose in providing material capable of receiving and reflecting images?' And he answers, 'Firstly her motive was to show us the sun with his glare dulled, since our eyes are too weak to gaze at him direct, and without something to reflect him we should be wholly ignorant of his shape . . . Secondly we should be unable to see or investigate that conjunction of the two heavenly bodies by which the daylight is wont to be interrupted [in eclipses] unless we could examine the reflections of sun and moon in basins on the ground with comparative freedom. Thirdly mirrors were discovered in order that man might know himself.'

Such a point of view appealed greatly to the Middle Ages. It was a standpoint very acceptable to the mediaeval Church, by which Seneca was regarded as a Christian. He was included by St. Jerome among the *scriptores ecclesiastici*, and is frequently quoted by later Christian writers. But this exclusively ethical attitude is inconsistent with the effective advancement of knowledge and has been one of the greatest enemies of science. In spite of the nobility of his sentiments, in spite of his lip-service to the advancement of knowledge, in spite of his belief in human destiny, Seneca's ethical attitude could do nothing to stay the downfall of ancient wisdom. To that downfall and to Seneca's relation to it we shall later return.

The works of Pliny and Seneca differ from those of most of

the authors that we have to consider in that they were not 'discovered' by the Renaissance humanists. Pliny and Seneca were indeed never lost, and their works formed part of the reading of the Dark and Middle Ages. For the understanding of mediaeval thought a knowledge of these authors is necessary.

§ 3. *Medical and Veterinary Knowledge*

The original native Roman medical system was quite devoid of scientific elements and was that of a people of the lower culture. Interwoven, as is all primitive medicine, with ideas that trespass on the domain of religion, it possessed that multitude of 'specialist deities' which was so characteristic of the Roman cults. Thus Fever had three temples in Rome, and was supplicated as the goddess *Febris* and flatteringly addressed as *Febris diva*, *Febris sancta*, *Febris magna*. Foul odours were invoked in the name of *Mephitis* to whom a temple was erected at a place where asphyxiating fumes emerged from the earth. Lassitude was implored in the name of *Fessonia*. *Uterina* guarded the womb, and *Lucina*, assisted by a whole group of goddesses, had charge of childbirth. The entire pantheon of disease and physiological function was presided over by the *Dea Salus* whose temple was on one of the summits of the Quirinalis. She was the deity who took the public health under her supervision.

Some of the surviving records of the original Roman medicine are of even lower material. Cato the Censor assures us that the ancient Rome, which he lauded, was *sine medicis sed non sine medicina*, 'healthy without doctors.' He advised that to a sick ox be given three grains of salt, three laurel leaves, three rue leaves and various other threes for three consecutive days, both patient and physician fasting and the drug being given when both were standing erect. For human patients his panacea was cabbage. He sought to reduce dislocations by reciting over them the euphonious formula,

'Huat hanat huat ista pista sista domiabo damnaustra.'

Students of folk-lore have shown that magical jingles can often be traced back to a forgotten tongue, but that of Cato suggests the expletive *lingua franca* still used by the victims of such accidents!

The entire external aspect of Roman medicine was gradually changed by the advent of Greek science. There is evidence, however, that the change hardly penetrated below the upper classes. Thus in medical works of the fourth and fifth centuries of the Christian era we still encounter numerous survivals of the older material. There are also many references in St. Augustine's *De civitate dei* which show that the ancient beliefs were widely current in Italy even among the well-to-do of his day. After the fall of the Empire they lingered among the barbaric peoples that entered into its heritage. Nor are they yet extinct, for prescriptions and practices of Pliny, of Marcellus Empiricus, and of Sextus Placitus Papyriensis may still be traced in the folk-customs and folk-beliefs of our own land and in the sayings and doings of continental peasantry.

Notwithstanding the large medical field that the Western Empire provided, and the wide acceptance of Greek medicine by the upper classes, it is remarkable that the Latin-speaking peoples produced no eminent physician. During the Republic medical education had been entirely a matter of private teaching. The relation of pupil and master exhibited by the Hippocratic oath was evidently that which prevailed under the early Empire. The initiate declared, 'I will reckon him who taught me this Art as dear to me as those who bore me. I will look upon his offspring as my own brethren and will teach them this art, if they would learn it, without fee or stipulation. By precept, lecture, and every other mode of instruction, I will impart a knowledge of this Art to my own sons, and to those of my teacher, and to disciples bound by a stipulation and an oath, according to the Law of Medicine, but to none other.'

Despite the Ionic Greek dress in which this formula is known to us, there is evidence that it is of Imperial date and of Roman rather than of Greek origin. The very form of the oath suggests the arrangements which were gradually made for medical instruction at Rome. The first important teacher there was the Greek Asclepiades of Bithynia (died *c.* 40 B.C.), a contemporary of Lucretius and like him an Epicurean. Asclepiades introduced the atomic view of Democritus into medicine. He deeply influenced the course of later medical thought, ridiculed the Hippocratic attitude of relying on the *vis medicatrix naturae*, 'the healing power of nature' which he regarded as a mere 'meditation on death', and urged that active measures were needed for the process of cure to be *cito, tuto, iucunde*, 'seemly, swift and sure'. He founded a regular school at Rome which continued after him.

An outline of the history of this school and of others formed in Rome can be made out with some approach to clearness. At first the school was the mere personal following of the physician, who took his pupils and apprentices round with him on his visits. At a later stage such groups combined to form societies or colleges, where questions of the art were debated. Towards the end of the reign of Augustus or the beginning of that of Tiberius, these societies constructed for themselves a meeting-place on the Esquiline, the so-called *Schola medicorum.* It had a president with the title of *archiatrus* and a secretary known as the *tabularius* or *scriba.* Finally the emperors built halls or *auditoria* for the teaching of medicine. The professors at first received only the pupils' fees. It was not until the time of Vespasian (emperor 70–79 A.D.) that medical teachers were given a salary at the public expense. The system was extended by Hadrian (117–138) and Alexander Severus (222–235).

Thus Rome became a centre of medical instruction. After a time subsidiary centres were established in other Italian towns. From Italy the custom spread and we meet traces of such schools at the half Greek Marseilles, as well as at Bordeaux, Arles, Nimes, Lyons, and Saragossa. From Marseilles, which had been the home of the geographers and astronomers

Pytheas and Euthymenes, came the physicians Crinas and Charmis. The latter, though accustomed to bathe his patients in ice-cold water in the depth of winter, received one of the highest medical fees mentioned in antiquity. Marseilles too was the home of Demosthenes, the most renowned of ancient oculists, who lived under Nero, and whose works were much sought after and survived at least as late as the fourteenth century. Bordeaux did itself no great honour in giving to the world Marcellus Empiricus, who had high office under Theodosius I (379–395) and Arcadius (396–408), and has left us a book which represents wellnigh the low-water-mark of superstitious folly. For the most part, however, these provincial schools produced workaday medical men, few of whose writings have come down to us. They were perhaps largely training places for the army surgeons. That class seldom had scientific interests, though Dioscorides, one of the most prominent physicians of antiquity and one who earned the respect of Galen and has deeply influenced the modern pharmacopoeia, served in the army under Nero. Dioscorides, however, wrote in Greek, and his work was probably not translated until the sixth century.

Before we leave the topic of medical instruction it will be in place to say a word concerning the study of anatomy. The practical study of that subject had been carried on at Alexandria, beginning with Herophilus and Erasistratus about 300 B.C. Physiology had been experimentally studied, and the terrible charge of vivisection of human beings is made against the school of Alexandria by Tertullian (*c.* 155–*c.* 222) and Augustine (354–430) who are supported by the very damning evidence of Celsus. Dissection of the dead body was still practised at Alexandria towards the end of the first century B.C. but it is probable that it had ceased by the middle of the second century A.D. It is clear that it was on the bodies of animals that Galen (130–200 A.D.), for instance, relied for his anatomical knowledge. Considering the indifference to human life which the Romans often exhibited, considering their brutality to slaves and the opportunities offered by gladiatorial combats, considering the obvious value of anatomical knowledge for surgical practice and the organization of the military medical service of the Empire, it is truly remarkable that the anatomical knowledge of antiquity was thus allowed to lapse. It did not revive until the rise of the mediaeval universities.

We may now turn to the literature of medicine. The earliest scientific medical work in Latin is the *De re medica* of Celsus which was prepared about 30 A.D. It is of great interest as our one adequate representative of the surgery of the Alexandrian period. Written in excellent Latin, it is in many ways the most readable and well-arranged ancient medical work that we have. All the evidence, however, points to this work of Celsus having been a compilation if not a translation from the Greek, and the sole surviving part of a complete encyclopaedia of knowledge. Many of its phrases are closely reminiscent of the 'Hippocratic Collection'. The ethical tone is high and the general line of treatment sensible and humane. Celsus, though almost unknown to the Middle Ages, was the first classical medical writer to be printed, his work appearing at Florence in 1478.

The treatise of Celsus is divided into eight books. It opens with an interesting account of the history of medicine containing a comparison of the rival sects of the so-called 'Dogmatic' and 'Empiric' physicians. The first two books deal with diet and the general principles of therapeutics and pathology, the third and fourth discuss internal diseases, the fifth and sixth external diseases. The seventh and eighth books, devoted to surgery, are perhaps the most valuable. Celsus professes himself a follower of Asclepiades of Bithynia (died *c.* 40 B.C.) but, unlike his master, he by no means despises the Hippocratic *expectant* method of 'waiting on the disease'. In many matters his comparative boldness as a surgeon will draw the attention of the modern medical reader. Thus he describes plastic operations on the face and mouth, and the removal of polypus from the nose. He tells too of the very dangerous operations for extirpating a goitre and of cutting for stone. He gives an excellent account of what might be thought the modern operation for removal of tonsils. Noteworthy also is his description of dental practice which includes the wiring of loose teeth and an account of what appears to have been a dental mirror. An idea of the surgical instruments in use in his time can be obtained from those which have been recovered from Pompeii, some of which are displayed in Fig. 8. At the top is shown a pair of forceps of a form used in removing a long uvula. Below, from left to right, are arranged a long forceps with pointed ends, a small pair of scissors, a pair of dental forceps, and a small pair of tweezers. To the right there is placed a pair of blunt forceps above and an instrument for scarification below.

The remaining Latin medical writings that we possess are not of high scientific value. Surviving works are ascribed to Antonius Musa, the medical attendant of Augustus. The attribution, however, is spurious and, after Celsus, the first Latin medical author whose writings have survived is probably Scribonius Largus, a physician of the so-called 'Empiric' school. He practised at Rome under Claudius whom he accompanied in 43 A. D. on his expedition to Britain, and he was physician to the Empress Messalina. His receipt book is derived entirely from Greek sources of the lower type. He follows the unscientific method, which became very popular in the Middle Ages, of beginning with the head and working down to the feet, entirely disregarding the relations and functions of the organs. This method of classifying diseases by their position in the body is very ancient and is encountered in an Egyptian medical papyrus of about 1700 B. C. Scribonius is the earliest writer who makes mention of the so-called *Hippocratic oath*, and has been praised because some of the unguents that he employed for wounds had antiseptic qualities.

After Scribonius Largus the most ancient Latin medical work is that of Pliny. He was a scorner of medical science and the starveling Greeks who practised it. 'Medicine, in spite of its lucrativeness,' says Pliny, 'is the one art of these Greeks that the serious Roman has so far refused to cultivate. Few of our fellow-citizens have been willing even to touch it, and if they do so they desert at once to the Greeks... Unfortunately there is no law to punish ignorant physicians, and capital punishment is never inflicted on them. Yet they learn by our suffering and experiment by putting us to death.' The collection of Pliny, which was to be a substitute for the works of these wretched Greeks, consists of a vast series of remedies built on the supposedly firm ground of 'experience'. It is based on no theory, it is supported by no doctrine, it is founded on no experiment. Yet it is the prototype of the medical output of the next fifteen hundred years. The cry of Pliny for 'experience' as against 'theory' has been plaintively echoed by the 'practical' man down the ages. Yet there are subjects and there are conditions in which the man without a theory may be the most unpractical of all. Medicine is such a subject and disease is such a condition.

When 'experience' is invoked in medical matters by Pliny and by later writers, the absence of the parallel to the 'experience' of many other affairs of life is often missed. In other matters the so-called experience is usually under some sort of control, and therefore in fact approaches the character of 'experiment'. Experience is thus frequently but the result of a series of *observations provoquées*. With clinical medicine, so long as it is uncontrolled by the ancillary sciences, this can seldom be the case. A single instance from Pliny will suffice. 'The herb dittany', he says, 'has the power to extract arrows. This *was proved* by stags who had been struck by these missiles which were loosened when they fed on this plant.' Had Pliny made any effort to verify such a statement? He had taken his 'experience', in fact, from

Fig. 8. SURGICAL INSTRUMENTS FROM POMPEII

By the courtesy of Prof. K. Sudhoff

Fig. 9. EWE AND LAMB. From a well-head at Vienna

an interpolated and spurious passage of a work by Theophrastus, and he omits to mention his source. Prepossession with the idea of the value of such experience led Pliny and the ages which followed him into innumerable absurdities into which it would be profitless to follow them. But if the multitudinous remedies of Pliny are always useless and often disgusting, yet his book contains some valuable material for the history of medicine, culled from many sources now lost. His very discursiveness and love of gossip are our gain, and though he can do nothing to advance medical knowledge he gives us much insight into medical practice in antiquity.

The later medical writings in the Latin language are hardly worth notice here. Some, such as those of Priscianus (*c.* 380), Marcellus (*c.* 400), and (pseudo-) Apuleius Barbarus (? *c.* 400), contemptible in themselves, are of interest for the influence they had on after ages. One writer, Quintus Serenus Sammonicus (*c.* 250), is remarkable for having introduced into Latin the foolish custom of writing medical works in verse. He is also the first to record the famous device or charm known as the *Abracadabra*. Another late Latin medical writer, Vindicianus (*c.* 400), less futile than most, was the friend of St. Augustine. Important for a special reason is Caelius Aurelianus, a Numidian physician of the fifth century. His work is of philological interest and is also noticeable as one of the few remnants of the so-called 'Methodist' school. It is, however, a translation from the Greek Soranus and not a native work. The last Latin medical writer of antiquity is probably Cassius Felix, an African, whose language is interesting but whose work, written in 447, consists only of extracts from earlier writers.

Veterinary medicine was a topic on which the Roman agricultural interests concentrated considerable attention. An important source for much of their material was a work by the Carthaginian Mago (*c.* 200 B. C.), which was translated into both Latin and Greek. The earlier Latin works on agriculture—

Cato, Varro, Columella—naturally include many passages which discuss the treatment of sick animals, and there is evidence that they draw largely on Mago. The *Georgics* of Virgil (written 31 B. C.) is really a manual of agriculture in verse. In the third book of the *Georgics* Virgil deals with the care and breeding of animals, and he speaks of epizootic diseases such as scabies in sheep, foot-rot, anthrax, rabies, and sheep-rot. Much veterinary information may be gleaned from the works of Pliny. A curious collection of remedies for diseases of cattle has come down to us under the name of Gargilius Martialis (*c.* 200 A. D.); it is interesting as an example of late Roman veterinary medicine with little or no Greek influence. The agricultural writer Palladius, who flourished in the fourth century, gives an account of the points of horses and describes how to tell their age by the teeth. The work exercised some influence on the Middle Ages and was translated into English as early as 1420.

By far the best known and most complete Latin veterinary work is the *Digestorum artis mulomedicinae Libri IV* by Flavius Vegetius Renatus (383–450), who is known also as a writer on military topics. The treatise is remarkably scientific and well arranged, considering the period at which it was composed; especially noteworthy is the contempt expressed in it for incantations and other superstitious practices. It had been studied by Petrarch and was the first veterinary work to be printed (Rome, 1487). Vegetius has been called the 'father of veterinary science'; it is certain, however, that he was a compiler, and among his sources is the *Mulomedicina Chironis* translated from Greek by one Claudius Hermerus (*c.* 300 A. D.?). The work of Hermerus survives and is of great philological importance as a record of Low Latin linguistic forms.

§ 4. *Hygiene and Organization of Public Health under the Empire*

If in Medicine itself the Roman achieved but little, in organization of medical service, and especially in the depart-

Fig. 10. OUTLET INTO TIBER OF THE CLOACA MAXIMA, THE MAIN SEWER OF ROME
From the engraving by Piranesi

Fig. 11. ADVANCED DRESSING STATION
From Trajan's Column
Left : a wounded legionary is aided by two comrades
Right : a surgeon bandages the thigh of an auxiliary

Fig. 12. A LATRINE near the Forum of Timgad in Algeria, flushed with water from a constant fountain

ment which deals with the public health, his position is far more honourable. All the writers on architecture—Varro, Vitruvius, and Columella—give much attention to the orientation, position, and drainage of buildings, and from an early date sanitation and public health drew the attention of statesmen. Considering the dread of the neighbourhood of marshes on the part of these practical sanitarians and in view of modern knowledge of the mosquito-borne character of malaria, it is entertaining to find the mosquito net (*conopeum*) ridiculed by the poets Horace, Juvenal, and Propertius!

Sanitation was a feature of Roman life. Rome was already provided with cloacae or subterranean sewers in the age of the

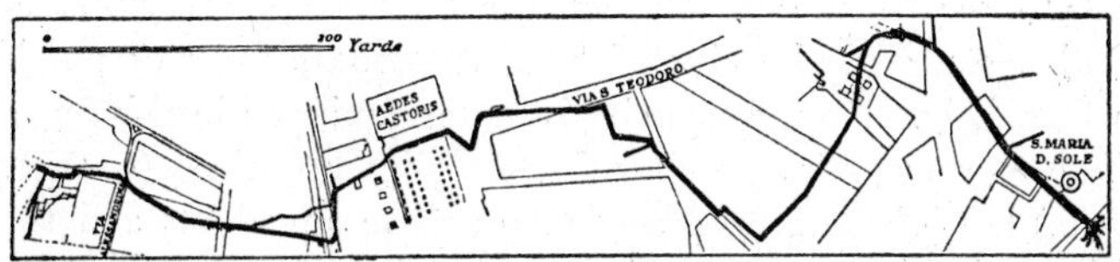

FIG. 13. Plan of the course of the Cloaca Maxima through the city to its outlet in the Tiber.

Tarquins (6th cent. B. C.). Similar conduits have been found in excavations in Crete of Minoan date, but there is evidence that the idea reached Rome from Etruscan sources. Tradition is probably just in referring the construction of the *Cloaca maxima* itself, the main drain of Rome [Figs. 10 and 13], to the period of monarchy.

The growth of hygienic ideas is seen in the interdict by the 'Law of the Twelve Tables' (450 B. C.) against burials within the city walls. It is noteworthy that this order is made without reference to any physician. The same absence of professional medical intervention may be noted in the instructions issued to the aediles to attend to the cleanliness of the streets and to the distribution of water. Nor is any medical help or opinion invoked by the ancient *Lex regia*, attributed to Numa, which directed the opening of the body in the hope of extracting a living child in the case of a pregnant woman who had died. It is the origin of the so-called ' Caesarean section ', the method by which Caesar himself is said to have been brought into the world.

At the date of these decrees physicians in Rome were either slaves or in an entirely subordinate position. Their status was greatly improved by Julius Caesar who, Suetonius (*c.* 120 A. D.) tells us, ' conferred citizenship on all who practised medicine at Rome . . . to make them more desirous of living in the city and to induce others to resort to it '. The finest monument to the Roman care for the public health stands yet for all to see in the remains of the fourteen great aqueducts which supplied the city with 300,000,000 gallons of potable water daily. No modern city is better equipped in this regard. The Roman military writer Sextus Julius Frontinus (*c.* 40–103 A. D.) has left us a good account of these aqueducts and their history in his *De aquis urbis Romae*. The distribution of water to individual houses was also well cared for, and excellent specimens of Roman plumbing may be seen in the British Museum [Fig. 14]. A large number of other sanitary devices have survived in many sites and are particularly well seen at Timgad in Algeria [Fig. 12].

Under the early Empire a definite public medical service was constituted. Public physicians or *archiatri*, as they were later called, were appointed to the various towns and institutions. Alexander Severus (222–35) organized the medical service of the imperial house. The archiaters of the palace were sometimes promoted to provincial governorships, as happened to Ausonius (*c.* 320), father of the poet, who became prefect of Illyria, or to Vindicianus (*c.* 400), the friend of Augustine, who became proconsul of Africa. At a yet later date the first archiater of the sacred palace was invested with the function of judging disputes between physicians. ' We decorate you from this moment ', says Cassiodorus (490–585) to one of them in his usual pompous and roundabout style, ' with the honour of being head of the archiaters, that you alone among the masters of health may be pre-eminent, and that all those who exercise their ingenuity on the subtleties of mutual contradictions may refer to your judgement. Be you the arbiter of this exalted art, and adjudge the conflicts of those who have formerly taken only their passions for judge. In healing them you will heal the

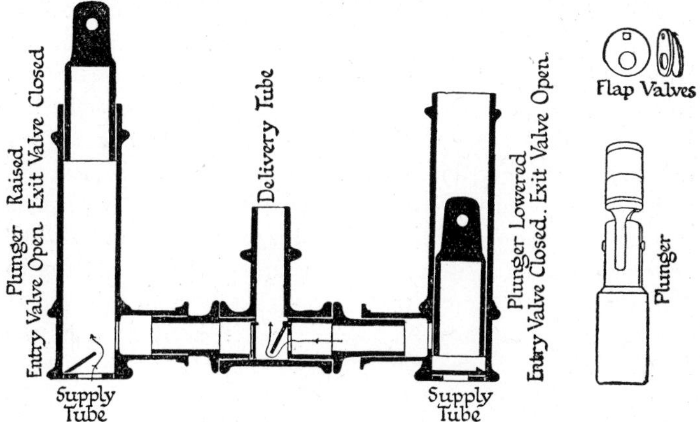

FIG. 14. Diagram of double action bronze pump from Bolsena in Etruria, now in the British Museum. The pump is constructed on a principle invented by Ctesibius of Alexandria (see p. 316). The pump is worked by alternating plungers raised and lowered by a single rocking beam which, for simplicity, is here omitted. The bottoms of the cylinders in which the plungers move were connected by pipes with the water-supply and are furnished with flap valves opening upward. When the plunger was raised a vacuum was created and the water lifted the valve and rushed in. When the plunger reached the highest point the valve fell again and retained the water. When the plunger descended it forced the water from the cylinder into the central delivery tube through another flap valve in the horizontal pipe.

sick if you terminate their quarrels prudently. It is a great privilege for you that these able men should be submitted to your authority and that you should be honoured among those whom all the world reveres.'

In Greek lands state physicians had been known for many

centuries and are mentioned by Herodotus (*c.* 484–425 B.C.). In the days of the Empire the custom of appointing district physicians spread early from Italy to Gaul and to the other provinces. A statute of Antoninus of about the year 160 A.D. regulates the appointment of these physicians. 'The smallest towns may have five physicians who may enjoy immunity from taxation. . . .The more important towns may have seven. . . .The towns of larger grade may have ten. . . . It is suitable for the largest number to be allowed to the capital cities, the second to cities with a court of justice. . . . These numbers may not be surpassed either by an ordinance of the curia or by any other means soever, but it is lawful to diminish them if this is done in view of the civil charges.' The main duty of these physicians was to attend to the needs of the poor. In the code of Justinian (533 A.D.) there is an article urging them to give this service cheerfully rather than the more subservient attendance on the wealthy. Their salaries were fixed by the *decuriones* or municipal councillors. They were encouraged to undertake the training of pupils. Inscriptions prove the existence of such municipal *archiatri* in many towns, and attest the respect in which they were held.

It is in connexion with the army that we see the Roman medical system at its best. The actual medical organization of the Roman army is, however, a very debatable topic, and information concerning it has to be gathered from very scattered sources. The matter may be thus summed up. 'Each of the 25–30 legions of 10 cohorts (numbering 6,500–7,000 men in all) had a legionary physician (*medicus legionis*); each of the 9 pretorian cohorts, the 4 urban cohorts, and the 7 cohorts of *vigiles* (who acted as police and firemen in the city) had four cohort surgeons (*medici cohortis*). Every body of auxiliary troops and every ship of the pretorian fleet had also its physician. All these physicians, as part of the military establishment, were regarded as *immunes*, exempt from guard and combat-duty or day-labour, and ranked among the *princi-*

pales (non-commissioned officers). In the Pretorian and city cohorts, they were required to be Roman citizens, while the physicians of the *vigiles* and auxiliary troops, serving in Italy and the provinces, could be freedmen or foreigners. For this reason, the staff surgeons of these latter organizations were called *medici ordinarii.* The legionary physicians were all of equal rank, had no other medical superiors, and were subordinated only to the camp commander (*praefectus castrorum*) or, in his absence, to the tribunes of the legions. The social status of the medical staff in this military hierarchy was that of the innumerable grades of non-commissioned personnel and of the highly elaborated bureaucracy attached to the army, which included accountants, notaries, registrars, secretaries, and civilian functionaries of all kinds' (F. H. Garrison). The actual administration of first-aid by Roman military surgeons is represented on Trajan's column [Fig. 11].

The great contribution of Rome to medicine—and it is a very great one—is the hospital system. It is a scheme that naturally arose out of the Roman genius for organization and is connected with the Roman military system. Among the Greeks *iatreia*, 'surgeries', were well known; they were, however, the private property of the medical man. Larger institutions were connected with the Aesculapian temples but there is no evidence of scientific medical treatment in these places. In Republican times the Romans were no better off, and the work of Cato shows that there was no provision for sick slaves. A temple to Aesculapius had been established on an island of the Tiber in Republican times. The island was shiplike in form. Part of it had been hewn to the shape of a ship's poop whereon the staff and serpent of Aesculapius and the head of the god were carved; remains of these symbols can be seen there to this day [Fig. 22]. 'On this island of Aesculapius', Suetonius tells us, 'certain men exposed their sick and worn-out slaves because of the trouble of treating them. The Emperor Claudius (41–54 A. D.), however, decreed that such slaves were free, and, if they recovered, they should not return to the control of their masters.' Thus the island became a place of refuge for the sick poor. We may regard it as an early form of public hospital.

Columella (first century A. D.) speaks of *valetudinaria*, 'infirmaries', for such persons, and gives humane directions for their management. Seneca tells us that *valetudinaria* were in use even by free Romans. The excavations at Pompeii show that a physician's house might even be built somewhat on the lines of a modern 'nursing home'. There are passages in Galen (130–201 A. D.) which seem to imply that it was in the provinces that private institutions first developed into subventioned public hospitals.

This development of public hospitals naturally early affected military life. At first sick soldiers had been sent home for treatment. As the Roman frontiers spread ever wider this became impossible and military hospitals were founded at important strategic points. The sites of several such military hospitals have been excavated. The earliest that has come to light is of the first century and is at Carnuntum, about twenty miles from Vienna. The best explored is at Novaesium [Fig. 15] on the lower Rhine near Düsseldorf. The military hospital at Novaesium was founded about 100 A. D. but has later elements. It is built on the corridor system. Entering from the north between the administrative offices we come on a large hall on which succeeds a long narrow room placed along the axis of the building. This room was probably used as a refectory. It is surrounded on three sides by a corridor out of which open chambers for the sick. Around this series of chambers runs another corridor also along three sides of the building, and around this outer corridor again is another series of chambers. These outer chambers are peculiarly arranged so that they do not open directly into the corridor but each pair is reached through a small vestibule. (See detail in Fig. 15.) The arrangement must be related to sanitation, and traces of the drainage system have been uncovered. The general scheme is much in advance of any military hospital until quite modern times.

From the military *valetudinarium* it was no great step to the construction of similar institutions for the numerous imperial officials and their families in the provincial towns. Motives of

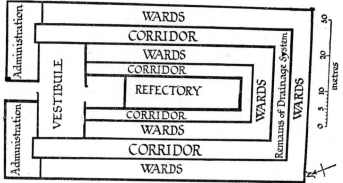

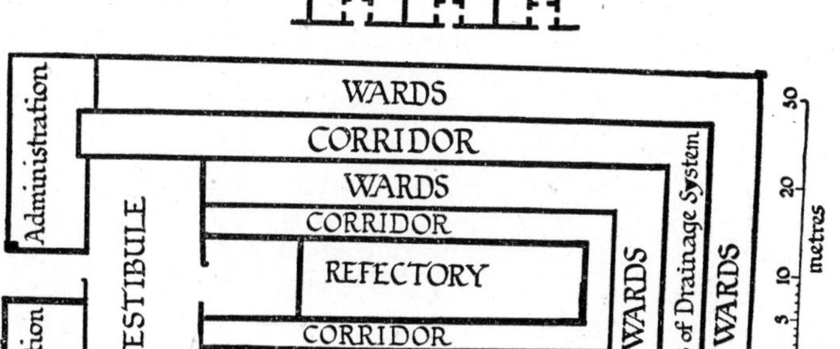

FIG. 15. General Plan of Roman Military Hospital at Novaesium near Düsseldorf. The assigning of the uses to the different parts of the building is conjectural.

benevolence, too, seem to have gradually come in, and finally public hospitals were founded in many localities. The idea naturally passed on to Christian times, and the pious foundation of hospitals for the sick and outcast in the Middle Ages is to be traced back to these Roman *valetudinaria.* The first charitable institution of this kind concerning which we have clear information was established at Rome in the fourth century by a Christian lady named Fabiola of whom we learn from St. Jerome. The plan of such a hospital projected at St. Gall in the early years of the ninth century has survived. It reminds us in many respects of the early Roman military hospitals. These mediaeval hospitals for the sick must naturally be distinguished from the even more numerous 'spitals' for travellers and pilgrims, the idea of which may perhaps be traced back to the rest-houses along the strategic roads of the Empire.

§ 5. *Mathematics and Physical Sciences*

As with all other peoples, the first system of numeration adopted by the Romans was based on finger counting. From it was developed a method of mechanical reckoning on a count-

Fig. 16. Carved Bone Counters employed in calculation, found in Pompeii and now in the British Museum. The positions of the hand indicate numbers, and are identical with symbols still used in England in the sixteenth century.

ing board. The simplest form was a board covered with sand divided into columns by the finger or by the stylus, counters being used in calculation. Cicero, referring to this method, speaks of an expert calculator as *eruditum attigisse pulverem*, 'clever at handling the sand'. The counters employed had graven upon them figures of the hand in various positions to represent different numbers. Many such counters have survived [Fig. 16] and their symbols are identical with those which remained in vogue till late mediaeval times.

A more complicated apparatus was the true *abacus*. This began as a board with a series of grooves in which pebbles or *calculi* could be moved up and down, hence the verb *calculo* and the modern use of *calculate*. The actual form of the

Roman abacus is well known, and several excellently preserved specimens have been recovered. In its more developed form the abacus consisted of an upper row of short and a lower row of long rods [Fig. 17]. Each of the short rods had a single perforated bead running on it and each of the longer ones four such beads. The first rod on the right was marked for units, the next on its left for tens, and so on up to a million. Its mode of application was very much more complicated than might be imagined. Persius had both forms of calculating board in mind when he derides the zany *qui abaco numeros et secto in pulvere metas scit risisse*, 'who sniggers at the figures on the abacus or the ridges of furrowed sand'.

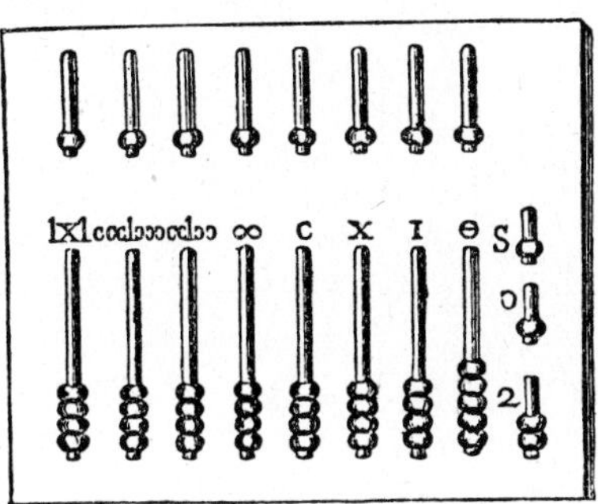

Fig. 17. A late form of Roman Abacus.

The whole mathematical system of antiquity was handicapped by its inadequate notation. The Roman numerals were, it is believed, derived from Etruscan sources. The decimal system with which we are nowadays familiar is of Indian origin, and reached Europe through Arabic channels in the Middle Ages. The Greeks often used geometrical methods where we should invoke the aid of algebra, and their mathematical developments made little impression on the Romans. How slight was the mathematical knowledge absorbed by Latin scientific authors may be gathered from the *Geometrica* and *Arithmetica* bearing the name of Boëthius (480–524 A.D.). Those elementary works ascribed to 'the last of the ancients' represent the mathematical legacy of antiquity to the earlier Middle Ages. Even when Rome had world dominion, Cicero bemoaned that 'the Greek mathematicians lead the field in pure geometry, while we limit ourselves to the practice of reckoning and measuring'.

The Romans held that the art of mensuration was at least as old as their city, and it was said to have been first practised by the priests for ecclesiastical purposes at a very early date. The knowledge of the subject advanced in Imperial times and a regular school for the teaching of surveying was established. The chief instrument in general use was known as the *groma*. It consisted of two lineals fixed at right angles and arranged to turn horizontally about a vertical pivot. From the end of each lineal a plummet was suspended. One of the lineals was used for sighting and the other to determine the direction in the field at right angles to the first. As both agriculture and town-planning were mainly on rectangular lines this instrument was of wide application. A figure of it has been found on the grave of a Roman surveyor, and an actual specimen has been recovered from Pompeii [Fig. 18].

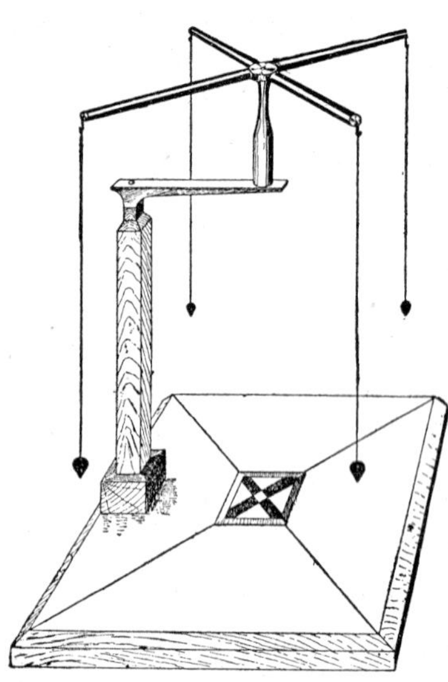

FIG. 18. The Groma. Reconstructed from descriptions, remains, and ancient representations.

That site has also yielded a number of compasses and other apparatus employed in mensuration [Fig. 19]. The inaccuracy of some Roman measurements is strange when we consider the exactness of these Pompeiian instruments. Thus $3\frac{1}{8}$ is given as the ratio of the circumference of a circle to the diameter by Vitruvius, a competent architect who must often have had occasion to examine the drums of columns. A better result might have been expected from any schoolboy provided with a compass and tape measure!

An interesting description of the method of estimation of the distance from the observer of an inaccessible point on the same level as himself, e.g. the opposite bank of a river, has come down to us. A line is traced along the near bank, and is measured off by rolling along it a *hodometer*, an instrument consisting of a wheel the length of the circumference of which is known and whose revolutions can be counted. Vitruvius has preserved for us a description of this apparatus which is in effect a 'taxicab' [Fig. 20]. From each end of this measured line a sight is taken by means of the dioptra—the Roman form of which was inferior to that described by Hero of Alexandria (*c.* 1st cent. A.D.). The angles and the base being thus available, a triangle, congruent to that formed by joining the point on the far bank to the extremities of the measured line, is constructed on the near bank. The vertical height of this triangle can now be measured by the hodometer and this will give the distance of the point from the observer, or the breadth of the river. We may here note that the work of Vitruvius was first printed in 1486 at Rome and was early circulating in an Italian translation. It was perhaps from such a version that Leonardo da Vinci (1452–1519) obtained hints which enabled him to design his 'taxicab'.

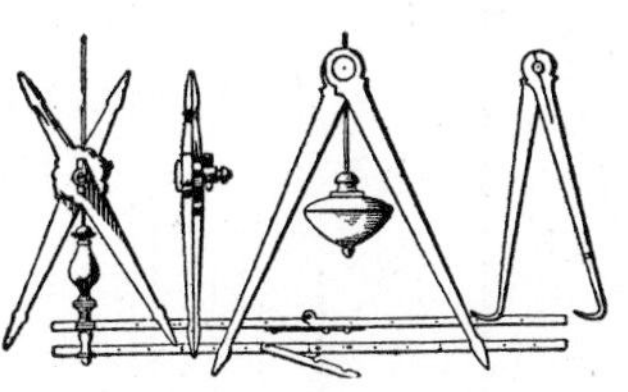

FIG. 19. Mathematical instruments. From Pompeii, after Oberbeck.

Mechanical knowledge among the Romans was very evident in certain departments; it had always a practical direction and was not cultivated for its own sake. Among the inventions that the Romans may have made independently is the steelyard. This instrument is a device of considerable antiquity among them, and may be traced back at least as far as the third century B.C. Its use was widely understood and many specimens have been recovered [Fig. 21]. The principle of the pulley, too, was well known. Thus on one of the monuments we can follow the mechanism of a crane. It is worked by a treadmill and raises blocks of stone by acting through a whole system of pulleys [Fig. 23].

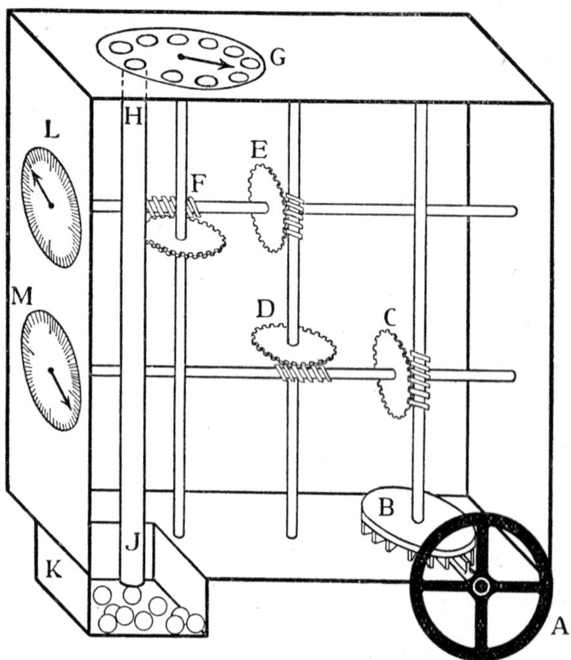

FIG. 20. 'Taxicab' or hodometer as described by Vitruvius. The wheel A runs along the ground. It has, eccentrically attached to its axle, a peg which fits into the cogs of wheel B. At every rotation of wheel A the wheel B therefore turns one peg. The rotation of B is transmitted to a vertical shaft and the rotation of this shaft is transmitted and reduced by passage through the series of joints C, D, E, and F. Finally the rotation at F is transmitted to a vertical shaft which is fastened to the disk G. This disk G is perforated with holes. As disk G rotates these holes come in turn opposite to the open upper end of the tube H J which leads to the reservoir K. Pebbles are placed on each of the holes in G and the machine is so geared that for every mile traversed one falls into the reservoir K. The distance traversed may be checked by counting these pebbles. Dials may be fitted to the horizontal shafts as at L and M.

The inadequate *theoretical* basis of the physical conceptions of Latin writers is shown in various directions. Thus Pliny recounts a fable of the Remora, a fish of the Mediterranean which has a sucker on its head. 'This tiny fish can restrain all the forces of the ocean. Winds may rage and storms may roar, yet the fish restrains their might and fury, and causes ships to stand still . . . by simply adhering to them.' Centuries before, Archimedes (287–212 B.C.) had demanded 'a *fixed* place on which to stand that he might move the world'. The full understanding of the works of Archimedes failed for the next millennium and a half. Yet his simpler practical devices, such as the water screw, were familiar enough to the Romans.

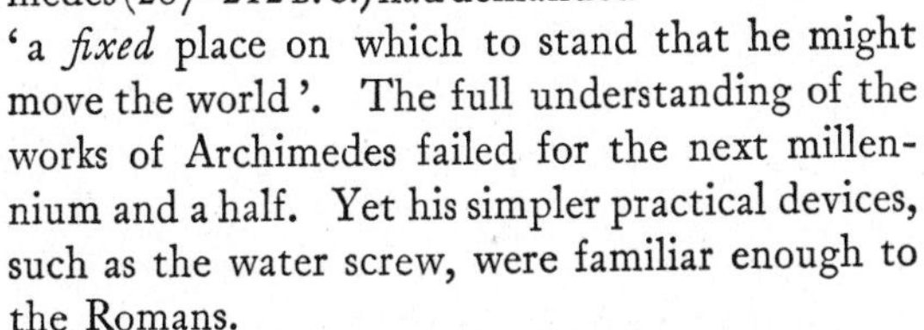

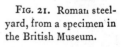

FIG. 21. Roman steelyard, from a specimen in the British Museum.

Seneca is superior, scientifically, to Pliny. This in itself is no great distinction, but there are several passages in the *Quaestiones naturales* which suggest that Seneca did occasionally take the trouble to verify some of the statements that he makes. He has a clear idea too of the value of astronomical observations. Thus he tells us that 'it is essential to have a record of all former appearances of comets. These bodies appear seldom and therefore we do not yet know . . . if they follow periodic laws and whether some definite cause is responsible for their reappearance at the appointed day. Such a development of astronomy is but recent.' In spite of this statement of Seneca there is a passage in the *Meteorologica* of Aristotle which seems to ascribe the knowledge of the periodic return of comets to the Pythagoreans and to Hippocrates of Chios (*c.* 425 B.C.), five hundred years before the days of Seneca.

Seneca's statement concerning the magnifying powers of glass globes is peculiarly noteworthy. Fallacious attempts have been made to show that the ancients knew of the effects of refraction of light at curved surfaces. That they knew of the burning-glass is clear from references in Pliny and elsewhere, and many glass or crystal spheres, probably used as fire-makers, have been recovered from Roman sites. These burning glasses do not, however, seem to have been used for magnifying purposes, and Seneca has bequeathed to us one of the very few passages in ancient writings that suggest that this power of transparent spheres had even been noticed. He records that 'letters however small and dim appear large and clear when viewed through a glass globe filled with water'. It has been claimed that globes of this type were used by the gem cutters of antiquity, but such suggestions are unsupported by evidence. The oft-repeated statement that Nero used a cut emerald as a lens to aid his defective vision has arisen from a mistranslation of a passage in Pliny.

Applied mathematics underwent some development at the end of the Republican period. Julius Caesar himself was an astronomical author and Pliny used a book of his as a source. Caesar had planned two undertakings of great scientific import. He wished to improve the Roman calendar which had fallen into great confusion, and to organize a general survey of the Empire. Both of these projects were ultimately realized.

The early history of the Roman calendar is obscure. We learn from Censorinus (*fl.* 238 A.D.) and Macrobius (*fl.* 400 A.D.) that the Roman year consisted at first of ten months and 304 days. Livy (59 B.C.–17 A.D.) and Plutarch (46–120 A.D.) give contradictory accounts of the reforms of Numa who is said to have introduced a year of twelve months. It is clear that at an early date there emerged a lunar year of 355 days which is almost exactly twelve lunations. Of this calendar Martius (the month of Mars) was the first month, Aprilis (probably for *aperilis* from *aperire*, 'to open'), Maius (perhaps related to *major*) and Junius (which may be related to *junior* and *juvenis*) were named in connexion with the opening, growth, and ripening of vegetation. The following six months Quinctilis, Sextilis, September, October, November, and December were given merely the numerical names which most of them still bear. Januarius was perhaps named from the god Janus, and Februarius, the last month, was the season of ritual purification (*februare*, 'to purify' or 'expiate'). To obtain some relation of this lunar reckoning to the solar year a cycle of four years had been invented of which the first year contained 355 days, the second 377, the third 355, and the fourth 378. The cycle thus covered 1,465 days and the average year was of $\frac{1465}{4} = 366\frac{1}{4}$ days. It is obvious that so variable a year was useless for agricultural purposes. The farmer had thus still to rely on the rising and setting of certain constellations, such as Arcturus and the Pleiades, for timing his operations. The year was variously modified at different periods, but until the reforms of Julius Caesar no adequate correspondence to solar events was attained.

In place of this system Julius Caesar, acting under the advice of the Alexandrian mathematician Sosigenes, substituted a solar year of 365 days and abandoned any attempt to adapt the years or months to the lengths of the lunations. In every fourth year one day called the *bis-sextus* was interpolated before the 24th of February (i.e. before 'dies *sextus* ante calendas Martis'). These fourth or leap years became known as 'bissextile' years. It is believed that this reform was a reproduction of the Egyptian calendar that had been enacted in 238 B.C. and had been perhaps designed at a yet earlier date by the Greek astronomer Eudoxus (*fl. c.* 350 B.C.). In 44 B.C., the second year of the Julian Calendar, one of the months was named *Iulius* in honour of its founder. In 8 B.C. another month was called *Augustus* after his successor.

§ 6. *Geography*

Geography in the limited sense as distinct from cosmography was a topic that might be expected to appeal to the practical and imperialistically minded Roman. We learn of the existence of maps from a variety of Latin authors—Cicero, Pliny, Seneca, Suetonius, and Vitruvius. From Varro we gain a hint of the early religious associations of land-surveying, for he tells us that a map of Italy engraved on marble had a place in the temple of Tellus.

The survey of the Empire planned by Caesar may have been suggested, like his calendarial reform, by ideas culled from Alexandria. The division of the provinces, the demands of trade, the distribution of the fleet, all made the need of this work evident. In the event the execution of the scheme fell to Augustus. The survey was superintended by his son-in-law M. Vipsanius Agrippa (died 12 B.C.) and was finally carried through in 20 B.C. after nearly 30 years' work. Agrippa wrote a commentary illustrating this map, quotations from which have survived in the writings of Ammianus Marcellinus (*c.* 325–92 A.D.) and Pliny. It was fairly accurate for the provinces of Italy, Greece, and Egypt, whereas other countries were only roughly surveyed.

The survey was rendered possible by the fact that the Empire was well furnished with roads marked out with milestones. There was a regular service of skilled *agrimensores* or surveyors whose work, incorporated in the reports of provincial governors and generals, would be available at headquarters. From this mass of material a huge map was prepared which was exhibited in a building erected for the purpose. This was the prototype of later strategical maps, a copy of one of which has survived to this day and is known as the *Peutinger table* after the sixteenth-century scholar who first published it. It was originally drawn in the year 366 A.D., but the copy we have, which is now at Vienna, was prepared in 1265. On it are shown the routes for armies throughout the Empire. These routes are indicated by lines which are notched at intervals

Fig. 22. SITE OF TEMPLE OF AESCULAPIUS, THE FIRST ROMAN HOSPITAL

On the ship-like island of S. Bartolommeo. Piranesi

Fig. 23. CRANE
Worked with human labour by treadmill
Lateran Museum

that correspond to a day's journey. The whole map is greatly distorted by being enormously prolonged in the east-west direction [Fig. 24 and Fig. 25]. It is evident that, in its construction, cartographical accuracy was less considered than the purely practical aim of a convenient view of the itineraries. It may thus be compared to the distorted maps issued by some of our railway companies. The unit is usually a Roman mile (a thousand steps = mille passuum = 1,651 yards). Distances are sometimes indicated by figures.

Some idea of the manner in which the main routes of the Empire were surveyed and marked out may be gained from certain monuments, notably the inscribed marble pillars of Autun (Augustodunum). The monument gives—or gave, for most of it is now lost—the distances of a number of places on the road from Autun to Rome such as Autessiodurum (Auxerre), Bononia (Bologna), and Mutina (Modena). Somewhat similar inscriptions—sometimes of the nature of simple milestones—have been found at Tongres in Belgium, in Luxemburg, at Valencia, near the Roman wall in Northumberland and in other places. Very remarkable are four silver bowls from Vicarello which give the route between Gades (Cadiz) and Rome. Of especial interest to English readers is a round bronze dish found in 1725 at Rudge Coppice in Wiltshire. Around its edge are written in second-century script the names of a number of places in the northern part of the country.

In addition to inscribed stones and vessels and besides maps or *itineraria picta* such as the Peutinger table, we have true route-books or *itineraria adnotata*. One of these, the *Itinerarium Antonini*, a remarkably complete register of the roads of the whole Empire, was probably put together in its present form about 300 A.D., though its original goes back at least to the beginning of the third century. Both principal and cross roads are indicated by lists of the towns and stations upon them, the distance from place to place being given in Roman miles. Of more limited scope are the pilgrim-books such as the *Itinerarium Burdigalense* of 333 from Bordeaux to Jerusalem and back to

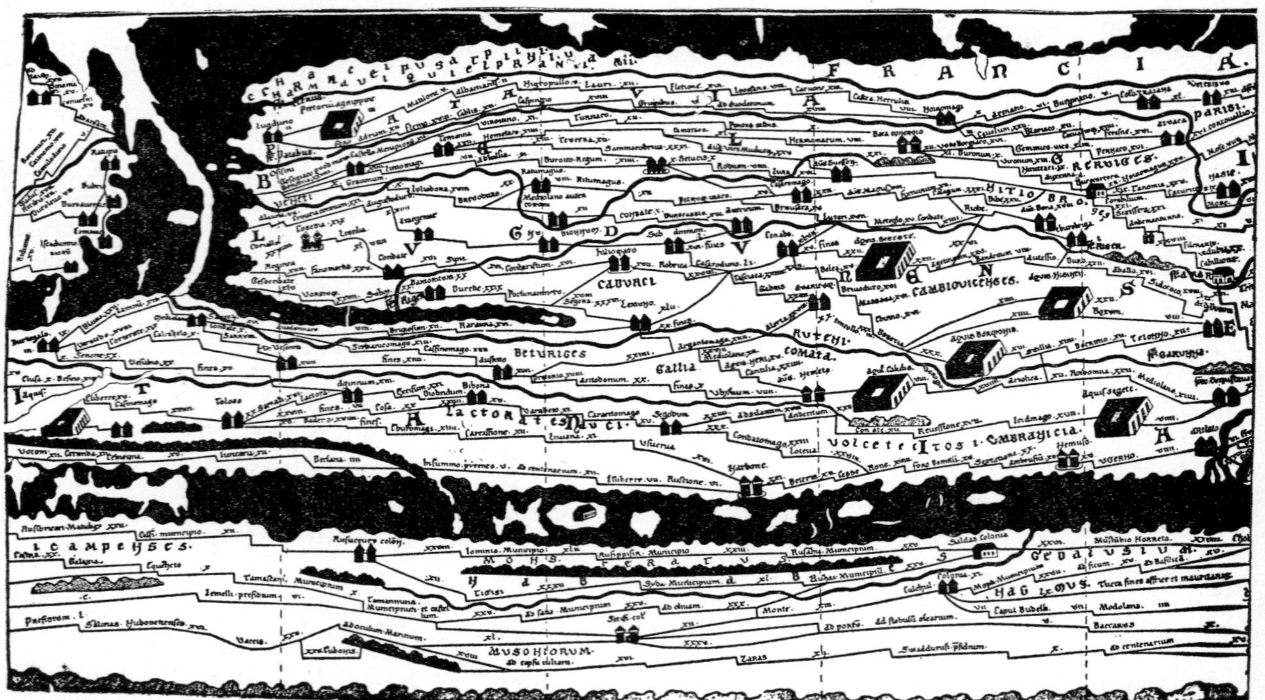

FIG. 24. Section of Peutinger map showing France and Belgium and parts of Britain and Spain.

FIG. 25. Roman Gaul, showing the area covered by the section of the Peutinger map on the opposite page and exhibiting the Roman roads included in that section.

Milan and the journey-book to Palestine of the lady-pilgrim called Silvia of Aquitania of about 380. Rutilius Namatianus of Toulouse wrote in 417 a versified *Itinerarium de reditu suo* which gave an account of a journey from Rome to Gaul. He was a pagan who fiercely attacked the monks,—men who dread the evils without being able to support the blessings of the human condition. His work naturally delighted the heart of Gibbon, and is of interest as still exhibiting the faith that Rome is immortal. The anonymous *Geographus Ravennas*, though put together as late as the end of the seventh century, contains, in a corrupt form, much valuable information concerning Roman roads and towns. The Ravenna geographer seems to have used sources employed by Ptolemy.

To general geography and cosmography as distinct from the limited subject of military and imperial surveys the Romans paid less attention. The only Latin writer of any importance who deals with the subject is Pomponius Mela. He was a Spaniard, and his date may be gleaned from his reference to Britain as about to be more fully explored by an expedition then in progress. This must refer to the visit of the Emperor Claudius in 43 A.D.

Pomponius Mela clearly meant his work to be an easy account of his subject. Beginning with a general description of the earth he avoids mathematical topics and does not give distances or measurements. The world is a sphere, and the land upon it is surrounded on all sides by sea [Fig. 26]. Five zones may be distinguished on the earth's surface; that in the middle is burnt up by heat and is as uninhabitable as are the two extreme zones by reason of cold. Between the torrid and frigid zones lie the two habitable temperate zones. In one of these we live, while in the other dwell the *Antichthones*. Our own hemisphere is completely surrounded by ocean from which it receives four seas or gulfs, one at the north, the Caspian, two in the south, the Persian Gulf and the Red Sea, and the fourth to the west, the Mediterranean.

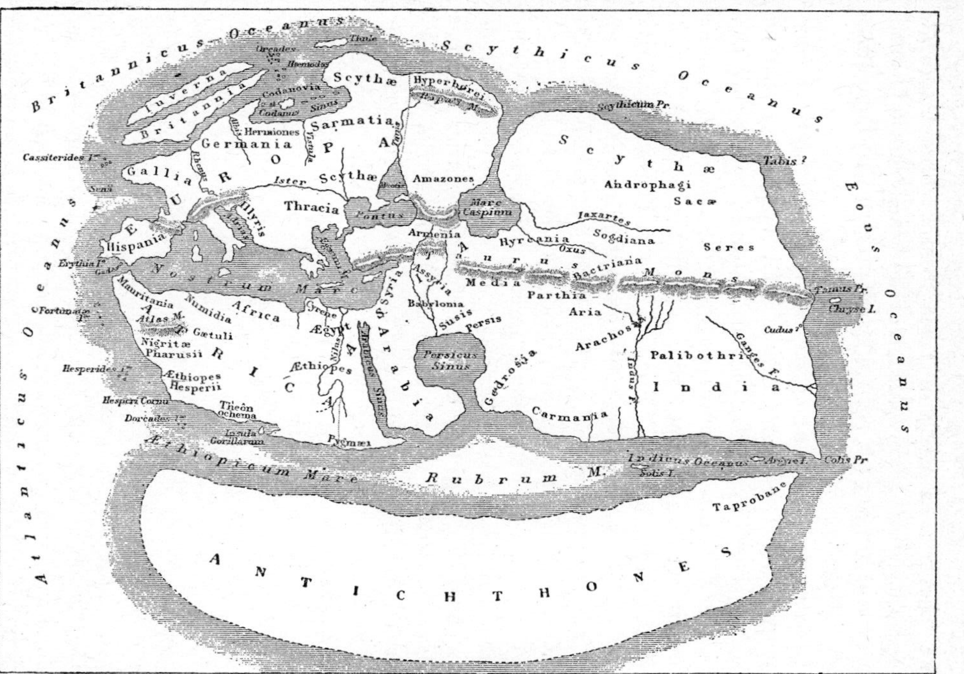

FIG. 26. Map of the World according to Pomponius Mela. From E. H. Bunbury, *History of Ancient Geography*, ii. 368; by permission of Messrs. John Murray.

The scheme as a whole is taken from Eratosthenes (275–*c.* 194 B.C.) whose geographical ideas governed the world until the time of Ptolemy (*fl.* 150 A.D.), and it is clear that Pomponius Mela is here borrowing mainly from Greek sources.

Mela next passes to a general description of the three continents, Europe, Asia, and Africa. It is noteworthy that he takes the river Tanais (the *Don*), lake Maeotis (the *Sea of Azov*), and the Euxine sea (Pontus Euxinus, the *Black Sea*) as the frontiers between Europe and Asia, while it is the Nile that divides Asia from Africa. Asia is as large as Europe and Africa together. These ideas were passed on to the earlier Middle Ages and are expressed in the first European world-map that has survived, which is in a seventh-century codex of Isidore (560–636) at St. Gall. Between the three continents is the Mediterranean which Mela speaks of as 'our sea'. Mela proceeds to a detailed description of the different countries which is sufficiently detailed for the lands and islands of the Mediterranean but becomes more vague as he passes from that area. He is singularly hazy as regards central Europe, which is remarkable when one considers the importance of the military operations in progress in that area. His account of Britain may serve as a sample of his descriptions of countries beyond his own immediate area.

'Britain, according to present knowledge, extends in the directions North and East. It offers a wide angle opposite the mouths of the Rhine. One arm of this angle looks towards Gaul, the other towards Germany. The two sides abut obliquely on a long straight line which terminates them behind and gives the land a triangular form like that of Sicily. Britain is flat, large, and fertile, but her produce is more suitable for cattle than men. She has forests, lakes, and considerable rivers which flow with alternating motion into the sea and towards their sources (according to the alternate movements of the tide); some of them produce pearls and precious stones. The inhabitants . . . are all savage and rich only in flocks. They paint the body either by way of ornament or from some other motive. They make pretexts of war and often attack each other, impelled solely by the ambition to command and to extend their borders. Armed like the Gauls, they fight not only on foot and on horseback but also in chariots which they call *covini* and which have scythes attached to their axles.

'Beyond Britain is Ireland stretching nearly as far and of an oblong form. Its climate is unfavourable for ripening cereals but it abounds in herbs of pleasant appearance and so sweet that the flocks fill themselves to repletion in a short part of the day, so that if not prevented from eating they would burst with fatness. The natives are rude and more ignorant of the virtues and devoid of piety than any other people.'

The haziness of the geographical ideas even of a very intelligent Roman of Imperial times may be gathered from the pages of Tacitus (*c.* 55–120 A. D.). He tells how, under Agricola, the Roman fleet rounded Britain and proved it to be an island, discovering at the same time the Orcades (Orkney islands) and coming in sight of Thule, by which the Shetlands are perhaps meant. Yet Tacitus, like Caesar and the elder Pliny, believes that Spain lies to the west of Britain [Fig. 27]. He describes the Pyrenees as running North and South. He goes on to explain the phenomenon of the midnight sun—which he brings as far south as the North of Scotland—by telling us that 'the flat extremities of the earth, casting a low shadow, do not throw the darkness up high, and the night does not reach to the sky and stars'. This statement implies the view that the earth is a disk with flattened edges.

The final geographical synthesis of antiquity was made by Claudius Ptolemaeus who worked and observed at Alexandria during the reigns of Hadrian (117–138) and Antoninus Pius (138–161), whom he survived. Ptolemy, who was no less important as a geographer than as an astronomer, wrote in Greek but worked on itineraries of Roman officials and merchants. Thus he may be said to preserve for us a summary of Roman knowledge of the earth's surface, presented, however, in a way of which no Latin writer was capable. Ptolemy is generally thought to have used the map prepared by M. Vipsanius Agrippa which was placed in the porch of Pollux at Rome (see p. 304).

Ptolemy developed his own manner of representing the curved surface of the earth on a plane surface. In his scheme of projection the parallels of latitude are arcs of concentric circles, the centres of which are at the North Pole. Chief among the parallels are the Equator and circles passing respectively through Thule, through Rhodes, and through Meroë. The meridians of longitude are represented by straight lines which converge to the Pole. He delineates in this manner the whole of the then known world, and the limits that he sets give a clear idea of the range of geographical vision in Imperial Roman times. The boundaries of Ptolemy's world are: on the north, the Ocean which surrounds the British Isles, the northern parts of Europe, and the unknown land in the northern region of Asia; on the south, the unknown land which encloses the Indian Sea, and the unknown land to the south of Libya and Aethiopia; on the east, the unknown land which adjoins the eastern nations of Asia, the Sinae (Chinese) and the people of Serica, the silk-producing land; on the west, the great Western Ocean and unknown parts of Libya. The portion of the earth thus

Fig. 27. Map of Western Europe reconstructed from the descriptions of Tacitus. From *Tacitus*, vol. i, translated by W. Peterson, by permission of Messrs. William Heinemann.

surveyed covers in length a hemisphere and in breadth between 63° north latitude and $16\frac{3}{12}$° south latitude.

The Γεωγραφικὴ Ὑφήγησις, *Geographical Outline*, of Ptolemy is the only complete scientific ancient geography that we have. As originally written it was furnished with maps. These have

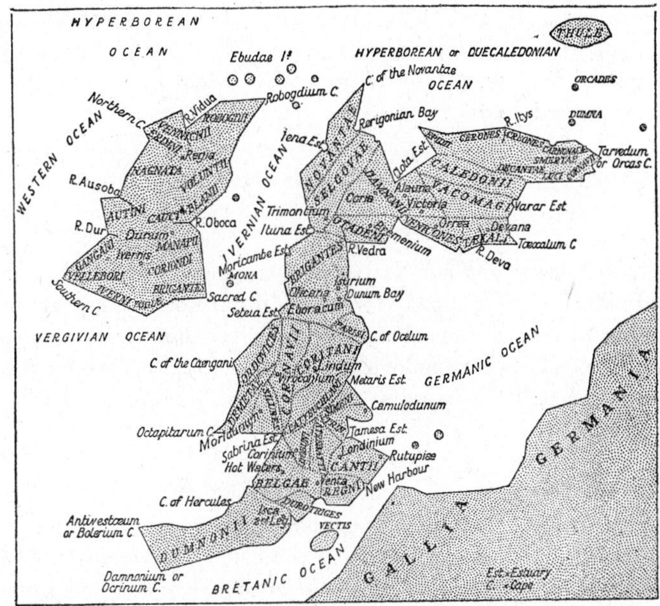

Fig. 28. Map of British Isles reconstructed by plotting out the fixed points given by Ptolemy and joining them together by straight lines.

long since disappeared, but as Ptolemy gives the latitude and longitude of the places that he mentions his charts can be reconstructed. A peculiar interest attaches to the map of Britain which can be thus put together [Fig. 28]. It would seem that Scotland was bent eastward with its axis at a right angle to that of England. This is an unusual degree of error for Ptolemy. It has therefore been suggested that he was here working not on records brought back by travellers, but on actual maps of the island, and that he made the mistake of fitting the map of Scotland on to that of England along the wrong side.

Ptolemy's *Geographical Outline* was not available in Latin until a translation was made by the Italian Giacomo Angelo who was Chancellor of the University of Montpellier early in the fifteenth century. That translation was printed at Bologna perhaps as early as 1472 and deeply influenced Renaissance geographical ideas. Many editions of it appeared adorned with reconstructed charts in the early years of printing. It was to errors in the work of Ptolemy that Columbus owed his belief in the practicability of a western passage to the Indies.

§ 7. *Astronomy and Cosmology*

The Romans did not deal with astronomical matters until fairly late and then mostly for practical purposes. They never developed a mathematical astronomy such as that which formed the basis of Greek cosmological speculations. A bronze plaque has, however, been found at Salzburg which is engraved with the names and figures of constellations. Pliny tells us that in his time there were 1,600 named stars. These bodies, he considered, were composed of fire and filled with air.

Popular astronomy and geography are represented in Latin by certain poetical works bearing the name of Avienus (*c.* 380 A.D.). The geographical poems of Avienus are adapted from Greek works by Dionysius Periegetes (*c.* 100 A.D.) which were rendered again into Latin by Priscian in the sixth century. For his astronomical works Avienus draws upon Greek treatises of Aratus of Soli (271–213 B.C.). To one of these known as the *Aratea Phaenomena* quite peculiar interest is attached. St. Jerome tells us that when, in the Acts, St. Paul is reported as saying 'In him we live, and move, and have our being; as certain even of your own poets have said, *For we are also his offspring*' (xvii. 28) he is quoting the *Aratea Phaenomena.* The words τοῦ γὰρ καὶ γένος ἐσμέν, *for we are also his offspring*, are in fact to be found in the opening invocation to Zeus in

Aratus, and in a slightly different form in a work of the poet Cleanthes (3rd cent. B.C.) and in an expanded form in Avienus. Aratus was a native of Cilicia, St. Paul's native province. Both Aratus and Cleanthes were claimed by the Stoics who, with the Epicureans, were opposing the apostle at Athens (Acts xvii. 18).

St. Jerome gives us also the approximate date of Avienus, for he speaks of the *Phaenomena* '*Arati, quem Cicero in Latinum sermonem transtulit et Germanicus Caesar et nuper Avienus*', 'which Cicero and Germanicus Caesar translated into the Latin tongue and lately also Avienus.' These three versions all still exist in whole or in part. That of Cicero is found in a certain very peculiar early manuscript. It is written with the words arranged to form figures representing the signs of the constellations. The figures resemble those engraved on the Salzburg plaque. They are important as exhibiting the passage of late Imperial into early mediaeval book illustration.

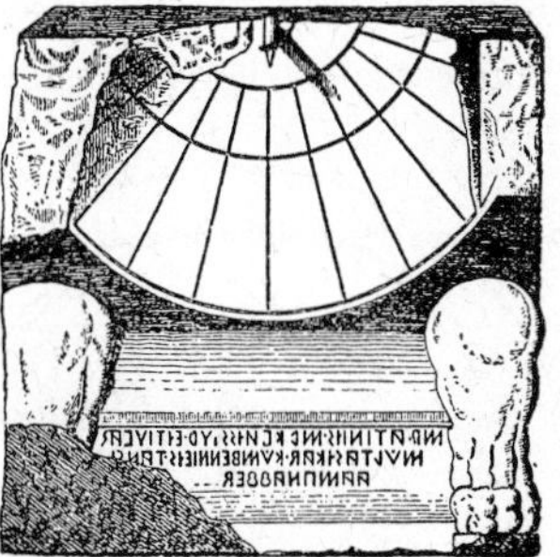

FIG. 29. Sundial found in the Stabian Baths at Pompeii in 1854. On the base are carved three lines in the Oscan script and language written from right to left, which may be read as follows:—

MR ATINIIͤS MR KVAIͤSSTUR EIͤTIUVAD MUͦLTASIͦKAD KUͦMBENNIEIͤS TANG⟨INUD⟩ | AAMAN⟨A⟩FFED

The Latin equivalent of this would probably be:

MARAS ATINIUS MARAS QUAESTOR PECUNIA | MULTATITIA CONVENTUS DECRETO | AEDIFICAVIT,

and it may be translated:

'Maras son of Maras of the gens Atinia, the Quaestor, built ⟨this⟩ by order of the Corporation out of fine-money.'

Though backward in astronomy the Romans had early developed a good knowledge of such elementary developments as the sundial, which was known to them in the third century B.C. and the results of which were early applied to calendarial reckoning. Several sundials have been recovered from Pompeii, one bearing an inscription in the old Oscan dialect [Fig. 29]. Full directions for the construction of sundials are given by Vitruvius, who tells of a number of different forms in use in his time. These he says were invented by Berosus the Chaldaean (*fl.* 250 B.C.) and by various Greeks of whom Aristarchus of Samos (*c.* 220–143 B.C.) and Eudoxus (*fl. c.* 350 B.C.) are the best known. The construction of these various forms implies command of considerable mechanical skill and some efficiency in the making and recording of elementary

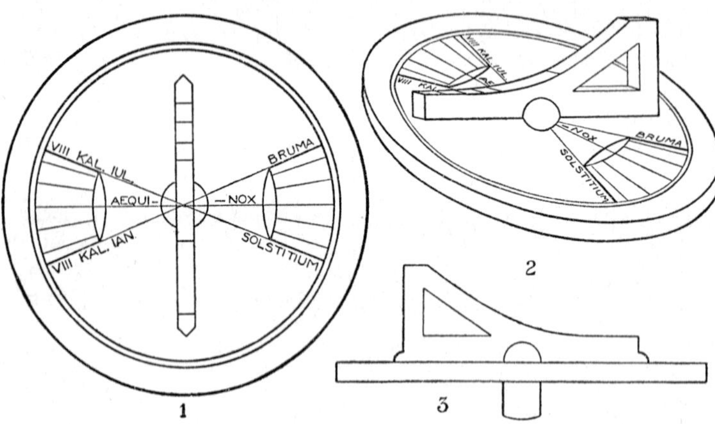

FIG. 30. Portable sundial found at Crêt-Chatelard in the Department of the Loire. The winter solstice (*bruma*) is given as the eighth day before the Kalends of January, i.e. December 23, and the summer solstice (*solstitium*) as the eighth day before the Kalends of July, i.e. June 22. The dates now given are one day earlier. The ground plan of the sundial is shown at 1, the complete sundial in perspective at 2, and in elevation at 3.

astronomical observations. Sundials suitable for use by travellers have been recovered from several sites [Fig. 30]. Vitruvius describes another form of time-measurer. It is a water clock working on an extremely simple and effective principle [Fig. 31]. He says he borrowed the idea from Ctesibius (*c.* 120 B.C.), an ingenious barber of Alexandria.

The difference in the length of day in different latitudes was well known to the Romans. From the fact that the longest day in Alexandria was 14 hours, in Italy 15, and in Britain 17 hours, Pliny deduces that lands close to the pole must have a 24-hours day around the summer solstice, and a 24-hours night in winter.

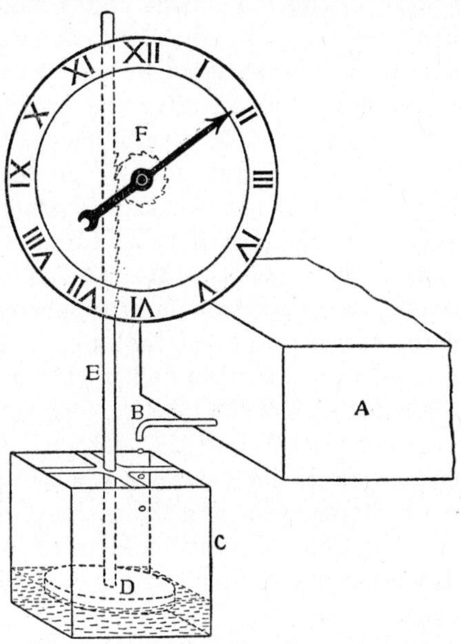

FIG. 31. Water clock described by Vitruvius. From the tank A water drips at a uniform rate through the small pipe B into the reservoir C in which is the float D. From the upper surface of D rises the shaft E the teeth of which, by their movement as the shaft rises, rotate the cog-wheel F. To this cog-wheel is attached a hand the position of which, on the surface of the dial, indicates the hour.

Many passages in Pliny reflect a contest concerning the form of the earth, reminding us of the similar dispute of the seventeenth century that turned around the name of Copernicus and the views of Galileo. Pliny opens his work with a description of the general structure of the universe. With the theory of the spherical form of the earth had come the view that man was much more widely distributed than had been thought. The general character of ancient mathematical geography had been fixed by Eratosthenes who presided over the school of Alexandria for more than forty years, till about 194 B.C. Geographical theory had altered but little since his time, but, with the dissemination of his sphericist view of the earth, the belief in the existence of antipodean races became not unusual among educated Romans.

'Science and the opinion of the mob', says Pliny, 'are in direct opposition. According to the former the whole sphere of the earth is inhabited by men whose feet point towards each other while all have the heavens above their heads. But the mob ask how men on the antipodes do not fall off; as though that did not present the opposite query, why they should not wonder at *our* not falling off. Usually, however, the crowd objects if one urges that water also tends to be spherical. Yet nothing is more obvious, since hanging drops always form little spheres.' Among his proofs of the curved surface of the earth is the gradual appearance of ships, mast first, then hull, as they approach the shore.

The teaching of the spherical form of the earth thus became the common belief of the educated during Imperial times. There were also individuals by whom the heliocentric teaching, of which the germ was among the Greeks, was not entirely ignored. Copernicus fifteen hundred years later sought to link his teaching to antiquity and quoted Cicero in support of his views.

To the moon and fixed stars the Romans had already in Pliny's time begun to attribute an influence on human affairs. 'Who does not know', he asks, 'that when Sirius rises it exercises influence on the widest stretch of earth?' The influence of the dog-star is an idea that may be traced back in Greek literature at least as far as Hesiod (8th century B.C.) and has given us our modern superstition of the 'dog days'. It was recognized that the moon had influence on tides and it was thought that influencing the outer world, the macrocosm, it had influence also on the body of man, the microcosm. With the waxing of the moon it was believed that the muscles became bigger and blood increased. This theory gave rise to the practice of periodical blood-letting.

The supposed influence of the heavenly bodies on the earth and on the life of man is a topic that leads on to judicial astrology. A knowledge of that subject became under the Empire a professional possession, illegal and prohibited but often tolerated and resorted to even by emperors. Astrology was beginning to spread in Rome in the first century of the Christian era. 'There are those', Pliny tells us, 'who assign [all human events] to the influence of the stars, and to the laws of their nativity. They suppose that God, once for all, issues his decrees and never after interferes. This opinion begins to gain ground and both the learned and the vulgar are falling in with it.' The art was of foreign origin. The credit of its invention is always ascribed to the 'Chaldaeans'. Orientals were certainly practising astrology in Rome from an early date but the main channel of transmission was Greek. 'As for the branch of astronomy which concerns the influences of the twelve signs of the zodiac, the five planets and the sun and moon on man's life,' says Vitruvius, 'we must leave it to the calculations of the Chaldaeans to whom belongs the art of casting nativities, which enables them to declare the past and future.'

It is largely against these Chaldaeans that Cicero directs his dialogue *On divination.* He misunderstands the basis of astrology and marshals ancient and fallacious arguments against it. Yet even Cicero accepted some astrological doctrine, and in his *Dream of Scipio* he spoke of the planet Jupiter as helpful and Mars as harmful. To the early Christian writers astrology was even more abhorrent, for it seemed to them to be the negation of that doctrine of free-will that was so dear to them. Tertullian (*c.* 155–*c.* 222), Lactantius (*c.* 260–*c.* 340), and Augustine (354–430) all inveigh against it. With the spread of Christianity in the West and the disappearance of the Stoic philosophy, astrology passed into the background to return with the Arabian revival and the rise of the Universities.

A large literature arose on the subject, of which we have remains in the works of Manilius (1st century A.D.), Censorinus

(3rd century A.D.), and Firmicus Maternus (4th century A.D.). Nevertheless, astrology seems on the whole to have been rather less cultivated in Rome itself than the general state of society and the wide spread of the Stoic philosophy might perhaps suggest. Lovers sought to learn of astrologers a lucky day for a wedding, travellers inquired what was the best day for starting on a journey, and builders asked the correct date for laying a foundation stone. All these may easily be paralleled by instances among the empty-headed in our own time and country. But Galen (130–201 A.D.) who practised among the well-to-do and educated assures us that they only bothered about astrology for forecasting legacies—and again a parallel might be drawn. The new astrology introduced by Greeks and 'Chaldaeans' tended, however, to replace the native magical system. The process can be observed in action in the work of Censorinus *De die natali.*

But astrology must not be considered only as a superstition and an occupation for empty heads and idle hands. The astrological system of antiquity was, after all, only a formal statement of the beliefs concerning the nature and working of our mundane sphere which the ideas of a scientific astronomy and cosmology had fostered. Faith in it was almost part of the Stoic creed. In the presentment of the world which science thus made, there was no room for those anthropomorphic gods, the belief in whom was still fostered by the priests and held by the multitude. The spread of science had led at last to a complete breach between the official faith and the opinions of the educated classes. The idea of 'universal solidarity', of the interdependence on one another of all parts of the universe, produced a new form of religion. The world itself must be divine. 'Deity', says Pliny, 'only means nature.' From such a view to the monotheism of Virgil, in which the world as a whole is regarded as the artistic product of an external god, is perhaps no great step.

On the whole, however, science, linked with Stoicism, failed to take that step, and assumed among later Latin writers a fatalistic and pessimistic mood. 'God, if God there be, was outside the world and could not be expected to care for it,' says Pliny. The idea of immortality seems to him but the 'childish babble' of those who are possessed by the fear of death, as Lucretius had once maintained. After death, so Pliny would have us believe, man is as he was before he was born—and this he tells us as he plunges into his magic-ridden pages!

Once and once only in these Latin scientific writings have we a clear note of real hope. It is significant that that note is sounded in connexion with a statement of a belief in the *progress* of knowledge, an echo of the Greek thought of the fifth and fourth centuries B. C. It is significant too that the note is sounded by one who approached, nearer perhaps than any other pagan Latin philosopher, to the idea of the divine immanence. In his *Quaestiones naturales* Seneca wrote:

> There are many things akin to highest deity that are still obscure. Some may be too subtle for our powers of comprehension, others imperceptible to us because such exalted majesty conceals itself in the holiest part of its sanctuary, forbidding access to any power save that of the spirit. How many heavenly bodies revolve unseen by human eye! . . . How many discoveries are reserved for the ages to come when our memory shall be no more, for this world of ours contains matter for investigation for all generations . . . God has not revealed all things to man and has entrusted us with but a fragment of His mighty work. But He who directs all things, who has established and laid the foundation of the world, who has clothed Himself with Creation, He is greater and better than that which He has wrought. Hidden from our eyes, He can only be reached by the spirit . . . On entering a temple we assume all signs of reverence. How much more reverent then should we be before the heavenly bodies, the stars, the very nature of God!

But the science of antiquity as exhibited elsewhere in Latin writings contains very little of this belief in man's destiny, this hope for human knowledge. The world in which the Imperial

Roman lived was a finite world bound by the firmament and limited by a flaming rampart. His fathers had thought that great space peopled by *numina*, 'divinities', that needed to be propitiated. The new dispensation—that *lex naturae* of the world that had so many parallels with the *jus gentium* of the Empire—had now taken the place of those awesome beings.

In the inevitableness of the action of that law Lucretius the Epicurean might find comfort from the unknown terror. Yet for the Stoic it must have remained a limited, fixed, rigid, and cruel law. His vision, we must remember, was very different from that given by the spacious claim of modern science which explores into ever wider and wider regions of space and time and thought. It was an iron, nerveless, tyrannical universe which science had raised and in which the Roman thinker must have felt himself fettered, imprisoned, crushed. The Roman had forsaken his early gods, that crowd of strangely vague yet personal beings whose ceremonial propitiation in every event and circumstance had filled his fathers' lives. He had had before him an alternative of the oriental cults whose gods were but mad magicians—a religion unworthy of a philosopher—and the new religion of science whose god, he now saw, worked by a mechanical rule. He had abandoned the faith of his fathers and had flung himself into the arms of what he believed to be a lovelier god, and lo! he found himself embracing a machine! His soul recoiled and he fled into Christianity. Science had induced that essential pessimism which clouds much of the thought of later antiquity. It was reaction against this pessimism which led to the great spiritual changes in the midst of which antiquity went up in flames and smoke.

CHARLES SINGER.

For suggestions and corrections I have to thank Miss M. V. Taylor of the Haverfield Library, Ashmolean Museum, and Prof. H. E. Butler of University College, London.

Books Recommended.

I. Roman Attitude to Nature.

Sir A. Geikie, *The Love of Nature among the Romans during the later decades of the Republic and the first century of the Empire.* London, 1912.

T. F. Royds, *The Beasts, Birds and Bees of Virgil.* A naturalist's handbook to the *Georgics*, with a preface by W. Warde Fowler. Oxford, 1918.

J. Sargeaunt, *The Trees, Shrubs and Plants of Virgil.* Oxford, 1922.

Franz Wickhoff, *Roman Art* . . . translated and edited by Mrs. S. A. Strong. London, 1900.

II. Latin Works on General Science.

F. Harrison, *Roman Farm Management* (Cato and Varro). London, second edition, 1918.

J. Masson, *Lucretius, Epicurean and Poet*, with notes and comments by J. S. Reid. London, 1907–9, 2 vols.

Lynn Thorndike, *A History of Magic and Experimental Science during the First Thirteen Centuries of our Era.* London, 1923, 2 vols. (Pliny and Seneca).

J. Clarke, *Physical Science in the Time of Nero*, with notes by Sir A. Geikie. London, 1910 (Seneca).

III. Roman Medicine.

Sir T. C. Allbutt, *Greek Medicine in Rome.* London, 1921.

M. Neuburger, *History of Medicine*, translated by Ernest Playfair. London, 1910.

J. S. Milne, *Surgical Instruments in Greek and Roman Times.* Oxford, 1907.

IV. Hygienic Organization and Public Health under the Empire.

F. H. Garrison, *Notes on the History of Military Medicine.* Washington, 1922.

T. Puschmann, *A History of Medical Education*, translated and edited by E. H. Hare. London, 1891.

E. T. Withington, *Medical History.* London, 1891.

V. Mathematics and Physical Sciences.

J. L. Heiberg, *Mathematics and Physical Science in Classical Antiquity*, translated by D. C. Macgregor. Oxford, 1922.

R. Steele, *The Earliest Arithmetics in English.* Oxford, 1922 (Abacus).

W. W. Rouse Ball, *A Short Account of the History of Mathematics.* London, 1915.

VI. Geography.

E. H. Bunbury, *History of Ancient Geography*, second edition. London, 1883, 2 vols.

C. R. Beazley, *The Dawn of Modern Geography*. London, 1897–1906, 3 vols.

H. F. Tozer, *Classical Geography*. London, 1876.

G. B. Grundy, *Small Classical Atlas*. London, 1894.

VII. Astronomy and Cosmology.

J. L. E. Dreyer, *History of the Planetary Systems from Thales to Kepler*. Cambridge, 1906.

E. V. Arnold, *Roman Stoicism*. London, 1911.

T. Whittaker, *Macrobius, or Philosophy, Science and Letters in the year 400*. Cambridge, 1923.

T. O. Wedel, *The Mediaeval Attitude toward Astrology*. London, 1920.

LITERATURE

'The Latin language is still the necessary foundation of one half of human knowledge, and the forms created by Roman genius underlie the whole of our civilization. So long as mankind look before and after, the name of Rome will be the greatest of those upon which their backward gaze can be turned. Behind the ordered structure of her law and government, and the majestic fabric of her civilization, lay a vital force of even deeper import, the strong, grave Roman character, which has permanently heightened the ideal of human life. It is in their literature that the inner spirit of the Latin race found its most complete expression. In the stately structure of that imperial language they embodied those qualities which make the Roman name most abidingly great—honour, temperate wisdom, humanity, courtesy, magnanimity; and the civilized world still returns to that fountain-head, and finds a second mother-tongue in the speech of Cicero and Virgil.'

No apology need be made for repeating here words written nearly thirty years ago; for the intervening years have only confirmed the conviction in which they were then written. They summed up the story of the six centuries of Latin literature. No attempt will be made here to repeat or summarize that story. The present occasion does not call upon us to trace the course of Roman history, or the growth of Latin literature as the authentic utterance and permanent expression of the genius of Rome; nor to follow through the ages the vital influence exercised by Latin writers on the thought and language, the ideals and achievements, of the commonwealth of European nations; nor even to set forth the continuous effect of Rome and the Latin classics on the growth of our own national life and of the English literature which is our peculiar heritage and our priceless possession. This last is of incalculable importance. Without Latin, neither the English language nor the literature which is the greatest glory of the English-speaking race would be what they are; it may be said broadly that they would not exist; and it may be said unhesitatingly that either for the historical study of English literature from Chaucer downwards, or for its intelligent appreciation, knowledge of Latin and of the great Latin classics is not merely important, but indispensable. This aspect of the legacy of Rome must therefore be touched upon. But the main object of this chapter is to emphasize the magnitude and variety of those Latin writings which are at the present day sources of vital unexhausted inspiration. If we speak in this connexion of the Legacy of Rome, we must not think of it as a treasure hidden away or only brought out for ostentation; we must not regard it as of the nature of the contents of a museum to be studied by experts, but as the furniture of our own house, as actual wealth upon which we live, and which enables us in our turn to contribute to the enrichment of life.

The main types of literature, the moulds into which human thought and emotion are run for permanence, were the creation of Greek genius. The Greek masterpieces in prose and poetry remain sources and models which, for the twentieth century as for its predecessors, are of unique value. They are still alive, they still keep their vitalizing influence. Greek can renew indefinitely—one can see it do so now—the power which it exercised when rediscovered for Europe at the Renaissance. The most daring modern speculation in ethical and social theory was anticipated by Plato. The analysis of the human soul was carried to its utmost limit by Euripides. The metaphysic of religion was wrought out in the Schools of Alexandria. But the civilization of Greece, including its literature as well as its thought and art, is a stimulant which, taken undiluted, is an intoxicant. The liberating power which has been justly claimed for it is often like the liberation of a high explosive.

For use, it had to be brought under control; to become a fructifying force, it had to be interpreted and recast by another civilization, that of Rome. The mission and the achievement of Rome was to transmute it into a substance adapted for universal use. Greek reached the Western world through Latin. It is largely through Latin, and still more through the latinized mind which we have inherited, that the Greek sources have to be approached, and Greek thought transformed (to use a metaphor from science) into the voltage for which the mechanism of our own minds, and of the world we live in, is fitted.

But this is not all. The Latin mind, as it expressed and recorded itself in Latin literature, was not only transforming, but constructive and creative. Civilization, as we understand the term, is of Greek origin, but it is of Latin substance. We think, and construct, and express ourselves both in words and in acts, not like Greeks but like Romans. Our feet are set, wherever we go, on the roads laid down by Roman hands. In the field of letters, as in our political and social institutions, in the machinery of our trade and commerce and industry, in our systems of law and government, in our municipal or communal life, we inhabit and adapt to our own needs and uses the structure created for us by Rome.

As if with an instinctive prevision of the task and mission that lay before it, Latin literature began with assiduous study and imitation of Greek models. This work began as soon as the Roman Republic, by conquest and absorption of the surrounding Italian tribes and by success in war with Carthage, had become a Mediterranean Power. National consciousness, and the sense of native genius which sought to find means of adequate expression, moved together on these lines. In the result, the literature of Rome not only absorbed and assimilated the technique of Greek writers, but drew from them new powers of its own. Captured Greece, in the well-known phrase of Horace, captured her rude conqueror. But it is equally true that Rome became the conqueror in this field also. Just as the conquered provinces were gradually romanized and became the members of a world-empire, so it was with literature. The provinces of history and biography, of oratory, of political, ethical, and social science in the field of prose, those of epic, lyric, dramatic and idyllic in the field of poetry, were occupied and mastered. To these the Latin genius added other spheres of its own. Law, as a science and an art, was in substance a Latin creation, and was an instrument as important as the Roman armies in extending and consolidating the Roman dominion. Latin religion, even when Greek influence on it was strongest, was the expression of a quite distinct body of belief and attitude of mind towards the powers which rule the world. ‘Satire’, that is to say, the portraiture and criticism, in prose or verse or a mixture of the two, of social life whether in its normal working or in its eccentricities, was claimed not unjustly by Quintilian as *tota nostra*, a field of literature in which there was little or no Greek influence to be traced. And the Latin language, by virtue of the weight and precision in which it stands alone, and for which it is the model and the despair of modern writers both English and foreign, was the fit vehicle for the criticism of life in its most concentrated form, for those ‘sentences’ which remain to the present day portions of our common speech and the expression, crystallized once for all, of human experience. All these forms of literature Rome handed down, through the night of the Dark Ages, to the new world which arose slowly and dispersedly out of chaos. That legacy has by no means lost its value. On the contrary, modern research presents it, in the clearer light of a wider and deeper knowledge, as a body of literature of unexhausted and inexhaustible interest, and no less remarkable for its light and guidance on the aims which all literature pursues. It may even be reasonably claimed that the value of the Latin classics as literature is enhanced by the fact that Latin is no longer in use for current purposes as an international language.

We can see and grasp their art more fully, we can find in them an even higher value, when they are not mixed up in our reading with masses of contemporary Latin, sufficiently like them in structure to be confusing, but lacking the authentic Latin virtue.

Other chapters in this volume deal with the legacy of Rome in the fields of law and jurisprudence, of religion and philosophy, and of the natural sciences. It is not necessary therefore here to enlarge upon these parts of Latin literature, beyond noting the point that to the Roman genius we owe not only the principles of law, but the handling of language so as to express these principles with elegance and precision; not only some of our most important religious and ethical conceptions, but practically the whole vocabulary of our theology and our moral philosophy; not only treatises which are the foundations of modern science in such subjects as agriculture (Varro and Columella), medicine (Celsus), architecture (Vitruvius), but our fundamental notions of applied science as an element of national civilization. To literature in its stricter sense, not as the vehicle of science but as the art of letters, we may now turn.

Clio, the Muse of History, was according to the Greek allegory the first in birth and rank of the daughters of the God of Light and the Goddess of Memory: and history, as an exquisite art and as a severe science, culminated in Greece in the works of Herodotus and Thucydides. To those two authors, one the Father of History, the other the creator of scientific history, we must always return as to vital sources and incomparable examples. But in both regards, the Latin historians hold a place which is hardly less important. They likewise were not merely recorders but creators. And while the history of ancient Greece is of unique fascination, that of Rome and the Roman world-empire is both larger in scale and more closely relevant to our own world and its problems. Livy has always been recognized as one of the greatest of literary artists. Now he is recognized also as one of the greatest of historians. Under his hands, the Roman Republic took shape both as an ideal and as a living reality. His achievement was the canonization of Rome, as the eternal city and the perfect commonwealth. He embodied once for all, he made visible in a series of living pictures, the lineaments of Roman character: the sanctity of the pledged word, the subordination of personal ambition to civic duty, the practical sagacity, the temperate wisdom, the exalted patriotism, through which a single city became mistress of the world and moulded the world into the fabric of a single citizenship. In the dark years of the war, many must (like the present writer) have found strength and comfort in reading Livy's *Historiae ab Urbe Condita*, 'Records of the City from its foundation', not only for the noble flow of the narrative and the charm of his incomparable style, but even more from the exalted sense by which the work is pervaded of human virtue finding its scope in the quiet fulfilment of public duty.

No less thrilling in its interest, and of hardly lesser practical value, is the history of Tacitus, that great arraignment of the Imperial system which the genius of its author has imposed on the world not as an arraignment but as a portraiture. It is a storehouse of mordant criticism which political writers have used as an inexhaustible treasury. In his portraiture alike of men and of scenes Tacitus is indeed one of the greatest masters. And perhaps the main lesson to be drawn from his history to-day is the fatal effect, in an age of laborious reconstruction, of a body of irreconcilable conservatism among the trained governing class, and of the exhaustion, in all classes alike, of a common civic spirit and of the instinct for self-government. We look through the eyes of Tacitus on a wrecked world, viewed by him and by the class he represented with sombre fatalistic acquiescence. *Deum ira in rem Romanam*, 'the wrath of God against Rome', one of his many unforgettable phrases, might be taken, it has been said, as a sub-title for his whole historical work. Never has this doctrine of despair been impressed with such point and weight. To have read Tacitus is to know the worst. To study the history of the Roman Empire in the lurid light which he throws on it is to realize, more vividly than one can do with the events of one's own time, how the reconstruction of a world and the organization of a larger civilization can be thwarted by failure in faith, hope, love; and how, without these, the springs of effective action (as well as those of great literature) dwindle away and run dry. The age of the Good Emperors, though Tacitus saw its dawn and hailed it with dubious approbation, was yet to come. But they were from the first fighting a losing battle; and after Marcus Aurelius, the Golden Age which had been proclaimed or prophesied by Virgil became a dream, only to be realized in a world other than that of earth.

Tacitus is the last of the Latin historians to whom the name of 'classical' in its stricter sense can be applied. His contemporary, Plutarch, whose lives of great Romans are not only standard biographies of intense interest but important sources of historical knowledge, and have been the schoolbook of the classical past for modern times, wrote in Greek, among his books in the quiet atmosphere of a little Greek town. But Tacitus himself is the author of one biography, which in its grace, restraint, and delicate beauty has been a model, striven after but unapproached by all subsequent writers of biographies —the short but perfectly executed life of his father-in-law Agricola, the conqueror of Britain and the founder, it may be said, of Latin civilization in our own country. Both biography and history after this period fell into swift decline. The reigns of the Antonines, in which the ideal of a prosperous, peaceful, well-administered and philanthropic world was more nearly reached than at any time before or after down to the nineteenth century, were chronicled by no historians even of the second rank, and the lives of them which have reached us are wretched compilations made long afterwards by incompetent authors.

It was later still, during the decay and in the approaching

dissolution of the Roman Empire and its civilization, that one last Latin historian appeared. The contemporary record by Ammianus Marcellinus of the latter portion of the fourth century is probably as fruitful in lessons for our own day as any other work of ancient history; for that was a world which in many respects bore a startling and instructive likeness to ours. It was a world upturned from its foundations, on the edge of bankruptcy, in which government had lost control, productive industry was crippled, life was harassed by a savage penal code and poisoned by frivolity and superstition. The picture of that sombre age is drawn by Ammianus with a grim and masterly hand, and with something of the older Roman temper. By a curious chance, the histories of Livy, Tacitus, and Ammianus have all come down to us incomplete. But the three great fragments are among the most precious in our inheritance from Rome, and the two former are, as pure literature, masterpieces for perpetual study.

The practical bent of the Latin mind, guided by strict logic, yet averse from theorizing or from abstract speculation, expressed itself in a body of ethico-political literature which bulks largely in the product of the two centuries immediately before and after the Christian era. As the Latin genius created Western civilization and moulded the forms of government and civil organization for the European world, so it likewise created a language capable of dealing with the range of social intercourse, the maxims of human conduct, and the handling of public and private life; and it produced a literature in which these matters were handled with copiousness, precision, and persuasive eloquence. The creation of this language was decisively achieved by Cicero. Under his hands the Latin language became a flexible and finished instrument; and this was the last and the largest conquest which Rome made from Greece. A statesman of high eminence and an orator of the first rank, Cicero does not owe his most enduring fame to the part he took in public affairs at the crisis of Roman history, or to the speeches (nearly sixty of them are extant) in which he proved himself the most copious, flexible, and splendid in the illustrious line of Roman orators. He has the still greater glory of having made Latin, both in its vocabulary and in its structure, a language in which the whole range of human thought could find exact, lucid, and noble expression. He was not a deep or an original thinker. His so-called philosophical works were in main substance adapted or even translated from the Greek. But those Greek works were, with a few brilliant exceptions, hardly literature. He not only translated but transformed them. His mastery of language and his sense of literary form gave them a wholly new vitality; and his genius brought Greek thought within the compass of the Western mind. European prose, as an instrument of thought, is Cicero's creation. For profound speculation we have to go to Plato. For insight into the laws of thought and conduct, and the scientific pursuit of knowledge alike in the moral and the material world, we have to go to Aristotle. But Cicero was the great interpreter and expounder. Ciceronianism means not only fluent grace and polished diction. It means something much more, power to wield with lucid ease and grace the whole armoury of language. Cicero may be called the great exemplar of essayists. Though not a searching thinker, he teaches the secret of making thought attractive, and presenting it in a way to appeal to common sense and humane feeling. He created a universal language, and did for the Republic of Letters what it was his unfulfilled ambition to do for the Republic of Rome, established in it the custom and law of civilized human life. The quality to which the Romans gave the name of *urbanity*, a combination of good taste, good feeling, and good sense, was their own creation, and is part of their legacy to us. Cicero, by the volume and splendour of his work, established it in universal currency.

The boundary between the essay and the pamphlet is undefined, and some of the most interesting of Latin writings dealing with national figures and public events should be called pamphlets rather than histories. This applies especially to two among the most celebrated books of the Ciceronian age, Sallust's account of the revolutionary movement of Catiline, and the famous Commentaries of Julius Caesar. These *commentarii*, 'notes', on the Gallic and Civil Wars, as with a calculated modesty Caesar entitled them, are unique in literature as written by the greatest general and statesman of his own or perhaps any age, who was also recognized by both friends and enemies as a writer of supreme genius. In them the pure Latin of Rome, not yet enriched and diluted by provincial influx, culminates; as does the imperial accent, *facultas dicendi imperatoria*, which was the study and the appanage of the Roman governing class. Their succinct lucidity, their masterly simplicity, remain unrivalled. Written at high speed in the intervals of military campaigns and amid the gigantic labours of organization and reconstruction, they give, with an apparent ease which conceals consummate art, a justification of his own political career, and a picture of the Roman qualities which subjugated and settled the world. The more familiar side of that picture is given in the priceless collection of Cicero's letters. In these (there are between eight and nine hundred in all) we can follow from year to year, and often from day to day, the fluctuations of politics, the social life of Rome, and the movements of a swift, intelligent, and sensitive mind. They enable us to realize the Rome of the dying Republic as vividly as if the scene were passing before our eyes.

That age was unique in its breathless interest, and in the magnitude of the spectacle which it presents to our observation. A century later, under the Empire, two Latin prose writers may be singled out as of special historical importance for the modern world. The voluminous ethical writings of Seneca are not now widely read. They are infected with the rhetorical vices of his age. But the neglect into which they have fallen can hardly be justified if we accept, as we may, the judgement of one of the most austere of English scholars. There is no modern writer, said George Long, the translator of Marcus Aurelius, 'who has treated on morality and has said so much that is practically good and true'. Seneca's writings amply repay study, not merely as the work of a brilliant man of letters who had for some years, during the youth of Nero, the government of the civilized world in his charge, but for the deep and long-continued influence they exercised on ethical thought, on standards and ideals of conduct, and, in particular, on the shape which the Christian religion took in the Roman world.

Hardly less potent in its effects, and equally full of practical wisdom for modern use, are the portions of Quintilian's great treatise, the *Institutio Oratoria*, which deal with the theory and practice of education. It was the rediscovery of this work in the fifteenth century which opened the age of the great educational movement of the later Renaissance; and to Quintilian modern educational theorists, as modern teachers might well do likewise, perpetually turn for statement of first principles, for analysis of educational methods and planning of school courses, and, above all, for a sane and high view of the meaning and function of education.

Of the legacy of Rome in science, and in the applied arts by which science is brought into practical service, an account is given elsewhere. But it may be noted here that there survive, out of an immense number of treatises, many lost, and others now only of historical or antiquarian interest, some which take rank likewise as literature, and which have been of much importance in stimulating, in more modern times, the interest and intelligence which it is one of the highest functions of literature to create. Among these, two may be specially named: the treatise on agriculture, *De Re Rustica*, by Varro, the most learned of Roman antiquarians and one who took all knowledge for his province, in which farming and rural economy are expounded with lucidity and grace, in such a manner as to make them widely attractive and bring them into relation with national interests; and the *De Architectura* of Vitruvius, a work indeed of small literary merit, but the inspiration of the revived classical architecture of the sixteenth and seventeenth centuries, and the text-book in which the whole modern literature of architecture originates. Larger and more important than either of these is the vast encyclopaedia compiled by Pliny under the title of *Historia Naturalis.* It was the chief source of general knowledge, both of nature and of the arts and crafts, throughout the Middle Ages, and remains a storehouse to which modern scholars or investigators have perpetual recourse: its value for the historical study of arts and industries, for a time discredited, is now once more fully realized.

There remains a whole province of Latin literature, the importance of which in human history and in the thought and life of Europe can hardly be overstated: the Christian writings. These begin (apart from a few earlier fragments) in the time of disintegration and partial anarchy which, at the end of the second century, came over the Roman world. They culminate two hundred years later in Jerome and Augustine; and they continue afterwards, in ever-increasing volume, down to the comparatively recent time when Latin ceased, so far as it has even now ceased, to be the common universal language of Catholic Christendom.

It is in a somewhat different sense from that in which we apply the phrase to the classical authors, that we can speak of this Christian literature as the legacy of Rome. Yet it is so in a very important degree. Western Christianity, as it developed in and permeated the countries which constituted the European Commonwealth, from the Adriatic and the Baltic to the Atlantic, took shape and colour from the Latin mind, and organized itself on Roman models. Any one who glances over the table of contents (themselves a substantial tome) of the two hundred and twenty-one volumes of Migne's *Patrologia Latina* must be struck by the fact that they represent a body of literature of incredible extent conveying a continuous tradition, which is not only written in Latin, but is powerfully affected by the Latin character. Nine-tenths of it belongs to the mediaeval, not to what is called the ancient or classical world. But the mediaeval world itself was the legacy of Rome and the successor of the Roman Empire. Further, the earliest and greatest of the Christian Latin writers were citizens of that empire while its main fabric yet stood; they were within the Roman culture; and their most celebrated writings, like the *Octavius* of Minucius Felix, the *Apologeticum* of Tertullian, the *Institutes* of Lactantius, the *Confessions* and *City of God* of Augustine, rank, not indeed as ancient classics, but as Latin classics in the largest sense. The cardinal point in the transition is the Latin translation of the Bible executed by Jerome and known as the Vulgate. It was completed by him in 405 A. D., and, with some later revision in detail, has been from then until now, that is to say, for more than fifteen hundred years, the scripture in daily use throughout the whole Catholic Church. Its language no less than its substance saturates all European literature, and in a sense it may be called the last and the largest single legacy of Rome.

When we turn from the sphere of prose to that of poetry, we enter on a more subtle and intricate inquiry. Latin prose is the foundation of common civilized speech. Latin poetry is a thing by itself. But here also, the legacy of Rome to the modern world, and to English poetry in particular, is of most high and vital value. To compare one kind of poetry with another is perhaps a futile occupation; to set one kind of poetry against another certainly is. Latin poetry, as art, stands on its own merits, and includes some of the noblest poetry in the world. But of all the external influences which have moulded or inspired English poetry, Latin is the most continuous and most potent. We owe to the Roman genius certain acknowledged and supreme masterpieces ; but we owe to it further a sense of disciplined form which has controlled the irregular impulses of the romantic or insular temperament, has civilized English poetry, given it a new elevation, dignity, and precision, made it classical. That influence reached us very largely through indirect transmission, through the channels of Italian and French poetry in which the classical note was revived or continued by a kindred instinct in the Latin races. But it is its direct impact on which stress has here to be laid.

Two names among the Latin poets, those of Virgil and Horace, stand apart from all the rest. They have been, and are, the schoolbooks and the companions of the whole world ; forming the mind of youth, and yielding more and more of their secret to prolonged study and inveterate acquaintance.

On Virgil's poetical supremacy it is needless to enlarge, for it is universally recognized and appreciated. He is, as he was to Dante six hundred years ago, ' the master ' : not only one of the greatest poets of the world, but the creator of ideals which have exercised the most profound influence on civilization and history. In his *Eclogues* he gave a new music to language, transplanted the Greek pastoral to Latin soil, and initiated the long and splendid course of idyllic poetry. Grace and tenderness, sometimes rising (as in the Fourth Eclogue, the poem which was for ages believed to have been written under inspiration and to be a prophecy of the birth of Christ) to majesty, sometimes (as in the Tenth Eclogue) to the highest pitch of romantic beauty, are the qualities of this earlier work. In the *Georgics* he moves with a more secure step in an ampler field. Dryden, in the dedicatory preface to his translation, places the *Georgics* in half a dozen brief words, ' the best poem of the best poet ', at the head of human achievement ; and there are few if any poems for which the claim of perfection can be so fully or so justly made. Technically and superficially a didactic poem, they present with consummate art, in language of liquid and faultless beauty, the picture of a Golden Age attainable in the actual world, the ideal of a life at peace with itself, with mankind, and with Nature. It is a life of hard work, of pious faith, of simple pleasures; subject to sorrows and disappointments, shadowed by death, yet presented, like the Italy which Virgil loved so passionately, as loaded with enrichment by the bounty of heaven and earth—

Nec requies, quin aut pomis exuberet annus
Aut fetu pecorum aut Cerealis mergite culmi,
Proventuque oneret sulcos atque horrea vincat.
Venit hiems: teritur Sicyonia baca trapetis,
Glande sues laeti redeunt, dant arbuta silvae;
Et varios ponit fetus autumnus, et alte
Mitis in apricis coquitur vindemia saxis [1]—

brought into intimate touch with the charm of mythology, the romance of science, and the glory of patriotism, and rising into the impassioned contemplation of life, nature, and destiny.

The constructive Roman temper sought its main poetical outlet in the larger, more massive forms of poetry; and the *Aeneid* is the national Roman poem. There were earlier national epics or epic chronicles. The *Annals* of Ennius were for long the chief Latin school-book, and helped largely to give Rome a sense of her own greatness and her imperial mission, and to embody the ideals of civic and individual virtue. These poems only survive in fragmentary quotations. But on the soil thus prepared, the *Aeneid* grew. What they had endeavoured, Virgil accomplished. In the *Aeneid* he became the voice of Rome, the spiritual founder of the Holy

[1] 'Unceasingly the year lavishes fruit or young of the flock or sheaf of the cornblade, and loads the furrow and overflows the granary with increase. Winter is come; the Sicyonian berry is crushed in the olive-presses, the swine come home sleek from their acorns, the woodland yields her arbute-clusters; and autumn drops his manifold fruitage, and high up the mellow vintage ripens on the sunny rock.' *Georg.* ii. 516–22. It is needless to add that no translation, in prose or verse, can render the Virgilian music.

Roman Empire, and the pilot-light for that universal Commonwealth or League of Nations on which men's eyes are now more and more earnestly fixed. He drew the picture of such a world's ideal ruler, the first servant of the commonwealth, regardless of fame and of pleasure, brave, patient, and merciful. He portrayed in him human strength and weakness, the vicissitudes of fortune, the tragedy of unhappy love, the deeds of war, and the glory of peace. He made him pass in a vision into the other world, to cross the River of Forgetfulness and traverse the Mourning Fields, to look on the punishments of Hell and the bliss of Elysium, and to see unrolled before him the long pageant of his posterity and the course of human history. He was the poet and prophet of the fusion of Rome with Italy (only in our own day imperfectly accomplished) and the incorporation of the whole world in the Italo-Roman civilization. He touched human things with the Virgilian magic, and enfolded them in the supreme Virgilian pity; 'stretching out his hands', in a final pathetic gesture of doubtful hope, 'to the further shore' of a Paradise in which life should find fruition. The *Aeneid* is the voice not only of Rome but of mankind.

Horace has been taken, perhaps even more closely, to the heart of the world. His *Odes* became a sort of Psalter of secular life; his *Satires* and *Epistles* have been, for the whole European world, the great handbook of good sense, good temper, and practical wisdom. No one has done more to spread and fix and make attractive that spirit of 'humanity' which, like its name, is of Latin creation. He gave mankind the type of the man of the world and the gentleman; he showed how it is attainable without birth or wealth, without anxiety or ambition, without either high intellectual gifts or unattainable saintliness of life. From the great idealisms and the deeper passions he keeps himself apart. He never touches what are called 'problems', whether social or individual. His thought and his feeling are both, in the literal sense of the word, commonplace; but in both, he is plumb on the centre. Just for this reason, what he gives us is of a kind to which the human mind instinctively and immediately responds. He touches and kindles minds which are refractory to the appeal of other and, it may be, of greater poets. His appeal is limited, but is central and universal; and many of his penetrating and mastering single phrases have been, for many thousands of people through many ages, keys to the whole of life.

Horace is at once the widest in his appeal and the most exquisite in his workmanship of Latin lyric poets. They are not many. The lyric was a form of literary expression to which the Roman temper did not take naturally; for lyric poetry, in nearly all its kinds, Greek and not Latin is the great exemplar. Even Horace's *Odes* are in a *genre* of their own, which has been a thousand times imitated but never quite recaptured. But in the generation before Horace, one of the great lyric poets of the world appeared in Catullus. He stands alongside of Sappho in Greek and of Burns in our own poetry. In him, language of faultless music and piercing simplicity ceases to be a mechanism and seems transmuted into air and fire. No poet perhaps has combined such perfect clarity with such intense passion. Of the little volume of his poems, many are lampoons, some are scholarly exercises—for he was as fine a scholar as Shelley—but what remains is the quintessence of poetry and is immortal.

Only second in importance to the *Aeneid* among Latin poems, and in the opinion of many showing an even more intense poetical genius and as wonderful, though less complete, a mastery over thought and language, is a work by a contemporary of Catullus, the *De Rerum Natura* of Lucretius. Its scope, as the title indicates, is even larger, its purpose more profound, than that of the epic: it is no less than the imaginative exposition of the whole system of the universe. Lucretius is the only poet who has essayed so gigantic a task and substantially accomplished it. The *De Rerum Natura* is not only an extraordinary literary achievement. It is not only a poem written in the purest Latin at the exact time when the Latin language culminated, and giving utterance, together with the Commentaries of Caesar, to the authentic Roman speech at its best and finest. It is the work of an intellect and imagination of the first order, of a scientific insight and an ethical elevation unequalled in the ancient world and hardly reached afterwards by any single writer. Lucretius wrote with a direct moral purpose, to disburden mankind of fear, to dispel the darkness of superstition and ignorance by the light of truth which is also the source of goodness and the soul of beauty. The scientific laws of the material universe are to him one with the laws of life and conduct. He is abreast of modern thought in his grasp of the principles and function of science. He anticipates some of the most important discoveries of the nineteenth century and of our own day in physics, in chemistry, in the theory of light and the doctrine of atoms : most remarkably perhaps in anthropology, and the history of the process by which civilization was created, and will finally—so he teaches—run its course and be resumed into the elements out of which it was built up. The prehistoric world and primitive man are to him an open book. But it is in his moral temper that he is greatest and of most enduring value. No nobler ideal of a pure and simple life, no higher message of strength and consolation, has ever been conceived and uttered. He may be called the Roman Milton; and the Epicurean philosophy takes in his hands the austere beauty and grave nobility which Milton gave, once for all, to our own Puritan theology. Both have a majesty unsurpassed in poetry, and a fire of genius which fuses intractable material; and if Milton is more consummate in the technique of his art, Lucretius is unequalled in his poignant humanity.

It was in the succeeding generation, that of Virgil and Horace, that Latin poetry touched its highest point; but a further conquest was made by Ovid, before the Golden definitely waned into the Silver Age. Ovid, more than any other single poet, was the model of the Middle Ages and the lamp of the Renaissance. He is a poet only of the second rank, but in that rank he is not only eminent but unique. He is a pattern of lucidity, fluency, lightness of touch, and grace of movement. He had by nature the rare narrative gift in perfection; he is the one great story-teller in Latin poetry. In the opinion of the best Roman critics, had he only controlled instead of indulging his brilliant rhetoric and still more brilliant wit, he might have been a poet second to none. That discipline was, from defects of character, beyond his power. Yet few poets even of the first rank have done work of such wide and effective importance. Not only did he handle, with seemingly effortless ease, and popularize for universal currency, the poetical forms created by his predecessors; not only did he light up, and transmit in its full fascination to later ages, the world of Graeco-Roman mythology; but he completed the work of Cicero and Horace in fixing a standard of accomplishment and civilized manners for Europe.

It was not, however, only, or even most largely, through his narrative poetry that Ovid made his mark on the history of European letters; it was even more through that less strictly defined type of lighter verse dealing with sentiment, with fashion, and with social life, for which he made the couplet (the so-called elegiac or 'long and short' metre) a vehicle of complete flexibility. This was in a sense his chief legacy to the world. The common intellectual occupation of the Middle Ages, it has wittily and not without a good deal of truth been said, was writing enormous quantities of bad Latin verse; and much the greater part of that verse was written in the Ovidian couplet. The Revival of Learning improved the quality but by no means lessened the amount of this production. The tradition still survives, though feebly, in our Public Schools: and its practice may be defended on the ground that it is an exercise hardly to be replaced by any other in the dexterous and accurate handling of words. From the Latin elegiac, as well as from the Roman oratory, we derive great part of such power as we have over pointed and balanced expression. It has touched our insular slovenliness and inconsequence with something of the Latin gift of clear thinking and the classical sense of form.

Of the post-Augustan Latin epic, important as it is in the history of literature, it is needless to speak here. The lofty splendour of Lucan, the equable grace of Statius, give these poets a claim on our regard. But in the essentials of their art they, no less than their feebler contemporaries or followers, were within the lines of the Virgilian tradition, and did not create a new poetry. The beginnings, a little later, of the movement of poetry towards romance are a chapter of fascinating interest; but they belong to the transition from the classical to the mediaeval world rather than to Latin literature in its stricter sense.

In dramatic poetry, the third of the three main types invented and named by Greek genius, the Romans were rather adapters and imitators than creators. For reasons to be sought in political and social history, the Latin drama never throve after its brilliant beginnings in the middle Republic. Republican tragedy only survives in fragmentary quotations. But from the period of the early Empire we have inherited nine tragedies by Seneca, which have an importance out of all proportion to their dramatic or poetical value. That value is little enough. They have no life, no dramatic insight or movement. They are declamations in dramatic form, written, it has been plausibly suggested, to comply with the craze for the stage which possessed Seneca's pupil, the Emperor Nero. But, historically, they are the chief source from which our own Elizabethan tragedy, as well as those of other European countries, was originated. For generations they were, for good and evil, the models which European dramatists followed. Greek tragedy was, until late in the revival of letters, practically lost and unknown; even when it became known, it was not until recent times that either its principles or its methods were understood. As the most recent study of the Senecan tragedy well puts it,[1] 'Seneca was near enough to Renaissance exuberance to appeal to it as a model; classic enough, when taken as a model, to impose upon it a wholesome sense of structure and style.' Not only in the earlier academic pieces produced in the schools and Universities (like the *Dido* acted by the boys of St. Paul's before Cardinal Wolsey in 1527), but throughout the whole of the national popular drama of the sixteenth century, Seneca is a stimulating and controlling influence: in Sackville's *Gorboduc* (1561), in Marlowe's *Tamburlaine* (1587), in Kyd's *Cornelia* (1592?), and his lost original *Hamlet* (1587?); throughout in Chapman and in Jonson (who places Seneca side by side with Aeschylus, Sophocles, and Euripides); and not less notably, in the earlier and middle plays of Shakespeare. *Titus Andronicus* (only retouched by Shakespeare) is pure Seneca from beginning to end. So is the *True Tragedie of Richard III* which Shakespeare remodelled; in his own play the influence of Seneca is still dominant. 'His work is little remembered,' Mr. Lucas concludes, 'still less regarded, now. But if you seek his memorial, look round on the tragic stage of England, France, and Italy.'

Even more important and far-reaching is the Roman legacy to the modern world in comedy. Latin comedy, like Latin tragedy, was framed on Greek models which it adapted and sometimes did little more than translate. But the Italian genius gave this exotic hybrid a wholly new vitality. Latin comedy was a real and fruitful creation. The modern rediscovery of large portions of the lost plays of Menander, the best as well as the most copious of the Greek comedians (if for the moment we set aside, as something wholly unique and incomparable, the Old Attic Comedy and the plays of Aristophanes), has emphasized our appreciation of Plautus and Terence as drama-

[1] F. L. Lucas, *Seneca and Elizabethan Tragedy*, 1922.

tists of high genius, who fully deserve their traditional fame, and who may be not only studied, but read, with unabated interest. Terence was, and is, admired most for the grace and purity of his language, which is a model of perfect Latinity. In ease and finish of dialogue he is an unsurpassed master and a perpetual model. Among our own English dramatists, Congreve alone stands alongside of him in this respect. In both the literary is stronger than the dramatic quality. Their art is too fine and delicate quite to get (in the modern phrase) across the footlights; it makes its appeal to a more refined and limited audience. It is interesting to note that more than one of the Terentian comedies, like Congreve's masterpiece, *The Way of the World*, 'the unequalled and unapproached masterpiece of English comedy', as Swinburne calls it, 'the one play in our language which may fairly claim a place beside or but just beneath the mightiest work of Molière', were failures when produced on the stage. Terence is a model for study by all writers of comedy; but Plautus is the first of Roman comedians. He is the parent and source of all modern comedy in its many varieties, the master and literary ancestor of Shakespeare and Molière no less than of a thousand dramatists of inferior achievement and less established fame. He is the creator for Europe of burlesque, in the *Amphitruo*; of the comedy of plot, in the *Captivi*; of farce, in the *Miles Gloriosus*; of the comedy of humours, in the *Aulularia* and the *Pseudolus*; of the comedy of domestic life, in the *Trinummus*; and in the *Rudens*, of the romantic comedy which is one of the chief glories of our own English literature.

The flowering time of the Latin drama was brief; it covered less than a century. To the Roman populace, shows, ballet-dances, and gladiatorial combats were more attractive. The fashionable world, as now, followed the mob. For the small appreciative public that remained, playwrights fell more and more into the habit of copying from their Greek and Latin predecessors. By the time of Cicero's youth, both tragedy and comedy were only kept alive in representation by the genius of a few great actors, in stock pieces which were a closed repertory. The plays which continued to be written were for the study rather than for the stage. Any original or vital dramatic work only lingered in the 'mimes' or *revues*. In these much sporadic talent displayed or wasted itself. Among the lesser Latin classics, a small but important niche is occupied by the collection of 'sentences'—single lines which had passed into proverbial currency—made from the mimes of Publilius Syrus, and enlarged afterwards from other sources of the same kind. The seven or eight hundred detached lines thus preserved bring us into close touch with the Roman character, with its shrewd wisdom and terse utterance. Many are as well known—perhaps in some cases even better—as the famous lines of the great poets; and they must be read and studied if we are fully to appreciate the Roman mind, and what we owe to it in matters of good sense, of clear insight, and of practical sagacity.

This sketch does not attempt to survey the whole field of Latin literature, even during the period of the classical writers and of the Roman dominion. It only singles out instances of what that literature was and what it means, as the legacy of a great civilization, to us and to the actual world. It was the essential product of a race and a language unique in history. What the Latin race did for civilization, what we inherit from their character and genius, is the subject of the whole volume of which this chapter is a part. The special point to be realized here is that their literature embodies, in the noble language which they created, not only the history of their achievements, but the quality of their mind and the lineaments of their character. Roman virtue is no idle phrase; nor was it inappropriately that the Latin language and literature received, as a subject of study, the name of Humanity. No language, and no literature, ancient or modern, has given utterance with such steady gravity to the voice of the human soul. *Magnanimitas* and *humanitas*, greatness of spirit and width of human feeling, are Latin words which express the two central qualities of the Roman character. From the Latin mind we inherit these qualities, as we find them expressed, alike with noble eloquence in the periods of their stately prose and the magnificent cadences of their poetry, and concentrated with pregnant brevity in monumental phrases. The same voice speaks, over a range of two hundred and fifty years, in the epitaph engraved and still to be read on the tomb of Publius Cornelius Scipio Africanus, *Mors perfecit tua ut essent omnia brevia, honos fama virtusque, gloria atque ingenium*;[1] in the marvellous lines of Lucretius,

> Iam iam non domus accipiet te laeta, neque uxor
> Optima nec dulces occurrent oscula nati
> Praeripere et tacita pectus dulcedine tangent;
> Non poteris factis florentibus esse, tuisque
> Praesidium: misero misere (aiunt) omnia ademit
> Una dies infesta tibi tot praemia vitae.
> Illud in his rebus non addunt, Nec tibi earum
> Iam desiderium rerum super insidet una;[2]

in the lamentation of Anchises over Marcellus,

> O nate, ingentem luctum ne quaere tuorum;
> Ostendent terris hunc tantum fata neque ultra
> Esse sinent: nimium vobis Romana propago
> Visa potens, superi, propria haec si dona fuissent;[3]

[1] 'Thy death has made all be brief, station, fame and virtue, glory and genius.'

[2] 'Now, now no more shall a glad home and a perfect wife welcome thee, nor darling children race to snatch thy first kisses and touch thy spirit with a sweet silent content, no more mayest thou be prosperous in thy doings and a defence to thine own; alas and alas for thee (say they) from whom one disastrous day has taken all these rewards of life! but this they do not add thereat, "and now no more does any longing for those things come over thee".' Lucr. iii. 894–901.

[3] Seek not to know, the ghost replied with tears,
The sorrows of thy sons in future years:

in the words with which Tacitus ends his exquisite life of Agricola:

Si quis piorum manibus locus, si, ut sapientibus placet, non cum corpore extinguuntur magnae animae, placide quiescas, nosque domum tuam ab infirmo desiderio et muliebribus lamentis ad contemplationem virtutum tuarum voces, quas nec lugeri nec plangi fas est. . . . Quidquid ex Agricola amavimus, quidquid mirati sumus, manet mansurumque est in animis hominum, in aeternitate temporum, fama rerum.[1]

Roma locuta est: it is a single voice, the voice of humanity. For the legacy of Rome in the field of letters has this further unique value, that it is an organic whole. Its compass is rounded and complete; it can be surveyed, and in its essentials grasped, in a single view. Latin literature has a definite beginning; and if it has not a definite end, that is because it became a literature for the whole world, in a language which remained for more than a thousand years the common inheritance and the habitual instrument of educated Europe. Throughout it is (to use a mathematical phrase) a function of Roman life and character. It gave voice to the greatness of the Republic. It created and fixed the ideal of the Empire. With the decay of the imperial system it decayed, but like the Empire, in its decay it fructified; in its disintegration it

This youth, the blissful vision of a day,
Shall just be shown on earth and snatch'd away;
The Gods too high had raised the Roman state,
Were but their gifts as permanent as great.
Virgil, *Aen.* vi. 868–71 (Dryden's translation).

[1] 'If there is a place for the spirits of the good, if as the wise deem, great souls do not perish with the body, may your rest be quiet; recall us, your household, from weak regret and womanish lamentations to the study of your virtues, over which grief and wailing are wrong. What we loved, what we admired in Agricola endures, and will endure in the souls of men, in the eternity of the ages, in historic fame.' Tac. *Agr.* c. 46.

became the soil and substance out of which a new world grew. Nothing in the world stands, it has been said, that does not come from Rome. The Latin language and Latin literature are the treasure we inherit from the race who organized and established civilization.

J. W. Mackail.

LANGUAGE

While in some other departments the Legacy of Rome to the modern world is apparent only to specially trained scholars and to those who have learned from them, in the domain of language the greatness, though not the full extent, of this inheritance is obvious to every person of ordinary education. It needs no exceptional learning, and very little reflection, to perceive that if the infant commonwealth of Rome had succumbed in the struggle with the Etruscan power, the languages known to us as Italian, Spanish, Portuguese, Provençal, and French (not to mention others of smaller importance) would not have existed, nor any languages resembling them. We all know that the little city state, by progressive conquests, became the mistress of the world, and that over the greater part of Western Europe the subject peoples learned to speak the language of their conquerors and forgot their native tongues, so that at the present day what was once the local dialect of the petty district of Latium is (diversely changed, indeed, in the lapse of time, but retaining its essential identity) spoken as their mother tongue by half the nations of the civilized world. And although the Germanic peoples, and the Celts of the British Isles, still preserve their native speech, their languages bear indelible traces of the influence exerted upon them by Latin in the days of Rome's supremacy. Even if this were all, the magnitude of the linguistic inheritance received by the modern world from Rome might well excite our wonder. But there is more to be said. Latin did not become a 'dead language' when it ceased to be the medium of everyday talk. Throughout the Middle Ages, and much later, it was (not in the Neo-Latin countries only, but also in England, Germany and the Low Countries, Scandinavia, Bohemia, Poland, and Hungary) the approved vehicle for writings on theology, philosophy, law, medicine, natural science, and (in many countries) also on history; and, as will appear later in this chapter, it continues to be employed, for certain scientific purposes, even at the present day. Lastly, every language of Western Europe (and not least our own) has in every age of its history added to its resources of expression by the adoption of words of Latin origin; nor does it seem likely that this process has anywhere come to an end.

The linguistic portion of the heritage received from Rome by later ages consists principally of three things. First, the colloquial speech of the later days of the Roman dominion, which survives as the nucleus of several modern languages. Second, the learned Latin of Christian times, which descended, by the unbroken literary and grammatical tradition of the schools, from the language of ancient Rome, and which—developed to serve the changing needs of expression, and from time to time more or less corrected by recourse to the classical models of diction—was through many centuries the common language of the learned of Europe, and still in some measure holds its place as the language of science. Third, the Latin preserved in the classical literature, the unexhausted treasury from which the modern languages have never ceased to supply the deficiencies of their own vocabulary.

The Latin which by gradual change developed into the vernacular tongues of Italy, Spain, Portugal, France, and other countries, was not the Latin of literature. It was the vulgar spoken Latin of the soldier, the peasant, and the artisan. In Roman republican days there was no doubt already a good deal of difference between the Latin used in familiar talk, even by educated persons, and the Latin of books and oratory; and between refined colloquial Latin and the dialect of the illiterate multitude the difference was still greater. All languages undergo gradual change; and even if the dialect of the lower classes of Rome had always been handed down from father to son in families of pure Roman descent, it would probably in the course of centuries have been very considerably modified. But under the later empire it would have been hard to find, in any class of society, from the lowest to the highest, a Roman of pure descent; very few persons, out of all the multitudes that spoke Latin, could claim even that it had been the mother tongue of their ancestors for more than three or four generations. The Vulgar Latin of Europe, in the ultimate stages of its development, was the language, not of Romans, but of Romanized Germans, Celts, Iberians, and people of other races, whose not very remote ancestors had learned Latin (often very imperfectly, no doubt) by oral intercourse with their neighbours, and had transmitted it to their children mixed with alien elements derived from their native speech. And in every generation it was exposed to fresh influences from the languages of barbarian invaders and of the still unromanized portions of the population of the Roman lands.

The investigations of modern philologists have been to a great extent successful in discovering what late Vulgar Latin was like before it became differentiated into what we call the Neo-Latin or Romance (better Romanic) languages. Of direct evidence bearing on this question there is indeed but little, for the obvious reason that people naturally did not begin to write in the vulgar tongue until it had become quite a distinct language from the standard Latin which every one able to write had more or less learned at school. Something may be learned from the unintentional lapses of imperfectly educated writers of Latin, and from the utterances of grammarians who warn their pupils against the use of current vulgarisms. But in the main it is by the comparative study of the Neo-Latin languages, especially as represented in their oldest extant texts, that scholars have been enabled in some measure to reconstruct the common substratum of unwritten language that underlies them all, and the local diversities of this common speech in various parts of the Roman world.

It would of course be impossible in this chapter—if the present writer were competent for such a task—to give, even in the merest outline, a comprehensive account of the characteristics of Vulgar Latin. We must content ourselves with presenting some few examples of the points in which this late development of Latin differed from the classical type. Of one of its most conspicuous and important features, the large number of words that came into it from the original languages of the Romanized peoples, nothing need be said here, as our concern is with the inheritance received from Rome.

It is a noteworthy fact that in two or three respects the late popular development of Latin supplied certain inconvenient deficiencies of the older language as an instrument of expression. Curiously enough, classical Latin had no word precisely equivalent to the Greek *ναί* and the English *yes*. The deficiency might under some circumstances be supplied by *etiam*; but this application was only one among the many uses of the particle. The early Latin translators from Greek could no doubt get over the difficulty by the use of an affirmative sentence echoing the words of the question ('Are you a soldier?', 'I am a soldier'), or by *aio*, 'I say (so)'. In colloquial Latin it was possible to express the meaning by using *sic*, 'so' (as often in Plautus and Terence). But it is hard to see what could have been done with such a passage as Matt. v. 37: 'Let your communication be Yea, yea (Ναὶ ναί) and Nay, nay.' The translator of the Vulgate found no better rendering for *ναὶ ναί* than *est, est*. A well-known pseudo-Virgilian poem shows that this application of *est* was not unique, but we do not know whether it was common except in echoes of the biblical use. In late popular Latin the ancient colloquial use of *sic* was continued and extended, so that in the south it became the regular word for 'yes' (Italian and Spanish *si*, Portuguese *sim*). In Gaul *sic* (Provençal and French *si*) served, like the Yorkshireman's *yea* and the German *doch*, to contradict a negative statement or suggestion, but in the south the ordinary word for 'yes' was *hoc*, 'this', while in the north this pronoun was combined with *ille*, giving rise to the Old French *oïl* (modern French *oui*). Hence the famous appellations 'Langue d'Oc' and 'Langue d'Oïl', applied to the two great groups into which the dialects of France are divided.

Again, ancient Latin, like the oldest stages of all languages, so far as we know (and like Russian to this day) had no articles. Late popular Latin supplied the need of a definite article (as Greek had done before, and as the Germanic languages did afterwards) by using the demonstrative 'that' in this function. Hence in all the Neo-Latin tongues the definite article descends from the Latin *ille* (*illa*, &c.). This is obvious in all the languages except Portuguese, where the initial *l* has been dropped, so that the article is *o* (feminine *a*, plural *os*, *as*). In Rumanian the article is expressed by *-l* (feminine *-a*; plural *-i*, *-le*) joined to the end of the noun. The want of an indefinite article was supplied in Vulgar Latin (as afterwards in the Germanic languages and in modern Greek) by the numeral 'one' (*unus*), pronounced with feebler stress than when used with its original meaning.

Another defect of the Latin language is the ambiguity of the perfect tense: *scripsi* may mean either 'I have written' (Greek γέγραφα) or 'I wrote' (ἔγραψα). The cause of this uncertainty of meaning is that the Latin perfect is in origin a confusion of two prehistoric tenses, corresponding respectively to the Greek perfect and aorist: its inflexions are derived partly from the one and partly from the other. The popular Latin from which the Romanic languages descend achieved a gain in clearness by restricting the inflected tense to its function as a mere preterite, and by using a combination of *habeo* with the passive participle to express the meaning of the Greek perfect; *scripsi* came to mean always 'I wrote' (ἔγραψα), while *habeo scriptum* was used for 'I have written' (γέγραφα). There are anticipations of this usage even in Classical Latin; the germ of it may be seen in expressions like Cicero's 'ea quae

Stoici habent collecta'; and a phrase like *compertum habeo* comes very near to being a periphrastic tense-form. So far, however, the auxiliary use of *habeo* was possible only with transitive verbs, which alone admitted of the passive inflexion. In order to make it a regular part of the grammatical machinery, it was necessary to evolve passive participles for intransitive verbs, so that one could say *habeo dormitum*, 'I have slept', and even *habeo potutum*, 'I have been able'; and, as may be seen in any grammar of a Romanic language, this step was actually taken. The same mode of combining the verb 'have' with a participle exists in English and other Germanic languages; but, although its history here is the same as in late Latin (first 'I have a letter written', where *have* retains its original sense of possession, and then 'I have written a letter', where it has become a mere auxiliary), yet the fact that it does not occur in the Gothic of the fourth century, or in the early writings of any Germanic language, seems to show that it was not a native development, but due to the influence of Vulgar Latin.

A quite different use of *habeo* as an auxiliary arose from the difficulty caused to barbarians trying to speak Latin by the eccentricities in the conjugation of the future tense. In some verbs the endings of this tense were *-bo*, *-bis*, *-bit*, &c., and in other verbs they were *-am*, *-es*, *-et*, &c. It is easy to see how puzzling these irregularities must have been to illiterate people who had not been familiar with them from earliest infancy. As a consequence, the inflected future went out of use, and a new tense-form was evolved, consisting of the infinitive followed by *habeo*. The words for 'I shall write' in all the Neo-Latin tongues—Italian *scriverò*, Spanish *escribiré*, French *(j')écrirai*, &c.—are contractions of the Vulgar Latin *scribere habeo*. This combination is alien to the genius of classical Latin, and there seems no decisive reason to suppose that it was inherited from the colloquial language of ancient Rome. But in the Gothic Bible of the fourth century we find expressions like *taujan haba*, 'to do (I) have', *wisan habaith*, 'to be (he) has ', where the Greek original had merely the ordinary future. The Goths, like the other Germanic peoples, had no inflected future; they commonly used the present instead. But when the need for an unambiguous future was urgently felt, they had recourse to the circumlocution above described, just as in later times the English evolved the auxiliary use of *shall* and *will*, and the Germans that of *werden*. It is an interesting possibility, though not a certainty, that the conjugation of the future tense in the Neo-Latin languages owes its form to the influence of Gothic and closely related dialects. The so-called conditional ('I should write') in these languages has two flexional types, which go back respectively to *scribere habebam* and *scribere habui*.

Considering the complexity of the inflexional system of the Latin verb, it is perhaps surprising that so much of it has survived in the modern vernaculars. None of the four regular conjugations died out in Vulgar Latin, though many verbs changed from one conjugation to another. The irregular verbs were a more serious difficulty, and anomalous forms were reduced to the normal pattern: *esse* was replaced by *essere*, *velle* by *volēre*, and *posse* by *potēre*. The inflected passive was wholly swept away, and its place was supplied by a combination of the verb 'to be' with the participle. Ancient Latin had this already, but *est amatus* stood for the perfect; in Vulgar Latin it was used for the present, and a complete set of passive tenses was formed on its model. The deponent verbs were assimilated to the pattern of ordinary active verbs (some of them, indeed, had always been so conjugated in popular Latin). Certain tense-forms of the active voice which survived underwent a change of meaning: the old pluperfect subjunctive became the imperfect (*scripsissem* supplanting *scriberem*); in Spain and Portugal the form of the pluperfect indicative (*scripseram*) acquired the sense of the conditional.

While in classical Latin the nouns, substantive and adjective, had three genders, in late Vulgar Latin they had only two, the neuter nouns having generally become masculine. This was really a relapse to prehistoric conditions, for the neuter gender of primitive Indogermanic was of later origin than the two others, being merely a differentiated form of the masculine. It was only in the nominative and accusative that the case-endings of neuter nouns in Latin differed at all from those of masculine nouns of the same declension ; in the most numerous class of nouns (the *o* stems) the terminations were identical even in the accusative (*dominum*, *regnum*). We cannot wonder that the Romanized barbarian, learning Latin by ear only, did not trouble himself with an elusive distinction that had no perceptible use. It is worth notice, as a parallel phenomenon, that though the Celtic languages had, in early historic times, the three genders, in their modern forms they have only the masculine and feminine. The only absolutely general rule relating to the inflexion of Latin neuters is that their plural nominative and accusative always ended in *a*. Some neuter plurals—of nouns in very common use—remained unchanged in Vulgar Latin. Italian has still a few plurals like *uova* (Latin *ova*), and *ossa*, and on the analogy of these has formed *mura*, ‘ walls ’, though the Latin *murus* is masculine. These forms are construed as feminine plurals, but some Latin neuter plurals have survived in all the Romanic languages as feminine singulars, on the analogy of the ‘ first declension ’. As was natural, this was what regularly happened to those plural adjectives in *-alia* that were nearly equivalent to substantives in the singular ; such, e. g., as the classical *sponsalia*, which in our Latin dictionaries is Englished ‘ a betrothal ’. Words of this type abounded in late Latin, and in the Neo-Latin tongues they were treated as feminine singulars. In imitation of these inherited words many new substantives were formed, especially in French, where the ending *-alia* had become *-aille*. Our own language took from Old French not a few words such as *espousaille* (from *sponsalia*), which became *espousal* ; and on the analogy of these it became usual to make substantives out of English verbs by the addition of *-al*, as in *betrothal* and *withdrawal.*

The ancient Roman system of case-inflexion was too deficient in uniformity and too full of ambiguities to survive under the conditions which produced the development of Vulgar Latin. It became needless to trouble oneself with the manifold forms of the genitive and dative, because an adequate substitute for them lay ready to hand. Already in classical Latin the prepositions *de* and *ad* sometimes came very near to expressing the sense of these two cases respectively, and, as time went on, their use became more and more nearly identical with that of the inflexions. Some traces of the genitive and dative of nouns occur in Rumanian and in the early stages of some of the other languages. The genitive plural *illorum*, and the dative singular *illi*, have been (of course in altered forms) preserved everywhere. But, speaking broadly, it may be said that the inflected genitive and dative had died out from popular Latin before it broke up into separate languages. The formal distinction between the nominative and accusative disappeared (though it survived in Provençal and early French), the form of the one or the other being employed for both. The ablative ceased to have any reason for its existence, for in its most prominent use as governed by a preposition it had been superseded by the accusative, and the various meanings which it had when standing alone could be expressed by the use of one preposition or another. Besides, the loss of final *m* had effaced the formal distinction, so far as the singular is concerned, between the ablative and the accusative; *domno* stood both for *dominum* and for *dominō*, *rege* both for *regem* and *rege.* Owing to the substitution of the 'analytic' for the 'synthetic' mode of declension, the Neo-Latin languages have much less freedom than Latin in the order of words in a sentence, as in them the object can be distinguished from the subject only by its position.

The pronunciation of late popular Latin differed in many

respects from that of the ancient language. Here we can only mention a few striking points. The *h* became everywhere silent, even in the pronunciation of the learned, though the grammarians preserved the tradition that the ancients did pronounce it. The sound of *k* (expressed in writing by *c*), when followed by *e*, *ae*, *oe*, *i*, was changed in some localities into that of *ts*, and in others into a sound resembling the English *ch*; the *g*, in ancient Latin always pronounced 'hard' as in *gold*, was, when followed by *e*, *ae*, *oe*, *i*, assimilated in sound to the Latin *j*; i. e. it was pronounced like our *y* in *youth*. The ancient Latin *v*, which was originally almost identical with our *w*, changed into the 'lip-teeth' consonant heard in *vain*, *very*. Between vowels *b* was sounded like *v*. Words like *filius*, *venio* became disyllables (*filyus*, *venyo*). An initial *s* followed by a consonant took a vowel (*i*, afterwards *e*) before it to facilitate pronunciation: thus *scribere* became in Spanish *escribir* and in Old French *escrivre*; in Italian this occurs only when the preceding word ends in a consonant, as in *per iscrivere*. An *n* before *s* had become silent, with lengthening of the preceding vowel, already in the colloquial speech of classical times: thus *mensa* was pronounced *mēsa*. At the end of a word, except in certain monosyllables, *m* had everywhere become silent; in the popular Latin of Italy final *s* was dropped, but in Gaul and Spain it continued to be pronounced.

In the pronunciation of the vowels there were some important changes. The ancient *ae* and *oe*, which were originally genuine diphthongs (i. e. consisted of two vowel sounds in close succession), had at an early period developed into the simple sound of *ē*,[1] even in educated pronunciation. Subsequently, the old distinctions of vowel quantity entirely ceased to be observed in ordinary speech and even in reading aloud; though they were still preserved in the tradition of the schools, so that correct verse could still be written. What happened, however,

[1] They did not, however, become identical. The *oe* became a 'close *ē*', like the ordinary *ē* of Latin; the *ē* which descended from *ae* was 'open'.

was not that no difference was made between an originally long *e*, *i*, *o*, or *u* and the short vowel written with the same letter ; *mĕrus* did not come to rhyme with *vērus*, *vĭdeo* with *rīdeo*, *bŏnum* with *dōnum*, or *hŭmus* with *fūmus*. The reason of this is that in the development of Latin sounds, even before the differences in quantity disappeared, the long vowels came to differ from the short vowels not only in their length, but also in the manner in which they were formed in the mouth, and consequently in their effect on the ear. When the difference in quantity ceased to exist, the difference in quality still remained. The consequences in late Vulgar Latin resulting from this development are somewhat curious. As a general rule (more strictly applicable to the dialects of Gaul than to those of the other regions) the long *e* and the short *i* of ancient Latin were, in accented syllables, replaced by the sound which phoneticians call 'close *e*', and the long *o* and the short *u* by the 'close *o*'; but these close vowels[1] were sharply distinguished both from the open *e* and *o* that stood for the old short *e* (and also *ae*) and short *o*, and from the close *i* and *u* which descended from long *i* and *u*. If the classical *lēvis*, 'smooth', and *lĕvis*, 'light', *pīla*, 'column', and *pĭla*, 'a ball', *lūteus*, 'yellow', and *lŭteus*, 'clayey', had all survived in popular use and undergone the regular change of pronunciation, there would have been no danger that the hearer would confuse the words that are spelt alike ; but *cētus*, 'a whale', and *cĭtus*, 'quick', *pōto*, 'I drink', and *pŭto*, 'I think', would have become homophonous. No doubt Vulgar Latin, like most other languages, had its long and short vowels ; but between the later quantity and the ancient quantity there was no fixed relation.

It was not only in grammar and pronunciation that late Vulgar Latin differed from the language of Roman literature. Its vocabulary, also, was widely different. If a classical scholar

[1] The terms 'open' and 'close', as applied to vowel sounds, refer to the larger or smaller degree of opening of the oral passage when the sounds are produced.

who knew nothing of the history of the Romanic languages were presented with a complete list of words and their meanings current in late popular Latin, it would contain for him many surprises. He would find that many of the very commonest and seemingly most indispensable words of the ancient tongue had altogether died out of use; that the words that had survived had often undergone extraordinary changes of meaning; and that an enormous crop of new words had sprung up, some of them formed from ancient words according to the familiar rules of Latin derivation, and others of quite obscure origin. It is possible that many of these apparent novelties were not really new. When our lexicographers, as they often do, mark a word, sense, or construction as 'ante- and post-classical', the meaning is that an expression which was used in the early days of Roman literature by Plautus or Ennius came to be considered unworthy of the dignity of literature, but survived in colloquial speech, to emerge into view in post-classical times, when the yoke of literary convention was loosened, and people began to write more nearly as they spoke. In the same manner, it is not unlikely that some Latin words, the existence of which is known to us only by their being represented in the daughter languages, may have come down in popular speech from the days of the kings of Rome. There are many words in familiar use among the lower classes of our own country which never occur in literature, though they can be proved to be as old as the English language. There can be no doubt, however, that by far the greater number of the peculiar words and meanings that distinguish late Vulgar Latin from the classical language were real innovations; and it is often easy to see how they must have originated. Sometimes a bit of ancient slang has taken the place of its more dignified synonym. *Testa*, 'a pot', is used for 'head' in all the Romanic languages (though *caput* has lived on everywhere in figurative senses, and its derivative *cabeza*, *cabeça* is in Spanish and Portuguese the commoner word in the literal sense). The French *joue*, ' cheek ', though the non-philological reader may be incredulous, descends from the Latin *gabata*, ' porringer '. *Crus*, ' leg ', died out everywhere ; the substitutes were *gamba*, ' fetlock ', and *perna*, ' ham '. Very many monosyllabic nouns, and some of two syllables, were dropped because (partly owing to phonetic change) they were found wanting in auditory distinctness. *Res* (*rem*) survives in Neo-Latin only as the French *rien*, ' nothing ' ; the word for ' thing ' is *caussa* (Italian and Spanish *cosa*, Portuguese *cousa*, French *chose*), which lost its original sense of ' cause '. *Ōs*, ' mouth ', gave place to *bucca* (Italian *bocca*, Spanish *boca*, French *bouche*), which in Classical Latin meant ' cheek '. (But *ŏs*, ' bone ', though also a monosyllable, was saved from extinction by being turned into *ossum*.) *Ignis* in late pronunciation lacked distinctness ; the word used for ' fire ' was *focus*, originally ' hearth '. *Equus*, ' horse ', fell out of use, and *caballus*, ' a nag, packhorse, hack, jade ' (Lewis and Short), took its place. Some very familiar verbs of Classical Latin lost their currency for similar reasons. One of these was *edere*, ' to eat ', which was generally replaced by *manducare*, ' to chew ', though in Spain and Portugal *comedere* (which of course is good Latin enough) was used instead. *Suere*, ' to sew ', was lost ; the Italian *cucire*, Spanish *coser*, French *coudre*, all come from *consuere*. *Scire*, ' to know ', was superseded everywhere by *sapere*, ' to be wise '. The regular classical words for ' to speak ', *loqui*, *fari*, were inconvenient as being deponents, and for phonetic reasons also. Their place was supplied in two different ways. The Spanish *hablar* and the Portuguese *fallar*, ' to speak ', represent *fabulare* (*-ari*), which in old colloquial Latin meant ' to chat ' (originally, ' to tell stories '). The other, more widely used, substitute for *loqui* had a very curious history. The Bible phrase *assumere parabolam* (a literal translation from the Hebrew : the English Bible renders ' to take up his parable ') somehow caught the popular fancy, so that *parabola*, which in the Old Testament passages means ' a figurative or poetical speech', came to be the ordinary word for 'speech', 'word' (Italian *parola*, Spanish *palabra*, Portuguese *palavra*, French *parole*), and from it was formed a verb *parabolare* 'to speak' (Italian *parlare*, Provençal *parlar*, French *parler*).

In popular Latin, as in most other languages, the development of the meaning of words often took a course that to us seems very strange, though we can usually discern something of the mental processes by which it was prompted. One would hardly have guessed that *pacare*, 'to pacify, appease' (whence the Italian *pagare*, Spanish, Portuguese, and Provençal *pagar*, French *payer*), would be adopted everywhere as the regular word for 'to pay (a creditor)', but so it was. Classical Latin, it may be remarked, had no transitive verb expressive of this meaning. By a further development, *pacare* came to be used also for 'to pay (a debt)', for which the proper Latin word was *solvere* (literally 'to loosen'). *Minari*, 'to threaten', became in late Latin *minare*, with the new sense 'to drive (cattle)'. Subsequently the word came to mean 'to lead', in which sense it has come down in nearly all the Neo-Latin languages (Italian *menare*, Old Spanish and Provençal *menar*, French *mener*). Even more remarkable, perhaps, than any of these examples is the change of meaning in *senior*, which ceased to have any reference to age, and became the ordinary designation of a superior in rank: Italian *sere*, *signore*, Spanish *señor*, Portuguese *senhor*, French *sire*, *(mon)sieur*, *seigneur*.

Some words that were very common in ancient Latin disappeared, not through phonetic causes, but because of the development of the sense of their approximate synonyms. The Romanic word for 'great' is not *magnus* (though the unclassical *tam magnus* survives in the Spanish *tamaño*, 'size'), but *grandis*, which originally meant 'full-grown'. *Casa*, 'cottage', came to be used for 'house', superseding *domus*. (The French word for a house, however, is *maison*, from *mansio*, 'dwelling-place'; but *casa* is preserved in *chez*, 'at the house of'.) *Ludus*, 'play', and the related verb, were supplanted by *jocus*, 'jest', and its derivative *jocare*. *Pulcher*, 'beautiful', gave place to *bellus*, 'pretty'. It was perhaps through its phonetic coincidence with this word that *bellum* ceased to be used in popular speech; the Romanic word for 'war', *guerra*, is of German origin.

Many of the short words that went out of use (as we have suggested, because of their exiguity of sound) were replaced by diminutives, used without any diminutive meaning. *Auris*, 'ear', was superseded by *auricula*, and *genu*, 'knee', by *genuculum*. *Aviolus* was used instead of *avus*, 'grandfather', and *vetus*, 'old', gave place to *vetulus* (Italian *vecchio*, Spanish *viejo*, French *vieux*), which came to include the meaning of *senex*. This use of the diminutive endings seems natural enough in *agnellus*, 'lamb', *avicellus*, 'bird' (Italian *uccello*, French *oiseau*), *apicula*, 'bee', or even in *ovicula*, 'sheep'; but some examples, such as the Gaulish Latin *soliculus* (French *soleil*) for 'sun', strike us rather oddly.

Of the words taken up by Vulgar Latin from Celtic and Germanic tongues we need not speak here, as they are no part of the Roman inheritance. But a few loan-words from Greek call for notice as being specially interesting. *Petra* became the universal word for 'stone', instead of *lapis*. *Blasphemare*, 'to speak evil of' (Italian *biasimare*, French *blâmer*, whence our *blame*), gained currency everywhere; probably not through the medium of the New Testament, as it was used in its original Greek sense, not in the narrowed sense 'to blaspheme'. *Platea* (πλατεῖα, 'broad way', 'street') came to mean 'an open space in a town', 'a square', and survives in all the Neo-Latin languages; the French form *place* acquired a more general meaning, which has been further extended in English. It is curious that in the south the Greek θεῖος, 'uncle', passed into popular Latin (Italian *zio*, Spanish *tio*, 'uncle, cousin'). A still more extraordinary borrowing is that of the preposition κατά, which seems to have been used by traders from the Levant pretty much as 'per' is used in English business language. *Cata unum* meant 'apiece'; hence the Italian *caduno*, Spanish *cada uno*, *cada*, Old French *chëun*, 'each'.

In post-classical Latin, and especially in the late popular dialect, a multitude of new derivatives of old words were produced by the extended use of resources inherited from the ancient Roman tongue. Thus from *jocus*, 'play', was formed *jocale*, 'plaything', whence our *jewel*; from *caballus*, 'horse', was derived *caballarius*, 'horseman'. The ending of feminine passive participles (especially of the form *-ata*) was very extensively used to form substantives from verbs, as in *armata*, 'arming of warriors', 'armed force' (Italian *armata*, Spanish *armada*, 'fleet of war-ships', French *armée*, 'army'). Hence the ending *-ata* came to be appended also to nouns. Thus in Italy and Gaul, where *diurnum* (Italian *giorno*, French *jour*) came to be the usual word for 'day', there was formed a derivative *diurnata* (Italian *giornata*, French *journée*), meaning 'a day's work'. The lexical inheritance of the Neo-Latin languages from Latin does not consist only of ready-formed words; it includes also a great number of suffixes of derivation which to this day can be used to form new words almost without limit. The Italian, Spanish, and Portuguese *-mente*, and the French *-ment*, which in those languages can still be appended to any adjective to turn it into an adverb, had its origin in Latin expressions like *tranquilla mente*, 'with a quiet mind'.

We cannot further pursue the interminable subject of the changes which the vocabulary of nouns and verbs underwent in popular Latin. But something must be said of the changes affecting other parts of speech. We will first give a few samples from words of a pronominal character.

As *ille*, besides surviving as a personal pronoun, had come to be used as the definite article, it was no longer serviceable as a demonstrative. It was kept alive in this function, however, by prefixing to it the interjection *ecce*, 'behold', or its later variant *eccum*. From combinations of this interjection with *illum* (*illam*, &c.) descend a great variety of Romanic forms meaning 'that', such as Italian *colui*, French *celui* (feminine *celle*), Italian *quello*, Spanish *aquel*. *Iste*, 'this', survives separately in the southern languages as *este*, *esto*; but the prefixed interjection is represented by the initial *qu* or *c* in Italian and Spanish *questo* and Old French *cest* (modern French *cet* before vowels). *Hic*, 'this', ceased to be used in the masculine and feminine, but the neuter *hoc* (in addition to its use for 'yes', which we have already mentioned) remains, with the usual prefixed *ecce*, in the Italian *ciò*. The place of *idem*, 'the same', was everywhere taken by a strange combination of *met* (evolved from the Latin *egomet*, *nosmet*, *semet*, &c.) with *ipsimum*, a sort of superlative of *ipse*: hence Italian *medesimo*, Spanish *mismo*, French *même*. *Nihil*, *nil*, entirely disappeared, and the problem of finding a word for 'nothing' was diversely solved in various parts of the Latin world. The Italian *niente* represents *nec entem*, 'that which is not'. The French *rien* is the Latin *rem*, 'thing', the negative notion being either expressed by *ne* in another part of the sentence or elliptically left to be understood. Similarly the Spanish and Portuguese *nada* stands for (*rem*) *natam*, '(thing) born', if we may venture to translate literally.

In the domain of the particles, the contrast between classical and late popular Latin is very great. The old adversatives, *sed*, *at*, *autem*, &c., went out of use; the usual word for 'but' was *magis*, originally meaning 'more', 'rather'. When two or three particles coincided in meaning, the popular speech usually retained only one of them. *Atque*, *ac*, and the suffixed *-que* disappeared, as *et* could always be substituted. *Haud* was superfluous, because its purpose was fully served by *non*; it could hardly have survived in any case, having become identical in sound with *aut*, 'or'. Many monosyllabic particles had by change of pronunciation become indistinct in sound, and ceased to be used: *ut* in the sense of 'that' was superseded by *quod*, and in the sense of 'as' by *quomodo* (Italian *come*, Spanish *como*,

French *comme*) ; *sub*, 'under', was replaced by *subtus* ; *ab* and *ex* became obsolete except in compounds. Many Romanic prepositions and adverbs are combinations of two or more Latin particles. The precedent of the classical *deinde* was followed in *de unde* (Spanish *donde*, 'where', French *dont*, 'of which') and *de ubi* (Italian *dove*, 'where'). The piling-up of particles was carried in Vulgar Latin to strange lengths. *Ab ante* (whence Italian *avanti*, French *avant*) and *in ante* (whence Italian *innanzi*), which go back to the early centuries, were treated as single words, and the combinations *de abante*, *de inante*, survive in the Italian *davanti*, French *devant*, and the Italian *dinanzi*, 'before'. From *abante* was formed a verb, *abantiare* (Italian *avanzare*, French *avancer*), 'to advance'. Many Neo-Latin particles represent Latin phrases containing substantives. (*Ad*) *hanc horam*, 'to this hour', has become the Italian *ancora*, French *encore*, 'still' ; the Italian *allora*, French *alors*, *lors*, 'then', is (*ad*) *illam horam*. Classical Latin had the Greek loan-word *tornus*, 'a lathe' (Virgil), and the derivative *tornare*, 'to turn in a lathe' (Cicero). The latter came in popular Latin to mean 'to move round, to *turn*', and gave rise to a verbal noun, *tornus* or *tornum*, 'a move round, a turn' (Italian and Spanish *torno*, French *tour*), which is contained in various Neo-Latin adverbs with the sense 'round, around' : Italian *attorno* (from *ad tornum*), *intorno*, *d' intorno*, *all' intorno*, and French *autour*, *alentour*.

It would have been easy to find abundance of additional examples of every one of the processes illustrated in the foregoing paragraph ; but for our present purpose those we have given are sufficient. A remarkable fact that calls for mention is that the Romanic vocabulary of pronouns and particles, unlike that of nouns and verbs, is all but entirely of Latin origin. Its ultimate etymological elements, though combined in novel ways and often surprisingly changed in signification, belong, with trifling exceptions, to the heritage received from Rome.

Having now come to the end of our survey (necessarily imperfect as it is) of the more prominent characteristics of the late popular Latin from which the modern Romanic languages have descended, we proceed to indicate briefly a few of the points of mutual resemblance and diversity in these languages as compared with each other. It will be convenient to confine our attention to the four great literary languages (Italian, Spanish, Portuguese, and French), and to speak almost exclusively of those features of these modern tongues that are inherited or developed from popular Latin, leaving out of consideration the large number of words which in all periods of their history they have adopted from literary Latin or formed from Latin roots. In the little we shall say about the special phonetic laws of the various languages, our chief purpose will be to enable the non-philological reader now and then to recognize a familiar Latin word under its strange Neo-Latin disguise.

As most people know, Italian is of all the modern languages the one that has the most obvious resemblance to Latin. To a great extent this is due to the fact that Italian has adopted a multitude of words from literary Latin, altering nothing but their terminations. But even if we consider only the popular kernel of the language, we shall find it in many respects nearer to its original than any of the sister languages. The first person singular present indicative of an Italian verb always ends in *-o*, a rule which is not found without exceptions in any other Romanic tongue; the Latin *sum*, *possum*, have become *sono*, *posso*. The sounds *p*, *t*, *k* (written *c*) between vowels, which in the cognate languages are regularly modified, are very frequently retained in Italian: *ape*, 'bee', *lato*, 'side', *amico*, 'friend', are Latin in all but the ending; *c*, however, is often changed to *g*, as in *luogo*, 'place' (beside *fuoco*, 'fire', from *focus*), *lago*, 'lake', *pagare*, 'to pay'. Italian agrees with the other southern languages, as against French, in retaining the late Latin vowels with comparatively little change. Speaking in terms of spelling rather than of strict phonetics, we may say that all the normal differences between the stressed vowels of classical Latin and those of modern Italian are those exemplified in the following words: Latin *paucum*, Italian *poco*; Latin *caelum*, Italian *cielo*; Latin *vĕnit*, *fĕrum*, Italian *viene*, *fiero*; Latin *sĭtim*, *litteram*, Italian *sete*, *lettera*; Latin *nŏvum*, Italian *nuovo*; Latin *longum*, Italian *lungo*; Latin *rotundum*, *ruptum*, Italian *rotondo*, *rotto*. The representation of Latin *ĕ* and *ae* by *ie* and of *ŏ* by *uo* occurs at the end of a stressed syllable. The constant avoidance of harsh combinations of consonants, which gives to Italian its character of the most musical of European languages, is shown in the change of *l* into *i* when following *p*, *c*, *b*, *g*, and *f*: *pianta*, 'plant'; *doppio*, 'double'; *chiave*, 'key'; *occhio* (from *oc'lum*), 'eye'; *biasimo*, 'blame'; *ghiaccia*, 'ice'; *fiore*, 'flower'. (In words adopted from literary Latin this euphonic change does not occur.) From the same cause has arisen the regular assimilation of the former of two succeeding consonants to the second, as in *otto*, 'eight', *sette*, 'seven', *sonno*, 'sleep'. The consonantal endings of Latin have all been smoothed away; *sum*, *sunt*, have both become *sono*; *amat* is represented by *ama*, *examen* by *esame*, *spem* (the only surviving word of its type) by *speme*. The fact already mentioned, that in Italy (and nowhere else except in Dacia) the final *s* became silent in popular Latin, has had some notable consequences. While in Italian, as in the other languages, the usual form of a noun in the singular represents the Latin accusative, in the plural Italian has been obliged to adopt the form of the nominative (*rose*, *campi*, not *rosas*, *campos*, as in Spanish). Where in Latin the nominative plural of a noun ended in *-es*, the ending was changed to *i*, as in *onori* for *honores*. The pronouns *nos*, *vos*, became *noi*, *voi*. In the verbs, *amas*, *amabas*, *amavistis* became *ami*, *amavi*, *amasti*. Apart from these changes, the only specially notable feature of Italian verbal conjugation is that in some verbs the inflexion of the Latin perfect has been discarded for a new formation, marked by the doubling of a consonant and sometimes also by change of the root vowel: thus for *habui*, *sapui*, *cecĭdi*, we have *ebbi*, *seppi*, *caddi*. A striking peculiarity of Italian is the great variety of diminutive and augmentative endings, which may be added almost at will to substantives of certain types of meaning. Examples of the diminutive formations are *casetta*, *casina*, *casuccia*, *casucciola*, from *casa*, 'house'; *ometto*, *omuccio*, *omicciuolo*, from *uomo* 'man'; *vecchietta*, *vecchina*, *vecchiarella* from *vecchia*, 'old woman'. The various diminutive endings have different shades of meaning, often expressing either affection or pity, or mild contempt. The augmentative endings are *-one*, as in *casone*, 'large house', and *-accio*, *-accia*, implying dislike, as in *capellaccio*, 'big ugly hat', *casaccia*, 'great ugly house'. In this connexion it is significant that Italian is the only Romanic language in which *frater* and *soror* have been superseded by the diminutives *fratello* and *sorella*.

In the degree of its resemblance to Latin, Spanish comes next to Italian. The final *-o* of the first person singular present indicative is retained (as also in Portuguese), but there are certain monosyllabic exceptions: *habeo*, *sapio*, *sum*, *sto*, *do*, *vado*, have become *he*, *sé*, *soy*, *estoy*, *doy*, *voy*. In one point, the preservation of final *s*, Spanish is more conservative than Italian, and it has some uncontracted forms where Italian has contractions, e. g. *decir* 'to say' (Italian *dire*). But, speaking generally, Spanish represents a more advanced stage of sound development than Italian. The change of *p*, *t*, *k* (between vowels) into *b*, *d*, *g*, which is occasional in Italian, is regular in Spanish. Similarly, while both languages represent the Latin *ĕ* and *ŏ*, at the end of an accented syllable, by diphthongs (*ie*, *uo* in Italian, *ie*, *ue* in Spanish), it is only in Spanish that these diphthongs occur in the middle of a syllable, as in *viento*, 'wind', *muerte*, 'death', for which Italian has *vento*, *morte*. The Latin *f* has mostly been dropped, though represented in spelling by *h*, as in *hacer*, *hijo*, from *facere*, *filius*. The Latin *g* before *e* and *i*, and the Latin *j*, which in late Vulgar Latin were pronounced like our *y*, retained this sound in some words, as *ya*, 'now', from the Latin *jam*, while in others they were represented in early Spanish by a sibilant like our *sh*, which afterwards developed into a guttural spirant resembling the German *ch*. As this sound is represented in writing by *g* or *j*, the spelling disguises the real amount of the change: such words as *gente*, 'people', and *joven*, 'young', look much more like Latin than they sound. The initial *g* and *j*, when followed by *e* or *i*, have disappeared in unaccented syllables, as in *hermano*, 'brother' (the *h* is silent), from *germanus*, and in *Enero*, 'January', from the Vulgar Latin *Jenuarium*. In the middle of words the Spanish *j* (pronounced as stated above) descends from the Latin *li*, as in *mejor*, 'better', or from *cl*, as in *ojo*, 'eye' (from *oc'lus*). The Latin initial *pl*, *cl*, *fl*, have all become *ll* (pronounced nearly like *ly*), as in *lleno*, 'full', *llave*, 'key', *llama*, 'flame'; though the modern Spaniard finds no difficulty in pronouncing these combinations in loan-words from literary Latin. The Latin *ct* has become *ch* (pronounced as in *church*), as in *ocho*, 'eight', *noche*, 'night' (*noctem*), *hecho*, 'made' (*factum*), *leche*, 'milk' (Vulgar Latin *lactem*); compare the Italian *otto*, *notte*, *fatto*, *latte*. Between vowels the Latin *d* and *g* have often disappeared, as in *ver*, 'to see', *creer*, 'to believe', *reir*, 'to laugh', *leer*, 'to read'. The final *e* of Vulgar Latin words, whether resulting from Latin *-e* or *-em*, is regularly dropped after *l*, *n*, *r* (preceded by a vowel), so that Spanish, unlike Italian, has a large number of words ending in those consonants; the terminations of the infinitive are *-ar*, *-er*, *-ir*. It is not necessary in this place to say more about Spanish phonology or to mention the few points in which the verbal inflexions of popular Latin have been superseded by new formations. But it may be worth while to point out some of the differences between the Spanish vocabulary (with which that of Portuguese closely agrees) and that which is common to the other Romanic tongues. *Frater* and *soror* have been supplanted by *germanus*, *germana* (Spanish *hermano*, *-a*). The verb *volēre* (Classical Latin *velle*), which is preserved in Italian, Provençal, and French, is entirely wanting; the word for 'to will' is *querer* (Latin *quaerere* 'to seek'), which also means 'to love'. The Latin *largus*, 'munificent, prodigal', which in the other Neo-Latin tongues has come to mean 'broad', in Spanish means 'long'; the word for 'broad' being *ancho*, from the Latin *amplus*. Of the two Latin words for 'more', *magis* was chosen in Spain (*mas*), *plus* in Gaul and Italy. *Locus* was superseded by its derivative *locale* (Spanish *lugar*). The Spanish *llegar*, 'to arrive', is the Latin *plicare*, 'to fold, bend', which in Italian (*piegare*) and French (*plier*, *ployer*) retains its original sense. (Compare *applicare*, in Classical Latin already used for 'to land'.)

The close original affinity between Spanish and Portuguese is greatly obscured by the divergent development of the sounds of Vulgar Latin in the two languages, and especially by the regular dropping-out, in Portuguese words of popular origin, of *l* and *n* between vowels. The omitted *n* usually leaves a trace of itself in the nasalization of the preceding vowel. (The nasal vowels are expressed in writing *ã*, *ẽ*, *ĩ*, *õ*; when final, the nasal *e*, *i*, *o*, *u* are denoted by the addition of *m*; the combinations *am*, *an*, *em*, *en*, &c., before a consonant are pronounced as nasal vowels. There are also nasal diphthongs, written *ãe*, *ão*, *õe*.) It is not easy at first sight to recognize the Latin *malus*, *solus*, *dolor*, *bonus*, *manus*, *tenēre*, *venire* under their Portuguese disguise of *mao* (feminine *má*), *só*, *dor*, *bom* (feminine *boa*), *mão*, *ter* (participle *tido*), *vir*. The Latin initial *pl*, *cl*, *fl*, which in Spanish have become *ll*, are represented in Portuguese by *ch*, pronounced like the English *sh*. (In loan-words *pl* becomes *pr*, as in *praça*, 'place'.) In some respects the Portuguese sound-system is more primitive than the Spanish. The Latin *ĕ*, *ŏ* have not become diphthongs, nor has *au* been confused with *o*: Portuguese has *cousa*, 'thing', *ouro*, 'gold', where Spanish has *cosa, oro.* The fact that *multus* is *muito* in Portuguese enables us to account for its Spanish form *mucho* and the adverb *muy*, 'very'. The Portuguese *venho* (*nh* pronounced nearly as *ny*), 'I come', *filho* (*lh* nearly as *ly*), 'son', *mais*, 'more', are nearer to their Latin originals than are the Spanish *vengo, hijo, mas*. The Latin initial *j*, and *g* before *e* and *i*, are represented by the sound of *zh* (or of the modern French *j*), as probably in the oldest Spanish. Both languages retain the Latin *g, j* in writing, so that a Spanish word and its Portuguese equivalent often are identical to the eye, but differ widely to the ear. The inflexions of the verb are, in the main, slightly more archaic than those of Spanish. The Portuguese conjugation, however, shows some novel features of its own: thus the present indicative of *perder*, 'to lose', is *perco, perdes, perde*, and that of *pedir* 'to ask', is *peço, pedes, pede*. The compound tenses are formed with *tenere* (Portuguese *ter*), not with *habere* as in Spanish and the related tongues. A remarkable characteristic of Portuguese is a fondness for metathesis, which often strangely disguises the identity of its words with those of Spanish. In its wealth of diminutive endings, each having its own special shade of emotional meaning, Portuguese vies with Italian.

The Neo-Latin dialects of France have, from their earliest appearance in written form, constituted two distinct groups, having many common features in which they differ from the other Romanic tongues. The dialects of the northern group—those of the 'Langue d'Oïl'—are usually spoken of as 'French', and their mediaeval form as 'Old French'. The southern group, the 'Langue d'Oc' (to which the Catalan of north-eastern Spain also belongs), is chiefly represented by the cultivated language commonly known by the convenient if not very accurate name of Provençal, in which the finest poetry of the twelfth and thirteenth centuries was written, and which continued in gradually decreasing literary use for three centuries longer. In many respects Provençal, even at quite a late period, was nearer than the earliest known French (ninth century) to the primitive type from which both languages descend; its forms, indeed, often represent a stage through which French must have passed. In some points (as in the treatment of Latin *p*, *t*, *c* between vowels, and the dropping of final *e*) the development of Latin sounds had in the Romanic of Gaul reached exactly the same point as in that of Spain; the infinitives *saber*, 'to know', *nadar*, 'to swim', *pagar*, 'to pay', are identical in Provençal and Spanish. But in certain other respects the common antecedent of Provençal and French had carried sound-change much further than the more southern tongues. Every vowel but *a* vanished altogether when it stood in the syllable, or one of the syllables, that came after the accented syllable of a Latin word; the only exception being that a final *e*, *i*, or *o* remained as *e* if preceded by two consonants that were difficult to pronounce without a following vowel. This change was of itself sufficient to produce a striking unlikeness between the Romanic of Gaul and that of the other countries. The Latin *amo*, preserved unchanged in Italian, Spanish, and Portuguese, here became *am*; the innumerable nouns of the second declension which survived ended everywhere else in *o*, but in Gaul had come to end in a consonant. Two other important peculiarities common to French and Provençal are the development of nasal vowels, and the passing of the Latin sound of *ū* into that of *ü* (the *u* in modern French *lune*).

In some of its features, however, the Romanic of Gaul is more conservative than any of the sister languages. The Latin final *t* was preserved, as we see in the modern French *disait* (from *dicebat*), *sert* (from *servit*), *fut* (from *fuit*). The initial *pl*, *bl*, *cl*, *fl*, *gl* remained unaltered. A far more important instance is that the distinction between the nominative and the accusative was preserved in Provençal and Old French (though lost in the modern language). In consequence of that dropping-out of the vowels of unaccented syllables, which we have already mentioned, the declension of a noun like *murus* assumed in Old French the following form: nominative singular and accusative plural *murs*; nominative plural and accusative singular *mur*. In later Old French the 'rule of *s*', as grammarians call it, was extended from the masculine nouns of the second declension to many nouns of the other declensions: the 'subject case' singular and the 'object case' plural were distinguished by the addition of *s* to the stem of the noun. Modern French has quite lost the case distinction. Most of its inherited nouns derive their form from the Latin accusative, as *couleur* from *colórem*, but some represent the nominative form, as *pâtre* from *pástor*. *Homme* descends regularly from *hominem*, but *homo* survives in the pronoun *on*. The only word that retains the Old French *s* of the nominative singular is *fils*, 'son'.

The changes by which 'Galloromanic' (as the common basis of French and Provençal is sometimes called) has developed into modern French are extraordinarily manifold and intricate. Yet the knowledge of a very few out of the many phonological laws of the language will be sufficient to remove the appearance of capriciousness from quite a considerable number of those points of unlikeness between French and Latin (or between French and any other Romanic tongue) which non-philologists are apt to consider strange. For example, let the reader, in addition to the facts we have already stated, take note of the following points: Almost from the earliest known period of French, a Latin *a* ending an accented syllable regularly became *e* (before *m* and *n* it became *ai*); an *a* in an unaccented syllable became *e*; the Vulgar Latin 'close *e*' (from Latin *ē*, *ĭ*) became *ei*, which developed later into *oi*; the Latin *t*, *d*, *g* dropped out between vowels and between a vowel and *r*; the Latin *c* and *g* before *a* became respectively *ch* and *j*. He will then see at once, without further explanation, that the French *cher*, *père*, *pain*, *main*, *vie*, *croire*, *moins*, *noir*, *jambe* are quite normally descended from their Latin originals. The conjugation of verbs in French has one feature that looks quite unlike anything in Latin or in the cognate languages—the final *s* in the first person singular (e. g. *suis*, *sers*, *sens*, *viens*, *aimais*, *vécus*). This, however, is really of Latin origin. The Latin *facio* became in French by normal phonetic development *faiç*, *fais*, and there were perhaps some other verbs in which the final *s* was similarly a natural growth ; from these it was extended to many verbs which originally had it not. The part of the French vocabulary which descends from Vulgar Latin is for the most part common to French with the other Romanic tongues. There are, however, many exceptions : e. g. 'to fear' was in Gaul not *timere* but *tremere*, which has become *craindre*. It is characteristic of French that a circumlocutory phrase has often been substituted for a simple word. Instead of the Old French *hui*, 'to-day' (from *hodie*), the modern language says *aujourd'hui*, 'at the day of to-day'. Similarly *le lendemain*, 'the morrow', has been built up by successive additions from the Latin *mane*, 'in the morning' (substituted in late Latin for *cras*) : first the preposition *de* was prefixed (already in Vulgar Latin : compare the Italian *domani*) ; next the adverb *demain* was felt to need a preposition before it ; then *en demain* became a substantive, which could be preceded by the article ; finally *l'endemain* came to be apprehended as a single word. Very many of the conjunctions and adverbs now in common use have been evolved in French itself from phrases, as *quoique*, 'although', *cependant*, 'meanwhile, yet, however', *maintenant*, 'now'.

The differences between French and the other Romanic languages have been much increased by changes in pronunciation of comparatively recent growth. One of these, the disappearance of *s* before a consonant, as in *tête*, *même*, *écrire*, *été*, for the Old French *teste*, *mesme*, *escrivre*, *esté*, has, since the seventeenth century, been recognized in the spelling. Other changes affect the spoken language only. Final consonants are for the most part pronounced only when the following word begins with a vowel, and not always even then ; and the written unaccented *e* is silent at the end of a word, and often in other positions. If French were written phonetically, it would look far less like Latin or Italian than it does in the traditional orthography.

The foregoing pages of this chapter have been concerned only with the first of the three instalments (if the expression may be allowed) in which, as we said at the beginning, the heritage of the language of ancient Rome has come into the possession of the modern world. With the other two we must deal much more briefly.

The conversion of the Roman Empire to Christianity had an important influence on the fortunes of the Latin language. Although the new religion found most of its converts among the poor and outcast, it was, from the earliest period of its promulgation in the West, accepted by a considerable number of the learned class, many of whom devoted their powers to the service of the Church. Hence, while pagan Latin literature declined, as its inner inspiration died out, a new and vigorous literature came into being, full of the enthusiasm of the new faith. Christianity never ceased to be, what it was from the first, a religion of books ; and in the West the language of its scriptures, its ritual, and its manuals of edification, was Latin. The Christian had motives of his own, in addition to those which appealed to his pagan neighbour, for desiring a knowledge of grammar, and the growing multitude of the Christian clergy gradually came to form a new learned class—in the end, the sole learned class that existed. As is well known, there was a long period in which it would have been impossible to say whether *clericus* meant ' a person ordained to sacred functions ' or ' a man of learning '. The question was not asked, because the two classes of persons were practically co-extensive ; if in certain royal and noble families there were laymen with more or less knowledge of Latin, these exceptions did not affect the general rule. Now while the Vulgar Latin of the laity went on departing more and more from its original form, the learned Latin of the clergy was, by grammatical studies and imitation of pagan as well as older Christian models of diction, maintained in a state of comparative purity. Nor was the use of the learned language confined exclusively to writing. The pupils in the schools were taught to use it as a spoken tongue; in many of the monasteries the inmates, whether their native speech was some form of Neo-Latin or some non-Latin language, were expected to carry on their conversation mainly in Latin. The practice of speaking Latin rendered the use of it in writing more fluent and spontaneous. Monastic Latin, like every living language, underwent a continuous development in accordance with the changing needs of expression. The more highly cultivated writers strove, not unsuccessfully, to avoid the barbarisms resulting from the influence of the current vernaculars; but ancient words insensibly acquired new meanings, and new derivatives were freely invented in conformity with the traditional rules of formation. The best monastic Latin—that, for instance, of Baeda—differs greatly from the language of ancient Rome, but as an instrument of literary expression it is not much inferior to Classical Latin.

The language of the cloister was naturally not without influence on the languages of the outside world. The learned, whether from ostentation or merely from habit, often made use of a Latin word when speaking in the vulgar tongue, and many of these words were caught up by the unlearned, and thus found their way into the spoken vernacular. As an example, we may take the common Romanic verb for 'to think'—Italian *pensare*, Spanish and Portuguese *pensar*, French *penser*. This represents the Latin *pensare*, which in the literal sense 'to weigh' passed into the Romanic languages in its colloquial form (with the regular loss of *n* before *s*), becoming the Italian *pesare*, Spanish and Portuguese *pesar*, French *peser*. In Classical Latin *pensare* was used figuratively for 'to weigh mentally, consider', and in Christian Latin this meaning developed into that of 'to think'. As thus used, being a word of the learned language, it was pronounced as it was spelt, and with this pronunciation it came into the popular speech.

The Latin words adopted in Old English—a considerable number—were for the most part taken from the spoken Latin of the clergy, not copied from books, and the early dialects of Germany (evangelized from England in the eighth century) received many words of clerical Latin, some of which survive in modern German and Dutch.

The great development of vernacular literature in the twelfth and succeeding centuries was not accompanied by any falling-off in the literary use of Latin. On the contrary, from various concurring causes, the literature written in the learned language gained fresh vitality. The rise of the universities, to which men from all the Western nations resorted as students and as teachers, resulted in the formation of an international republic of learning, for which Latin served as the common medium of intercourse. The increased opportunities of intercommunication among scholars led to a quickening of intellectual activity, manifested in the development of the scholastic philosophy and the beginnings of the study of natural science. For many ages Latin continued to be the universal vehicle of higher instruction; and even so late as the end of the seventeenth century it was felt that a work of scholarship, philosophy, or science ran grave risk of missing its due effect unless published in Latin. To speak only of our own country, it was in Latin that the discoveries of Gilbert, Harvey, and Newton were given to the world (the *Principia* was published in 1688). In the eighteenth century Linnaeus used Latin for the works in which he laid the foundations of botanical and zoological method. The use of Latin still survives to some extent in works of classical and Oriental scholarship, though since the middle of the last century it has gradually become more and more rare. The technical terminology of botany, zoology, and the medical sciences is still Latin, and the English physician writes his prescriptions in an abbreviated Latin that gives little trouble with the concords. When we consider how at the present day scientific men wail over the necessity of consulting publications in half a dozen languages in order to keep in line with the progress of investigation, and how some of them are inquiring hopefully or with regretful doubt into the possibilities of Esperanto or Ido, it seems not unreasonable to think that the advance of mathematical and physical science in the seventeenth century owed something to the possession of an international language inherited from ancient Rome.

In other spheres than those of literature and science the ancient language yielded only after a long struggle to its rivals. It was not until the last quarter of the seventeenth century that Latin completely ceased to be the medium of formal diplomatic intercourse between the nations of Europe. The technical language of English (and perhaps still more of Scottish) lawyers still abounds in Latin phrases and formulas handed down from the long-distant days when the pleadings of the courts were conducted in the learned tongue. The victory of the modern languages is now, indeed, almost complete. But the Roman Church, in its ritual and its official documents, still retains (and may for ages yet retain) the language which it inherited from ancient Rome.

We have now to speak of the last of the three portions of the Roman legacy of language : the vocabulary of Latin considered as a treasure on which the modern languages have from time to time drawn for the enrichment of their own stores. In the Romanic languages the adoption of words from literary Latin began very early. The oldest vernacular literature, which consisted largely in translations, was the work of clerks, and was intended not for the laity, few of whom were able to read at all, but for readers who had some knowledge of Latin, though not enough to enable them to make free use of books written in that language. The writers could therefore venture, without great risk of not being understood, occasionally to introduce into their compositions a Latin word or a derivative from Latin where the resources of the vulgar tongue failed to supply any satisfactory expression for the intended meaning. In succeeding ages, when literary instruction was no longer confined to the clergy, the layman who was sufficiently well educated to be interested in the more ambitious kinds of literature could be presumed capable of understanding a word of learned origin which he had not before met with as part of his native language. Hence in every century down to the present, each of the Neo-Latin languages has received new additions to its literary vocabulary from the inexhaustible storehouse of Latin.

In England before the Norman Conquest it was far otherwise. The rise of vernacular literature here was much earlier than on the Continent. The native speech, being wholly unlike Latin, commanded a respect which could not be accorded to what were regarded as mere corrupt varieties of the learned language; in the schools it was the vehicle of elementary instruction. Already in the eighth century a large body of written poetry, secular as well as religious, came into being; in the following century King Alfred became the father of English prose. The writers in Old English, though themselves men of learning and sometimes treating of learned themes, hardly ever resorted to the use of Latin words. Abbot Ælfric, at the end of the tenth century, instead of adopting the Latin technical terms of theology, science, and grammar, rendered them by new compounds or derivatives of native words. But these artificial formations did not survive. After the coming of the Normans, owing partly to the large influx of foreigners into the monasteries, the native literary culture fell into decay. Children were no longer taught to read and write English, but only French and Latin. When Englishmen began once more to write in their native language, it was in a tentative phonetic spelling based on French, and owing very little to the native orthographical tradition. Although colloquial English survived (even here, however, many words had given place to their French synonyms), literary English was dead, and had to be recreated. It was natural that when an idea had to be expressed that was outside the range of popular discourse, the writers should find it easier to adopt a ready-made term from the literary languages with which they were familiar than to form a new compound or derivative from native elements. In this way a multitude of Latin words came into English, at first chiefly through the medium of learned adoptions in French and afterwards directly, the endings being cut off as in French words. In the Elizabethan age the formation of new words from Latin was extravagantly common, and though most of the neologisms of that period promptly disappeared, not a few of them have proved permanently useful. The passion for bold experiments in language abated in the seventeenth century; but fresh additions to the literary vocabulary from Latin have never ceased to be made, and probably will long continue to be made. A writer who has been classically educated and who is conscious of addressing classically educated readers, may often find a new Latin derivative the handiest way of expressing his meaning. This resource is so obvious that it is sometimes adopted without any consciousness of innovation. It is not an unknown thing for an author who is scrupulous about the purity of his English to consult his dictionary in order to see whether there is precedent for some word of Latin etymology that has slipped from his pen. That the legacy of Rome has rendered valuable service to the English language there can be no reasonable question. But its benefits have not been unqualified. The Latinized vocabulary is one main cause of that wide divergence between the language of much of our best literature and the popular speech, which foreigners have often justly regarded as a weakness of the English tongue.

In modern German, if we take merely the evidence of the dictionaries, the Latin element is excessively small. Modern purism, indeed, has banished from the language many Latin derivatives which were current in the seventeenth and eighteenth centuries. Yet we can seldom read a German work on science, philosophy, theology, or even history, without now and then meeting with some word of Latin origin, which is ignored by the lexicographers, and which the foreigner often finds puzzling because he does not know the precise shade of meaning that it has acquired in German literary tradition.

There is yet one more portion of the Legacy of Rome which, though it does not strictly come under the head of language, may fitly be mentioned in this chapter, because there is no other place which would be so nearly appropriate for it. The Roman alphabet is not only the possession of the speakers of the Neo-Latin, Germanic, and Celtic languages, but is used also by several of the Slavonic peoples, by the Hungarians and Finns, and by many thousands of natives of Asia and Africa who never heard the sound of any European tongue.

H. Bradley.

ARCHITECTURE AND ART

ROMAN architecture has always held a definite and distinguished, if not undisputed, place in the world's estimation. But Roman art has had, so to speak, to fight for its existence. We have been told before now that the artistic endowment of the Roman people was small, and that all the culture of the Roman Empire was Hellenic. And so, at the beginning of our survey, we are faced by the question whether there was such a thing as Roman art. Are Roman art and architecture (at least in outward guise) merely Hellenic art and architecture in a later stage of development; and is the legacy of Rome in these matters only the legacy of Greece under another name?

These questions did not vex our forefathers. To them the remains of Greece and Rome presented the spectacle of Classical Antiquity as a whole, with a long history but a single one; and their knowledge of it was mostly confined to what they found in Rome and Italy. The discovery of unadulterated Greek art entirely altered the situation. The study of Greek art and architecture almost monopolized the interest of archaeologists; everything was judged by the Hellenic standard; and everything Roman was depreciated or ignored.

In our days there has been a reaction. This is not the place to tell the story of the rehabilitation, or rather the discovery, of Roman art. But we may note in passing that Wickhoff's book, which first clearly expounded the theme, was published little more than twenty years ago. Its advocates cannot be said to have overcome all opposition; but the case for a Roman art, with a history and character of its own, has won wide acceptance. Let us see what the claim amounts to.

In the first place, then, a somewhat vague and tentative

claim is made on behalf of an indigenous Italian or Romano-Etruscan art, which was not altogether overwhelmed by the invasion of Hellenism in the latter days of the Republic. As we noticed above, there are those who say that the artistic endowment of the Romans and the allied peoples of Italy was negligible. And yet the efflorescence of Italian art, especially in Tuscany, from the 'Trecento' onwards might raise a doubt, even if the racial changes or infiltrations of the intervening centuries be taken into account, whether such a judgement be not too sweeping. It would not have been surprising to find that there was an original indigenous Italian art, of distinct quality and independence; but, unfortunately, the material evidence for it is disappointing and unconvincing. Wickhoff and others have boldly claimed for this native Italian art a decisive influence in remaking the imported Hellenistic art, so that there came into being that Roman art, with its 'illusionism' and other characteristics, which he so brilliantly described. But the theory, it must be confessed, is very much in the air; and, in any case, it has never yet been followed up and worked out in detail. A more obvious and tangible expression of Italian art is to be seen in the humbler form of gravestones (often of soldiers) with their simple and direct reliefs, which are found mostly in the homelands and the western provinces of the Empire. Rarely, as in the great stone military trophy at Adamklissi in the Dobrudsha, this art appears on a larger scale. At its best it may be interesting from its subjects and their realistic treatment: it can be vigorous and even impressive. But, on the whole, its artistic value is inconsiderable; and, in any case, it cannot be regarded as forming an appreciable part of the legacy of Rome. A great deal more can be said on behalf of a real and independent Roman art of portraiture, but we will reserve our remarks on this till we deal with it in its proper place.

On the other hand, it may fairly be claimed, and indeed

Fig. 32. TRAJAN'S ARCH, BENEVENTO

Western face. 114 A.D.

Fig. 33. RELIEF OF EAGLE IN OAK WREATH

Time of Trajan. 98–117 A.D.

it is generally admitted, that there grew up in the Roman Empire a Roman Imperial art, based upon and continuous with the Hellenic tradition, but infused with a new and ample life of its own. It was called upon to deal with Imperial subjects, and it worthily responded to the call. One of the great needs of art is that from time to time it should find fresh inspiration, a renewal of youth, an unexhausted soil. The subject-matter that inspired one age to great artistic achievement becomes tired and threadbare, and art tends to appear conventional, traditional, or merely ingenious. The old religious and patriotic inspirations of Greek art were things of the past; the meteoric career of Alexander the Great was too transient to furnish a new theme of world-wide interest; and it was rarely that the Hellenistic monarchs, or the events in which they bore a part, were of a sufficiently elevated character to stir the deeper emotions that are necessary for high artistic attainment.[1] But the Imperial position and destinies of Rome provided a theme or a background of unparalleled grandeur; and, before the first century was out, a Roman Imperial art had come into existence. For us it is represented primarily by the state monuments, such as the triumphal columns and arches (Fig. 32). But these Imperial works do not stand alone, for beside them we find in Rome and Italy a contemporary art of distinct and high quality which must have been due to the stimulus of the new conditions. It is towards the end of the first century that Roman portraiture produced some of its best work, and to the same period belongs the decorative yet realistic sculpture which Wickhoff used to illustrate his theory of ' illusionism ' or impressionism. Perhaps no one work better summarizes the aesthetic and Imperial qualities of this Roman art than the famous panel, carved with an eagle in a crown, now in the church of the Apostoli at Rome (Fig. 33). The important thing is that we should

[1] An obvious exception is the great altar of Zeus at Pergamum, commemorating the national victory won by Attalus I over the Gauls.

not think of Imperial Roman art as an exotic, like the imported Greek art of the days of the Republic. It grew on the soil of the Empire, in a new world, with new sources of vitality. Nor need we assume that the artists were always Greeks by origin. At first, no doubt, they were so, predominantly. But as time went on they must have had, one would think, Italian assistants and pupils. And so there would grow up, especially in the cosmopolitan conditions of Rome, a world of artists and craftsmen, the result of a fusion of East and West, which might fairly be called Roman. Indeed it is possible to exaggerate the importance of the question. The more we learn about the Hellenistic world, the greater appears the debt of Rome to it. But, so far at least as art and architecture are concerned, it was sometimes only the germ that was transmitted; and when these Hellenistic ideas were absorbed by the Roman Empire, they were transformed by the medium of the new world-state into something larger and grander than they had been before. Or, to put it in another way, the Roman Empire used these ideas for its own ends, and thereby gave them a new lease of life in ampler and richer fashion than they had enjoyed before. And thus we are justified in speaking of Roman Imperial art and architecture, whether the artists and architects were of Greek origin or not. But, in spite of the fact that many of the names handed down to us are Greek, we may well believe that, in the western half of the Empire at least—and it is that with which we are concerned—much of the work was done by Western hands.[1]

[1] The name of Nero's court painter, Fabullus (there is some uncertainty about the form), who decorated the Golden House, and Pliny's anecdote (*H. N.* xxxv. 120), that he always wore the toga even when at work, show that he was a Roman. He must have had the help of a school of assistants to carry out so large a scheme. The case has a special interest for our subject, because, after their rediscovery at the Renaissance, these paintings were studied and copied by artists from many parts of Europe, who have left their names on the walls. Some fragments of the work are in the British Museum (Gem Room: wall to left of entrance, 3rd and 4th compartments).

The case for the independence of Roman architecture is much stronger. One has only to think of the ruins of Athens compared with those of Rome to realize how great is the contrast of the two architectures, and how different is the character of the buildings in the two centres of the Hellenic and the Roman worlds. Everybody knows that the pride of Roman architecture was the development of the arch and the vault. We will not spend time in discussing their country of origin, though we may notice once again that it was at the end of the Republic, in the age when Rome was learning most from the civilization and art of the Hellenistic monarchies, that the Roman vaulted building first becomes important. It is through Rome that the arch and the vault (with its offspring the dome) have come to us, and that is what is important for our purpose. It was under Roman auspices and in the service of Roman Imperial architecture that they became the essential and fertile elements, big with possibilities, on which the whole future progress and history of European building on the great scale was to depend. Greek architecture was summed up in the Greek temple; a perfect creation in its way; but without a future.[1] The system of column and architrave could get no farther, and the Greeks showed no serious signs of abandoning it. It may be that they were lacking in architectural imagination and inventiveness. Rivoira makes an interesting comparison between the careers of the Greek temple and the Greek church, in the hands of an architecturally unprogressive race.[2] From the time when 'the central plan', as it is called (which he believed to be

See F. Weege in *Jahrbuch d. k. deutschen archäol. Instituts*, xxviii (1913), pp. 134, 140 ff.

[1] The only types of modern buildings for which the Greek colonnade architecture seems to be adapted are the public hall and the museum. St. George's Hall, Liverpool, and the front of the British Museum are instances. But the interior of the former, at least, is quite Roman.

[2] *Architettura Romana* (Milan, 1921), p. 107.

ultimately of Roman origin), was adopted for Byzantine churches, it has remained stereotyped down to the present day; so that when an 'Orthodox' church is built in a Western city it has to conform to the traditional type. Whatever progress or inventiveness Greek architecture showed was in the Hellenistic states; and it is a more than plausible theory that this was the result of its contact with the buildings of Syria and the near East.

The reason why architecture developed so rapidly in the Roman Empire is that it was one illustration of the practical and constructive Roman genius; that which made them also good law-makers and good road-makers. We may note, by the way, that we know of far more architects with Roman names than artists. If it be incredible that the 'Roman citizen' Cossutius, who, we are told, built the temple of Zeus Olympius at Athens for Antiochus Epiphanes, was an Italian by birth, we can set Rabirius, the architect of that very characteristic Roman work, the Flavian Palace on the Palatine, against Apollodorus of Damascus, who was responsible for Trajan's principal buildings, but seems to have worked largely in the Roman spirit. One can see from Vitruvius how wide was the conception of the Roman architect's knowledge and functions.[1] One might almost say that he was as much an engineer as an architect proper. External ornament—the 'orders', as they are called—they borrowed or adapted from Greece; but the main interest of the Roman architects was in the planning and construction

[1] Vitruvius, i. 1. As we have mentioned Vitruvius, it may be as well to add that, though his name is popularly connected with Roman architecture, he is, as the contemporary of Caesar and Augustus, too early to tell us anything about the great Imperial buildings. As Sir R. Blomfield puts it: 'Of the true vitality and creative power that was latent in Roman architecture I doubt if any glimpse is to be caught in Vitruvius's treatise' (*The Mistress Art*, p. 234). Sir T. G. Jackson has well described the unfortunate influence exercised by the *De Architectura* after it became known again in the sixteenth century (*The Renaissance of Roman Architecture*, Part II, pp. 156, 205).

of the great public buildings required for the service of the state or the needs of the people: not temples, but palaces, government offices, the great baths and places of entertainment. As we shall see, it was the Roman achievements in these fields which provided the models or the ideals on which nearly the whole of our modern conceptions of public building are based. The Greek temple would never have supplied them, any more than the Gothic cathedral. An architecture which has been developed in the service of a religion is inadequate for the needs of a great community, especially a modern one; and in this sense Roman architecture is 'the architecture of humanism',[1] the source from which our secular public building has sprung. It is hardly too much to say that Rome was the first city in the world to have a great secular architecture. A parallel might almost be drawn between the epoch of civil construction at Rome which began with the foundation of the Empire, and the outburst of secular building at the Renaissance and the Reformation, though it would not do to press the comparison too far. Great churches have been built in Western Europe since the fifteenth century; but churches are no longer the normal expression of architecture, and church-building has tended (as our own country shows) to fall back on conventional and traditional styles, and so to drop out of the line of architectural development and progress. In the sixteenth century the activities which had been almost monopolized by the church were diverted to the creation of great houses, and ultimately of great public buildings. Human interests had come into their own again. And so in the Roman Empire, though temples continued to be built, great buildings for the service of the state or public purposes, and, in a less degree, great private houses in town or country, became the chief forms of architectural expression.

[1] I have, of course, borrowed the phrase, with some restriction of its meaning, from the title of Mr. Geoffrey Scott's brilliant apology for Renaissance architecture.

But it is time that we should take stock of some of the ways in which our modern art and architecture is indebted to Roman achievements in those fields. As the debt of architecture is far the greater, we will begin with that. Let us start with general ideas.

The two features of Roman architecture which have most impressed and most influenced the mediaeval and the modern world are solidity of construction and magnificence of conception. Masonry of squared stone blocks had been practised by other races long before it appeared in Rome, but the Roman *opus quadratum* was second to none in durability; and, in any case, it was Roman stonework which handed on the tradition, and provided the models and the standard for the next great age of Western architecture, the Romanesque. How conscious of the influence our Anglo-Saxon ancestors were, comes out in the fact that, though their first churches were rough and rude work, those that were made of stone and not of wood were proudly described as built 'after the manner of the Romans'.[1] But it was not till the eleventh or twelfth century that we get Norman churches with fine ashlar walls which are comparable with Roman work, though the stones are generally smaller. From that time the tradition, revivified by the Renaissance and by fresh contact with the ancient models, has been continuous. At the present day fine dressed stonework is still the main way of expressing the solidity and dignity required by great public buildings.

The two other chief materials of modern building, brick and concrete, are also the representatives of Roman traditions. Both were of importance for the progress of architecture under the Empire, for it was largely the use of these light and relatively plastic materials that enabled the Roman architects to vault great spans with comparative ease, and thus show the way to the vaulted mediaeval church and its descendants. Roman concrete construction was always concealed by a skin of brick, marble, or other decorative facings; but the very

[1] Bede, *Hist. Eccl.* v. 21.

fact that these were the first to disappear left the constructive material uncovered, to tell its tale and transmit its lesson to future ages. Here, as always, it must have been the great Imperial buildings of the city of Rome, the best known as well as the most instructive remains of antiquity, that provided the suggestions which were to bear fruit in the modern world. It is only in recent times that the world has again seen the use of concrete construction on a great scale. And though the manner of its application, and especially the use of steel reinforcement, is something quite new and unconnected with anything in ancient work, we may remember that, so far as the material is concerned, the Romans were the first to make use of it for great buildings.

Of the great brick-using countries of the ancient world, Babylonia, Egypt, and Italy, it is obvious that our tradition of brick-building is derived from the last, but with this difference that, whereas Roman brickwork was mainly used as a facing for concrete construction, mediaeval and modern brickwork is generally solid. Except perhaps in Italy, the brick tradition is hardly continuous. Even in the latter days of the Western Empire, the output of the Roman kilns fell off or came to an end; but abandoned or ruined buildings supplied plenty of the handy material to be re-used, as we often find it in the earlier mediaeval work. When we pass to the richer and fuller life of the thirteenth and fourteenth centuries, brick once more becomes important, especially where stone was not easily procurable, as in the Low Countries and our own eastern shires,[1] where at the end of the Middle Ages buildings like Tattershall Castle and Layer Marney Towers show the use of brick on a grand scale. The seventeenth- and eighteenth-century architects, like their modern successors, were not afraid to use it, in combination with stone, even for palace

[1] The early use of brick in English mediaeval work is being recognized. The foundations of Coggeshall Abbey Church (twelfth century) were of brick, and at Little Coggeshall there is a complete brick chapel of about 1220. *Inventory of the Historical Monuments of Essex*, iii, pp. 165, 167.

and public buildings. The fine English brickwork of that period was, no doubt, due to the direct influence of the unequalled brick facing of the first century which Rome has to show. But even the ordinary brickwork, which has become the common material for so much of our domestic building, may be regarded as part of the legacy of the Roman world.

Roman Imperial architecture was not only massive, it was also magnificent. Piranesi had justification for the title which he gave to one of his volumes: 'Concerning the Magnificence of the Romans.'[1] Magnificence as applied to art and architecture is a complex idea, and it contains at least two elements, largeness or grandeur of scale and richness of decoration. Egyptian architecture could be sublime; the greatest Greek temples were both sublime and beautiful; but the grand scale and splendid decorative treatment, both external and internal, of the Roman Imperial buildings produced an effect of magnificence which was all their own. The capacity for this seems to have been inherent in the Romans. Magnificence is a relative term. The Republican Tabularium, the relics of which still look down on the Roman Forum, was a plain and modest structure compared with the Coliseum or the Baths of Caracalla; but in its own day, and judged by contemporary standards, it was an expression of the consciousness that the growing Imperial destinies of the Roman people demanded magnificence in its public buildings. The memory and the examples of this Roman magnificence in building were never forgotten. After the old Roman world and its works passed away, and building on the grand scale once more became possible under new conditions, when the idea to be expressed was no longer the Roman Empire but the Catholic Church which occupied its place, it was this inherited spirit of magnificence which dominated the designers of the great Romanesque and Gothic cathedrals. With the Renaissance and the emergence of the great European powers,

[1] *De Romanorum Magnificentia et Architectura* (Rome, 1761).

the tradition of Roman magnificence was again provided with a field in secular architecture; and it has found world-wide expression in the public buildings of modern states, whether it be the garden front of Versailles, or the Capitol at Washington, or the Houses of Parliament at Westminster where the Gothic dress is only an architectural fashion clothing a state building of grander scale and more regular design than the Middle Ages ever contemplated.

The decorative element in Roman magnificence has been sharply criticized. Let us examine it rather more closely.

Roman architecture is often accused of having borrowed its decorative features from the Greeks, and of using them in an unconstructional, tasteless way, which deprived them at once of their meaning and their charm. When the Romans, by the help of the arch and the vault, raised their piles of masonry or concrete, it occurred to them to make these presentable by applying the Greek column and entablature as a decorative facing. The applied or engaged column, with the architrave, cornice, and other members, were used to build up towering façades with tiers of colonnades or arcades, or both combined. This system of the Roman 'orders', as they are called, has been described as, at the best, dreary and monotonous, and, at the worst, blatant and vulgar; and it is contrasted to its detriment with the purity of Greek and the variety of mediaeval ornament. The question interests us directly, for this system of façade decoration with engaged columns and architraves and all the rest is, as every one knows, the most prominent characteristic of modern city architecture; and through the Italian Renaissance it is one of our most obvious inheritances from Rome.

Now this sort of thing may be well done, or it may be ill done. It can be oppressive, uninteresting, meaningless; or it can be splendid, impressive, significant. Roman ornament was often enough overdone or mechanical, just as there are plenty of instances of tasteless and uninspiring work in our 'classical' or Renaissance town architecture, especially of the last century. But, at its best, it corresponds to a genuine instinct which demands that the importance of the uses or service of a building shall be expressed by a certain outward dignity and splendour. The tradition from which we derive our practice in these matters is that of the Roman Empire, and the question is whether it has ever been improved upon. Ultimately this is a question of taste. Great architecture, it is true, must be constructive, and the Roman achievements in construction are unequalled. But we may also ask whether the Roman architects did not make a great discovery when to their vast Imperial buildings they applied in a decorative way, which never altogether lost sight of their constructional origin, the column and other members which had reached the term of their original use in the simple and limited public structures of the old Greek world. The exterior of the Coliseum (Fig. 34) satisfies the eye with the combined solidity, majesty, and grace of its treatment; and at the same time its forms and parts have a connexion with the internal construction. It is not like the skin of ornamental stone-work which veils the steel skeleton of some modern buildings. The eye is not less satisfied with the same treatment as it appears in the works of the great Renaissance architects who learned their lesson from the ruins of Rome. Nor have the architects of modern times, we venture to think, as yet discovered any better way. The great majority of public and city buildings still follow the Roman decorative system, and the latest architectural developments do not show much signs of abandoning it. The new government palaces at Delhi, the latest public buildings in London such as the County Council Hall and the Port of London Offices, and, we may add, no less those of America, have alike been faithful to the precepts of Roman architecture.

There was a time when Pugin and Ruskin had almost succeeded in scolding British public opinion out of the Roman tradition, so that even the state buildings of the British

Empire began to be designed in the Gothic style; and at the beginning of the Victorian Age we had the new Houses of Parliament, and almost at its end the new Law Courts. Mr. Lytton Strachey has reminded us that, if it had not been for the firmness of Lord Palmerston, we should have had a third.[1] But the fashion did not last, and the reason is not far to seek. The mediaeval styles will not bear comparison with the classical, either for plan or elevation, when it comes to constructing the great public buildings of a modern state. The sublimity and mystery which are the secrets of the mediaeval cathedral are inappropriate or inapplicable to the secular public building, and result in fatal defects for its lighting and convenience. Apart from castles, mediaeval secular buildings of importance are chiefly to be found in the towns of Flanders and of Northern Italy. All of them, even what was the Cloth Hall of Ypres, are inadequate for the complexity of modern needs. The grandest, perhaps, and most complete mediaeval public building that has come down to us is the Doge's Palace at Venice. We will deal with the question of plan presently. But, apart from the impressiveness of mere bulk, it is at least arguable that its exterior, in proportions and the beauty that comes from line and symmetry and the proper distribution of ornament, is inferior to the front of Sansovino's building which faces it across the Piazzetta. Even the beauty and interest of its sculptured capitals are not peculiar to the style, for the Renaissance in its freer moods, and with the mediaeval tradition behind it, knew how to make use of figure sculpture to embellish its façades; and the architects of to-day seem to be increasingly alive to the possibilities of monumental and decorative sculpture applied to public buildings.[2] However, these are later developments,

[1] *Queen Victoria*, p. 235.

[2] The remarkable group of public buildings at Cardiff will at once occur as an illustration to those who are familiar with recent developments of British architecture.

and we must be content to claim for Roman architecture the creation of the decorative façade with its long lines of columns and pilasters and arches, expressing and emphasizing the extent and dignity of a great building of public character. In fact the monotony of which the system is accused is really an essential element in producing that imposing effect necessary for public architecture. It is the repetition of the column, the long-drawn lines of architrave and cornice, which help to impress upon the spectator the mass and ordered spaciousness of the building, and, indirectly, the importance of the service to which it is dedicated. The attempt to construct a modern state building on mediaeval lines almost inevitably results in a similar uniformity, or if you will, monotony, for which Gothic ornament is less well fitted than the Roman or Renaissance systems of decoration. The Houses of Parliament are undoubtedly imposing and dignified, but one of the charges that has been made against them is that the decoration of the exterior is too uniform. It was bound to be so under the circumstances. Street's Law Courts, on the other hand, have variety and irregularity of the parts, but it is at the cost of the dignity and impressiveness of the whole.

The creation of this system of façade decoration may have been aided by what seems to be an instinctive Italian capacity for theatrical and scenic presentation. It appears in the Roman triumph (with, perhaps, a Hellenistic suggestion); in the spectacular productions which were such a feature of Roman public amusements; in the development, largely at Rome, of the ritual of the Catholic Church; in the history of the opera and the modern stage; in the creation of the baroque style of architecture; in the lay-out of the Italian villa garden. Stage scenery is depreciated, partly on account of the unsubstantial nature of its materials. But, granted its temporary purpose, it may display a largeness of imagination and composition which has intrinsic merit; and in this quality the Italians seem to have been the teachers of the world. Expressed in noble and permanent materials it takes the form

Fig. 34. THE FLAVIAN AMPHITHEATRE OR COLISEUM AT ROME. 80 A.D.

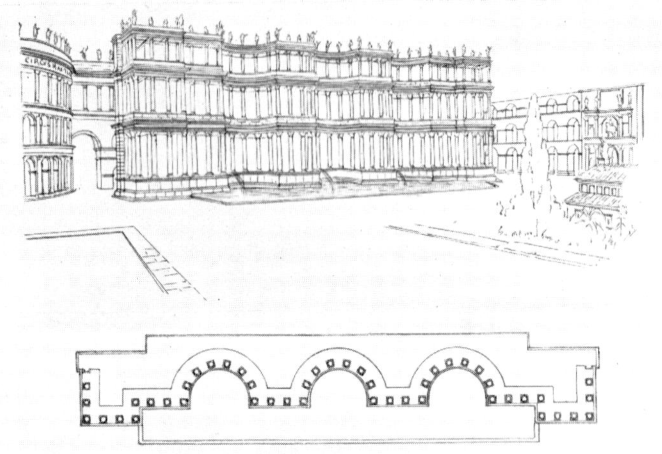

Fig. 35. THE SEPTIZONIUM, ROME. 203 A.D.
Restoration by Prof. Hülsen

Fig. 36. ROMAN BRIDGE AT RIMINI. 22 A.D.

of great monuments and imposing architecture; and in this way there is an affinity between, for instance, the Septizonium of Septimius Severus (Fig. 35)[1], the conceptions and imaginations of Piranesi or the Italian scenery designers of the eighteenth century,[2] and the marble masses of the Monumento Nazionale which now towers over Rome from the Capitol, the lineal descendant of the monuments of Imperial Rome.

It is unnecessary to dwell on our obligations to the Roman development of the arch, for its importance in all subsequent construction is obvious. But we may recall one application of the arch pure and simple which comes to us through Rome, and that is the bridge. The Nile had no bridges, and we are told that the bridge over the Euphrates at Babylon consisted only of a set of stone piers connected by wooden platforms.[3] At Assos in Asia Minor there are the remains of an ancient Greek bridge of the same form, all in stone;[4] but there is nothing in the Greek world to suggest that the arched bridge was invented there. Central Italy, however, contains a number of early vaulted tunnels and culverts; and this makes it probable that the Romans developed the stone arched bridge from the monumental *cloacae* and culverts which the Etruscans taught them to build. Anyhow, the fact remains that Rome was the first great city which had a series of monumental stone arched bridges; and from Rome the practice spread along the lines of the great roads to the farthest provinces of the Empire (Fig. 36). From the bridge was developed the aqueduct, specimens of which have survived to be the models for later architects and engineers. And though roads belong neither to architecture nor art, the bridge may remind us

[1] I have to thank Prof. Hülsen for the illustration, a modification of his former restoration (*46 Winckelmann-Programm*, 1886). Recently another treatment has been published (T. Dombart, *Das Palatinische Septizonium*. Munich, 1922); but the general effect is much the same.

[2] Sir R. Blomfield, *Architectural Drawing and Draughtsmanship*, p. 61.

[3] Herodotus, i. 186; Diodorus, ii. 8. 2.

[4] Clarke, Bacon, and Koldewey, *Investigations at Assos*, p. 129.

how important the example and tradition of the great Roman roads has been through all the succeeding centuries.

The history and extent of Roman achievement in the construction and development of vaulting is too large and too technical a subject to be discussed here, and we must content ourselves with the barest summary. The simplest form is the barrel vault, which was known in principle to the older civilizations, but was used by the Romans on a scale never thought of before in, for instance, the Flavian palace on the Palatine and Hadrian's twin temple of Venus and Rome. From the Roman it has come down to mediaeval and still more to modern architecture, and is peculiarly applicable to corridors and narrow halls. On a larger scale it becomes oppressive, and it was this defect of the grandest specimen in existence, the nave of St. Peter's, that warned Sir Christopher Wren to avoid it in St. Paul's, where each bay is vaulted by a small dome. But with its effect of strength or massive solidity, and the impressiveness which comes from its unbroken lines and vistas, the barrel vault is characteristically Roman. Two barrel vaults intersecting at right angles produce the groined or cross-vault, a much more important discovery, for it enabled the separate bays of an arcaded building to be vaulted in a lighter and also more scientific way, by concentrating the pressure on certain points where it can be controlled by counter-thrusts of various kinds. Groined vaulting begins to appear in Roman buildings soon after the middle of the first century, and by the time of the Flavian Emperors it was well established, as the corridors of the Coliseum show. In the great central halls of the Imperial Baths (Fig. 37), and, above all, in the Basilica of Constantine (Fig. 39, and for plan see Fig. 67), it was used for roofs of very wide span ; and in the Basilica the outward pressure is met by walls set at right angles to the central space. These transverse walls are pierced with arches, and thus form aisles which have barrel vaults ; while the side walls of the central hall rising above them are lighted by large

Fig. 37. BATHS OF CARACALLA, ROME. Restoration of interior of the Great Hall, from a drawing by the late R. Phené Spiers

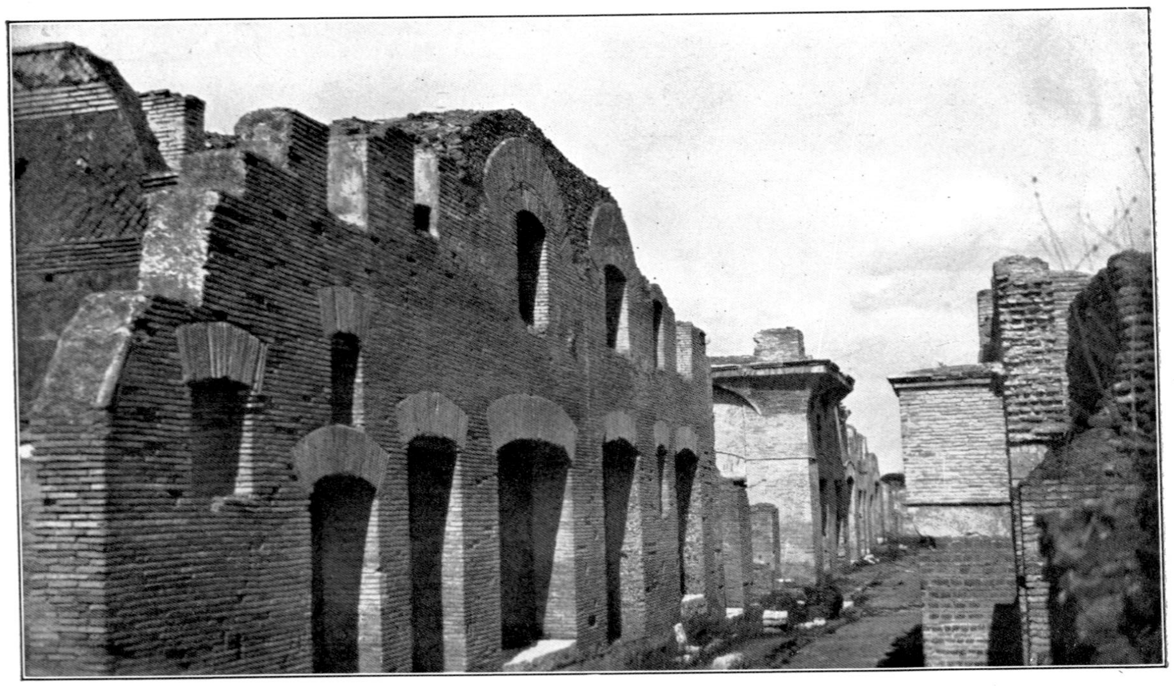

Fig. 38. A STREET FRONT IN OSTIA. 1st or 2nd cent. A. D.

windows, and so form a clerestory. In this way we get the principle of the church with vaulted nave and aisles. It was not, however, in the power of the earlier Lombardic or Romanesque church builders to reproduce the Roman vaulting of considerable spans, and it was only with the development

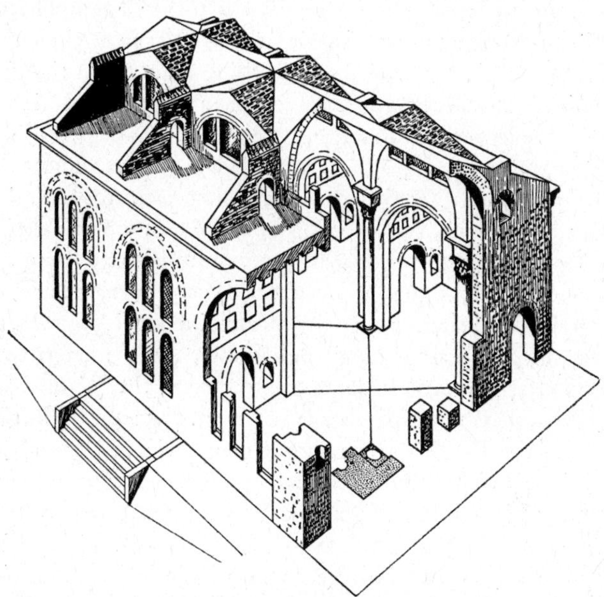

FIG. 39. Sectional reconstruction of the Basilica of Maxentius or of Constantine, Rome (312 A. D.).

of the groined vault, reinforced by diagonal stone ribs, in the eleventh and twelfth centuries that it became possible to vault the naves of the great Romanesque or Norman churches. Whether these were suggested by the diagonal brick ribs which are found in Roman groined vaults from the time of Hadrian onwards is uncertain. Gothic architecture completed the evolution by the introduction of the pointed arch, and the development of the external, and ultimately of the flying buttress. The Romans were well acquainted with the external buttress for walls, and by the third century they were using the arch as an abutment for vaulting, as well as for arches of large span. But without pressing these anticipations or germs of the chief elements of Gothic architecture too far, we may be content with seeing in the great halls of the Roman Thermae and in the Basilica of Constantine the prototype of the church with vaulted nave and clerestories rising high above the aisles. That idea, and all that it involved, may truly be described as part of the legacy of Rome.

After the vault comes the dome. While various rudimentary forms of domical vaulting and cupolas seem to have been known in the East, and probably something more in a Hellenistic capital like Alexandria, it was in Italy and at Rome that dome-construction on a large scale was developed; and, partly by tradition, partly by direct influence, the Roman domes are the source of all our Western and modern ones. Even to-day the earliest dome of great span, that of Hadrian's Pantheon, has never been surpassed in diameter. But the dome of the Pantheon is a simple one, developed from a circular base of the same size and outline. It was a greater discovery to set a dome on a square or polygonal base by means of pendentives, that is, the triangular pieces of vaulting which form the transition from the angles of the base to the circle of the dome above it. Pendentives of this kind appear as early as the time of Domitian in the rebuilt 'House of Augustus' on the Palatine; and they were developed in various ways, and later found a special field in Byzantine church architecture, where the dome plays such an important part. In the West it was not till the rise of the Renaissance in Italy that dome construction again became important; but it is significant that the first great Renaissance cupola, that of the cathedral of Florence, was erected within sight of the eleventh-century baptistery, which has a dome of considerable size, constructed on the lines of the Roman tradition.

Another Roman achievement of great importance for the future was the development of public buildings with elaborate or complex plans. Greek architecture, as we have said, was represented mainly by temples. We know comparatively little about Greek secular buildings, but their planning seems to have been of a simple character. If we knew more about the buildings of the Seleucids and the Ptolemies, we might, perhaps, be able to trace the source of some of the Roman plans. As it is, the meagre account we have of the famous Museum or Library of Alexandria does not suggest that its plan was very elaborate; and the remains of the Library at Pergamum tell a similar tale.[1] It was in Imperial Rome that the needs of the public service and of city life were first provided for on a grand scale; and, with regard to the future, the two most important forms were the palace and the Thermae or baths. The Palatine hill is covered with the remains of the vast structures which housed the Imperial court and administration. The intricate plans show complexes of rooms and halls, connected by courts and corridors, and ingeniously fitted into one another so as to provide the maximum of accommodation for a highly organized life and service, and at the same time give one another mutual structural support. But it was not a single creation. One Imperial residence after another was added as Caesar's household, which became identical with a large part of the Imperial administration, grew.[2] One can hardly suppose that these added 'houses', which ultimately covered the whole quarter, were used only as the personal residences of the emperor for the time being, and then abandoned. They were required for the service of the state, and it is this which explains their continual growth. In our days the residence of the head of the state has been

[1] Strabo, xvii. 1. 8. Collignon and Pontremoli, *Pergame*, p. 137.

[2] Strabo's account (loc. cit.) of the palace of the Ptolemies at Alexandria, with the additions made by successive kings, reads curiously like the story of the growth of the Imperial palace at Rome.

almost entirely separated from the government offices; and to realize what the Palatine was like, with its Imperial residence, its judicial, financial, administrative departments, its temples, libraries, and museums, we must go to the Vatican as it still, more or less, exists, and think of what it houses under its many roofs. The Vatican carries on the tradition of the Lateran Palace, and the tradition of that went back to the days when the Palatine was still a living institution, or at least a living

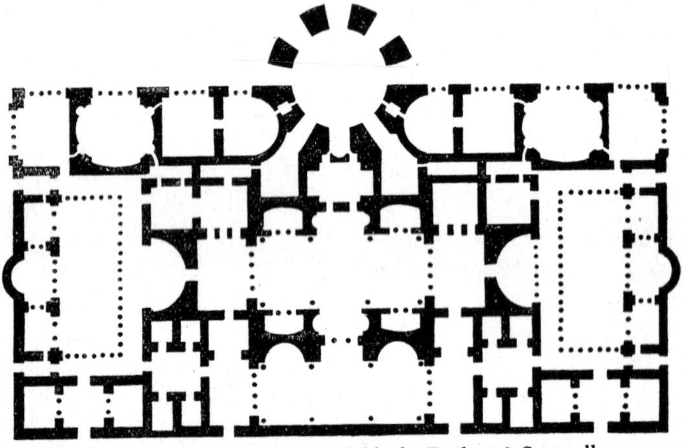

FIG. 40. Plan of the central block, Baths of Caracalla.

memory. In this way the tradition of the *Palatium*, like its name, was perpetuated in the 'palaces' which housed the governments of the European states, though the process of differentiation has tended to separate the residential from the administrative buildings, and to isolate the various departments from one another. And we must not forget that the ruins of the Palatine, far more complete in the fifteenth century than they are to-day, must have directly influenced the Renaissance architects by suggesting actual forms as well as general conceptions, which they embodied in the works to which our modern public building is so much indebted.

The Palatine, however, has no unity of plan. To see at its best the Roman achievement in the creation of an elaborate plan which forms a unity and is self-contained, one must go

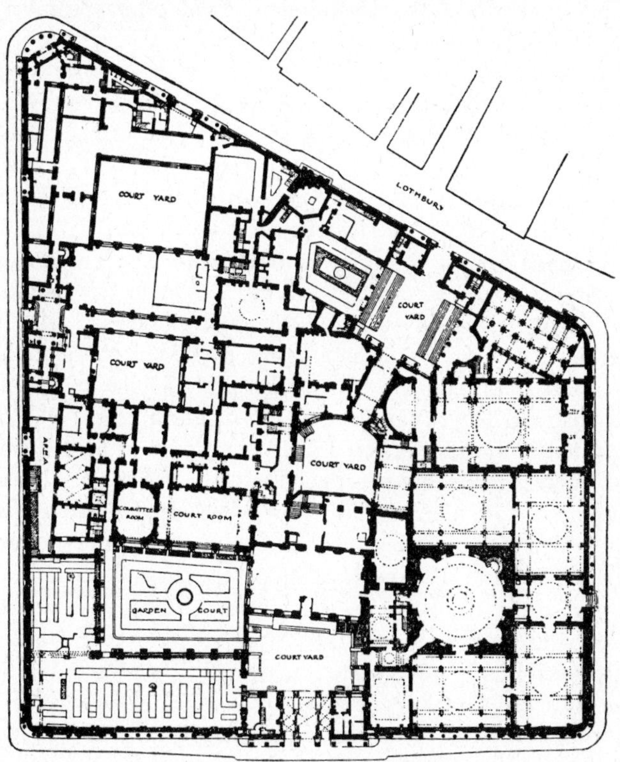

FIG. 41. Plan of the Bank of England (1788).

to such buildings as the Baths of Diocletian or of Caracalla (Fig. 40). The Imperial Thermae, with their annexes providing for recreation, edification, and exercise, created the type of a great building of many parts and purposes, but forming a unity of design and service, which had a powerful influence on the architects of the Renaissance; and partly through them, partly by direct study of the ancient plans, and always through the ideal which they set up, on the planning of all the large buildings in which the administrative and commercial life of our great cities is carried on. Irregularity of site, inevitable in the conditions of a city like London, may sometimes make the perfect symmetry of the Roman Thermae impossible; but one cannot look at Sir John Soane's plan of the Bank of England (Fig. 41)—to take what may be called a classical example—without feeling how much it owes to the bath and palace architecture of ancient Rome.

We have seen in the great central hall of the Thermae the prototype of the Romanesque vaulted church, of which the Gothic church is, in turn, merely a development. But the thermal hall was not the immediate model for the church in the form most familiar to us, and the Romanesque basilica did not take shape before the eighth or ninth century. What preceded it was the early Christian or Constantinian basilica. We know practically nothing about the form of Christian churches before Constantine; but when, as the outward and visible sign of the establishment of Christianity as the emperor's religion, he built a series of great churches in and about Rome, he gave them all one form, that of the basilica, with its nave, aisles, and apse, and sometimes transept as well. It is not unreasonable to suppose that these basilicas, erected in the last great epoch of Roman construction, were the continuation on a grander scale of an already existing type. Of late it has become pretty clear how that type originated. We will not spend time in demonstrating the improbability of either the temple, or the civil basilica, or the private basilica, or the atrium of the house, having been the model of the Christian assembly-room, for the arguments may be found in all the text-books. But there was another and obvious form of religious meeting-house, with which the Christians would be familiar, and the suitability of which was already tested by

Fig. 42. THE ARCH OF CONSTANTINE, ROME. 315 A.D.

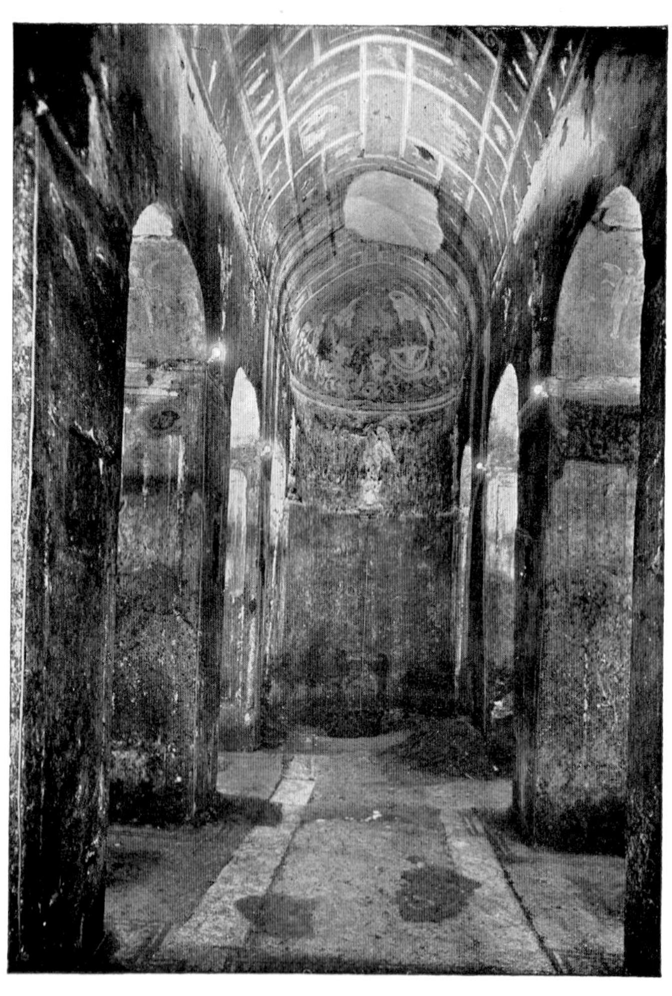

Fig. 43. INTERIOR OF SUBTERRANEAN BASILICA
Near the Porta Maggiore, Rome. 1st cent. A. D.

experience.[1] From various points of view Christianity may be classed with the mystery-religions, those private associations, mostly of Eastern origin, which offered individual salvation to the initiated, and played so large a part in the personal religion of the ancient world. For their meetings and worship they did not build temples like those of the ancient official cults; for their rites took place in the presence of large congregations, for which the temple was quite unfitted. They therefore adopted a form of the basilica, with its nave flanked by passage-aisles, and terminating in an apse, or, as

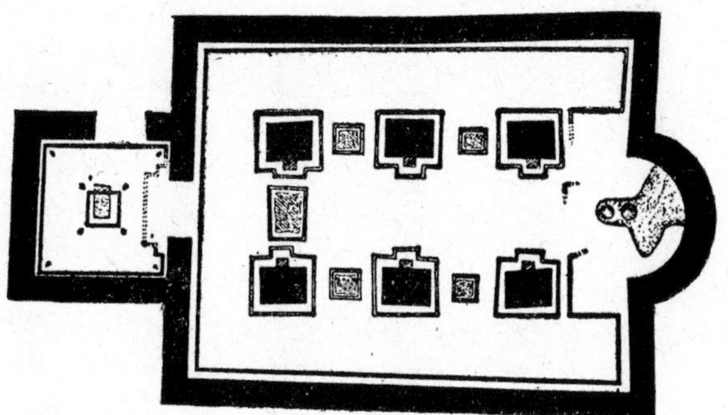

FIG. 44. Plan of the Basilica of Porta Maggiore.

we should say, chancel. In Greek lands this type goes back to Hellenistic and pre-Christian times, but it was in the Roman Empire that the mystery basilica had its chief development. The subterranean basilica, discovered not long ago at Rome near the Porta Maggiore (Figs. 43, 44), and probably connected with one of the mystery-religions, appears to contain almost every element of the later Christian church: narthex, nave, and aisles, terminal apse with some indications of sacrificial rites, and even the central seat of the chief officiant. Were it not for the imagery on wall and vault, we might have asked whether it were not an early Christian church. And all this

[1] What follows is mostly based on the account by G. Leroux, *Les Origines de l'Édifice hypostyle* (Paris, 1913), pp. 318 ff.

at a date (perhaps not later than the middle of the first century A.D.) when the Christians can only have been beginning to require such elaborate places of assembly.[1]

Two essential features of the early Christian basilica are the wooden roof and the ranges of columns, carrying sometimes an arcade, sometimes a straight architrave, which form the communication between the nave and the aisles. The vaulted thermal halls and the Basilica of Constantine had only three bays, so that it is clear that the many-bayed naves and choirs of Romanesque churches were, to that extent, the descendants of the Christian basilica. But if vaulting was to be substituted for the timber roof, the column had to be replaced by the articulated pier (to which the clustered shafts of the later Gothic correspond) from which the groining could spring, and a system of buttresses to meet the outward thrust had to be developed. The Romans knew of both the compound pier supporting groining (as in the Basilica Julia), and the external buttress; but the tradition handed on to the mediaeval builders was enormously developed both structurally and decoratively, so that in Gothic churches the buttress becomes one of the most important and characteristic features.

We can hardly leave the Early Christian buildings without a word about their most characteristic decoration—the apse and wall mosaics. The mosaic tradition survived till far on in the Middle Ages, both at Rome and in the East; but it came to an end with the Byzantine school of the twelfth century, which has left such splendid monuments of the art at Venice and Monreale and Cefalù. It never gained a footing north of the Alps, where its decorative equivalent is the stained glass which, in the later Middle Ages, converted the walls of churches into sheets of transparent gold and colour, the true counterpart of the glowing splendours of San Marco.[2]

[1] *Journal of Roman Studies*, ix (1919), pp. 78 ff.

[2] The older use of mosaic for pavements, remains of which are so frequent all over the Empire, and not least in our own country, may be said to have

After the church comes the house, and here we must distinguish between the town with its streets of house-fronts, and the country house standing isolated in its curtilage or garden. The most obvious feature of the cities of European or Western civilization is the streets of many-storied buildings. Familiar passages in Latin writers tell us that the same thing was to be found in Rome, though it was, no doubt, a characteristic shared with other ancient cities where land was valuable and the pressure of population great. The literary evidence is confirmed by two portions of house-fronts of the Imperial

FIG. 45. House of Saints John and Paul, Rome. 4th cent. A.D.

age still standing at Rome. One was in the Gardens of Sallust, and belonged to a building with at least four stories. The other, on the Caelian, forms part of the street front of what is known as the House of Saints John and Paul (Fig. 45), and, with its open arcade surmounted by two stories of square-headed windows, is exactly like a modern street front, with its shop windows below and its residential or business floors above.[1]

died with the Roman world. Its revival, whether in mediaeval or modern times, has been fitful and artificial.

[1] Recent excavations at Ostia have helped us to understand the nature of the tenement-blocks or *insulae* of Rome. Mr. H. Chalton Bradshaw describes those of Ostia (Fig. 38) as 'very much like a modern block of flats' (*The Town Planning Review*, Jan. 1923, pp. 11–13: *Rome: a note on housing conditions*).

The tradition, in fact, has been continuous, descending to us through the mediaeval town. The streets of Italian towns like Bologna, which preserve much of their mediaeval appearance, have their footways covered by the arcades which support the first and highest floors of the houses, and form part of the façade. The plan made the ground floor too dark for the northern climates ; and in our own land, for instance, we find it only exceptionally, as at Chester. In the north the footway was generally outside the house, and the arcade was replaced by the shop-front on the ground floor. But in one way or another our street fronts reproduce a type which was normal in ancient Rome.

The Roman house on the Caelian, which we have just mentioned, like most of our town houses had not that interior court which is such a general feature of the larger Italian houses, and is clearly a descendant of the atrium of the Roman mansion, sometimes adapted from or combined with the Greek peristyle. But, except sometimes in the houses of the great, this was not the common form of northern habitation, where the exigencies of light made it desirable that rooms should look outwards and not inwards. There is, however, one type of building with which we are familiar, which has inherited the atrium or peristyle plan, and that is the academical college through the monastic cloister ; and at the end of the Middle Ages, and later, even private houses were planned in the same way. The monastic cloister is probably derived, not directly from the ordinary atrium, but from that modification of it found in Roman dwellings designed, not for a single proprietor or family, but for a corporation or collegiate body, or, by analogy, for a military body. In these cases the ordinary peristyle-atrium was lengthened so as to provide a large number of rooms round it for administrative purposes, or as chambers for the members of the body or force. We find this in its simplest form in the 'Atrium Vestae', the house or convent of the Vestal Virgins under the Palatine, where the private rooms of the six Vestals open out of the *tablinum* or 'common room'; while round the cloistered court are chambers for the household and offices, and perhaps also for novices. In this earliest model of the convent or college, the church or chapel (the temple of Vesta) was outside the building. But in the military examples, based on the same type, the chapel of the emperors and the Imperial standards takes the place of the *tablinum* in the most important position at the head of the cloister court. We find this arrangement in the barracks of the detachment of the Roman city-guards (*vigiles*) stationed at Ostia; and the head-quarters (*principia*) of permanent camps and garrisons followed a pattern, based on the same principle, which occurs all along the German and British frontiers, and must have been normal throughout the Empire. We have here the characteristic features of the monastery; the church, the cloister, and the living-rooms. But naturally in the Christian system, the conventual church generally took the form of the Christian basilica and its descendants, for the Roman military chapels were not meant to hold a congregation. Moreover, the tendency for monasteries to grow up as adjuncts of great churches contributed to the same result.

When we turn to the country house, the evidence of origins is more imperfect and less easy to estimate. It must be through mediaeval forms that the Roman tradition, if any, has descended; and the question is, can we trace any Roman elements in the two chief forms of mediaeval residence outside towns, the castle and the manor-house? So long as mediaeval castles and manor-houses are inhabited, we may be said to have a direct interest in their origin; and besides, the ordinary houses in which most people live are derived from them by processes of elimination and development. Diocletian's palace at Spalato might be thought of as the earliest castle that we know; but though, except on the sea face, it had the walls and towers of a frontier *castellum* of the period, its interior was like a small town, and has nothing in common with the castles of the feudal age. On the other hand, a description by a sixth-century poet of the bishop of Trier's *castellum* on the Moselle, in a district where Roman culture was deeply rooted and long survived, reads exactly like the account of a mediaeval castle. The top of a hill was enclosed by a circuit wall with thirteen towers, and on the highest point, like a keep, stood the residence (*aula*).[1] Conditions of insecurity may well have led to similar arrangements elsewhere; but it seems a far cry from the stronghold of Nicetius to the Norman castles of the eleventh century, and the evidence does not enable us to fill the gap. But for the other type, the fortified manor-house, there does seem to be something like a Roman analogy or prototype in the fortified farm or country houses which, in the days of the Empire, are found in districts and provinces where conditions were unsettled or dangerous. Some of the best preserved examples are in Roman Africa, but they occur also near the Rhine and in North Gaul; and recently, near Cardiff, a Roman 'villa' has come to light, which, apparently in the fourth century, was enclosed by a rampart and a moat.[2] In some cases the residence was in this way isolated in the middle of a fortified 'enceinte', but in others the house itself takes the form of a *castellum*; and the dedicatory inscription of one of the African examples describes the whole thing as a 'tower',[3] a usage which may be paralleled in some mediaeval dwellings in our own country. It may be, however, that these are only cases of similar conditions having produced similar results. In the present state of our knowledge there is nothing like a chain of evidence to connect the 'moated grange' in Glamorgan with the earliest mediaeval fortified houses that we know.

[1] Venantius Fortunatus, *Carmina*, iii. 11 (*Mon. Germ. Hist.*, *Auct. Ant.*, iv. 64).

[2] Dr. R. Mortimer Wheeler in the *Journal of Roman Studies*, xi (1921), pp. 67–85.

[3] *C.I.L.* viii. 22774.

One might have expected to be able to trace some survival of the common forms which the Roman *villa* took in Gaul and Britain; but the evidence we have almost invariably tells a story of destruction and ruin, not of adaptation, at the hands of the barbarian invaders and their descendants. And yet it is difficult to believe that the arrangements of the Roman country house had no influence whatever on the planning of the early mediaeval residence in the same districts. One possibility suggests itself which may be worth mentioning. In the northern provinces, where the exigencies of climate modified the Italian plan, there is a frequent type of late Roman house (the villa near Cardiff is an instance of it), which, whether it has an interior court or not, is characterized by a front of two projecting wings connected by a long room or corridor in which was the entrance. So too, the simplest form of the mediaeval manor-house is the hall, flanked by the kitchen at its lower end, and the private room of the master at the upper. If we could believe that the hall grew out of the ancient vestibule (just as, by a reverse process, in the smaller modern house the hall has shrunk into a passage), we might regard it as a survival of the Roman plan. But again the connecting evidence fails us.[1]

Two features of our modern dwellings are found in Roman provincial houses: glass windows and central heating. Both, of course, were directly due to the desire for protection against the northern climate. Glass has, indeed, been found at Pompeii; but it is in the northern provinces that the evidence of its use is most abundant. But when the Roman civilization disappeared, glass windows seem to have survived only in churches; and their return to houses was slow and fitful till quite the end of the Middle Ages. Roman house heating was an

[1] K. Swoboda has recently endeavoured to establish a connexion between this type of villa and some of the Romanesque palaces of Germany, *Römische und romanische Paläste* (Vienna, 1919), pp. 192 ff.; a book to which I am indebted for some other suggestions.

extension of the hypocaust system of heating baths, by carrying hot-air pipes up the walls. It was fairly common in the British and Gallic provinces, but it seems to have left no tradition behind it; and we cannot claim for it more than that it provided the suggestion for the modern system.

The most important department of the Roman art which has bequeathed its legacy to us is intimately connected with Roman architecture, and, like it, is mainly Imperial in character. Naturally, therefore, it is largely represented by monumental sculpture. The Romans developed the public monument, the memorial of great rulers or of great events, in ways of their own, and on a grand scale. The Arch of Titus (Fig. 56) and the Column of Trajan form landmarks in the history of Western art; and the sculptures of these and similar Imperial monuments (Fig. 46), together with innumerable subordinate works produced in the same conditions and atmosphere, have remained as permanent influences, the force of which is hardly yet exhausted. Let us look at some of the ways in which this influence has worked.

So far as form is concerned, the two peculiarly Roman kinds of memorial, the triumphal arch and the triumphal column, left no direct descendants. The triumphal arch has been reproduced sporadically from the time of the Renaissance onwards, and especially under the neo-classical fashions of the Napoleonic Empire. But whether it be the arch of Alfonso I at Naples with the free treatment of the earlier Renaissance, or the stricter Roman pattern of Napoleon's arches at Paris and Milan, or our own Marble Arch in London, these are revivals which represent no continuous tradition, and still less have any root in religious ideas, as the Roman arch probably had. In the same way the memorial columns of the Place Vendôme and Trafalgar Square are derived directly from the Roman columns of Trajan and Phocas, and are alike the offspring of the classical taste of the First Empire. As far back

Fig. 46. ANTONINUS PIUS AND FAUSTINA carried to Heaven on the wings of the Spirit of Eternity. Below, the Goddess Roma (right), and Personification of the Campus Martius (left) where the cremation took place. After 161 A.D. Now in the Vatican

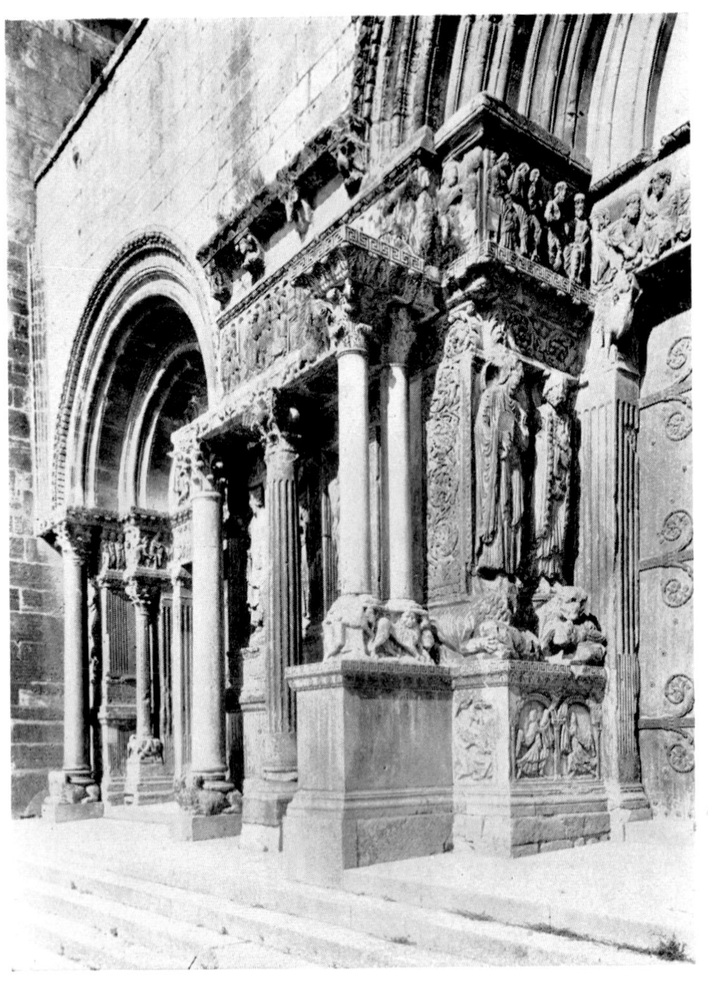

Fig. 47. PORTAL OF ABBEY-CHURCH
Saint-Gilles (Gard). About 1150–1180

as the eleventh century, Bishop Bernward of Hildesheim had imitated the column of Trajan in a great bronze candlestick for his cathedral, but the case was exotic and isolated.

On the other hand, the figure-sculpture with which these monuments were decorated had a far-reaching influence. The sight of the sculptured chronicles of the wars of Trajan or Marcus Aurelius, winding round their columns at Rome, must often have stimulated later artists who had to tell a story, not by way of providing models to be copied directly, but by offering an example of clear and orderly narrative—that the Middle Ages had forgotten the real meaning of the reliefs was indifferent—presented with all the dignity and detail that the subject required. Still more important was the influence of the historical or symbolical reliefs and statues of the Imperial triumphal arches, above all, perhaps, of the best known of them, the Arch of Constantine (Fig. 42), that epitome of Roman sculpture from its zenith down to the transition to mediaeval art. They may even have provided the suggestion or the germ of a special development in the future. With the end of the Western Empire, sculpture sank to positive barbarism. When the revival of art began in the eleventh and twelfth centuries, accompanied as it was by a perception and appreciation of the remains which the ancient world had left behind, sculpture found two main fields for its activity: the figure-capital and the church portal. On the latter all the resources of twelfth-century figure and decorative carving were lavished in northern Italy and especially in southern France. It is obvious that both figures and decorative motives owe much to the Roman remains which were abundant in the same regions. But more striking, perhaps, is the analogy between the portals of Modena and Verona, and still more those of Saint-Gilles (Fig. 47), of Saint Trophime at Arles, or of Moissac, and the Roman arches with their display of historical sculpture. The analogy is not, of course, so much in form : the porch and the tympanum, for instance, are new elements in the mediaeval design. It is rather in the conception of a monumental (sometimes triple) passage-way forming the basis of a scheme of sculptured decoration which has for its subject the victory and glory, in the one case, of Christ, in the other, of a Roman emperor. In no other form of monument did Roman art accumulate historic and symbolic sculpture for this purpose; and therefore there is an analogy, and perhaps something more, between the Roman triumphal arches and the portals of Saint-Gilles and Vézelay with their descendants at Chartres and Amiens and Rheims.[1]

But Roman sculpture was not confined to triumphal monuments, and there were other forms which were more fertile in providing suggestions and models for the artists of later ages. There was the portrait-statue and the portrait-bust; there was the storied sarcophagus front; and there was the whole range of formal decorative design applied to frieze or pilaster or doorway. When the age of barbarism had passed, and art awakened to a new life in the eleventh and twelfth centuries, it was the ancient examples of Roman sculpture, surviving in comparative abundance in parts of Italy and southern France, which provided the chief stimulus and the most obvious models. One of the most prolific forms of later Roman sculpture was the sarcophagus, elaborately carved with reliefs, generally mythological or symbolical, but sometimes historical. The form was a Greek, that is to say, a Hellenistic creation, but it attained its fullest development in the Roman Empire. Rome was one of the great centres of production; and there was a time when Italy and Southern

[1] There is an even closer approximation to the decorative schemes of the Romanesque portals in some late Roman provincial arches; e. g. the arch of Besançon, and that of Dativus Victor at Mainz, with their 'storied' voussoirs and (in the French example) panels covering the piers and even the shafts of the columns. S. Reinach, *Répertoire de Reliefs*, i. 78–82; iii. 527.

Gaul must have contained more specimens than any other countries. During the Middle Ages these sculptured sarcophagi were not only to be found *in situ* in Roman tombs, but were familiar objects in churches and streets and gardens, because they were converted into coffins for the bodies of saints and great personages, or into tanks and fountains. Probably no form of ancient art had a more direct influence on the rising schools of Italian and French sculpture in the twelfth and thirteenth centuries, not so much by way of providing models to be copied, as by exhibiting a standard of design and technical accomplishment which, though it may often have been that of a decadent period, was generally in advance of anything that the earlier mediaeval artists were capable of. But those artists possessed one essential quality that the past could not give them, the breath of new life and inspiration which urged them to look forwards and not backwards. Mere copying of ancient work would never have carried them appreciably forward. Again and again we see them going back to Roman models for motives, for details, for whole figures at times, as Niccola Pisano did on his pulpit in the baptistery at Pisa; but it is only to gain by contact with the ancient tradition fresh strength for the new achievements to which the vital force of their own art impelled them. The new life of mediaeval sculpture was above all things independent and real, and yet its growth and development would have been almost inconceivable without the background and foundation which Roman art provided. The modern art of sculpture has a continuous history from the Tuscan works of the transition, for which the doors of the baptistery at Florence, separated as they are by nearly a century, stand as types. And thus we may say that, by virtue of this descent, it has its share in the legacy of Rome.[1]

[1] We have no space to dwell on the ways in which the influence of the minor forms of ancient relief, such as the cameos or intaglios preserved (like the ivories) in church treasuries, or the coins and medals turned up

While its artistic importance is secondary as compared with the relief, the influence of Roman decorative sculpture in mediaeval and modern art has been more simple and direct. The magnificent scroll-work, with its convolutions of acanthus foliage, or sometimes, of the vine, which became so characteristic a feature of Roman decorative art from the first century onwards, has had, in one form or another, a continuous history from ancient times down to our own day. It shrank into meagre trails of barbaric leaves and flowers in the decadence, but with Romanesque art it regained some of its strength and richness; and where ancient examples were ready to hand, as they were in Italy and southern France, they were often directly reproduced (Fig. 47). With the Renaissance it took its place as a regular decorative element in neo-classic architecture; and beside it no less prominence was given to the Roman pilaster ornament of fantastic plant and animal forms wreathed about an upright stem, or to that other motive which had come to Rome from Hellenistic art, and there attained a world-wide celebrity—the festoon or swag of fruit or leafage (Fig. 48). And all these forms hold their place to-day, not only on account of their architectural fitness and the satisfaction which they give to the eye, but even more because they are capable of infinite variety and play of fancy.

Coming now to sculpture in the round, two of its forms, the portrait statue and the portrait bust, are so important in modern art that it is well for us to recall the facts about their Roman origin. The isolated portrait statue was not, of course, a creation of Roman art, but an old Greek fashion, votive in origin. But it had a quite unprecedented development in the Roman Empire, when the passion of state and municipal officials for getting themselves immortalized in marble attained

from the soil, forms part of the legacy of Rome; and we must be content to note in passing that two features of our coins, the sovereign's head and the Latin legend, are a continuous tradition from the days of the Roman Empire.

Fig. 48. Relief representing a tomb. To illustrate Roman swag and pilaster decoration. From the monument of the Haterii, end of 1st cent. A. D. Lateran Museum

Fig. 49. Rome. Equestrian statue of the Emperor Marcus Aurelius. 161–180 A. D.

Fig. 50. Venice. Equestrian statue of Bartolommeo Colleoni, by Andrea Verrocchio. 1488

almost ludicrous proportions. Though the commercial production which made this multiplication of statues possible inevitably degraded their artistic standard, it was to a great extent rediscovered works of this kind which stimulated the Renaissance sculptors to revive the memorial portrait statue, which had filled a very subordinate place in the Middle Ages. Thenceforward the tradition has been continuous and increasingly abundant down to the present time. We no longer think it desirable to clothe our worthies 'in a Roman habit', like many of their predecessors down to the eighteenth century; but, on the other hand, we may be inclined to ask whether some of our statues of public men, erected in the last hundred years, are much better than the average Roman ones.

A definitely Roman origin may be claimed for the equestrian statue, a form of the portrait statue which was revived quite early in the Renaissance, and has never been more popular for military memorials than at the present day. It has obvious attractions for the artist. Equestrian statues were not unknown in Greece, and it is significant that Alexander the Great had one in his new capital. We may be sure that the precedent was not neglected by his successors, and so the tradition was handed on to the founders of the Roman Empire. It was at Rome that the isolated monumental figure of the sovereign, mounted on his war-horse as commander-in-chief of the Imperial armies, first took its place as one of the most impressive forms of state portraiture. The earlier ones have vanished, though a contemporary poem by Statius enables us to realize to some extent what Domitian and his steed in the Forum looked like. It is to the preservation and celebrity of a single example, the bronze Marcus Aurelius of the Capitol (Fig. 49), that we can trace the revival and development of the equestrian statue from the fifteenth century down to our own days. Seldom has a single work of art had so distinct and so prolonged an influence. That influence, though indirect, may even be seen in the fourteenth-century stone and wood mounted figures of princes and generals which crown their tombs in North Italian cities, such as Milan and Venice and Verona. But Donatello's Gattamelata at Padua and Verrocchio's Bartolommeo Colleoni at Venice at once challenge comparison with the Roman model by their composition and material, and produce a far finer result (Figs. 49, 50).

The weakest part of Roman statues was usually the conventional and commonplace treatment of the figure. Such interest as they have comes from the head. Accordingly, a much more favourable impression is conveyed by the bust, which dispenses with the figure altogether. The extraordinary merit of the Roman portrait busts of the Early Empire has long been recognized, and we may regard them as a definite achievement of Roman art. We have been reminded, indeed, that the portrait head, generally in the form of a herm, was a Greek development; that in the later Greek art portraits with a high degree of individuality were produced; and that, so far as the evidence goes, the artists who made the Roman busts were predominantly of Greek origin. But when all is said, the fact remains that, as portraits of the individual which have seized on all that is characteristic and personal and discarded the merely typical, the Roman busts are independent and unsurpassed. They are the creation of an art which we may call Roman, because it belonged to the Roman Empire and flourished on Italian soil. Indeed, it is worth considering whether native Italian elements and characteristics may not have contributed to make Roman busts what they are. The Etruscan sepulchral portrait-effigies have a remarkable individuality and naturalism. Then there is the long tradition of the ancestral *imagines*, the wax masks which preserved the features of the past members of great Roman families. That tradition may have influenced the memorial busts in stone or marble of a later age, sometimes set (as in the tomb of the Haterii) in similar shrines (Figs. 51, 52), and hardly less realistic, especially as their life-like effect was helped by colour. Moreover, though portrait heads were not a new thing, what has been called 'the shoulder bust', which is the characteristic Roman form, was a new development; and it has a distinct and important artistic value, which has been admirably summarized in the following passage. 'As compared with the herm, the shoulder bust enabled the Flavian artist to free the pose of the head, thus intensifying its expressiveness . . . as compared with the figure, it compelled him to eliminate anything savouring of the dramatic or the theatrical . . . and concentrate all his import in the face.' [1] In somewhat the same way, with the modern painted portrait, which, though the art of portrait sculpture still flourishes, may be compared for relative popularity and abundance with the Roman statues and busts, one of the reasons why the quarter-length or half-length has been favoured by even the greatest painters is because it helps to enhance the personality portrayed, by concentrating attention upon its most expressive part—the face—without depriving it of its natural setting in the figure, which is necessary for a complete presentation of the individual. The bust had no continuous history through the Middle Ages, but at the Renaissance the Roman examples were quickly appreciated by connoisseurs and sculptors; and with that stimulus Donatello and others produced their masterpieces of individuality and beauty. All succeeding ages and schools have, in their several ways, maintained the importance of the bust as the most individual form of realistic portraiture.

One other form of figure sculpture, the recumbent sepulchral effigy, has been so prominent and continuous from the twelfth century down to the present day, when it shows no signs of being exhausted, that one is tempted to ask whether its origins can be traced to the ancient world. While we look for them in vain in Greece, it is on Italian soil that we find some of the closest analogies to the mediaeval effigy in the figures lying flat on the lids of some Etruscan sarcophagi. The

[1] J. W. Crowfoot in *Journal of Hellenic Studies*, xx (1900), p. 41.

Etruscans may have borrowed the idea from the Phoenicians or Carthaginians; for Carthage can show recumbent effigies of priests and priestesses of the age of Hannibal, which might almost be the prototypes of the mediaeval figures. But the idea does not seem to have borne fruit when the traditions of Etruscan art were absorbed by Rome, and it is only very rarely that we find anything of the kind on Roman sarcophagi, where, following the commoner Etruscan fashion, the dead person, often with his wife by his side, generally reclines supported on the left elbow. The mediaeval form has been traced to the practice of exhibiting the actual corpse, or an image of the deceased lying on the bier or coffin during the funeral (a practice which, we may note in passing, was itself of Roman origin)[1]; and certainly this was not without its influence on the form of the permanent effigy in stone or marble. But it is characteristic of many of the earlier mediaeval effigies that, though laid flat, with a pillow under the head, the person is represented as alive, and even in action; the ecclesiastic giving his blessing, the knight drawing or sheathing his sword (Figs. 53 and 55). The niche-like architectural setting of such figures also suggests that the whole thing was originally upright, and has simply been laid flat in order to cover the grave or tomb-chest. Now, at a rather earlier date, we actually find these portrait-effigies, framed in niches or quasi-niches, standing upright as part of the sculptured decoration of walls or piers. There is an abbot-bishop Durandus, carved in low relief on the face of a pier in the cloister of Moissac at the very beginning of the twelfth century, which, with his attitude, accessories, and architectural frame, is exactly like the horizontal tomb effigies later in the century. Such upright memorial figures, framed in a niche or arch, may have a Roman origin in one of two ways, perhaps both. They may have some connexion with that form of the late Roman sarcophagus-front which has a row of figures in niches or in the openings of a continuous arcade. Yet the

[1] Herodian, iv. 2, where the ritual of Imperial funerals is set forth.

Figs. 51 and 52. BUSTS FROM THE MONUMENT OF THE HATERII
End of 1st cent. A.D. Lateran Museum

Fig. 53

EFFIGY OF A BISHOP

13th cent.

Fig. 54

GRAVESTONE OF M. FAVONIUS FACILIS. 1st cent. A. D.

Fig. 55

EFFIGY OF A KNIGHT

13th cent.

framed portrait-effigy is isolated, and it may be that it is more nearly related to a Roman type of upright gravestone in which the figure of the deceased as he was in life (sometimes only a half-length) stands in a recess above the epitaph. Such tombstones are specially frequent for soldiers in the frontier provinces of the Rhine and Britain; but we also find them used for civilians in other parts of Gaul. As it is just in these countries that we find the earliest mediaeval effigies, it is not impossible that they may owe something to surviving specimens of the Roman type; and, in this way, gravestones like that of the centurion Marcus Favonius Facilis at Colchester (Fig. 54) may be the ancestors of the mailed knights who still lie in many of our churches.

The influence of ancient painting on the modern art which has its source in the Renaissance is almost negligible. The traditions of painting in the Roman Empire are, indeed, for long traceable in wall-pictures and illuminated manuscripts both eastern and western. But by the time that the new-born Italian painting of the Trecento was emerging from its cradle in Byzantine art, those traditions had become faint; and Roman influence of this kind is, at the best, remote and indirect. Nor were the discoveries of actual Roman paintings sufficiently important to have had much influence on the practice and ideas of the Renaissance artists, except in the matter of decorative design. It was only with the systematic excavation of Pompeii, from the eighteenth century onwards, that any considerable body of ancient painting was available for study; and here, as we now know, the art was purely Hellenistic and Alexandrine.

There is, however, another way in which the art of the Roman Empire has affected modern painting; and that is by the inspiration which has come, not from pictures, but from sculpture. It was the marbles which formed the most important, as they were the most permanent, record of the achievement of ancient art. When the age of iconoclasm was past, and the dawn of humanism and antiquarianism had begun to shine, the eyes of the mediaeval artists and scholars were opened to the strange ideal beauty of these figures of gods and heroes which belonged to a world so different and so distant from their own. A northern visitor to Rome, somewhere about the year 1200, has recorded in a vivid way the impression made on him by a marble Venus which he was taken to see. Like other images, it had, no doubt, been deliberately hidden, and then rediscovered by accident; and it may be that Venus of the Capitoline Museum which has come down to us in an almost undamaged condition. At any rate, when 'Magister Gregorius' saw it, it was perfect, and still retained some of its delicate colouring; so that it seemed as if alive, with the blood pulsating under the fair skin. 'And', he continues, 'such was its wondrous beauty and magical charm, that I was constrained to go three times to see it, though it was two miles distant from my lodging.'[1] But it was not till the great age of the Renaissance in the fifteenth and early sixteenth centuries that deliberate search and the formation of collections exhibited the works of ancient sculpture in considerable quantity before the eyes of the artists of the day, and restored them to almost exaggerated honour and appreciation. Their influence was the greater on account of the 'all-round' training of the Renaissance artist, fitting him to be as much an architect or a sculptor as a painter; for this must have made the painters more susceptible to the lessons to be learned from Roman sculpture. That those lessons were important for the progress of painting we cannot doubt. We are not thinking of the direct influence of the marbles, which is most marked in the school of Padua; for that was something exceptional, and it left little or no tradition behind it. Mantegna, saturated with the Roman spirit and Roman forms, so far as he knew them, in the grandest and most Roman of his works, the Triumph of Caesar (Fig. 57), achieved all that

[1] *Journal of Roman Studies*, ix (1919), p. 24.

was possible in that direction; but it was not that way that the path of progress lay. What the remains of ancient art really contributed to the advance of painting was that, unequal and commonplace as much of the rediscovered work was, it provided, with all the accomplishment of a long artistic tradition behind it, standards of form and composition which stimulated and fertilized the new-born energies of both painter and sculptor, without fettering or sterilizing them as mere imitation would have done. Above all, it was largely through the Roman statues and reliefs that the study and the presentation of the nude was recovered as one of the great fields of the artist's activity. The sight of the ancient examples gave the early Renaissance artists a sanction, as it were, and courage to venture on what had been almost a forbidden form of art, and thus inevitably led the way to the study of the life-model. It is in painting rather than in sculpture that the greatest achievements of modern art in representing the nude are to be found. And so we may remember that, in this way, Giorgione's Sleeping Venus and all her descendants owe their existence to the antique marble goddesses which enraptured the Renaissance artists.

But it was not only the practice and scope of painting which were affected by Roman sculpture. There was also the lesson of style—and particularly what is called the grand style—imparted to the monumental painting of Raphael and Michelangelo at Rome by the historical and symbolical sculptures of the Imperial age, especially when seen in their local setting, with all the glory and glamour of the legend of Roman greatness about them. It has often been noticed what a stimulating effect Rome exercised on the architects and artists summoned thither to carry out the works planned by the Popes of the great age of the Renaissance. Some of that effect, no doubt, was due to the force of competition, and the experience gained from contact with other men's work in these gatherings of the first reputations of Italy.

But the fact remains that it was at Rome that they produced the best work of which they were capable, so that even a second-rate Florentine (as he appears to us) like Cosimo Rosselli figures in the Sistine Chapel as a not altogether unworthy associate of Botticelli and Pinturicchio. And so we may suppose that the spirit and atmosphere of Rome, together with the serene dignity and ideal beauty of the Imperial statues and reliefs, contributed to that largeness of treatment and grandeur of form which Michelangelo displays in the Sistine Chapel and Raphael in the Stanze. The 'Parnassus' and 'the School of Athens'—still more 'the Disputa'—do, indeed, in their vision and its presentation soar far beyond the range and comparison of ancient art. But in the symbolic figures of the four great fields of human intellect, which fill the medallions on the vault of the Camera della Segnatura, the connexion with the past is less remote and more apparent; and they seem to be instinct with the Roman spirit at its highest power (Fig. 58). And we may remember that, with all the changes of taste or creed, these works have remained the starting-point and standard of monumental painting down to the present day.

Looking back at the various ways in which we have traced the influence of Roman architecture and art in our own world, two points seem to call for special emphasis, and we may state them shortly by way of conclusion. One is that Rome has mainly influenced later ages by unconscious tradition, or by the force of example. In the long run, mere reproduction of ancient forms has nearly always been barren. The twelfth-century imitations of Composite capitals are little more than archaeological curiosities, and nowadays no one thinks of building churches like the Madeleine at Paris, in imitation of a Roman temple. It was the spirit and not the letter of ancient art that had most influence on the future. The other is that, wide as was the field of the Roman Empire and its remains, the city of Rome has always been the most powerful force for

Fig. 56. TRIUMPH OF TITUS OVER THE JEWS
Relief from his arch at Rome. After 81 A. D.

Fig. 57. TRIUMPH OF JULIUS CAESAR
By Andrea Mantegna. 1485–1494
Hampton Court Palace

Fig. 58. 'POETRY' BY RAPHAEL
Camera della Segnatura in the Vatican. 1509

transmitting the Roman tradition. As it was in Rome that all the artistic resources of the Empire were concentrated and fused, we must go to Rome to see what Roman art was like, and what it meant. Pending the rediscovery of Greece, it was mainly from Rome that the world got its ideas of ancient building and ancient art. The celebrity of her remains was assured when she became the capital of the spiritual empire of the Roman Church, and not less when the revival of humanism made her the goal of pilgrims of a different kind. At all times, for Western Europe, the Eternal City has retained its supremacy as the capital of the ancient culture and all it has to teach.

G. McN. RUSHFORTH.

BIBLIOGRAPHY.

F. WICKHOFF, *Roman Art*. Translated by Mrs. S. Arthur Strong. London, Heinemann, 1900.

PROFESSOR H. STUART JONES, *Art under the Roman Empire*. *Quarterly Review*, cciv (1906), pp. 111 ff.

MRS. ARTHUR STRONG, *Roman Sculpture*. London, Duckworth, 1907.
For a more recent statement of Mrs. Strong's views on Roman Imperial art see the *Introductory Address to Students* in her *Apotheosis and After Life* (London, Constable, 1915).

H. B. WALTERS, *The Art of the Romans*. (Includes a survey of the architecture.) London, 1911.

PROFESSOR PERCY GARDNER, *Professor Wickhoff on Roman Art*. *Journal of Roman Studies*, vii (1917), pp. 1 ff.

W. J. ANDERSON and R. PHENÉ SPIERS, *The Architecture of Greece and Rome*. 2nd edition. London, 1907.

SIR R. BLOMFIELD, *The Mistress Art* (especially Lecture VII, *Rome*). London, 1908.

BUILDING AND ENGINEERING

ROMAN civilization, which an Italian poet has described as *intera e diritta*, was essentially constructive in all its manifestations; in architecture and technical methods as in jurisprudence and in the art of government. It did not confine itself to abstract judgements and sophistical futilities, it did not study philosophy for philosophy's sake and practise art for art's sake, but aimed always at practical, positive ends, and created a wonderful technical organization in order to attain them. Admitting the many points of resemblance which unite it both directly and indirectly with the civilization of the Greeks, we must nevertheless insist that the two civilizations are to be regarded from two entirely different points of view.

It would be easy to defend this attitude against those preconceived ideas, still in vogue, which find their expression in the term 'Graeco-Roman', a term almost without meaning when applied to a whole civilization and a whole architecture. These ideas are due, first, to the serious dearth of researches into the art and the technical methods of the Romans; secondly, to the exaggerated attention hitherto paid to Vitruvius, whose work is so largely based on earlier treatises of the Alexandrine period that he is not a reliable guide if we wish to understand the engineering and architecture of his time; lastly, to confusion between technical and artistic methods, which were definitely separate in Roman practice.

On the other hand, to understand the great phenomenon of Roman culture as expressed in its architecture and engineering, and to follow its offshoots in the Middle Ages and the Renaissance, it must be judged by standards not very different from those by which we judge modern civilizations, especially those of great nations which are rich in colonies, such as Great Britain. Then, as now, we shall find that the chief characteristics are: (*a*) the great political and financial power of the central State; (*b*) the essentially calculating and materialistic spirit of the peoples, so that art and religion become means but not ends in life; (*c*) the regulated, orderly expansion of the public services; (*d*) the organization of technical methods and the gradual perfection of technical ideas, whether scientific or practical. It is plain that the last two points have acquired a vital importance in the nineteenth and twentieth centuries, giving our civilization a mechanical and scientific character which finds no parallel in the Roman period. But it is also certain that in no other epoch of the past are these four elements to be found so closely united as under the Roman Empire.

In explanation it must be said that to the Romans the chief aim of architecture and of the applied sciences was essentially utilitarian. Temples were no longer their chief monuments, but palaces, baths, amphitheatres, granaries, bridges, aqueducts, and drainage work. For the people, 'panis et circenses'; for rich private individuals, the satisfaction of luxury and of material comforts; for the State, the government of the conquered peoples through the conferment of prosperity and through the impression of magnificence and power: so that it has been justly said that the construction of public buildings and public institutions had a real political function, corresponding to that of the systems of government, which were almost always tolerant and far-sighted, allowed an ample measure of administrative autonomy, and respected religions and customs.

The chief practical means by which the Romans strove to attain these ends—setting high standards before themselves, and acting with a practical sense of organization on a large scale never again to be found in the Latin peoples—can best be seen in their handling of the problems of communication, in their management of working materials, and in their organization of labour.

The organization of labour was particularly important, constituting, as it did, the force behind all constructional and technical achievement. By means of the data furnished by Marquardt and Choisy,[1] we can prove that the social system which prevailed in these undertakings was that of workmen's corporations, sharply distinguished according to trades and united by religious bonds; these corporations were the guardians of constructive traditions which were passed on from generation to generation, from the experienced workmen (*magistri*) to the apprentices; and it was perhaps among them, that is, by practical experience rather than in schools, that the architects [2] and the *mensores* were formed.

Choisy, practically ignoring the usual system of agreements with contractors (*redemptores*), supposes that the *collegia* of the *redemptores* were real co-operative unions, compelled to lend their labour to the State when required, obliged to respect

[1] Marquardt, *Privatleben der Römer*, Leipzig, 1886, vols. xiv and xv of Mommsen's *Handbuch der römischen Alterthümer*; Choisy, *L'Art de bâtir chez les Romains*, Paris, 1873; cf. also Bouché-Leclercq, *Manuel des Institutions Romaines*, Paris, 1886; Mané, H., *Die Vereine der Fabri*, &c., Frankfurt, 1886; Waltzing, J. P., *Étude sur les Corporations professionnelles chez les Romains*, Louvain, 1895.

[2] The professional status of the Roman architect was naturally uncertain and ill defined, just as we find it later in the Renaissance; on the one hand, there is the aristocratic type portrayed by Vitruvius, e.g. Apollodorus, Alypius of Antioch, and the Emperor Hadrian himself, which received its training in the schools mentioned by Lampridius in the *Life of Alexander Severus*, and later by the *Codex Theodosianus*; on the other, the practical, humble type of architect risen from the ranks, who was at the same time a *redemptor*, whose lack of education was the butt of one of Martial's epigrams; there were also the military architects, under the direction of the *Praefectus fabrum*; these sometimes had the rank of private soldiers. Cf. on this subject de Montauzan, op. cit., ch. v; Daremberg and Saglio's *Dictionnaire d'Antiquités*, s.v. 'Architectus'; also the recent article 'Ueber römischen Baumeister' in *Zeitschrift deutscher Arch. u. Ing.* (August 1922), which collects the evidence of many inscriptions.

fixed tariffs in private undertakings, and compensated for these obligations by the enjoyment of endowed funds granted to the corporation and administered by it. But even if this cannot be proved, it is nevertheless quite logical to assert that these corporations had a professional as well as a trade-union and religious character, and that in large undertakings (and especially in mason's work) they controlled the whole multitude of unskilled workmen, the labourers suited only for transport and unloading work thus being controlled by intelligent, technically trained workmen. In public works they may be regarded as the peace legions of the Roman State; in private undertakings they took the place of slaves.

This type of organization, this social arrangement of the working classes, long survived the Roman Empire in all the western parts of Europe. We find it again under the Lombard kings, who established rules and tariffs for the 'magistri commacini'; we find it when art begins to revive at Rome in the thirteenth century, when the guild of marble-workers exercised a real jurisdiction, subject to the consuls. And it is not improbable that even the guilds of the Gothic period had some distant relation to these ancient corporations, which they resemble in their exclusiveness, in their dominant religious idea, and in their preservation of the building tradition.

In the Roman period the following facts in the general course of technical development are closely connected with this particular social system:

1. The sharp division between the arts, which became almost independent of each other, so that, for example, in the construction of a building the marble facing was often executed long after the building of the walls and had no real aesthetic connexion with them: this principle of facing or *doublure* is opposed to the essentially organic nature of Greek architecture; the result is that we are unable to reconstruct in our minds the true external aspect of many buildings, such as the Pantheon and the great Roman Baths.

2. The evolution of technical knowledge independently of the arts of architecture and decoration. These arts were derived, in great measure, from Greek art of the Alexandrine period—an old art which had completed its cycle, and which was not rejuvenated but merely made hybrid by being grafted on to local tendencies to which Rome allowed free expression; thus, no longer upheld by a constructive spirit, and transplanted from its original home, its life was short, and after the splendour of the period between the end of the Republic and the time of Hadrian, it decayed rapidly, falling into an excessive ornateness combined with poverty of execution. The technical side of building, on the other hand, had a continuous progress in every field, as was natural under an organization which valued cumulative experience and the progressive improvement of theoretical and practical discoveries. What modern science and industry accomplish by laboratory research, tests, theoretical hypotheses expressed in formulae, and the organized contributions of students and scientists, was accomplished for the science and industry of ancient times by the transmission of technical knowledge, by the application of the results of experiment to the processes and principles of building, and by empirical formulae, jealously guarded and handed down in mysterious symbolic form.

So it comes to pass that the third and fourth centuries—generally considered to be an era of great decadence in Roman art—are, on the contrary, the period of the greatest triumphs in the field of building; the energy seems suddenly to fail (though in reality it was but transferred to the Eastern Empire) only when political uncertainty and eventually political ruin, with the collapse of public and private prosperity, put an end to all building on a large and costly scale and broke the continuity of the great tradition.

This is also the cause of the varying degree of decadence in the different branches of art: the decadence is almost complete in everything connected with marble ornamentation, and especially in the decoration of the ancient architectural orders; it is almost absent in the new elements directly connected with actual construction, such as the arch and the vault.

It follows from all these observations that the essential fact in Roman construction, from the end of the Republic (when the period of the formation and assimilation of the various ethnographical strains concludes) to the end of the Western Empire (when the necessary conditions for further development ceased to exist), is the comparative independence of the several crafts: without which it would have been difficult to satisfy the varied and complex practical demands of public and private life. This is the point of view from which we must consider the architecture and engineering of the Roman Empire.

We shall now examine in detail, from the technical point of view, the constructional methods employed in building; we shall not concern ourselves here with the type of the building as determined by its purpose, or with its external form in relation to its decorative facing. It must, however, be remembered that it was precisely these constructional methods which made it possible to enclose vast covered spaces, to adapt the proportions of these spaces to the design of a harmonious whole, and in fact to give expression to the main artistic intention of the Roman architect. This intention was first and foremost *spatial*: expressed in the magnificence of the dimensions, in the harmony of the relation between empty and filled spaces, and in the variety of the forms of the enclosed spaces in plan and in elevation. This variety was an organic feature with respect both to the purpose of the building and to its construction; it took the place of the monotonous uniformity of the Greek scheme, the beauty of which lay instead in its admirable grace and in the perfect reasonableness of its elements.

The chief problem was that of spanning large openings and large enclosed spaces; it was solved by the arch and the vault. Timidly attempted by the Egyptians, used sparingly by the

Assyrians, and systematically on a comparatively small scale in Etruscan bridges and tombs from the seventh to the first century B. C., the arch and the vault advanced with slow but certain progress to greater and greater magnificence and complexity.

In this vast and completely new problem (since up to that time the width of a room had been limited by the measurements of the timber obtainable, or else it was necessary to divide the room by series of intermediate columns),[1] the minor proposition was the efficient construction of walls, arches, and vaults, but the main proposition was to find a system which would get rid of lateral pressure, giving beauty to the enclosed space and securing its illumination.

These two propositions, the first of which provided a field for the executive activity of the mason, the second for the creative activity of the architect, were closely bound together towards one single purpose: from the point of view of stability, this led to an abundance of resisting power which enabled these buildings to defy time with only a minimum of upkeep, or even, in practice, with none at all, and in the face of wanton destruction.

Walls. The character of Roman wall-structure was not unvarying either in time or place. In the East, and particularly in Greece, in Asia Minor, in Syria, and in North Africa, the survival of the Hellenistic tradition, as an ethnographical and artistic element, and, as a material element, the abundance of stone suitable for squaring, frequently caused the adoption of masonry in large blocks of cut stone; in Central Italy there are signs of the continuance, even throughout the first century A. D., of the Etruscan type of masonry in squared stone, the stone being employed either as skeleton-

[1] An analogous limitation can be seen in Christian basilicas, the planimetric and constructive scheme of which is merely derived from the halls of basilican type already in common use under the Romans, cf. G. Giovannoni, 'Nuovi contributi allo studio della genesi della basilica cristiana', in *Atti della Pont. Accademia di Archeologia*, Rome, 1919.

work or as facing. But when the masons' guild-organizations predominate, and those of the stone-cutters take second place, the concrete type of masonry, contained within its appropriate moulds, is widely used: these moulds were sometimes temporary, sometimes they became permanent factors in the mass of the masonry; and this type became the most truly characteristic in Roman building.

These facts of course require classification and comment; the terms employed by Vitruvius in his treatise (particularly in his second book) will be retained, but not his sub-divisions; the latter correspond to certain artificial standards in which the Hellenistic school, of which Vitruvius is the direct heir, failed conspicuously to adapt itself to the realities of his time.[1]

Walls in cut stone, *quadrati lapides*, in those rare cases where the cut stones constitute the actual skeleton of the wall, usually follow the Etruscan method of (1) courses of uniform thickness, (2) blocks of parallelepiped form (in which the width is equal to the height and the length is double or triple, and all the dimensions are multiples of the linear units of measurement), (3) layers in which the blocks face the outside wall alternately in headers and stretchers, (4) *diatoni* (bond-stones), the end view of which is square. One of the most typical and magnificent examples exists in Rome in the boundary-wall of the Forum of Augustus, in which this arrangement of coursing is emphasized by the appearance of cushion-shaped bosses. In the same place can also be seen, faithfully copied, the pattern of the stone walls of the time of the kings and of the Republic, such as those of the rampart of Servius, of the Marcian aqueduct, of the substructure of the so-called Temple of Vesta, &c.

But much more commonly cut stone serves as a facing for an interior mass composed either of masonry in layers of random rubble or of mass concrete; this is the *structura*. In this case the arrangement of the blocks in alternating courses of headers and stretchers has not yet been adopted, but headers and

[1] Cf. G. Boni in *Notizie degli Scavi*, vol. x, p. 495.

stretchers are found in the same course; the former (i. e. the *diatoni*), placed across the wall, serve to bind the facing to the body. It is in fact these bond-stones which, where the cut stone facings, as has almost always happened, have been torn away, have remained with their square ends truncated, and which, in the base of the tomb of Cecilia Metella, for example, can still be seen built into the shapeless mass of the *structura*. In the temple of Jupiter Latiaris these bond-stones had at their inside ends a kind of re-entrant curve, shaped like a raven's beak, to reinforce their hold.

Vitruvius gives the Greek name *emplecton* to this type of masonry, and distinguishes the Greek from the Roman emplecton, the Greek being composed of blocks of stone, the Roman of slabs forming a kind of chamber in the wall; this system can only have been rarely used. One partial example of it can be quoted in Rome in the so-called Temple of Vesta (or of the Mater Matuta) in the Forum Boarium.

The *opus incertum* is related to these methods: in this the external wall is formed of blocks, either large or small, polygonal in shape and joined at the corners, which are fitted together. This is a survival of those polygonal walls of large blocks, conventionally called Cyclopean or Pelasgic, which were largely used in Central Italy from an early period (contemporary with the Mycenaean) up till the time of the Roman Republic, as in the walls of Norba or Alfedena; since, as has been justly observed, this method is attributable less to an historical than to a geological factor, namely, to the character of the limestone used. One of the most interesting examples of this *opus incertum*—a real piece of polygonal face-work—exists in the wall of an aqueduct which brought water possibly to Angitia in the basin of Fucino.

Examples of the *incertum* with small materials are much more common, as at Palestrina and at Anxur (now Terracina), and at Rome in the Porticus Aemilia at Marmorata, and in the Rostra of Caesar at the western end of the Forum.

At this point we already find concrete masonry-work, the most characteristic Roman work in Italy and the western regions of the Empire; in this the exterior face-work gave form to the interior filling of plaster, i. e. the *caementum*, which was practically the same as our concrete or *beton* ; it was used as a substitute for the primitive fillings and constructions of earth which had attained a high development in earlier times in the form of the *murus terreus*, in altars built of turf-clods, and in bricks of unburnt clay.

The vast dimensions of these concrete-built walls (called *structura*) generally allowed the two stages of construction to be entirely separate, making a cunning correspondence between the system and the organization of the work; the guilds of masons carefully finished the facing, and meanwhile the rest of the workmen completed the labour of filling and punning the *caementum*; by this means they were officered and utilized a great number at a time by efficient overseers. It must not be thought that this was done everywhere, as Choisy affirms, with his usual tendency to generalize and reduce the complex facts of building almost to formulae. There are not lacking, even in Latium, Roman walls of lesser thickness, e. g. in the Villa of Hadrian near Tivoli, in the Villa of Nero near Subiaco, in the so-called Temple of Minerva Medica in Rome, in which it is obvious that the mass-work and the facing were constructed simultaneously by the same workmen, and the former really consists not so much of concrete as of rubble and broken brick—that is, of material not cast into shape, but placed in irregular layers by hand. It is not without interest to note that this is the method which the Roman masons of to-day still follow in making brick walls.[1]

The term 'concrete' is not really a precise description of

[1] Interesting pictures of masons occupied on the construction of a wall—in a fresco in the vault of Trebius Justus on the Latin Way and in the bas-reliefs on the Column of Trajan—show methods of work and systems not at all unlike ours.

the composition of this filling, which usually consists of alternate layers of rubble and mortar tightly compressed, and not of a mixture made before placing. Real concrete, on the other hand, was used for what Vitruvius (viii. 7) calls *signinum opus*—layers of water-tight facing for the sides of reservoirs or the pavement of terraces, like the kind still used to-day for areas and terraces.

The face-work of these concrete-built walls most commonly consists of baked bricks (*cocti lateres*). The shapes and proportions of these bricks are extremely varied: according to Vitruvius the brick was theoretically 1 foot (0·296 m.) in width and 1½ feet (0·444 m.) in length (*longum sesquipede latum pede*), and half-bricks were made from them simply by breaking. There were also bipedales (2-foot bricks), large bricks about 60 cm. square, used not only in arches but also in the continuous levelled courses running through the structure of the wall. There were also *laterculi bessales*, two-thirds of a foot (about 20 cm.) square, and about 4 cm. in thickness. But actually the proportions used were much more varied, and it has frequently been noticed that bricks originally shaped for *tegulae* have been afterwards transformed into ordinary bricks by cutting off their projecting edge and grinding them down on slabs of stone.[1]

Frequently these bricks, whatever their original type may have been, were cut into isosceles triangles and placed with their base flush with the external surface of the wall and the apex (a right angle) turned inwards, so as to form a toothing and hold to the body of the wall (Fig. 59); the body of the wall, as has been shown, was interrupted and regularized at uniform

[1] Boni has shown, after long research, that the above-mentioned type of *tegulae fractae* was extremely common in Rome in the first and second centuries A. D.; they were used for wall-ornamentation and were part of the material derived from the great fires which were frequent in the city at that time; they were generally cut into scalene triangles. Isosceles bricks, however, began to be adopted, made by sawing diagonally the square bricks (⅔ ft. square) from the *suspensurae* of the hot baths.

distances by courses of large bricks, usually 2-foot bricks, which crossed it through its whole thickness.

On a basis of the external dimensions of the facing bricks, the width of the joints, and the regularity of the workmanship, minute classifications have been made (by Parker and Miss Van Deman in particular [1]), to which a strictly chronological value has been attached; and as always happens when an attempt is made to determine the progress of a constructive spirit by mechanical developments, exaggerations and serious errors have resulted. Let it suffice here to say that masonry of the first century was generally composed of bricks which were not very thick (2–3 cm.), all the same size, laid with great accuracy, and with very close joints (less than a centimetre); that in the following centuries bricks increased progressively in thickness, till, in the Baths of Diocletian and the basilica of Maxentius, they are almost 5 cm. thick; their frontal lengths became unequal and their joints as much as 3 cm. in width. This, if it shows less love, but greater haste and carelessness in the building, was nevertheless in no way detrimental to its solidity; this was completely assured by the excellent quality of the cements used (in Italian building these almost always contained pozzolana), and by the close union between facing and mass.

FIG. 59. Wall with surface of triangular bricks.

A well-known and very singular arrangement of the facing is that of the *opus reticulatum*, obtained by small blocks of tufa in the shape of square truncated pyramids, placed with the square base outwards and the sides at 45 degrees from the

[1] Cf. Van Deman, 'Methods of determining the date of Roman concrete Monuments', in *Journal of the Arch. Inst. of America*, vol. xvi (1912).

vertical. The *reticulatum* was almost always enclosed by squares of bricks: it had a rather short period of development, from the time of Sulla, when it was gradually substituted for the *incertum*, till the time of Hadrian, after which it was almost entirely abandoned.

There is no need to linger here over the numerous other methods, such as that of the *opus mixtum*, with alternate courses of bricks and tufa-blocks, frequently used in the time of Constantine, or of small stones in a herring-bone pattern, fairly common in Northern Italy; or finally, that curious arrangement, common in Africa, of walls with an independent framework of long slabs of stone, forming vertical pillars and horizontal joists, the rectangular spaces being filled in with ordinary light masonry. The object of these notes is not to make a complete analytical study, but to give a summary of the more important types and methods of Roman technique. This technique, in the field of architecture, survived long into the Middle Ages, both in Byzantine building and in western buildings in that *opera romanensis* mentioned by the chroniclers of the Lombard kings Rothar and Liutprand.

In the same way, too, the construction of walls in unburnt bricks, the *lateres* with which Vitruvius deals at such length, deserves only a brief mention. This method was indeed used in country buildings, and sometimes even in the *insulae* in cities;[1] but it came from a desire for economy, and is an example of a tendency, not uncommon in many great periods (for instance, in the Egyptian), to give an ephemeral character to the buildings constructed for ordinary use, in contrast to the magnificence and durability of the great monumental structures.

Arches. The form of the Roman arch appears in the full

[1] Rome in the Republican period was largely built of *lateres*, that is, unburnt bricks: and it was the boast of Augustus that he had partly transformed it into a stone-built city, i. e. by using tufa, peperino, or *lapis tiburtinus* (travertine).

arch in its ordinary applications, in the segmental arch of the windows of baths and in many relieving arches, and in the platband surrounding any small opening. The structural character of the arches is closely related to that of walls, except of course that their construction is more organic and more characteristic.

The chief prototypes of ashlar arches are found in the doors, bridges, and sewers of Etruria; often, indeed, Roman arches appear from outside, like these, completely extradorsal, for example, in the theatre of Marcellus in Rome, in the amphitheatre of Verona, &c. Next, the scheme of the arch in pentagonal ashlar came into use, resulting from a new idea of closely uniting the materials of an arch with the corresponding materials of the wall; the wall of the Forum of Augustus and the gate of the *Templum Sacrae Urbis* in Rome are the best known examples of this construction, which is of a simple beauty in direct relation, new as this method of building was, with the structure. From these examples arose later, during the Renaissance, all the infinite derivative forms of the embossed arch, especially in the work of Sangallo and Sammicheli.

But intermediate examples are not lacking. In the Coliseum and in the arch of Drusus in Rome can be seen the extradorsal arrangement, here stylized in the slender archivolt which, with its continuous line, represents the survival of a traditional method, while the voussoirs are pentagonal and go across the archivolt.

The architectural type seen in porticoes like those of the Coliseum is perhaps the most characteristic of Roman architecture, because it seems almost to symbolize its formative process. The vital essential of the constructional scheme (borrowed from the Etruscans) lies in the rows of arches supported on piers, and in turn supporting the whole of the fabric above them: this scheme, like all elementary forms, embodies an organic or pseudo-organic type of architectural expression. On the other hand, the principle of half-columns and trabeation which squares the arches has become the old-fashioned element derived from Greek art and now finding an expression which is merely formal and devoid of any constructional function.

The only successor to this great characteristic motive—and that after a long interval in spite of earlier sporadic appearances in Pompeii—was the alternative scheme of the arch carried directly by the columns, the columns thus reverting to the purely static function of support: the halls of the palace of Diocletian at Spalato are a magnificent example of this scheme employed on a monumental scale. Whatever its origin, it leads up to the systematized plan of the Christian basilicas and, later, of the Byzantine churches.

Arches of bricks embedded in concrete mass-work were generally composed of large bricks (usually 2 feet in length), placed with greater or less accuracy in conformity with that of the masonry facing. Sometimes, in the first century A. D., the desire for perfect workmanship led to the adoption (as, for instance, in the Coliseum in Rome) of cuneiform bricks, which allowed of the arch being built with uniform layers of cement of the least possible thickness. For arches of exceptional size and resisting power a double or triple ring of bricks formed the type best adapted; the Pantheon offers the most characteristic examples.

Sometimes, too, the arches were of a mixed structure analogous with that of the masonry; an arch of bricks in the outside facework, but inside, an arch in concrete, with bricks of 2 or 1½ feet in length placed radially at intervals, forming in this way separate keys of artificial stone and controlling the internal stresses of the concrete work, by determining the line of thrust and preventing deflection.

A function of Roman arches almost as important as that of spanning openings was that of the relieving arches in the mass of the wall. These, made of brick and very strong, appear to penetrate the wall, but in reality give a rhythmic stability to the whole structure. To examine the most typical of these: the recent excavations at Ostia, which have unearthed whole Roman dwelling-houses of more than one floor, show in the windows traces of timber architraves, above which stood segmental relieving arches, which still survive and show of what type the present ruins were. The embedding of the platband into the semicircular relieving arch is very common, and becomes the characteristic type of constructional, and sometimes of architectural, design. It appears, for example, in the apertures in the theatre of Orange and in the fine stone-built side gate of the *Templum Sacrae Urbis* in Rome already mentioned, which is attributed to the time of Vespasian and which had so many imitations and derivatives in the architecture of the Italian Renaissance (e. g. in the palace built in Rome for Raphael by Bramante, in the Alberini in Rome, in the Palladian Palazzo de Porti at Vicenza), and in the neo-classic architecture of the beginning of the nineteenth century; so also in the mural structure of the rotundas in the Baths of Diocletian, in the so-called tomb of S. Urbano on the Appian Way near Rome, in the theatre of Ferento, &c.

These relieving arches are used sometimes in the same massive mural structures for the purpose of locating its stresses at given points on to foundations sometimes interrupted and sometimes not. For instance, the whole exterior of the circular wall of the Pantheon is intersected by very large arches of this kind constructed in more than one row, and corresponding to the recesses and niches hollowed out in the mass of the wall. The *Templum divi Augusti* under the Palatine shows this same scheme in a form even more regular, but less logical, inasmuch as it lacks the constant relation of the arches to the empty spaces below; and presumably from that time onwards (that is, from the time of the Flavii) it became the normal procedure for Roman builders to subdivide the masses of the wall, to unite the facework securely with the heart of the wall in order to prevent its becoming detached, and finally, to preserve as a matter of routine elements which were almost useless, for example, in the buttresses of the so-called Temple of Minerva Medica in Rome.

With regard to relieving arches, this highly significant fact must not be forgotten—that often, in cases where the Greek architectural scheme of columns and epistyles was adopted, as it still was in merely useful, as well as in ornamental, porticoes (that is, in peripteral or pseudo-peripteral arrangement), the resistance of the architraves to deflection was assisted or replaced by platbands; these were either hidden in a strip of frieze, as in the Porta Maggiore and in the Forum of Trajan in Rome, or they formed the actual structure, with cuneiform voussoirs, of the architraves (themselves visible); this can be seen in the Temple of the Dioscuri in the Forum Romanum, in the famous Mausoleum of Capua, in the *Theatrum Maritimum* of Hadrian's Villa, in various porticoes at Pompeii, in the Porta Nigra of Treves, &c.; or again, they stood immediately above the trabeation, as in the colonnades inside the Pantheon, and in the Temple of Concord in Rome.

Vaults. The scheme of Roman vaulting for the spanning of large enclosed spaces is so important as to constitute the characteristic of the spatial building and architecture of the whole great period of the Empire.

The geometrical forms of these vaults were generally very simple; the barrel-vault, which Vitruvius calls ‘camera’, with semicircular arch, built over rectangular or circular spaces (porches of amphitheatres, tombs with a central pillar); the groined or cross vault, formed by the intersection of cylindrical vaults (which Vitruvius does not mention); the spherical vault or dome on a circular ground-plan.

But many other secondary types are derived from these main sources. The cloister-vault is uncommon, but can be seen in the Tabularium at Rome and in the almost pyramidal roofs of many tombs; the very fine entrance-pavilion of the Piazza d'Oro of Hadrian's Villa is also roofed with a lunetted cloister-vault. The groined vault or that interpenetrated by other cylindrical arches, was used in many cases in the very varied plans of the rooms in Hadrian's Villa, especially in the large and small baths, where the builders have performed wonderful feats of construction. But most interesting of all are the Bohemian-vaults and domical vaults, enclosing not circular but polygonal spaces, for these embryonic constructions have given rise to theories concerning the Roman origin of Byzantine building.

There are a few unimportant and imperfect examples of these, at Albano, at Chaqqa, at Tripoli, &c., in which the joining of the corners is effected by means of a triangular stone placed horizontally and out of the perpendicular. The following, however, are examples of the different solutions arrived at to reconcile the polygonal base with the surface of revolution—solutions which up till a short time ago were held to be completely foreign to Roman building.

The tomb near Rome called the 'Sedia del Diavolo', which has been studied by Durm and by Rivoira,[1] shows a complete example of a Bohemian vault on a square plan; another instance can now be added to this—a tomb near S. Stefano Rotondo, a drawing of which, by Topham, is among those preserved at Eton College and published by Ashby.[2] A real cupola on spherical consoles is found in a tomb of the second century on the Via Nomentana,[3] and forms a counterpart to the Oriental cupolas at Gerasa and on the Maeander in Asia Minor. A tomb of cut stone at Cassino shows in its magnificent construction the transition from the irregular octagon to the cupola, and there are even more complete solutions of the problem in an octagonal room in the Baths of Caracalla and on a decagonal plan in the Nymphaeum at Rome known as the Temple of Minerva Medica. The architectural form which

[1] Works quoted at the end of the chapter.

[2] Cf. T. Ashby in *Papers of the British School of Rome*, vol. viii.

[3] G. T. Rivoira, *Architettura Romana*, p. 193.

shows the transition from the square to the octagonal ground-plan can be detected in various examples (in the *domus Augustana* at the Palatine, in the villa of the Gordiani, &c.) by the use of niches in the wall at the corners ; and the Villa of Hadrian likewise provides instances of elementary trumpet-arches of conical form.

Already, therefore, in the forms of Roman building there is the germ of Byzantine principles on the one hand, on the other, of those which matured in the west, first at Ravenna, then in the Romanesque period.

The construction of Roman vaults in ashlar is exceptional, and is almost entirely limited to eastern countries, especially Syria, and to North Africa. The truly characteristic system, however—even more so than the system of wall-building—is that of concrete vaults, composed, that is, of cast material, placed in the form, given to it by the centering, of a complete semicircle : this material, when set, becomes actually equivalent to an artificial monolith, and this system, like that of the filling of walls, has its origin in the masses of earth of the tumuli.

In this system, which corresponds very closely to all the material and social conditions affecting the organization of Roman activities, is to be seen the precursory type of the structures in cement concrete (not reinforced), which are used so much in modern bridges. There are other points of comparison ; the advantages of economy and rapidity of construction ; the defects resulting from the necessity of a complex frame to sustain the immense weight, which changes its position and causes heavy lateral pressure on the piers ; defects resulting also from the dangers to stability either through the giving of the foundations which thus causes derangements which break the continuity of the mass, or through the sundering of the masonry owing to the inclemency of weather. Roman builders as they gained experience sought to overcome some of these obstacles by introducing a series of ingenious improvements into their work and their methods. But it must not be thought, as would appear from the somewhat imaginative treatise of Choisy, that these improvements were introduced systematically from year to year, so that each construction was more perfect than the last. On the contrary, there are types of very late vaulting which revert to the primitive method. The whole of the constructive architecture of the Romans, in this as in other branches, may be compared to a vast forge where many different experiments and tests are carried out, and where sometimes through a long period of failure the way is prepared for methods which are to bear fruit in later periods.

One of the most widespread of the expedients used was an attempt to get rid of the complex timber falsework, previously required as a continuous and complete centering and consisting of boards in a straight line with the falsework beneath the vault: these boards often left their imprint on the soffit, as if to preserve a record of the type of lined surface so often adopted. Then there was the system of the mould of bricks: a preliminary vault of large bricks placed edgewise, their sides joined with quick-setting cement (ordinary plaster or cement with plenty of lime), represented exactly the shape which the centering usually provided and upheld the concrete casting. The mould then remained adhering to the soffit in the mass of the masonry. The Baths of Caracalla and Hadrian's Villa afford fine examples of this arrangement; the examples in the houses at Ostia, on the other hand, are on a smaller scale; in these can sometimes be seen, still in place, a mould of this kind, but double, that is, reinforced, so as to be thoroughly safe in its resistance under great weight.

The intrinsic improvements in wall-building were sometimes concerned with the lightening of the mass. Terra-cotta crocks were then inserted into it, sometimes at random, as in the baths of Stabiae at Pompeii, in the Villa of the Gordiani on the Via Prenestina, and at the tomb of S. Elena (Tor Pignattara) near Rome; sometimes, on the other hand, in a thorough and regular manner, as in a bakehouse at Pompeii quoted by Overbeck [1] and by Mau,[2] and in North Africa at Tipasa [3] and at Aïn Tunga [4] in buildings of the third and fourth centuries. These are, it must not be forgotten, exceptional cases; but these ideas, carried on in more frequent and more important instances during the fourth and fifth centuries, were forerunners of the systematized methods—which really amount to a definite style—as used in Ravenna, in the Basilica Ursiana (370–96), in S. Agata, in the Baptistery of Neon (449–58), and in S. Vitale (526–47).

Fig. 60. Ribs in the cupola of the so-called Temple of Minerva Medica at Rome.

The introduction of brick arches into the mass of the masonry represents another innovation of a different kind, much more widespread than the chamber-system for lightening the weight. By this method the structure was subdivided into a resisting framework and a solid bulk of filled masonry; the framework was composed of ribs, placed, in the barrel-vault according to the main curves, in the groined vault according to the diagonals, in the domical vault according to the meridians. These ribs located the stresses of the masonry at a few points where the resistance of the piers was also concentrated. Important examples in Rome are at the Villa di Sette Bassi on the Latin Way, in the 'pulvinar' of Septimius Severus at the Palatine, in the Baths of Diocletian, in the so-called Temple of Minerva Medica (Fig. 60), in the

[1] Overbeck, *Pompei u. seine Bauten*, Leipzig, 1884.

[2] Mau, *Leben u. Kunst in Pompei*, Leipzig, 1900, p. 379.

[3] Cf. Gsell, in *Mélanges d'Arch. et d'Hist.*, 1894, p. 348.

[4] Cf. Carcopino in *Mélanges d'Arch. et d'Hist.*, 1907, p. 34.

arch of Janus Quadrifrons, &c.; but probably not in the Pantheon, where the real structure of the vaulting, from above the relieving arches in the interior attic-story, is not exactly known, but may perhaps (from some of Sangallo's drawings) have been simple and without ribs.

Here, then, is the great origin of the principle which in the later Middle Ages was to produce the ribs of Romanesque and Gothic vaulting, and it is not improbable that the survival of the tradition may have been due to the Lombard guilds which were distributed over the civilized world from the centres of late Roman culture in Northern Italy (one of which, Milan, now preserves nothing from ancient times but the church of S. Lorenzo).

But their importance and significance once established, we must not exaggerate, as Choisy has done, the importance of ribs in Roman vault-construction. Formed as these ribs were, not by massive brick arches, but by a species of hollow caissons between which the concrete casting penetrated, it is absurd to think that they could have been used before the introduction of these caissons, or that for them any part of the sustaining falsework could have been spared. Nothing is more obvious in them than a principle of canalization of the thrusts of the vault and possibly also a method of lightening the falsework itself, inasmuch as the arches, when closed, at once held in check the heavy dead weight of concrete, just as in pillars of reinforced concrete the steel rods at the corners hold in place and reinforce the mass of cement.

Certainly the organic, or more often pseudo-organic, expression of style in these ribs is shown by the external appearance of panels or lacunars in the soffit of the vault. Sometimes these panels were rhomboidal in form (the apse of the Temple of Venus and Roma, Temple at Baalbek, &c.) corresponding to an oblique interlacing of ribs: of this, even if there remain no actual monuments, we have reliable authority in Renaissance drawings by Giuliano Sangallo [1] and Guido Guidetti.[2]

The organic structure of the Roman vaulted building. All these elements, which have now been considered separately, are merely the parts of a great whole, manifestations of a single idea, a single energy; and in this lies the greatness of Rome. The Roman vaulted building achieved the perfect balance of all its parts, both as regards construction and design, in a planimetric arrangement which allowed the counter-balancing of the thrusts caused by heavy superstructures.

In internal enclosed spaces of a complicated nature, as for example in the building of baths, the equilibrium is chiefly based on the elimination of these thrusts by means of a mutual opposition of thrust on the inside walls. But the encircling wall of the building was supplemented by the addition of buttresses, which were sometimes external, as afterwards in the Gothic period, but were more commonly and characteristically internal.

These two general methods of solving the problem of resistance to thrusts had already been employed in simpler cases in smaller constructions for the supporting of earth or water. Frequently the outer walls in these buildings have projecting abutments, which are logically connected by arches on the horizontal, forming recesses (as in one wall of a villa near Frascati, and in a reservoir in the villa of the Gordiani on the Via Prenestina); cases are likewise common in which the mass of the wall was divided up on the inside by arches which connected radiating buttresses. In the mass-work of many tumuli (on the Via Appia and the Via Salaria), can be seen a regular star-shaped plan, which divides up the mass of earth and locates its thrusts on to separate points (Fig. 61).

[1] Cf. *Il libro di Giuliano da Sangallo*; Cod. Vat. lat. published by Hülsen.

[2] Cf. a drawing (1330) in the Uffizi Collection.

Not unlike are the foundation-plans of the theatre of Basle and of the Poecile of Hadrian's Villa.[1]

In the large public buildings all this acquires imposing character and architectural form. We need not discuss the simple types of external buttress which appear, for instance, in the theatre of Aosta and in the great precinct near Santa Costanza in Rome, but monuments like the round temple of Baalbek, the Augusteum, and the Nymphaea under the Claudium in Rome are worthy of attention, for in them the plan of a succession of recesses in the shape of *exedrae* exactly fulfilled the function of connecting the projecting buttresses in a perfectly logical manner (Fig. 69).

FIG. 61. Tomb on the Via Salaria (diameter 31 m.). Plan.

As has been said, the arrangement of interior buttresses was even more typical. Quite often the wall was not bounded on the inside by a simple vertical surface, but contained a whole rhythmic design of recesses and projections, caused by a succession of niches, which gave an aesthetic value to the architectural form, and constructionally increased the moment of inertia of the pier, by enlarging its base and forming sections of transversal wall between the niches.

The Temple of Venus and Roma, like the Temple of Diana at Nîmes (Fig. 62), and the Pantheon provide good examples of this arrangement, the first in conjunction with a rectangular building and a barrel-vault, the second with a circular building and a domical vault. In the Pantheon (Fig. 63) the outer wall is smooth and continuous; the total thickness amounts to about 7 m., but it is not actually solid, because recesses

[1] Miss Taylor has called my attention to an almost similar example in England in a tomb at West Mersey in Essex.

and niches are cut into it, alternately semicircular and rectangular, forming between them the interior buttresses.

Two important structural methods arise from the accentuation of this fundamental form.

One is that of a central hall flanked by transversal halls, which in their subdivisions have interior buttresses which support the roofing of the central hall. The *tepidarium* of

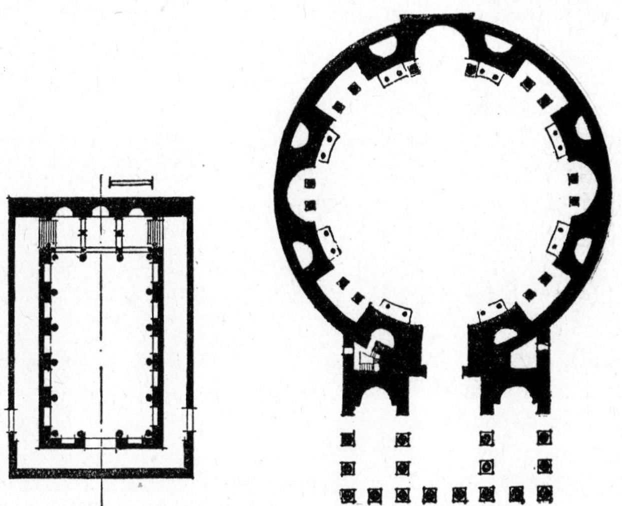

FIG. 62. Temple of Diana at Nîmes. FIG. 63. Pantheon.

the Baths of Caracalla, like that of the Baths of Trajan which no longer exist, affords a fine example of this method: the basilica of Maxentius (Fig. 67) not only carries it to proportions of extraordinary size, but also introduces another new element into the system of resistance. The great rectangular hall (about 25 m. wide and roofed by three cross vaults springing from supporting columns of over 18 m. in height) was flanked on each side by three large transversal enclosed spaces. But the necessity of raising the roof of the principal hall to allow of good illumination brought about the heightening of the transversal walls into diaphragms, which, rising above the level of the roofing of the wings, were continued upwards, so that from being internal buttresses in the ground-plan they became external buttresses above.

Here then is the complete principle of equilibrium as used in the Christian vaulted church. The mediaeval church is simply more fragile and lighter, having all its masses cut up and pierced and even the transverse walls opened up by the arcades of the side-aisles, just as at a later date the external abutment-diaphragms were to become flying buttresses. The complete stability of the basilica of Maxentius is seen again in its entirety in the churches of the Renaissance, especially in those erected during the great building period—the second half of the fifteenth century, after the Council of Trent. The church of the Gesù in Rome and all the innumerable other churches derived from it, which have side-chapels substituted for side-aisles face on to a single central space, and have large external consoles as continuations of the transversal walls, are the direct descendants of the halls of Roman baths and of Roman civil basilicas, not only in their constructional and architectural scheme, but also, it may be, in their scheme of decoration.

In the *tepidarium* of the Baths of Diocletian, a little earlier in date than the 'basilica nova' of Maxentius, the method adopted is even more complicated, since the transversal walls and the abutment-diaphragms join on to the large exterior towers and to the recesses between them (Fig. 68). The two typical constructional systems are thus interwoven in what is perhaps the most magnificent and the best-designed monument of ancient building (Fig. 64).

The other derivative of the structural designs of the Pantheon arose when the builders boldly transferred the recesses from the inside of the wall-mass to the outside, breaking the continuity of the inside line of the wall. Hence the pavilions of Hadrian's Villa, hence the central hall of the Baths of Constantine (Fig. 70) on the Quirinal, the great Triclinium of Trèves with its three apses, and, more important than all, the nymphaeum of the Horti Liciniani (Fig. 71), well known under the name of the Temple of Minerva Medica.[1] The points where the apses met (by a method complementary to that used, as already mentioned, in the small interior vaults of tumuli or in the niches in the walls of mausolea) formed the essential centres of resistance to the thrust located there by the main vault and by the arches placed in the perimeter.[2]

If we trace the connexion between these buildings and the early Byzantine churches of S. Vitale at Ravenna, S. Lorenzo at Milan, SS. Sergius and Bacchus and S. Sophia at Constantinople, the church of the Nativity at Bethlehem (through all the many intermediate buildings such as S. Costanza and Tor Pignattara in Rome, the tomb of Galla Placidia and the baptisteries of Ravenna, S. George at Salonika, the churches of Syria and Asia Minor) it is possible to reconstruct a long continuous chain which links the great Roman with the great Byzantine vault-construction. All the petty discussions about priority of date, all the theories (especially those connected with the name of a distinguished, but by prejudice anti-Roman, student, Strzygowski [3]), which, founded on monuments all of uncertain date and derivation, try to explain the origin of Byzantine architecture as an Oriental phenomenon produced in Asia Minor, in Persia, in Iran, in cycles which are

[1] Cf. G. Giovannoni, 'Il ninfeo della Villa Liciniana e le cupole romane', in *Annali della Soc. degl' Ingegneri e degli Architetti Italiani*, 1904.

[2] It may be of interest to note that there have been many derivatives in modern buildings from the structural design of the Nymphaeum of the Horti Liciniani; as, for example, in the great hall of the Sorbonne in Paris, and in the Exhibitions of Palermo and Breslau.

[3] Cf. J. Strzygowski, *Kleinasien*, &c., Leipzig, 1903; *Spalato*, &c., Freiburg, 1906; *Altai-Iran*, Leipzig, 1917; *Ursprung der christlichen Kunst*, Leipzig, 1920. For a clear treatise summarizing the Orientalist tendencies, but much more balanced and closer to the main conception, see Monneret de Villard, *L' Architettura Romana negli ultimi Secoli dell' Impero*, Milan, 1915.

connected with each other outside Rome,—these theories all fall to the ground in face of this other cycle, of Roman formation and derivation, or rather, it should be said, they all unite in a wider cycle. It is useless to attempt to confine in one single line of development a complex and manifold fact such as the evolution of a great constructional and architectural system, which may come into existence by various ways that yet finally re-unite. And to disconnect this development from Rome, from that great centre of organization, that vast constructive forge which assimilated and gave unity to all the different tendencies and then transmitted them to outlying points, to shut the eyes to this vast phenomenon which for four centuries maintained an unbroken tradition and an organic unity in the whole architecture of the Empire, and even in spite of the immense variety of free manifestations in the various provincial schools, formulated a style more compact, more creative, and more fertile in methods than any that had ever existed—this is not archaeology, but political science. Even if it were proved—which is still far off—that the palace of Chosroes I at Ctesiphon is built on the same scheme as the halls of Roman baths and is of earlier date than these, that the Asiatic tradition of cupolas was brought to Rome by eastern architects, that certain secondary schemes which were to be considerably developed later—such as arches on columns, or trumpet-arches supporting the cupolas of square-planned buildings—were derived from Persia, there must always remain the firmly established fact that Roman builders assimilated these elements in an embryonic state and then put them to their own calculated uses on a larger scale, in a continuous series of vast, complete monuments, all of which corresponded to a single idea and a single civilization, though developed differently by the different provincial schools; and it was inevitable that these monuments and these provincial schools should have derivatives in succeeding periods. It would be equally logical to deny the existence of the Latin language

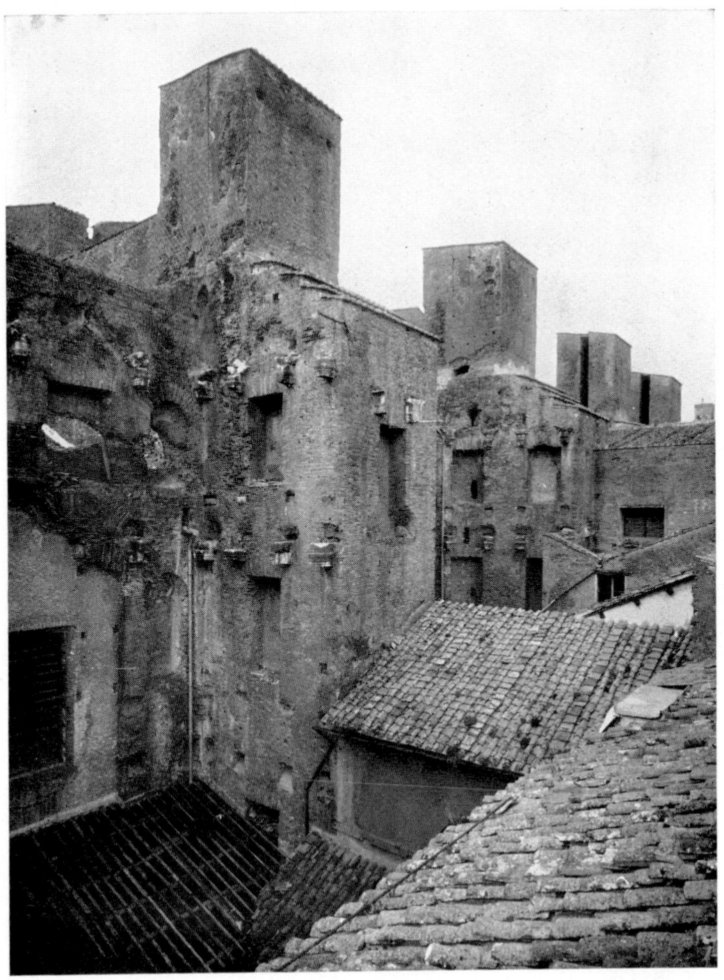

Fig. 64. WALLS OF THE BATHS OF DIOCLETIAN

Fig. 65. ROMAN BRIDGE AT MERIDA

Fig. 66. AQUEDUCT OF SEGOVIA

and its Romance descendants by asserting that its origins were eastern, and that certain terms were introduced into it from the Greek.

There is no need to spend time upon other accessory methods of construction. Thus, for example, among the many constructional schemes and experiments which the study of Roman civilization reveals, flying buttresses appear to be an exception. However, to claim these exceptional cases as the prototypes of those which appeared during the twelfth century at Vézelay, St. Denis, and Soissons, would also fall within the sphere of political science. In the main, the two great styles of vaulted architecture, the Roman and the Gothic, even if they have some ideas in common and have a certain relationship—inasmuch as the second derived by a long and indirect line certain experimental notions from the first—yet differ fundamentally, as has been shown, with regard to their directing principles. The one is the expression of permanent stability and of calm, sure equilibrium; it created monuments which have remained standing through centuries of almost complete neglect, and established in Italy a tradition which the Gothic style impaired only superficially. The other is an aspiration towards boldness and movement; it reduced the building to a skeleton whose resisting power is subjected to the strongest possible forces, and in dominating the factor of space disregarded the factor of time; so that if the delicate flying buttresses of the French and German cathedrals have endured to the present day in spite of weather conditions, it is due to the constant care of an unbroken period of civilization, which has seen to their preservation and timely restoration.

Such, then, are the main principles connected with the great wall-structures, the masses of which the Roman architects and builders controlled with such admirable skill—drawn, as Vitruvius says, *ex fabrica et ratiocinatione*. The different processes of building, the most usual working methods,

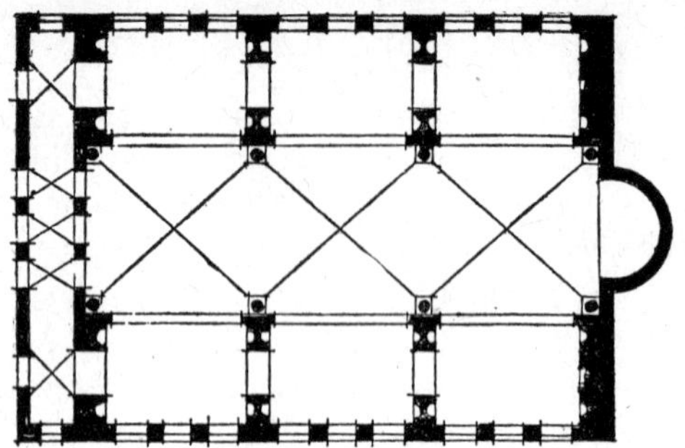

Fig. 67. Plan of the Basilica of Maxentius at Rome.

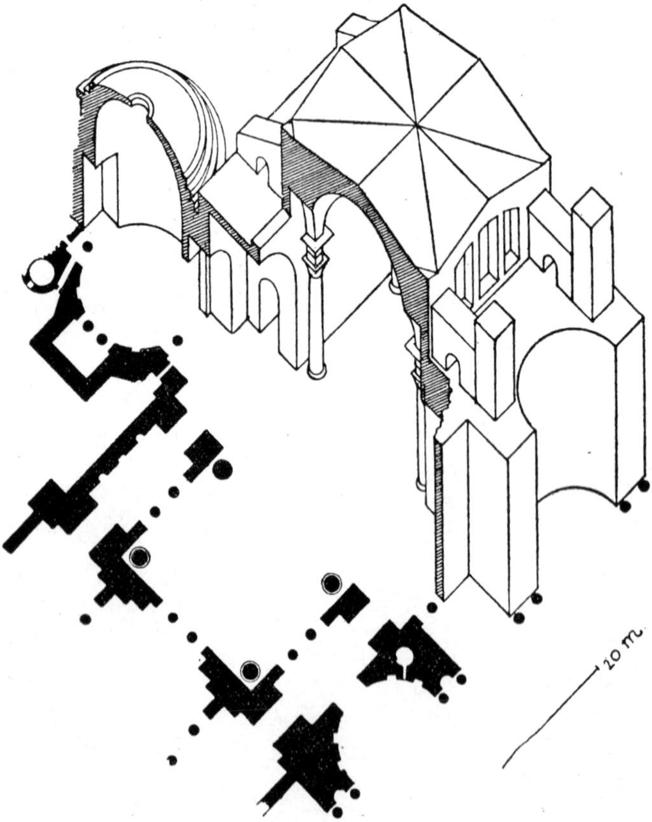

Fig. 68. Baths of Diocletian at Rome. Sectional reconstruction.

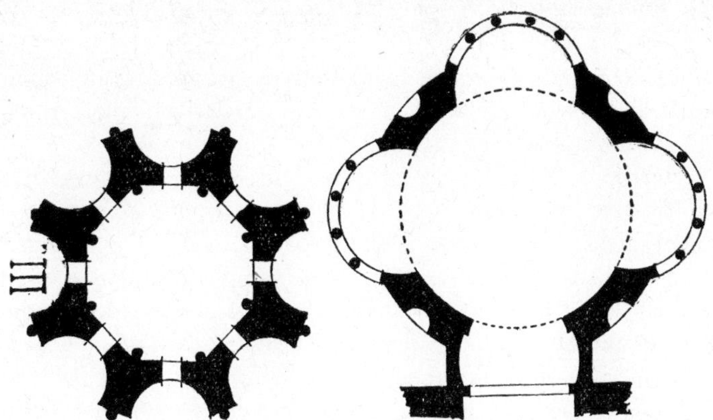

FIG. 69. Round temple near Rome (from a drawing by Sangallo).

FIG. 70. Central Hall of the Baths of Constantine at Rome.

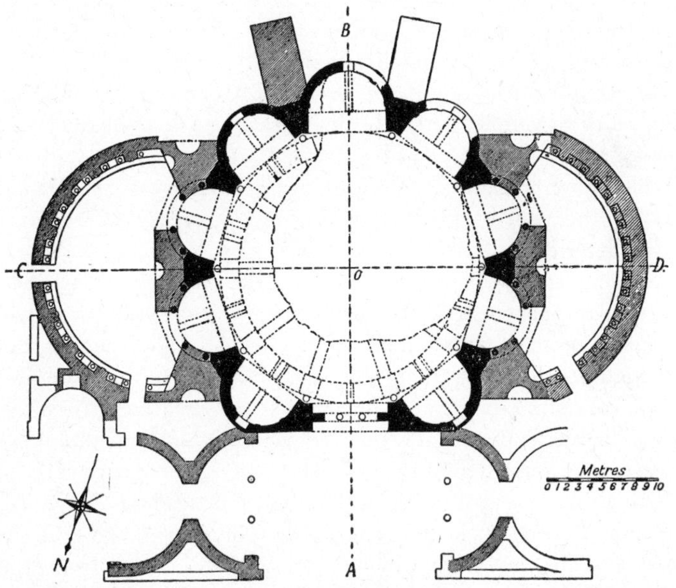

FIG. 71. Hall of the Horti Liciniani, known as the Temple of Minerva Medica at Rome.

and the organization of the workshops capable of accomplishing such an immense amount of work in a relatively short time, must also be considered.

On the whole the complex systems of construction were not unlike modern systems and methods (apart from recent mechanical inventions). The wooden scaffoldings, called *machinae*, used as temporary staging, were very similar to those still in use in Rome (the valuable evidence of the fresco in the hypogeum of Trebius Justus has been mentioned). Often, by some ingenious and remarkable arrangement, great inclined planes for bringing up and raising materials were formed in the structure itself, or sometimes the building was completed with great speed in its essential constructional lines and then finished off at each separate point by forming independent centres of operation—which is exactly what is done in American sky-scrapers built on metal frames.

Recent researches by the architect Cozzo in the Flavian amphitheatre in Rome[1] have shown that the slope of the *cavea* was first made on a complete framework of pillars and arches, which then remained enclosed in the masonry of the radial walls, and which served for raising the blocks of cut stone for the exterior galleries. It is not impossible that the great relieving arches of the walls of the Pantheon may have had a similar purpose, that is, to facilitate the completion of the roofing in the first rapid phase of the work, and then, in the second period, to complete the ballast covering of the structure.

A common arrangement is that of stones projecting from the masonry as supports for the temporary wooden scaffolding; these then remained in the finished fabric as decorative corbels. The Coliseum and various bridges and viaducts (e.g. the Ponte Cestio in Rome, the bridge of Narni, &c.) afford examples of this plan, which is sometimes exalted from the

[1] Cf. G. Cozzo, 'La costruzione dell' Anfiteatro Flavio', in *Rivista d'Architettura ed Arti decorative*, Rome, v. 1923. Fig. 72 is reproduced from this article.

merely constructional to the architectural, just as in a preceding period projections and recesses in the moulding of arches represented the stylization of the supporting arch-centering.

FIG. 72.

Clearly, even if all the decorative facework in slabs of marble was applied subsequently to the construction of the wall and formed a husk independent of the framework, the same is not true of the squares of cut stone which were solidly embedded in the essential part of the fabric and must therefore have been placed there at the same time. Sometimes haste must have compelled the placing of the blocks in position when they were barely hewn out, and they were then worked and finished off in position, but it is absurd to assert, as Choisy does, that this was the usual procedure in building.

There must have been many different kinds of apparatus for raising large blocks of stone, but they were almost all based on a system of pulleys with a multiple purchase, which Vitruvius classifies according to the number of parts on a single shear-legs, by the names of *trispastos*, *pentaspastos*, *polyspastos*. Sometimes they had real cranes, generally of a movable or travelling type, furnished with a tall vertical mast and derrick, multiple purchase pulley, and a large wheel or windlass. An interesting illustration of this is to be seen in a bas-relief in the Lateran Museum; it is complete in every detail, and is exactly comparable with the type of crane used up to the present day, especially in France, and minutely described by Rondelet in connexion with the construction of Ste. Geneviève in Paris.

These, then, are the essential characteristics of the most typical, the most important, and the most fully developed branch of Roman technical achievement—that is, the construction of walls (but without any specification of its various other elements in relation to special purposes). A brief review is now required of the principal activities of civil engineering, apart from building, that is, of bridges, roads, aqueducts, systems of drainage, &c.

Bridges and viaducts. Many fine bridges and viaducts still remain all over the Roman Empire. They sometimes consist of a simple succession of semicircular arches (as at Rome, at Rimini, at Narni, at Vaison, at Sommières), sometimes of a complex series of different kinds of arch, or of a direct superposition of arches on more than one level, as in the Pont du Gard, or again of continuous vertical piers with multiplex arches between them, as in the Spanish viaducts (Alcantara, Merida (Fig. 65), Termez, &c.).

It is interesting to note that the Romans, in spite of their mastery of arch-construction, preferred multiplying the intermediate piers to using a series of wide-spanned arches, which would subject the abutments of the bridge to heavy lateral pressure. And the way in which these great structures have lasted shows how completely the Romans solved the most difficult of the problems which faced them in this type of building—that of foundations under water.

The text of Vitruvius (Book V) shows how all the original ideas relative to such foundations were noted and made use of; there was the system of partitions with double walls of piling (*taleae et catenae*) forming a coffer-dam from which the water was drained by means of wheels, Persian-wheels (*noria*), or the *coclea* of Archimedes, and perhaps also by pumps [1]; sometimes a layer of lime was put down in the water, after the bottom had been excavated by means of a hand-dredge, the *rastillum*; or sometimes they had recourse to a layer of proper artificial parallelepiped blocks. Piling was also commonly used, either as foundation or for damming; it was placed at the bottom after the course of the water had been carefully deviated.[2]

Modern technique, therefore, has inherited everything from the Romans in this most important branch, as well as in the parallel branch of harbour-construction. It has then added to these systems new mechanical developments for drainage of water by means of pumps, for excavation by dredges, and, finally, for sinking caissons by compressed air; but it has followed the same principles as were used experimentally in the great and lasting works of the Romans.

[1] Vitruvius (x. 7) describes a double pump invented by Ctesibius; but it is not known if its use was common.

[2] The ruins of the harbour of Civitavecchia also show the system of caisson-foundations, filled with concrete and sunk in the sea by means of rafts.

Roads. A great network of roads stretched over all the provinces of the Empire, and constituted a most important means of communication and organization. Traced out chiefly for military purposes, they were made often in long straight lines, and encountered steep slopes. They were narrow (between 2·50 and 3 metres) but along the sides of the principal carriage-road ran two other roads; these were without artificial foundations and were for ordinary use.

The laying of the road-bed shows clearly the intention to render upkeep unnecessary by an initial construction of more than sufficient thickness and resisting power. Sometimes (as in the roads on the Rhine) roads were of the ballasted type (*glareatae*); these had a series of layers of substructure, partly of dry material, partly of concrete and gravel masonry, the total thickness varying between 0·80 and 1 metre. More often roads were paved (*stratae*), a most important example of this being the Appian Way: then also they had at least four layers, the *statumen* and the *rudus* composed of small stones put down with a little cement, the *nucleus* which was of real concrete, or sometimes contained chalk and compressed earth, the *summum dorsum*, which was actually the paving, formed of big blocks of basalt stone, 0·50 to 0·60 metres high, shaped polygonally and joined together in a similar manner to that already mentioned as used in walls of the polygonal or cyclopean type.

Remains of these great roads still exist throughout the whole Roman world. It is not without interest to observe how they may still serve as a model for many streets in modern cities. In these indeed, owing to the intensity of traffic and the violent shocks produced by the quick movement of heavy loads, systems of light paving, with the use of thin slabs, and small-sized products of stone and wood, have now become unsuitable. So it is necessary to return to ancient methods: substructures of great thickness, composed of layers of different materials (which for this reason do not form too rigid a mass), and paving with stones of great bulk and resisting power bound tightly together. The recent granite-paving of many streets in Milan does not differ much from the ancient roads except in the rectangular, instead of polygonal, shape of the stones; and it is not unlikely that before long in Rome there may be a return to the *summum dorsum* of lava from the volcanoes of Latium, similar to the *crusta* of the Via Sacra or the Via Triumphalis.

Aqueducts. Perhaps the most characteristic of all Roman structures are those built to carry water in large quantities to the cities for drinking purposes, for public and private baths, for ornamental use in nymphaea and fountains, and possibly also for land-irrigation and for country villas. Quite justly do Frontinus (*Com.* Tit. xvi)—curator of the waters in Rome under Nerva and a valuable technical authority on the subject[1]—and Pliny, in his *Natural History* (lib. xxxvi, ch. 24), affirm that no work in the world, however magnificent, can be compared to them. From long distances the waters of springs and rivers were collected and conveyed partly by subterranean tunnels, partly by channels supported on walls and arches, till they arrived at a reservoir (*castellum*), from which the distribution to the city began.

Apart from some exceptional cases to be mentioned later, the downflow of water was at that time controlled not by pressure but by an open channel, and this fact compelled the builders to avoid either an adverse slope in its course or an obstruction resulting from a too sudden change of gradient, inventing a remedy, if necessity arose, against any over-rapid change of speed, and also to keep the course of the water at a higher level than that of the distributing reservoir, by bringing it at the necessary height across the plains which surrounded the cities. Thus the line of an aqueduct was planned in much the same way as the line of a railway is studied

[1] Cf. R. Lanciani, *I Comentari di Frontino*, 1878–80; C. Herschel, *Frontinus and the Water Supply of Rome*, London, 1913.

nowadays, its course sometimes being considerably lengthened—as happened between Tivoli and Rome on the Marcian and Claudian aqueducts and the Anio Novus—so as not to exaggerate the gradient, mountains being negotiated by tunnels and valleys by large structures of masonry.

This was accomplished sometimes with great precision, sometimes, on the contrary, in a rather rough and ready fashion. In the aqueducts near Rome the gradients, which are generally maintained between 2 and 15 per thousand, sometimes descend in connecting sections to 1 or rise to 140 per thousand; [1] and the expedients mentioned above were often very primitive, as for instance that of making sharp angles to diminish velocity. There is no doubt that all this inaccuracy was due to the usual methods of levelling, by means of water and plumb-line,[2] and of measuring, by calculation of the content of a cup or pipe; [3] methods which gave exact results only when used with minute care, but were insufficient when used in haste.[4]

Certainly in the construction of aqueducts the Romans

[1] Cf. V. Reina, *Livellazione di antichi Acquidotti*, Rome, 1917; T. Ashby in *Papers of the British School of Rome*, 1900–15.

[2] The topographical instruments used by the Greeks and Romans were: the *groma*, a kind of set square; the *libra aquaria* (water-level); the *chorobates*, a level of large dimensions with a plumb-line; and the *dioptra*, a complex instrument corresponding to our theodolite. Vitruvius (viii. 5) seems to have faith only in the *chorobates*; and perhaps he is right, because the *dioptra*, an apparatus which is perfect in theory and seems admirable from its description by Heron of Alexandria, must have been a theoretical conception rather than a practical instrument, so complicated was its mechanical realization. Cf. de Montauzan, *La Science et l'Art de l'Ingénieur*, &c., Paris, 1909, and an article in *The Engineer*, 16 Dec. 1921.

[3] Cf. de Fenizio, *Sulla Portata degli antichi Aquedotti*, Rome, 1916. Here the *quinaria*, a unit of hydraulic measure, is exactly determined as having a discharge of 0·48 litres a second.

[4] Pliny cites an example of this insufficient accuracy in levelling, and Frontinus admits instances where the discharge differed considerably from predicted calculations.

showed themselves greater as builders than as experts in hydraulics. The tunnels cut out of the mountains are sometimes almost $2\frac{1}{2}$ kilometres in length, as for instance the one which goes from the lofty valley of the Liris towards the ancient Angitia; the masonry structures crossing the valleys were sometimes on as important a scale as large bridges, as in the aqueduct of Segovia (Fig. 66) and many others in Spain. The superposition of the channels of more than one aqueduct often lent them a particularly imposing appearance, as in the case of the Porta Maggiore in Rome.

The weak point of such structures lay in the fact that they were not permanently water-tight, because the *opus signinum* which covered the inside walls of the channel was liable to be damaged by any accident in construction or any disturbance of its stability. Unlike any other Roman building they therefore required continual repair and reconstruction; and the cessation of regular upkeep meant that they automatically ceased to work; so that mediaeval Rome, deprived of its former incredibly abundant water-supply of about 1,200,000 cubic metres a day, brought by its fourteen aqueducts, was compelled to make use of the yellow waters of the Tiber, round which its habitations clustered.

The system of pressure-conduits in vogue nowadays was not, as has been said, the ordinary system of the Romans, but was employed in some fairly important examples, either with the use of metal pipes (these were generally of lead, but sometimes of terra-cotta or wood, which were also used at that time for piping[1]); or again with pressure-conduits of masonry. Examples of the siphon-system and of adverse gradients in the transit of valleys, though not found in aqueducts near Rome (perhaps on account of their very large capacity) are quite common elsewhere, for instance at Termini Imerese, Caerwent,

[1] Cf. in the text of Palladius, lib. ix, ch. 11: '*Cum vero ducenda est aqua ducitur aut forma structili, aut plumbeis fistulis, aut canalibus ligneis, aut fictilibus tubis.*'

Aspendos. The above-mentioned aqueduct of Angitia and that of Lyons [1] are better examples: the first is completely in masonry, the walls covered with *opus signinum*, the second has a battery of leaden pipes. Choisy [2] has observed a special arrangement of openings in the conduit to avoid water-hammer and to form air-holes—a plan by which the water rises through a vertical column into a reservoir at its natural level, from which it again descends. He quotes examples at Pompeii and at Aspendos in Asia Minor.

The system of pressure-tubes was generally used, however, not so much in main aqueducts as in the distribution of the water from the reservoirs to which it was brought (of these there survives in Rome that of the Aqua Julia near the Porta S. Lorenzo, and in Sicily that of Termini [3]). A complicated system of leaden pipes, of cylindrical cisterns also of lead, worked by pressure or by unrestricted level, of embryonic taps, of subdivisions with doors, &c., of which many evidences are still preserved both in monuments and museums, and in drawings of Renaissance artists—all these permitted a regular flow of water to the many different places for which it was intended.

Reservoirs and dams. The reservoirs were directly connected with the aqueduct system. They were sometimes of enormous capacity, like the *Piscina mirabilis* of Bacoli, which covered an area of almost 2,000 square metres; or the immense reservoir built by Constantine at Byzantium, on the plan of which many Byzantine works of the same kind were modelled later; or the numerous cisterns constructed in Africa, at *Julia Caesarea*, at Malka, at Bordj, at Stora, &c. The plan of construction was simple and did not differ in idea from the straightforward and simple method employed in bridges and aqueducts: there were no large arches or ceiling-vaults, but the rectangular space was divided at regular intervals by partitions formed of

[1] Cf. G. de Montauzan, *Les Aqueducs antiques de Lyon*, Paris, Leroux.

[2] Choisy, *Histoire de l'Architecture*, vol. i.

[3] Cf. B. Romano, *L' Acquidotto Cornelio a Termini*, &c., Palermo, 1827.

a series of arcades, and between one partition and another there were barrel-vaults. Sometimes the divisions between the compartments were closed and communicated only by doors, perhaps to allow of the cleaning of each compartment in turn.

On the outside walls, which were directly subjected to the lateral pressure of the water when the reservoir was above ground-level, the same principles of resistance were adopted as have already been described in the case of earth-retaining walls and of the piers of vaulting. One very common method of construction included the use of external buttresses, often connected by horizontal arches forming recesses between them.

The inside of such reservoirs was covered with *opus signinum*, which found here, as Vitruvius observes (viii. 7), its most satisfactory use. He gives also in this connexion details of the composition of cement (*materia*) most suited for uniting with small pieces of stone and fragments of brick: two parts of lime to five of sand. Later, Faventinus prescribes a richer mixture, i. e. one part of lime to two of sand. The sand throughout Central Italy and often also in very distant parts was the substance known as pozzolana.

As regards the great water-retaining dams, that of Subiaco,[1] constructed at the same time as Nero's Villa, can be described. It consisted of a wall 14 metres thick, surmounted by a bridge of perhaps 40 metres in height, which formed a long lake going back about 2 km. into the valley. Its chief purpose was as an ornament for the villa; then in the time of Trajan the scheme of the *Anio Novus*, which had its *piscina limaria* here, was incorporated in it. The exact constructive methods of this great achievement are unknown to us, because it collapsed in A. D. 1305 and little remains of it; but certainly (since apparently it was not used for industrial purposes) it can be claimed to have been the prototype of all the great modern barrages.

[1] Cf. G. Giovannoni, *L'Architettura nei Monasteri Sublacensi*, Rome, 1904.

Drains and overflow channels. The Romans inherited their technique for the drainage of marsh-districts and lakes from the Etruscans, whose admirable systems are known to us (though very imperfectly), such as, for example, the system employed for the drainage of the swamps in the marshy district near Ansidonia; and probably for a long time it was Etruscan workmen who kept up the tradition. It was owing to the spread of this technical knowledge and the various precautions taken in the use of overflow ditches and subterranean channels (very common in the Roman campagna), owing also to big enterprises like the digging of the so-called Rio Martino as an overflow channel for the Pontine marshes, that the Tyrrhenian country districts were partially freed from marsh and malaria, and highly cultivated; and the water, collected and regulated, could sometimes be converted into a fruitful agent for this cultivation.

The *Cloaca Maxima* in Rome (Figs. 10, 13) belongs to this type of enterprise. It was constructed after the period of the Kings to drain and carry to the Tiber the waters of the valley where the Forum Romanum was built, and was afterwards, in the time of Augustus, modified and to a great extent reconstructed on a higher level, till it has become a proper sewage-channel, which in its tortuous course collects the waters which come from the Viminal, the Quirinal, the Capitol, the Palatine, and the Caelian hills.[1] It is interesting for its construction in ashlar, but even more so from the point of view of the history of hydraulics and town-drainage.

The drainage and regulation of lakes by overflow channels was the most important achievement in this branch of Roman engineering. The most famous example is the overflow channel of the Alban lake, constructed in a single year at the time of the taking of Veii. This channel is actually a tunnel with its sides covered with stone masonry, and it still works steadily for

[1] Cf. Hülsen in *Neue Jahrbücher für den klass. Altertum*, I, xiii. 1, Leipzig, 1904.

the purpose of regulating the waters of the lake and irrigating the fields of the surrounding country.

But the achievement which excels all others in size is the overflow channel of the Lago Fucino, carried out under Claudius to drain the basin of the lake and put it under cultivation. It consisted of a tunnel 5,600 metres in length and on an average 5 square metres in section (it is rectangular and surmounted by an arch), cut through ground which is partly rocky, partly of clay; it is therefore in part cut in the virgin rock, and in part lined with masonry, which had to be constructed for safety with a very strong bond between the layers. There can still be seen at Monte Salviano, which was also traversed by an overflow conduit, the great inclined shafts, used for descending to the bottom and for removing the excavated material; elsewhere, on the other hand, there must have been vertical shafts dividing up the course of the tunnel into short sections, to allow of excavation, and also to employ simultaneously the thirty thousand workmen who, according to the evidence of Suetonius and Tacitus, were at work there. It was exactly for this reason that the channel, before reaching its outlet in the valley of the Liris, was rather tortuous, passing under the level ground of the plains of Palentum to seek places where the shafts would be less deep: this would not be a rational method in modern drainage operations.

The overflow channel of Fucino, which turned out to be insufficient owing to the mistaken calculation of its capacity, and perhaps also owing to its faulty execution (it was an official undertaking of the Imperial government), lasted only a short time, then fell in and was closed; but it serves to indicate a power of initiative and a wealth of resources unparalleled till modern times.[1]

A work of an importance almost comparable with the

[1] Cf. Brisse, *Il Prosciugamento del Fucino*, Rome, 1883. Here are described the actual drainage operations and the function of the ancient overflow channel, the course of which was exactly followed in the new channel.

Fucino channel is the canal which was made about 272 B.C. by the consul Manius Curius Dentatus, to drain the plains of Rieti by carrying off the waters of the Velino, till they emptied themselves into the Nera, thereby creating the waterfall of the Marmore, which is about 200 metres high. The canal is about 1 km. in length and is partly cut in the rock; a point of interest about it is a vast lateral basin, which seems to have been enlarged by Piso in the time of Tiberius and was then called the Fossa Tiberiana. The object of this basin was evidently to draw off the waters of the Velino for short periods (perhaps two or three days) during the digging operations, or during operations of enlargement or repair, which we know to have been carried out more than once in the canal, and which occasioned lively discussions amongst the experts in hydraulics and bitter disputes between the inhabitants of the mountain and valley zones.[1]

Military architecture. The military architecture of the Romans, as indeed their strategy in general, was perhaps more manifest in offence than in defence. The great fortification-walls are, of course, not without importance—that of Rome, for instance, which was hastily constructed by Aurelian against the barbarian menace, and consists of curtain-walls with rectangular towers at intervals, with a patrol-path inside and a battlemented top. There are also isolated towers and ravelins, many examples of which are found in the provinces, and temporary enclosures, large palisaded entrenchments, of which, even if none remain, representations can be seen in the reliefs on Trajan's Column. But in these on the whole there is very little that is new, beyond what the Greeks had produced, of which the tower of Euryalus at Syracuse remains as a record.

In the great field-entrenchment works, on the other hand, and in siege manœuvres, those, for instance, mentioned in Caesar's *Commentaries*, the enormous scale of Roman organization is apparent. The whole army, transformed into a vast

[1] Cf. Degli Effetti, *Dei Borghi di Roma*, &c., Rome, 1675.

guild of labourers, was employed on towers of wood or masonry to reinforce the lines of circumvallation and contravallation, on engines of assault or helepoles, on the completion of great terraces, as much as 80 feet high, built to dominate the ramparts and to furnish the viaducts on which the helepoles were brought forward. They were controlled by the *praefectus fabrum* and organized in sections by maniples of experienced workmen, who were specialists akin to the engineers of to-day.[1] It is quite possibly here rather than in the free *collegia* of workmen that we may trace those centres of technical organization, in which the great constructive tradition was preserved and developed.

In this way the great conception of labour-control came to be an all-important means of conquest, just as in times of peace it was an essential factor in the construction of all the magnificent, practical, and soundly-designed buildings of Rome.

A study of Roman constructional technique and engineering-works should not rightly end at this point. Nothing has been said of their marine structures—harbours and light-houses—of all the buildings of a strictly practical nature, such as the *horrea*, of the timber structures, which include many fine bridges (of which those of Caesar on the Rhine and of Trajan on the Danube have remained famous), of the great advances in agriculture, the different decorative methods in bronze, terra-cotta, stucco, and encaustic, the control of a supply of river-water in houses, the excellent heating systems as seen in the Baths (the heat circulating in the intervals between the walls and floors), or of the application of mechanics and gnomonics, so closely connected, as can be seen from the treatise of Vitruvius, with practical architecture. This chapter only serves to indicate the necessity for a complete treatise, a Roman encyclopaedia, which, though badly needed, is still

[1] Cf. E. Rocchi, *Le Fonti storiche dell' Architettura militare*, Rome, 1908; G. de la Noé, *Principes de la Fortification antique*, vol. ii, Paris, Leroux.

lacking. It has only been possible to summarize the more salient characteristics of the organizing power of the Romans in the field of construction and of their vast and complicated technical knowledge, which needed only scientific precision to enable them to attain to modern perfection and adjust their experiments in hydraulics, mechanics, or the use of metals to their high standard of achievement in masonry-work. The superb remains that have survived owing to their structural stability are the evident and lasting proofs of the immense progress made by Roman civilization in the development and gradual conquest of technical and constructional means, and of the great tradition which it bequeathed to be taken up and variously amplified by succeeding generations.

GUSTAVO GIOVANNONI.

BOOKS RECOMMENDED.

On the subject dealt with in this essay see the general discussions in Rondelet, *L'Art de Bâtir*, Paris, 1820; Canina, *Architettura romana*, Rome, 1830; Lanciani, *Ancient Rome*, Boston, 1888; Parker, *Archaeology of Rome*, Oxford and London, 1874–83; Choisy, *L'Art de Bâtir chez les Romains*, Paris, 1873; Durm, *Baukunst der Römer*, in *Handb. der Arch.* ii. 2; Choisy, *Vitruve*, Paris, 1909; Rivoira, *Architettura romana*, Milan, 1921; Middleton, *Ancient Rome*, Edinburgh, 1885; Blümner, *Technologie und Terminologie der Gewerbe und Kunst bei den Griechen und Römern*, Leipzig, 1887; C. Merkel, *Die Ingenieurtechnik im Alterthum*, Berlin, 1899; A. Terquem, *La Science romaine*, &c., Paris, 1885; C. G. de Montauzan, *La Science et l'Art de l'Ingénieur aux premiers siècles de l'Empire*, Paris, 1909.

AGRICULTURE

The very name of Agriculture is full of suggestions. It is a record of mankind's advance to settlement from the ever shifting conditions of nomad life. It means that man has broken away from the roaming consumption of nature's bounty in the manner of other animals; that he has noted the steady operation of natural forces in the course of seasons, and is turning his human wits to employ those forces year by year for his own profit; that memory of past experience has given him skill, and taught him to face the future with growing confidence. It means that he has learnt to rely on his own labour, while supplementing it by that of any trusty helper; that he turns his cattle to account by inventing the plough, and generally procures his sustenance with greater certainty and ease.

If this step was taken while primitive conditions of conflict and insecurity rendered the individual unable to stand alone, and membership of some group was necessary for survival, we must not lay too much stress on the stage of common operation and common ownership by tribes or clans as depicted by ancient tradition or modern inference. For it is surely clear that a movement to settled tillage, however rudimentary, contained the germ of a movement towards individual responsibility and individual rights. In the long run the superiority of some individuals to others was certain to be manifest in this department as on the battle-field. That it would find some recognition, however tardily, was a mere matter of time. And such recognition, the reward of labour and skill, meant the eventual opening of economic possibilities to men of foresight and thrift. Then the invention of coined money multiplied the effect of these qualities, facilitating exchange and extending opportunities, as wealth could now be hoarded and was no longer represented solely by perishable goods such as live stock.[1] All through there was slowly developing the notion of Property, which gradually reached the stage of recognizing property in land. With this momentous step land took its place as a subject of economic exploitation, from which the most important consequences followed in due course. And nowhere are these consequences more clearly marked than in the history of Rome.

Whatever may have been the detailed steps by which the early Roman community made this advance, it is at least certain that property in land appears in tradition as recognized from the first. A few dim survivals serve to indicate the former system of gentile or communal tenures, but the normal condition is one of land held severally in lots of small size. Besides these there are stretches of common state land (*ager publicus*) used for the grazing of flocks and herds, and we hear of a small payment (*scriptura*) levied by the state for this privilege. Tradition firmly represents this use of common land as the subject of the most persistent and deep-seated troubles that beset the Roman state. While the Commons (*plebs*) strove to get a fair share of the privilege in order to keep the necessary live stock, the old citizens employed their superior political power under the existing constitution to promote their own interests. So the land-question appears as the great political question of early Rome. The Licinio-Sextian legislation of 367 B.C. necessarily combined restrictions of the right of user of the state pastures with concession of equal political power to the Commons. Only thus could the gain of equal rights over the state pastures be maintained in practice. This settled matters for a time. Henceforth the vital division in Rome was between the Rich and Poor. The old Nobility of birth (*patricii*) was gradually absorbed into a new Nobility

[1] *pecunia*, money, connected with *pecus*, live stock, the earlier unit of value.

of wealth and official rank. The scruples based on religion, in effect a claim that none but members of the ancient clans could lawfully bear office in the State, had been overcome, and internal differences more and more put on an economic character.

The great period of Roman expansion shows the change thus effected in full work. The planting of settlements (*coloniae*), in which each *colonus* received as his full property an allotment of land, was a means of appeasing land-hunger and at the same time of securing the hold of Rome on newly conquered districts. Whether new fortress-towns were founded as centres of districts, or old strongholds made seats of resident garrisons, the effect was to push forward the Roman frontier in charge of farmer-soldiers. In some parts no such fortified centre was established, but a district divided among a number of settlers, each with a farm of his own. As citizens of Rome liable to military service, all these Roman farmers could be trusted to bear arms in defence of the borders, and to send prompt news of impending raids to the government in Rome. But an even more remarkable feature of Roman advance in Italy is to be seen in the so-called Latin Colonies. Alliances with neighbours on terms favourable to Rome were an important part of Roman policy. Not only was this policy steadily pursued: it was further developed by the creation of new communities of Allies. It was indeed a momentous discovery, that mere crude conquest and annexation was not the only method by which a State could extend its power. Rome sent out large bodies of settlers, both her own citizens and others, to found new cities at points of strategic value and become citizens of these new cities. Each city had its proper territory, and the allotments of land to the new settlers were on a liberal scale. There was little likelihood of their coalescing with the old inhabitants of the district, who suffered by their intrusion and resented their presence. Relying on Rome for support, and bound to her service by the terms of their alliance, while enjoying freedom in their own internal government, they were more secure than they could have been in independent isolation, and were centres of Roman influence in peace and bases of Roman operation in war.

Into details of this systematic expansion we need not now enter. The point on which it is needful to insist is that it was a land movement, in which the plough was, to say the least, an instrument as powerful as the sword. Citizens or Allies, the spread of a population devoted to the interests of Rome was an occupation by farmers. And this is the soundest and surest of all forms of occupation, when the conquest of former holders is followed by conquest of the land. What we have to collect from fragmentary tradition is some notion of the character and conditions of agriculture in Italy during the period in which the country was brought under the control of Rome. This is not easy to do. Not only is tradition slight and capricious; it comes to us almost entirely from ages already conscious of degeneracy and prone to moralize on the glories of a golden past. We may accept the outlines of the picture without much attention to the deep shades of colouring.

Whatever advantage Rome had as compared with her immediate neighbours in being better situated for commerce—and this advantage was surely considerable—the farther she pushed on and occupied fresh country, the greater became the importance of agriculture as the backbone of the State. The well-being of this fundamental industry meant the power to keep what had been won and the opportunity of assimilating the conquered peoples. And it was this power to keep and the ability to assimilate that gave Rome her hold on Italy and enabled her afterwards to use the resources of Italy in union against a disunited world. The typical Roman citizen of full rights was a man with a landed property, a man 'settled on the soil' (*adsiduus*), whether actually residing there or not. Farmers in permanent residence were probably the great majority. It was characteristic of the Roman love of order that the art of land-surveying was early developed. Land-allotments laid out by measure on a strictly rectangular plan were the regular feature of 'colonies'. In the assignations of land to individuals (*viritim*) the same method was followed, perhaps with somewhat less regularity. Each allottee thus received ground for a homestead and a portion of arable soil. It was the practice to leave some space unallotted, as pasture-land for the live stock belonging to a particular group. There were also many odd pieces of irregular shape that had not been included in the rectangular lots. It can hardly be doubted that these were from the first turned to account in various ways by the owners of the adjoining land. Spaces for foot-paths and cart-tracks were provided in the survey. The lie of the ground would often make it necessary that access to one lot should be through another next to it, or that water from one should drain off through another. Such matters were recognized in some form, and eventually were the subject of an important chapter of Roman Law; but no doubt local custom, gradually hardening into rule, effectively solved most questions of the kind.

A great part of Italy, mountainous and wild, would not lend itself to this formal organization. Some of the upland country, held by poor rustic peoples, did not easily pass under the control of Rome; but in the end her centralized power prevailed against their loose cantonal systems. And the annexation of hilly districts meant the acquisition of wastes suitable for summer pastures. This enabled flocks and herds to be kept on a much larger scale by changing the grazing ground according to seasons, as is usual in Italy. The custom of keeping such lands as State-domain (*ager publicus*), and granting rights of use to lessees at a rent, still remained. But we do not hear so much of the rich unfairly engrossing these privileges, and of attempts of the poorer classes to secure their due share. That abuses still existed is fairly certain. But the large distributions of land in the course of conquest, and the much wider area over which they were scattered, seem to have made the claims of ordinary citizens less insistent or less numerous, at least for many years. And to small farmers who kept few beasts it could hardly have been worth while to send one or two cattle or a few sheep to distant grazing, which would only pay on a larger scale. We can guess that the farmer and his family relied chiefly on tillage of the soil for a living, and made the best use they could of the local woodlands and wastes.

There is no reason to regard such households as models of agricultural enterprise practising intensive cultivation with minute care and skill. On Roman homes, each ruled by the Head, the Father, with arbitrary power under the strict customary domestic law, and bound to strict observances of religious cults proper to each family and to any groups in which the family was included, there lay a moral burden of precedent. Local events, too, such as fairs, markets, and festivals, had their fixed dates and rules. Even the times of farming operations were often determined by ancient custom, sometimes it may be traditions of a primitive age of common husbandry. The tyranny of superstition died out very slowly in Italy. In short, we must conceive Italian agriculture in the period of Roman expansion as being laborious and unintelligent, no doubt learning something by experience, but mainly guided by mere precedent and rule of thumb. We must allow for some improvements in detail, due to contact with foreigners such as the Greeks of Sicily and southern Italy, with Etruscans and Phoenicians. But on the whole it was a domestic industry, concerned with the maintenance of families rather than with exploitation of natural resources for accumulation of surplus wealth. On this supposition we can understand what befel it in the next period.

When we speak of it as domestic, we must bear in mind that the family over which the Father ruled included others than those related to him by the tie of blood. The bondman and bondwoman, enslaved directly or indirectly through the fortune of war, were as yet not mere alien chattels. They were a part of the family, inferior and without legal rights, but still a part not unrecognized by the family religion. In these days they would be all or nearly all of Italian origin and well able to take the colour of the family circle as humble dependants. That they bore their full share of work is not to be doubted, and the work was normally farm-labour. But the slave could be set free, discharged from the power or 'hand' (*manu missus*) by his master, remaining as a customary dependant on favourable terms. That he could even become a citizen, and be his master's heir, proves that he was not regarded as a wholly debased creature tainted by the fact of servitude. So the labour-problem for the present generally solved itself on a household basis, whatever unhappy results may have followed in individual cases.

We must not, however, picture to ourselves the whole Roman dominions (and those of their Allies) in Italy as parcelled out in equal portions of arable land supplemented by portions of waste and woodland. Private property-rights implied power of sale, and it is not to be supposed that years went by without changes of ownership due to the success or failure of the various holders of land. Nor must we forget that an age of warfare is an age of accidents. The average Roman was ever a keen, grasping man, not given to neglect opportunities offered by fortune or the necessities of his neighbour. It is therefore highly probable that by the time when Rome had won the control of Italy there was already much inequality in the comparative size of landed estates. Tradition represents the development of great holdings (*latifundia*) in the next period as more sudden than it was in reality.

The crops raised would naturally vary a good deal according to differences of climate, situation, and soil. Of cereals, wheat and barley, also the chick-pea (*cicer*) and millet, seem to have been commonly grown, and the old-fashioned spelt (*far*) was still cultivated to some extent. The oat (*avena*) was not in favour. Vegetables[1] were of many kinds, and human diet mostly vegetarian. Of fruits, the fig was nearly everywhere, and apples and pears apparently plentiful. Hay was made for the cattle, but the leaves of some trees were in use for fodder and for litter, and the hay, perhaps small in quantity, eked out by the grazing on lands in stubble. Vines were grown and a rough wine made. The olive, introduced by Greeks, was probably now beginning to appear; but its general adoption as a leading feature of Italian farming belongs to a time when men of capital could afford to wait for slow and profitable returns. The appliances in use were few and simple. The farmstead (*villa*) was a simple house with its storehouses and stables according to the scale of the farm. The ox and the ass were needed for the labour on the land. The goat and cow gave milk, and the poultry supplied eggs. A rude cart or two served for the transport required. The plough seems to have undergone little improvement from the earliest days. Other tools were the spade (*pala*) and several of a different type combining in various degrees the characteristics[2] of a pick and a hoe. For on some soils and on steep slopes neither plough nor spade could be used with effect. There was the sickle (*falx*) for mowing, and the fork for many purposes. The axes, knives, and many other tools hardly need mention, but we must not forget the threshing-floor and the wine-press, or the inevitable dunghill. Among the differences caused by circumstances we may note the practice of irrigation (an immemorial art) in suitable places, and the keeping of swine chiefly near forests of oak and beech.

Rome, emerging from a period of internal strife, victorious in her early border wars, employed the century 366–265 B.C. in becoming mistress of Italy, and agriculture was apparently all the better for the advance of security and order. But times of great strain were at hand, bringing changes in the

[1] For instance, beans, lettuce, garlic, cabbages, nuts.

[2] *rastrum*, *ligo*, *sarculum*.

conditions of rustic life, changes that were destined to affect for evil the fortunes of the Roman State. Two matters need to be kept in view at this stage, not as striking changes already recorded in tradition, but in relation to what we hear of the sequel. In the course of conquest large areas of public domain-land were certainly acquired. According to custom, most of this would be let out to recognized occupants as grazing-land at a light rent. That this process received great extension in this period of expansion can hardly be doubted; and surely it was the larger landholders, in a position to keep live stock on a large scale, that chiefly profited thereby. That such an advantage favoured the formation of large landed properties, worked in combination with large state leaseholds, is no rash inference. That economy of labour resulted from this plan, and that the net return from such mixed farming on a large scale opened up a prospect of wealth, was an easy discovery. Another step was the delegation of management, suggested by the larger scale of operations, too large for direct personal control. In the next period, when we find a steward (*vilicus*), the normal manager of a *villa*, responsible to the landlord (*dominus*), we are surely not justified in supposing that this momentous change was a sudden revolution in rustic life rather than an extension of a system already beginning to appear. Rightly or wrongly, I believe that large farming and delegation of management are phenomena developed from small beginnings in isolated cases during the conquest of Italy.

How agriculture fared during the First Punic war (264–241 B.C.) we have no means of guessing. Italy provided good soldiers, but the clumsy war-machine was ill suited for warfare abroad. The final victory was won at sea, and the help of Greek naval allies, eager to be revenged on Carthage, had more to do with Roman success than Roman tradition would admit. After this war Rome took in hand a further expansion to the North, overthrew the troublesome Gauls of the Po country, and began to plant settlers in frontier districts and in colonies at important strategic points. But before things had time to settle down the invasion of Hannibal took place. For the space of seventeen years a great part of Italy, particularly the South, was wasted by war, the effects of which, even directly serious, were indirectly, through the remodelling of agriculture, an irresistible influence controlling all later Roman history.

A careful student of the second Punic war cannot but be struck by the appearance of capital operating in masses during the struggle. State contracts were indeed no new thing, but the equipment and feeding of the forces gave a new importance to this form of enterprise. An empty treasury and urgent need eventually placed the State at the mercy of capitalists. These gentry not only combined to make fraudulent profits at the State's expense, but (unless our record is wholly false) consented to let repayment of moneys due from the State be deferred, receiving security therefor in the form of public land held on beneficial lease at a nominal quit-rent. That they made a good bargain for their own pockets is manifest: patriotism had chosen a favourable moment for a remunerative venture. And the close of the war soon offered fine opportunities for wider speculation. Thousands of farms had been laid waste. Heads of families had fallen in battle: wives and children had sought refuge in Rome or other towns: many of the surviving men had lost the habits of rustic patience and toil in the excitements of military life. Above all, it was clear that the restoration of a derelict farm would be a long and painful process. It meant building up from the beginning all the establishment, the fruits of past labour and thrift, destroyed in the war. No wonder that men, lacking the free capital to make a fresh start and play a waiting game, often shrank from going back to their ruined holdings. So the land-market was glutted, and men with money bought farms cheap.

Nor was this in itself a sign of revolutionary change. That the rich should buy land and form large estates was not a matter for public dislike or surprise. In 218 B.C., at the very beginning of the war, the commercial opportunities of Roman senators had been restricted by statute; but this only tended to make them invest more of their fortunes in land. What was new was the effect of more direct contact with systems of agriculture (particularly the Carthaginian) in which a more scientific farming prevailed, and by which speculators in land made it a regular source of industrial profit. Now, the more highly organized the system, the more it must depend on the exact co-operation of labour and skill. Skilful direction needed a certain supply of toiling hands to give it full effect: and this brings us to the age of overseers and slave-gangs.

Slavery was a time-honoured institution in the ancient world, but on a small scale it could exist without any great disturbance of economic conditions. The employment of slaves in the mass as so much brute force to be turned from task to task at an owner's will was, wherever practised, a rough attempt to do what nowadays we do by machinery. A human chattel followed the precedent of the ox and the ass, and the profits of his labour belonged to his master. We must not confuse him with the serfs who tilled the soil in some Greek states. He was not bound to the soil, rendering certain dues as a subject to his conqueror. He could be moved anywhere and sold to any one at the will of his lord. He stood above the brute beast in his human power of understanding the motive of punishment and seeking to escape it; and through this capacity could be converted into a mere labour-unit such as the new economic system required. It was also possible to influence him to some small extent by prospects of reward: but these would generally consist of little privileges not to the advantage of other slaves, or even to their disadvantage. For instance, promotion to be an overseer meant that the promoted 'hand' had to keep his position by ruthless slave-driving. And naturally enough the landlord did not adopt the system of slave-gang labour with the intention of burdening himself with the incessant worry of resident direction. The rise of Rome was rendering political life more engrossing, not to say more profitable. Therefore the aim of the wealthy Roman was to remain at the centre of power for the sake of his ambitions, drawing an income from his estates, and doing their management by deputy. The beginnings of corruption in politics made money necessary, and the use of money further corrupted politics. So the resident steward became a characteristic figure of Italian agriculture, and it was soon found convenient that he should be a slave, even if he was not (as is probable) a slave from the first.

Here we have a system of agriculture openly designed for the production of surplus profit, profit to be absorbed and used for his own purposes by the owner, owner not only of the land but of all the live and dead stock thereon, including the whole staff of human slaves. More and more the arable lands were put together in huge estates by the acquisition of derelict farms, and a series of wars provided a supply of slaves. That the early stages of the movement were wasteful and cruel is only too probable, particularly if, as seems to have been the case, the production of cereal crops for market was at first attempted on a large scale. Importation of corn from abroad to satisfy the urban demands soon began to divert Italian agriculture into more profitable channels. But the culture of the vine and the olive could also be undertaken on a large scale, and came to fill the leading place in Italian farming. Some however of the processes necessary for the production of wine and oil called for more care and intelligence than ordinary slaves could be trusted to show. It seems therefore that the employment of hired men (*mercennarii*) did not wholly cease. They were often employed in gangs under responsible gangers (*mancipes*), for instance, in the gathering of olives (the *leguli*) or in the more delicate operations of the vintage. Payment might be in cash, or in shares of produce (the contract *partiario*), and the relation was duly recognized by the law.

But the employment of free men for special operations did not supersede the responsibility of the slave steward: he had the general direction of labour, slave or free.

Side by side with tillage was the stock-farming. It seems to have been still on the increase, for the much smaller amount of labour required made it very profitable. It could be conducted on a very large scale, indeed more easily than on a small one. Moreover it suited the slave-owner. The work was light compared with labour on arable land; and for a great part of the year the *pastores*, tending flocks and herds on the hills, were left pretty much to their own devices. This free life made slaves fairly contented with their lot, and minimized the difficulties of control. The chief herdsmen and shepherds would not wish to be transferred to heavy labour on the farm, and the work called for few subordinate slaves, being largely performed by dogs. The pastoral staff consisted of strong, hardy men, kept in fine condition by life in the open. For dealing with wolves and robbers they were armed at least with a spear. But they were in effect responsible for their conduct to none but their owner, and he cared little for any wrong they might do to others. No wonder that, having no rights of their own, they became regardless of those of strangers, that they pilfered from farms within reach, and robbed travellers; and that in no long time the pastoral service became a school of brigandage. Thus in the course of some fifty years (200–150 B.C.) the new system changed the face of a great part of the most eligible districts. Huge estates swallowed up little farms, and slaves were dislodging free rustics from the countryside. Only in some highland regions, lying off the main lines of traffic, there still flourished a native peasantry industrious and brave, the salt of Italy.

The period which saw Rome become supreme in the Mediterranean world is one in which we get a clearer light on the conditions of agriculture through the evidence of Cato, a Roman of strongly-marked type, a practical farmer (among many various activities), warm in likes and dislikes, who laid down the law with a self-confidence that makes us think of our own William Cobbett. The chief importance of his book *De agricultura* for us lies in its attitude towards the land-question of his day. Though a stern reformer in public life, a champion of old Roman simplicity and thrift against the new school of politicians growing up under Greek influences, Cato seems to have taken the agricultural situation as he found it, and not to have aimed at impracticable reaction towards the vanished past. He treats of an estate on a considerable scale, but still of manageable size. While it comprises all departments of rustic enterprise, the culture of the vine (on 100 *iugera* = about 62½ acres) and the olive (240 *iugera* = about 150 acres) receive special attention. But he was well aware that a good net profit was in general most surely derived from the pastoral side of husbandry. The point on which he insists most strongly throughout is the avoidance of waste, and the need of the master's watchful eye to enforce economy. Evidently he saw that, while landlords desired the highest possible returns from their estates, they were too indolent or too preoccupied to give the necessary personal attention to their economic interests. The slave steward (*vilicus*) was chiefly concerned to see that his master did not expect too large a return from the estate, since any falling off in a bad season was likely to involve his own punishment. The interest of the staff was to minimize labour. We may be sure that under such conditions the land did not produce crops up to the full standard of its fertility. The precepts of Cato clearly show that by unremitting and skilful vigilance a landlord could exact a satisfactory return from his estate. But this was an ideal probably seldom realized; and the advice of Cato was addressed to a generation that needed it. The average landlord, suffering in pocket through his own slackness or incompetence, was more likely to flog or degrade his steward than to direct the management with patient efficiency himself. Cato was a man of quite exceptional energy and knowledge, and must be regarded as one rebuking his contemporaries rather than representing them.

Yet, for all his devotion to the welfare of the landed interest, Cato seems to have been under no delusion as to the difficulty of wringing a good and steady income out of agriculture. He himself engaged in many various enterprises slightly or not at all connected with land-farming. But he loved the land, and took pride in a farmer's life, to him the best of any: a Roman of Romans, to him the Roman farmer-citizen seemed the highest of human types. Yet he accepted the new development of slavery, which was destined to be the ruin of a vast number of Roman farmers. Nowhere will you find the treatment of slaves prescribed in a more callous spirit than in the precepts of this Good Old Roman. Fed and worked on the same principles as the ox, the slave, like the ox, is to be sold for what he will fetch, when he can no longer be worked to profit on the farm. In truth the system described by Cato is one based on the utter ignoring of human rights as such. It is derived from the rule of force as applied by man to man in primaeval struggles for existence: its inhumanity is so striking because it is combined with a positive and rigid view of the sacredness of a free citizen's property in material things. A man so much the child of the past could not look forward to the future and forecast the evils to come.

It was therefore to little purpose in the long run that he gave instructions in detail for all the working of an estate. How to buy and sell (particularly to sell), under what conditions of season and weather to engage in this or that operation, how to turn every moment of time to account, in particular how to find useful occupation [1] for hands in the winter months, how to keep the staff in health and regulate their rations in proportion to the labour exacted at a given time—these and many other precepts were well enough in their way. But they were

[1] A good instance is basket-work with osiers grown on the farm. Flax and reeds were also turned to account, and women spun and wove wool.

merely making the best of a bad system: the economic fallacy of slavery remained.

In the absence of statistical records we have to grope our way very carefully if we want to form a notion of rural Italy during the period 200–146 B.C. The course of foreign policy was affecting it profoundly all the time. Of the three main theatres of war, each was producing peculiar results at home. In the East, the overthrow of great monarchies and the ruin of Greek Federations opened up countries of old civilization and accumulated wealth. Military service offered chances of plunder, demoralizing the soldiers, while capitalists soon discerned possibilities of gainful enterprise. In the West, Spain had to be held, that it might not again fall into the hands of a revived Carthage. But piecemeal warfare against rude tribes was unprofitable and the losses enormous. Rome took to laying the burden of this blood-tax chiefly on the contingents of her Allies, thus creating a discontent which had serious consequences at a later day. In the North, the conquest of the Po country was now really carried out and followed by effective occupation. The Gaulish tribes were driven out or absorbed by a great Italian immigration. No doubt many dispossessed or disheartened Roman and Italian farmers found a new home in these rich lands. Strong fortress-colonies secured the control of Rome; and the Province of Cisalpine Gaul, not officially a part of Italy, soon became in fact the most prosperous agricultural region of the whole peninsula. No doubt estates there varied in size, but it seems certain that the management of land remained on a sounder footing than the new-fashioned system prevalent in the richest parts of Italy proper. Productive farms, thriving towns, and a growing population, made this district the best surviving nursery of Roman strength.

But wherever there were wars there were captives, and the slave-market was full. The slaves were of very various quality. In particular, the hellenized East supplied, besides mere labourers, not a few skilled men versed in agricultural arts, accustomed to methodical industry. Supple and cunning, such men were able to combine servile obedience with deceit not easily detected. As stewards, they were on the face of it invaluable to landlords who desired to enjoy a great social position and a good income without distraction from the calls of public life. But, as I have hinted above, the interest of the slave was to prevent his owner from expecting too rich a return from his estate. It is, I think, beyond all doubt that these stewards generally kept down the productiveness of estates, and that in their hands agriculture quietly declined. The custom was spreading of 'improving' the *villa*, making it into a 'country-house' rather than a plain farmstead, a place at which the great landlord might stay in comfort and entertain fashionable friends. This movement played into the hands of stewards, furnishing excuses for sundry shortcomings. In the course of the second century B.C. this fashion carried all before it, and parks and mansions became the bane of Italy. The system rested on no foundation of native Italian economy. It was only the money exacted, officially or unofficially, from the subjects abroad that kept it going. What with the nobles who went out to govern the Provinces and made fortunes by blackmailing the natives, what with the capitalists who farmed revenues and squeezed the people iniquitously, the world was being cruelly exploited to maintain an unwholesome magnificence in Italy.

The years following the destruction of Carthage in 146 B.C. present a blood-stained record. New Provinces were acquired, and old ones reduced to passive order. A terrible invasion of northern barbarians was successfully defeated, and a firm foothold gained in Gaul beyond the Alps. Spain was at last really conquered, and northern Italy (Cisalpine Gaul) secured by the subjection of the Ligurian hill-men in a series of petty campaigns. The power of Rome was asserted against Jugurtha in Africa and Mithradates in Greece and Asia Minor. Externally the great Republic seemed to have put down her rivals. But her inner unsoundness was all the while being demonstrated by repeated evidences of incapacity. The real government rested with the Senate, now a clique of selfish nobles greedily absorbing the perquisites of office: public opinion was impotent, for the constitution worked in such a way as to defeat all popular movements of reform. Wars waged by armies of discontented troops under incompetent commanders normally began with disasters and ended without glory. The levies of citizen soldiers had to be made from a class declining in numbers, and Marius saved the military situation only by the enlistment of landless men who volunteered for service in hope of loot. In short, the army was becoming professional rather than patriotic, serving a successful general rather than the State. To raise an army was easier than to disband it. Money pensions being unknown, the discharged soldier clamoured for an allotment of land; that he meant to spend his later years in unremitting bodily toil is most unlikely. Meanwhile the captives, of whom the spoils of war largely consisted, were passing through the slave-market on to the great estates of the rich, and the slave-gang system was tightening its grip upon the land. To compete with the great estates by slave-husbandry on a small scale was probably quite impossible. Yet the large-scale husbandry was wasteful and full of horrors, and attempts to solve the land-problem were notable phenomena of the period.

The occurrence of two bloody wars with revolted slaves in the Province of Sicily, where the system of *latifundia* (chiefly for cereal crops) had reached an extreme development, sufficiently exposed the danger to which the abominations of that system had brought the Roman State. The risings were at last crushed by military force after appalling destruction of life and property, but then the system resumed its course. The beginning of the first rising may date from 139 B.C., the suppression of the second was completed in 99. In the space of these forty years fall the attempts of the Gracchi (133 and

123–122 B.C.) to put back a free Roman farmer-population on Italian land, and (more striking still) the reaction which recorded their failure. The battle-ground of land reform was inevitably the question of the individual tenures of public land. It was true that the legal property of the State had not been extinguished by the recognized occupation (*possessio*) of individuals. But the laxity of the government and connivance of officials had in the course of many years allowed *possessores* to make changes and combinations for their several convenience. So complicated was now the tangle of legal rights and equitable interests, that to unravel it without hardship inflicted on some persons was impossible. The Gracchi failed and fell, because there existed no political means of carrying out a reform-policy in a succession of continuous years. Their work was undone, the lands allotted to the needy passed back by sale into the hands of waiting capitalists, but with a difference. What had been left to the great landholders had been left to them as private property, not as leasehold from the State, and the portions now reacquired followed this precedent. So lands that had before been merely 'possessed' were now owned by the great private landlords, and the State had renounced its legal claim to resume them.

Unhappily we have no sufficient means of testing the genuineness of the land-hunger that the reformers endeavoured to satisfy. It seems certain that they wanted to regenerate rural Italy. But, of those who were willing to accept offered allotments, how many were seriously prepared to cultivate them patiently and thriftily for the rest of their lives? And how many had the means of stocking even a small farm? We do know that the government had for some time been driven to pacify the urban poor by providing them with corn below cost price, and that a Roman mob now existed, half pauperized and wholly untrustworthy. A statesman was compelled to court it—sometimes to his ruin. It is not likely that many sturdy farmers could be drawn from this source. It may be that some of the remaining landless rustics were allottees under the Gracchan scheme, but we have no special ground for thinking so, or for believing them to have been a numerous class. And, urban or rustic, we cannot now appraise the difficulties to be faced by men trying to make a fresh start on land probably in the rough and not of the best arable quality. An attempt was made to find them tools and stock for the venture, by appropriating to this purpose a windfall that came to the State treasury; but we know no details, not even whether the proposal took effect at all. How many men in all received allotments we do not really know; still less, how many of the recipients really became working farmers. Whether it was that impracticable designs were doomed to fail, or that a wise and practicable reform was thwarted by the arts of a selfish nobility, or that some middle verdict is the true one, it is at least clear that Italian agriculture was not restored to health by the efforts of the Gracchi.

The years following the Gracchan movement were full of internal troubles. The Italian Allies were smarting under the continued refusal of the Roman franchise. In 90–89 came the great rebellion, and Rome had to fight for existence. After two years of fierce and destructive war the desired concession had to be made, but the complete merging of Italy in the Roman State was only achieved after further years of civil war marked by frightful bloodshed and devastation. That agriculture suffered is obvious; but it is most important to note that it was now assailed by a new and portentous evil. The victory of Sulla left him with two pressing tasks. He had to destroy or reduce to impotence the party opposed to him. This he effected for the time by massacres and proscriptions, and by remodelling the constitution so as to bestow on the senatorial nobility, in the form of legal power, that virtual control of government of which recent upheavals had deprived them. But he had also to satisfy the claims of his supporters, both his soldiers and the miscellaneous partisans and minions who had helped him on to victory. This he effected by wholesale confiscations. Communities as well as private individuals suffered. Informers and spies were rewarded, and in a scene of betrayals and murders much of the best land in Italy was made available for transfer to new owners. These new owners were often disbanded soldiers who had little qualification for patient and intelligent farming, whose aim was not labour but ease, and who were doubtless unused to respecting the rights of others. As farmers they were a notorious failure, and the impending troubles of Rome and Italy were very largely due to the presence of this element among the population, enraging those whom they dispossessed, and discontented themselves. The grants to the victor's favourites were as mischievous in their own way. The favoured took their chance while it lasted ; that is, while the fear of Sulla gave his partisans the control of the market ; and bought up valuable properties for a trifle. That the prevailing uncertainty of tenure, and the well-founded dread of appearing to have money, were a check upon the useful employment of capital, is beyond doubt. The Sullan reaction, forcible and unenlightened, was an agricultural disaster. But here, as ever, we can only speak of its effects in general terms, owing to the absence of statistics.

There are, however, certain matters on which our capricious record now and then throws light and indirectly gives us hints on the rustic situation. Piracy in the Mediterranean was no new thing. The maritime republic of Rhodes had earned general gratitude by repressing it: but ever since 167 B.C., when the Roman government weakened and humiliated Rhodes, this evil had been growing worse than ever. Its most remunerative branch was the capture of slaves for the great market at Delos, where there was an unfailing demand. Kidnapping on land supplemented captures at sea. Roman capitalists, buying to sell in Italy or Sicily, were deeply interested in the trade, and the fruit of their operations had been painfully evident in the Sicilian slave-wars. In Italy the public security

Fig. 74. VIRGIL'S FARM, conjectural site between the Carpenedolo ridge and the river Chiese five miles from Calvisano

Fig. 75. VIRGIL'S FARM. The Lower Alps seen from Calvisano

and the Provincial governors, they throve at the expense of the subject peoples. Thus no small percentage of the active and enterprising elements of Italian population were scattered over the Roman Empire, and became men of importance, leaving Italy to the parks and fishponds of the nobles.

It is to be wished that we were in a position to describe fully and vividly the surroundings of a Roman *villa* and the life of its inhabitants. But to attempt such a picture is hardly possible with due regard to truth. The establishments referred to under the title of *villae* varied infinitely in type, from the rural seats of rich men scattered over Italy in pleasant spots, and the seaside villas planted on such lovely shores as the bay of Naples, to the farms worked for profit in less attractive districts, the smaller holdings on mountain slopes, and those of the genuine free working farmers still surviving in the highlands. Every type, not to say every *villa*, had its special characteristics. These characteristics, if we only had statistical detail, might be described at length, not unprofitably. But to piece together casual references in poets such as Horace, Tibullus, Ovid, or Virgil, and construct a picture of the average *villa* out of these materials, would surely be misleading. Nor do the technical writers help us much. Their business was to suggest what ought to be done or left undone; not to record existing conditions, to which they of course refer, but only as serving to confirm or illustrate their argument. This is not a statistical bottom on which we can build. From it we may draw many significant inferences, but from such inferences we can hardly compose a picture that would be at once instructive and true.

The presence of *vernae*, young slaves born on the estate, is a good instance of our difficulties. That they were to be found on most farms is fairly certain; and they seem in general to have been kindly treated in their childhood. The mere fact of their existence suggests a sympathetic treatment of the adult slaves. But that they were, when grown up, the objects of any special consideration is hardly to be affirmed on existing evidence. Their condition must have varied greatly on various estates, and the pretty scenes of gambolling children find a natural but rather unconvincing place in the works of idealizing poets. A more trustworthy detail of rustic life is found in the observance of rural festivals, at which all, slave or free, made holiday. But this was rather a palliation than a remedy of the forced-labour system. Most striking was the difficulty of keeping a due proportion between the residential *villa* and the landed estate (*fundus*) worked as a farm. This problem exercised the writers on *res rustica*, mainly because of the growing tendency to make the residence a luxurious country seat. But this difficulty was mainly confined to choice localities: in remote or dreary surroundings the *villa* proper was apt to be neglected, and the landlord deterred from needful visits to his property by the fear of personal discomfort. One significant feature of the country life was the need of keeping on good terms with the neighbouring owners. Cordial relations meant mutual accommodation, such as the loan of auxiliary labour at a pinch. Hostility could take effect in various ways, such as damage to crops or live stock; a landlord had in his slaves a force not unwilling to exchange field-labour for raiding, sometimes even under arms. For such outrages there were legal remedies: but redress procured by hard swearing and the eloquence of counsel could not disguise the wastefulness of misdirected energy or restore neighbourly feeling. It is not for nothing that questions of boundaries, rights of way, &c., occupy an important place in Roman Law. After all, the best security against molestation was to be known as a man of private resources and political influence, a neighbour, in short, whom it was not expedient to offend.

Another movement of not less consequence than the tendency to seek a living abroad seems now to have been in progress. No doubt landlords had from early times occasionally let lands to tenant farmers. There is no reason to think that this had been a common practice. There is reason to think that the position of such tenants was a weak and dependent one. In a contract between rich and poor, the former was better able to insist on terms favourable to his own interest, and the strict enforcement of bargains was a marked feature of Roman Law. A change in the connotation of the term *colonus* (' cultivator ', often implying praise) was giving it the sense of ' cultivator of another's land ', contrasting it with *dominus*, the proprietor. Varro, Cicero, Caesar, all recognize the farm-tenant as a rustic figure, but either without any special implication or as a social and economic inferior. How far the relation of tenancy was becoming commoner in rural life may be difficult to judge. Its prevalence in a later period, rivalling the system of steward and slave-staff, rather suggests that it was coming into vogue in the last age of the Republic. We hear of a landlord calling out his *coloni* as armed retainers in the great civil war. As to labour, Varro advises the employment of hired freemen for duties requiring intelligence or entailing risk of malarial infection. But it appears that free wage-earners were chiefly, if not wholly, itinerant gangs from the highland districts, who went back home with their wages. Slave labour was still the normal equipment of the farm, great or small.

When the civil wars were over, and the ruler of armies became the real master of the Roman world, one of his cares was to revive agriculture. But in Italy the renewal of wholesale confiscations, to provide lands for discharged soldiers, had once more given farming enterprise a rude shock. As in Sulla's time, active cultivators were turned out to make room for men less able or less willing to give due attention to the business. Some of the new men failed and sold their land to speculative buyers. Some judiciously kept on the former owners as tenants at a rent. Things gradually settled down, as the older generation died out, but old evils remained. And, with the ' Roman peace ' established by Augustus, the supply of slaves from capture in war was no longer so plentiful, and the market depended on the ordinary abominations of the trade. It is significant that the Emperor had to take measures to repress an infamous abuse, the kidnapping (*suppressio*) of freemen in Italy itself and their sale into slavery on Italian estates. That the favoured and imperial country became a happy land under the new dispensation is not to be believed on the authority of court poets. Speculation in Provincial agriculture, and grants to imperial favourites, promoted the formation of great estates abroad, some of them very large. These necessitated the employment of a host of stewards and other agents, mostly skilled freedmen or slaves, and elaborate organization. That a part, often a large part, of such estates was let to humble tenant farmers grouped on small holdings around the lord's central Home Farm, was probably already the case: at all events we find this system in existence in the first century of the Empire. Moreover, the establishment of a virtual Monarchy naturally brought with it not only an Imperial Treasury but the creation of funds at the personal disposal of an Emperor. This arrangement, at first carried on by the ruler's private agents, was developed into a regular, highly organized department, with a special bureau for the administration of the imperial domain-lands. The bulk of these domains tended to grow gradually through bequests from individual testators; occasionally by leaps and bounds, when an Emperor, jealous of great landlords, or needing money for his own purposes, made away with the present owners and confiscated their estates. Africa in particular was the scene of such appropriations.

Imperial or private, these great Provincial land-units tended to a certain uniformity. A body of cultivating tenants (*coloni*), humble folk, farmed parcels of land on fixed conditions. At the head of the local organization stood the man in the Home Farm, whether he were the agent of the absentee landlord, or a tenant-in-chief to whom the whole estate was leased, the *conductor* or 'hirer' as he came to be specially called. But whatever were the rules in force on the estate, the *coloni* were freemen with full legal rights and duties, bound only by the conditions of their tenure, and able to go or stay as suited their own convenience. The law of landlord and tenant guarded the interests of both parties, and it is not easy to find fault with the system, so long as it was fairly worked. Its corruption we shall see later. We must, however, not forget that holdings of a different kind existed through State action in the Provinces. For retired soldiers to settle down in districts favourably known to them in the course of service was no new thing: it had happened long ago in Spain. With the establishment of a standing army quartered on the frontiers by Augustus, the grant of land-allotments became the ordinary means of pension on discharge. Settlements of veterans were scattered about the empire, generally in organized communities. These veterans were probably from the first persons of local importance; certainly they were a very notable class under the later Empire. That there were besides other landholders of various types is clear. But that the 'Roman' settlers of any kind were mere handworking peasants, doing their own drudgery as a matter of course, we have no reason to believe. We hear of slaves; and, when we find reference to free manual farm-labour, there is reason to believe that the toiling *coloni* are native tenants of a 'Roman' overlord.

In the middle of the first century A. D. we get some light from the significant treatise of Columella. This is not only the fullest of our ancient authorities: incidentally it reveals to us what were the most urgent agricultural problems of the age. Taken together with the somewhat later evidence of the younger Pliny, it helps us to get a notion of rural economy in Italy about 50–100 A. D., more solid and trustworthy than the stray notices on which we too often have to depend. Neither of these writers directly points out that agriculture was on the downward road, with small prospect of recovery. But we learn that, if the system of cultivating for the landlord's own account by a steward and slave staff was to continue, it would need reform. The organization must be elaborated and tightened, to make it economically efficient. Waste and labour-costs were eating up the profits, and the blame for so pitiful a result really rested on the landlords themselves. They often chose worthless or incompetent slaves for stewards, and did not keep a watchful eye on their doings. In short, the system, thoroughly well devised, was only not a success because owners would not take trouble for their own interest. That this highly qualified critic, despairing of a personal amendment of landlords, could only suggest improvement of the organization in detail, was surely ominous of failure. Yet he clearly thinks this system economically superior to the alternative plan of letting farms to tenants. A bad tenant will exhaust the soil for his own immediate gain, or cultivate badly through ignorance or carelessness. To get good tenants, and to keep them, is far from easy, indulge them as you may. The experience of Pliny, a great landlord, fully bears out this view of the rustic dilemma. He enjoyed the country, and was not indifferent to the social distinction conferred by the ownership of great estates. But he could not make them pay as they ought to pay. The returns from them were poor and uncertain; he was always in trouble with tenants; if he granted them abatements of rent, they did not regain their solvency; if he sold them up, the proceeds did not cover their arrears. Moreover, it being the custom for landlords to start tenants by advancing equipment (*instrumentum*, including slaves), he would have to sink more capital in the venture, not to mention the expense of getting the farm into good condition again when it had been let down by an outgoing bankrupt. True, the law furnished means of enforcing proper cultivation, but in practice legal proceedings against a tenant were evidently often vain. The truth surely is that in the conditions of this outwardly prosperous age both landlord and tenant were commonly in a bad way. Advice from Columella and the kindly efforts of Pliny could not restore vigour to a rotten agriculture. What was needed was a race of practical working farmers; things were not to be mended by specialists or amateurs.

We must bear in mind the general economic situation in Imperial Italy. The country was not industrial, producing goods for export sufficient to pay for its imports. Some cities, Rome in particular, were great centres of consumption. With exception of the Po region (now included in Italy), and certain highland districts, it was not really producing all the food and clothing required for its population. Its imported supplies were, as Tiberius said, at the mercy of winds and waves: the capital city was at times exposed to the risk of famine. So long as revenues from abroad poured in, it paid better to produce dainties for the tables of the rich than plain bulky food-stuffs. There was, however, a small-scale agriculture that managed to thrive, perhaps even to grow, under present conditions. It was that of market-gardens and small vineyards, chiefly in the neighbourhood of Rome. In the hands of men not too lazy or too proud to attend to their business, such enterprises were often remunerative. Personal devotion was the secret of success. Many of these small cultivators were freedmen, who in this as in other walks of life turned to account lessons learnt in their days of slavery. Such men, keen and not distracted by ambitions, adapted themselves to circumstances and prospered, while native 'Romans' decayed in their pride or pauperdom. On their holdings slave labour was employed as on great estates, but on a smaller scale, and the proprietor himself saw to it that work was done, and done properly. The fall in supply of slaves is indicated by the development of the old practice of slave-breeding. Columella treats it as one of the phenomena of a large estate, and makes allowance for it in his system: slave children had long been an ordinary element of farm-households. But it would seem that comparative scarcity of imported slaves, and the resort to breeding, were beginning to improve the prospects of the rustic slave. It was becoming not unusual to set up a deserving slave as virtual tenant (*quasi colonus*) of a small farm, stocked by his master. He had every inducement to make the holding a success. Good and regular returns, whether of money-rent or share of crops, were what his master wanted. He had fair hope of manumission under his master's last will; even the farm might be bequeathed to him by his master's gratitude. In these arrangements, duly recognized by the jurists, lay a germ of improvement in the economics of agriculture, but the course of Roman history did not allow it to produce its possible result.

For some ninety years (70–160 A.D.) the empire enjoyed a peace hardly broken by wars; Trajan even made new conquests, and Hadrian did much to strengthen the frontier defences and reorganize internal administration. But the quiet period, often represented as a golden age, was probably a time of unperceived decay. Behind the screen of military posts the Provinces were at ease in fancied security, and were becoming unwarlike in an age when what had been won by force could only be secured by force. Over the borders Germanic and other barbarous tribes were increasing at a rate with which the 'Roman' population could not compete. They were chronically in need of more food, and the spectacle of an agriculture which was at least systematic, compared with their own shiftless efforts, was a temptation to seek a sure and bountiful subsistence sword in hand. The Roman frontier was long and its guardian armies insufficient to hold it at all points. Once it were pierced, though but for a time, would the resources and machinery of the empire be able successfully to bear the inevitable strain?

In the reign of Marcus Aurelius (161–180) the strain on the resources of the empire became actual and severe. Successful war in the East was followed by a terrible plague, brought by infected troops, and plague by famine. Then came inroads of barbarians from the North and a series of campaigns, desperate efforts to drive out the invaders and restore the frontier. To raise armies Marcus had to enlist even slaves and barbarian mercenaries. The need of money was extreme. After hard-won victories, there was still the problem how to repopulate wasted lands. To leave them waste was to leave open the northern barrier. Marcus settled large bodies of German and other barbarians within the Roman border; they were to hold their lands on condition of military service to Rome. The scale on which this was done made this measure very different in kind from the occasional admission and employment of barbarians by earlier emperors. Moreover, the 'Roman' world was now so much weakened that its motley population could not Romanize new-comers.

The effects of these efforts and sacrifices were undoubtedly felt in agriculture. The mere feeding of great armies in distant seats of war, with little or no local supplies, must have been a heavy burden on somebody. Probably it fell first on the Po country. The bulk of Italy was in no condition to give much help. It is hardly possible to resist the conclusion that those parts of the empire which were great food-producers, and which were not troubled by the wars, were subject to disproportionate squeezing under the pressure of necessity. The case of the great corn-province Africa invites consideration from this point of view. The great estates referred to above were a principal source of Roman supplies. From inscriptions we get glimpses of what was going on there in the second century A.D. The ordinary terms on which chief tenants took over such domains made them each responsible not only for payment of his own rent but for collecting those of the *coloni* on behalf of the imperial government. The *coloni* paid in shares (*partes*) of produce; that is, they were *coloni partiarii*. Collection was probably a tiresome business, but the chief tenant had his compensation in the liability of the *coloni* to render him certain days of compulsory service on the Home Farm. He was tempted to exact more labour than was due, and also to increase the payments in kind. These encroachments could be withstood by the help of the Emperor's agents who represented him in the Province, but these agents could be influenced by bribes and favours. It was still possible to appeal direct to the Emperor, a troublesome process, and liable to be defeated by corruption of the departmental officials in Rome. That the *coloni* sometimes did take this course, we know from the surviving records of some of their appeals that succeeded. How far and how long the orders for redress of grievances were obeyed in practice, we do not know. Only by the vigilance and justice of the central bureau in Rome could the rights of the *coloni* be secured. Any weakening or corruption at the centre might be depressing or even disastrous to a class of men devoted to the production of more food than they consumed.

The food-question, I repeat, was already a serious one. In the long, troubled century that followed the death of Marcus it became even more so. We have evidence of grave anxiety at head-quarters in the recorded efforts of Emperors to promote reoccupation of derelict lands and reclamation of the waste. How far the offers of holdings rent-free for a series of years were successful in extending cultivation, we cannot tell. It is quite clear that to find squatters, and bind them to the soil by the tie of their own improvements, was to confess the empire's pressing need. It was the past bestowal of their own labour and capital that bound the *coloni* to farms from which they were free to remove. It was doubtless their reluctance to go that made them sometimes submit to irregular exactions. But at present their interests and those of the government agreed fairly well. It was the chief tenant, who was in fact a middleman, that needed watching. These huge Provincial domains were outside the municipal organization, so the collection there was not provided for by the municipal machinery. It seems therefore that the officials in Rome would sometimes have to weigh delicate considerations in deciding what action was most expedient. In short, one of the most important departments of agriculture depended for its continued prosperity on the continuance of the government machine in efficient function.

Now the third century of the Empire (180–284 A. D.) was full of troubles. Invasions, civil wars with pretenders, mutinies of licentious soldiery, were accompanied by financial distress which was only aggravated by debasement of the currency. Government tended to become a succession of military tyrannies, meeting momentary needs by the readiest application of armed force. In such circumstances the machine of government got out of gear. That it did so, and with disastrous consequences, we may be sure: the absence of particular record is only a symptom of a fatally disordered age. Even the series of great lawyers died down in this period. Therefore, when we find the agricultural problem pressing for solution at the beginning of the next period, there is no ground for surprise. Evidently the government, always in straits, had lost effective control of its subordinates, and tendencies never easily checked now operated without restraint. Chief tenants of great estates were squeezing the sub-tenants in order to satisfy the growing demands from Rome. Their encroachments had to be winked at, for fear of an interruption of supplies. So in the competition of selfishness the weaker went to the wall. The *coloni* were practically losing the freedom of movement that was legally theirs. The real issue was now this—was enterprise to be revived by a great administrative effort, or was the creeping stagnation to be recognized and regularized by law?

When Diocletian attained supreme power (285 A. D.), he remodelled the Imperial system in the hope of restoring efficiency. Four colleagues held Imperial powers, each in a division of the empire. For a time the plan, as a mechanical improvement, had considerable success. But four elaborate Courts of Oriental type, and an immense hierarchy of officials, were very costly, and every expedient had to be tried in order to meet the financial needs of the government. Italy had to lose its privileged position. It was parcelled into Provinces and taxed like the rest. The system of payments in kind received great extension, and was applied not only in collection of dues but in payment of salaries. To agriculture this was a deadly blow. A remodelled census was established on the principle of subdividing the territories into an ascertained number of farm-units each of which stood charged with an equal fixed tax. It seems certain that in practice no such theoretical uniformity was possible, but the principle was not abandoned. From the farmer this system took away all hope of profiting by the turn of the market for food-stuffs. In a bad season he would have to deliver as much produce as in a good one. This was discouraging to enterprise and industry. Farmers began to desert the land and seek refuge in towns, adding to the indigent populace there. Of the endless hardships of these poor *coloni* we have no complete impartial picture; but the pressure that drove men to leave the holdings on which they had spent their toil and care must have been cruel. Every effort was made to prevent their flitting, for any decline in production menaced the whole fabric of the empire. Another side of the change in progress seems to have been a rise in the power and importance of the chief tenants on the great estates. We have seen that their presence was serviceable to the central authority, which had only intervened now and then to check their selfish encroachments on the sub-tenants. Henceforth they seem rather to illustrate the general working of the Imperial mechanism, in which the upper man ground the lower for his own interest and security. To seek the protection of men of influence (*potentes*) became a social custom and canker in town and country alike, but the most fatal symptom of the age was that all rested on an agriculture that had ceased to hope.

Constantine (306–37) reunified the Empire after civil wars, and made a final choice of a land-policy. The *coloni* had been so bound to the soil by gradual effect of past circumstances, that they could no longer find release save as fugitives at any sacrifice. Constantine faced facts, and bound them to the soil by positive law. But this was recognition of a complicated disease, not a remedy. The forcing of all trades and professions into permanent guilds had for some time been a regular policy of Emperors. The same rigid fixity was now legally applied to agriculture, utterly inconsistent though it was with the nature of the occupation. Food-supply was more than ever the prime need. We even find legislation to prevent liability to military service or auxiliary transport from impairing the food-productive efficiency of the rustic population. The army covering the empire was now mainly barbarian. Barbarian settlers were also numerous in some Provinces: assimilation of these aliens had practically ceased. They were, however, not idle. Evidently they carried on a simple agriculture with success, for their crops and general well-being lured further swarms of hungry warriors over the frontier.

The partition of the empire into Eastern and Western, following the line of a vital difference, was accomplished in the period after Constantine, and the Empire in the West was finally extinguished in 476. From the point of view of Rome's agricultural 'legacy' we are only concerned with the West, and it happens that we have some information, chiefly bearing on Gaul. In the years 356–60 Julian (afterwards Emperor), then in charge of this great group of Provinces, successfully defeated the invading Germans, and by good administration relieved the distressed Provincials. He remedied grave abuses under which agriculture was then suffering. It is significant that the supplies for Roman armies on the German frontier were generally drawn from Britain. Now the northern seas were infested by Saxon pirates, and these rovers had to be humbled by Julian in order to restore the traffic. But Britain, ever a troublesome dependency, once more rebelled, and was finally abandoned in the time of Honorius (Western Emperor 395–423). The hold on Gaul was loosened, and Germanic tribes pushed in. If we may put trust in the pictures drawn by Christian writers in the middle and latter part of the fifth century, it seems that the way was paved for their occupation by the iniquitous oppression under which the Roman Provincial farmers were groaning; an oppression that had made them *coloni* in the newest sense, mere serfs of greedy landlords. Such a rural population was not likely to offer a stubborn resistance to the warlike invaders, and the serf of a Roman lord might find himself on the whole better off as the serf of a barbarian chief. The 'Romans' were not massacred, and some Roman landlords evidently came to terms with the intruders. Sidonius (about 430–80) depicts for us a Roman civilization still existing not only in towns but in country seats of wealthy nobles. How the blending of peoples laid the foundations of France is a theme beyond the scope of these pages.

To appraise the legacy of Rome in the field of agriculture is no easy matter. In the material development of cultivation we can hardly credit the Romans with notable advances as pioneers of an originative kind. In this as in other departments of civilized life they were primarily borrowers and carriers; their readiness to adopt the means and methods of others was remarked by Polybius. Thus on their native system were grafted in the course of centuries many foreign notions derived from Greece, from Carthage, and later from Gaul or elsewhere. Of the pains taken to improve Italian agriculture we have ample evidence in those of the treatises on *res rustica* that have come down to us. The functions of tillage were minutely studied, and results observed. Not to mention manuring and the careful distinction of qualities of manures, the use of lime, clay, and ashes was well understood; also the ploughing-in of stubbles and certain fodder-crops after grazing. Fallows were a part of the system: true rotation of crops can hardly be traced. In the matter of appliances there seems to have been very little advance. This stagnation was no doubt mainly the effect of slavery. The development of agriculture on a large scale for profit was undertaken with labour so heartless and unintelligent that there was little or nothing to be gained by improving tools. The same phenomenon has been noted in modern times. Free hired labour was but seldom employed, and in agriculture only as an occasional resource. The mere wage-earner was necessarily a mean figure in ancient civilization, in the Roman perhaps most of all.

That political influences deeply affected the fortunes of Roman agriculture is obvious to every student of Roman history. When we remark the disappearance of the old triune character of citizen (*civis*), farmer (*colonus* in original sense), and soldier (*miles*), the three functions that the early Roman was ready when called upon to assume, we are taking note of the most vital change that came over the Roman State. Rigid and formal law sanctified the rights of property, but political power was needed to prevent unfair dealing with the land-questions of a growing community. Under the Roman constitution, every expansion of dominion rendered the mass of farmer citizens more unable to assert themselves. Under an individualistic land-system, the individual landholder became in practice politically impotent. Momentary agitations became ineffective in the long run. So the Few prevailed, and the corruption of politics and the decay of sound agriculture went hand in hand. The acquisition of a vast empire only continued the process. Luxurious villas spread over more and more of Italy, while openings in the Provinces enabled 'Roman' emigrants to win a good living abroad by means less laborious than rustic industry. The development of tenancies, and the steps by which the *coloni* sank into the condition of virtual serfs, slaves of the soil, have been sketched above. Agriculture deprived of hope, labour deprived of its reward, lost the breath of life, and undermined the empire that depended on their vigour.

The last stages of Roman expansion betray the failure of that power of assimilation by which Rome had consolidated her hold upon her earlier conquests. Most interesting are the results of recent inquiries into the case of Britain. We know that no small pains were taken to Romanize the Province. But the distribution of town-centres, and particularly of rural villas, indicates that the spread of Roman civilization proceeded along determined lines in chosen districts and in relation to the military posts that gave security. Britain when abandoned did not remain a 'Latin' country.

Perhaps we may name organization as the most evident legacy of Rome in agriculture. To have carried a systematic method of farming into so wide an area of western Europe was surely no small achievement. Barbarians looked on, admired the results, and eventually, when settled in conquered Provinces, learnt something better than their own crude methods. But there is in Italy at least one region in which Roman agriculture at its best has left a living picture of itself. The tourist who looks out from the top of Milan Cathedral over the Lombard plain sees a scene of continuous cultivation and fertility. In essentials it is probably much what it has been ever since the Romans firmly occupied Cisalpine Gaul. Its appearance suggests the Roman land-surveyors that laid out holdings for Roman settlers in this district favoured by nature, where the system of monstrous *latifundia* never reached its worst. Even there, however, we must not forget the rustic slave. In one of his letters Pliny, lamenting the costliness of trusty slaves, remarks, 'as for chained slaves, I never keep that sort on any of my estates, and in those parts [the Cisalpine] nobody does'. So the slave was there also; and we may fairly wonder that agriculture under such labour conditions prospered so long and so well as it did. For in this brief sketch we have been reviewing its fortunes over a space of more than a thousand years.

W. E. HEITLAND.

BOOKS RECOMMENDED.

LLOYD STORR-BEST, *M. T. Varro on Farming.*
W. E. HEITLAND, *Agricola.*